820.9
VAR

DATE DUE

Thomas Hardy's desk, Dorset County Museum, Dorchester

A READER'S
GUIDE *to*
WRITERS'
BRITAIN

Sally Varlow

PR ON

x

First published in Great Britain by Prion Books Ltd.,
32–34 Gordon House Road
London NW5 1LP
Reprinted with revisions, 1997

Published with the support of the
National Tourist Boards of England, Scotland and Wales.

A catalogue record of this book can be obtained
from the British Library

ISBN 1–85375–201–0

Cover design by Design Revolution
Cover images: Robert Louis Stevenson, John Betjeman (Hulton Deutsch);
George Bernard Shaw, Jane Austen (Mary Evans Picture Library);
Shelley Memorial (Oxford Picture Library/Chris Andrews).
Book design by Kelly Flynn
Maps by Malcolm Swanston
Colour origination by Global Colour, Malaysia & London

Printed and bound in Italy

CONTENTS

INTRODUCTION

Once upon a time, storytellers and poets travelled the country, singing ballads of brave deeds, retelling old tales of young lovers, weaving magic in the glow of great-hall fires.

Then came William Caxton, who first put the legends of King Arthur into print, and it was the turn of the readers to take to the roads. Searching for 'story-book' settings and hunting down writers' haunts grew into an honourable pastime. Poets do it. Playwrights do it. Even educated dons do it. Wordsworth made a pilgrimage to Burns's grave within 10 years of Rabbie's death. Matthew Arnold made it to Charlotte Brontë's Haworth Parsonage within months.

It became a truth universally acknowledged, as Jane Austen put it, that a reader in possession of a good book gains further pleasure from knowing where the author lived, loved and found inspiration.

But it is not just a highbrow habit. Booklovers seldom keep solely to serious reading, especially during holidays and weekends away. So this guide covers places linked with all sorts of writers and books – ancient and modern, classic and popular, fact and fiction, serious and fun – throughout England, Scotland and Wales.

Sometimes it is a sentimental journey, a reminder of stories and poems once learnt but long forgotten. It points the way to landscapes where great writers left a large imprint: Dylan Thomas on the 'heron priested' shores of Wales; R. L. Stevenson on Scotland; Thomas Hardy on Tess's Wessex.

At other times it brings in writers who don't often appear in guide books: Hugh MacDiarmid crossing paths with John Buchan in the Scottish Borders; Rosamunde Pilcher in Cornwall as well as Daphne du Maurier; Tolkien in the Midlands alongside George Eliot.

Always it is a selection. It highlights writers whose work has strong local links and places that readers can visit. Nearly every house and collection named is open at some time and though many churches are locked on weekdays, keys are generally kept nearby.

The chapters are organised by region, (see map on page vi) and each has an area map and a gazetteer (at the end of the book) listing places to visit. For readers who want to follow one writer there is a detailed index of authors and places, so you can trace Beatrix Potter or John Betjeman, from the West Country to London or the Lake District.

Once you've decided which area to explore, local Tourist Information Centres (TICs) are the best places for further help. They often have trails and brochures about major authors, can name more local writers to read and follow up, and have lists of nearby events.

Regular literature festivals, such as Cheltenham, Brighton, King's Lynn (it has two) and Bath (the newest, good on books for children), usually fix dates well ahead to help you plan staying visits. But many more events are 'impromptu'.

Call at a TIC and you could discover library exhibitions on local authors; readings by countless current writers producing new work; and, hooray, storytellings. All over Britain there is a welcome revival of the age-old custom that led Taliesin through Wales, Walter Scott's Last Minstrel across the Borders, and Alan-a-Dale deep into Sherwood Forest.

Sally Varlow

*For Grandma, who first led me to 'Louisa's steps'
at Lyme Regis – with* Persuasion *in one hand
and an ice-cream in the other.*

ACKNOWLEDGMENTS

Writing a book like this would be impossible without the advice, comments, information and good cheer supplied by dozens of people and organisations. In addition to the national tourist boards for England, Scotland and Wales, valuable help and support was provided by: England's 11 Regional Tourist Boards; Edinburgh, Isle of Wight and the Scottish Borders tourist boards; Birmingham Marketing Partnership; and the local authorities for Bedford, Cornwall, Cumbria, Devon, Nuneaton and Bedworth, South Hams, Stoke on Trent, and Walsall.

A number of other bodies also gave generous assistance and time: the National Trust for Scotland, Scottish Arts Council, and Book Trust Scotland; the Arts Council of Wales, the Welsh Academy, and the Centre for Advanced Celtic Studies; and each of the Regional Arts Boards in England.

Particular thanks go to: Olga Davies of Wales Tourist Board and Peter Reekie of the National Trust for Scotland; to Paul Clough, Lady Dunpark, David Hart, Bob Mole, John Munro, Gilbert Summers, Ian Weightman, Emyr Williams, and Pat Woodfine.

I should also like to thank, in England: Kathleen and Bill Adams (George Eliot Fellowship), Elizabeth Bates, Chrispher Dean (Dorothy L. Sayers Society), Alison Maxam, Julie Obada, Connie Pickard, John Potter (Arnold Bennett Society), Jane Randall, Rose Willis, and Sam Warnock. In Scotland: Walter Cairns, Iain Crichton Smith, Lindsay Fraser, Brian Lambie, Dame Jean and Mrs Patricia Maxwell-Scott, Maurice Mullay, and Hamish M. Paterson. In Wales: Dr Rhiannon Ifans, Meic Stephens and, representing every unnamed helper, the lady at Llanbadarn Fawr church who kindly waited to lock up while I lingered over Dafydd ap Gwilym's poems one sunny spring evening.

But above all, special thanks are due, for unstinting help and research, to Iris Ivinson and to my husband, Peter.

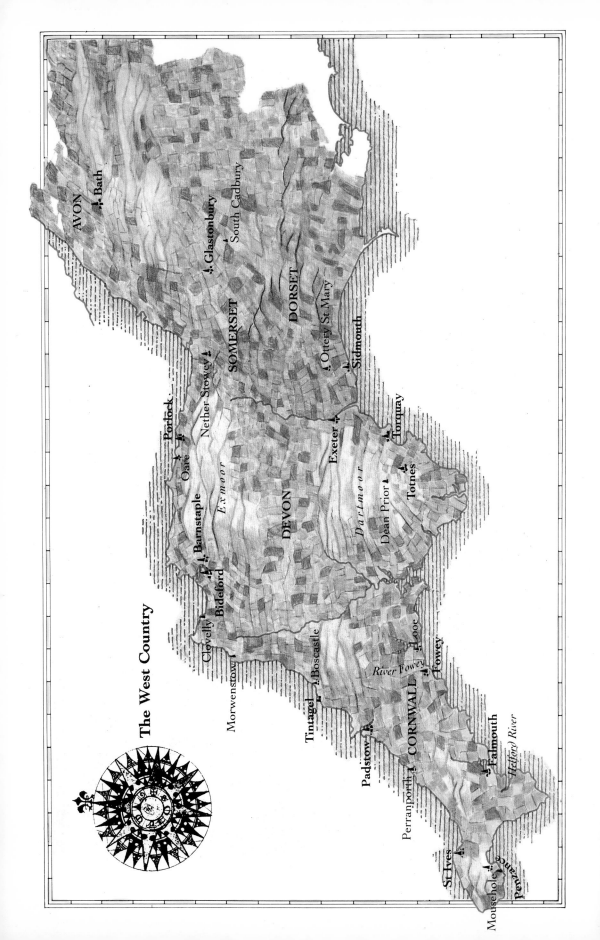

CHAPTER 1

The West Country

THE
WEST COUNTRY

TALES OF KING ARTHUR

In July 1485 William Caxton's new printing press was busy setting a book of eight stories written in prison by an obscure knight who had died a few years earlier.

Caxton titled it *Le Morte Darthur* and despite its curious origins it was the most important piece of 'modern' Arthurian fiction. The 'hoole book of King Arthur and his noble knyghtes of the Round Table' was the first structured story of Arthur's life and the break-up of the Round Table fellowship. It was an astonishingly modern narrative that followed Arthur from his birth at Tintagel to the final battle with his evil nephew Sir Mordred, 'uppon a downe bysyde Salesbyry', and his burial on the Isle of Avalon.

It would inspire every subsequent Arthurian poet and storyteller down to John Steinbeck's *The Acts of King Arthur and his Noble Knights*.

Almost nothing is known for sure about its author Sir Thomas Malory, except that he came from Warwickshire, went to jail and died in 1471. He was probably sent to prison eight times on different charges; fought at the siege of Calais in 1436; and died aged about 60, maybe still in London's Newgate jail.

He had certainly consolidated into a fixed tradition all the earlier versions of Arthur (part real, part fantasy; the Celtic warlord and medieval king) with the stories of Merlin, the Holy Grail, Tristram and Iseult, Launcelot and Guinevere.

Malory had also given it a brilliantly sad finale, with Launcelot following on foot as Guinevere's funeral procession makes its way from Amesbury Abbey in Wiltshire, where she had retired as a nun, to her resting place beside Arthur at Glastonbury.

'Thenne, al these thynges considered,' Caxton wrote in his preface, 'there can no man resonably gaynsaye but there was a kyng of thys lande named Arthur.' First, Caxton urged his readers, 'ye may

'Now put me into the barge, said the king...And there received him three queens with great mourning' – Sir Thomas Malory's account of the life and 'piteous death' of Arthur sent readers searching Somerset and Cornwall for the sites he named.

Glastonbury Tor, believed to be the burial place of the Holy Grail, sought by every Knight of the Round Table but seen only by 'Sir Galahad, the good knight'.

John Steinbeck (1902-1968) read Malory as a boy of nine and spent years touring Britain in search of King Arthur.

'*A beautiful England this must have been, if it contained many such abbeys as Glastonbury*' – Henry James, English Hours.

see his sepulture in the monastery of Glastyngburye.'

The Somerset market town of Glastonbury was claimed to be Arthur's resting place at least by the 12th century. Geoffrey of Monmouth said the wounded king was carried to the Isle of Avalon, and Avalon was identified as Glastonbury by two of his contemporaries: Gerald of Wales and William of Malmesbury.

Once upon a time Glastonbury and its conical hill, Glastonbury Tor, rising from a vast inland lake that covered the present-day Somerset Levels, had been a sacred site of the Old Religion. Here, according to William of Malmesbury, Christ's follower Joseph of Arimathea came carrying the Holy Grail, the Cup of the Last Supper, and founded Britain's first church.

When Joseph buried the Grail containing some of Christ's blood at the foot of the Tor, William explained, a spring gushed open (now Chalice Well) spreading miraculous, healing water that turned red on the ground. When he planted his staff on Wearyall

Hill just west of the town, it took root and grew into the Holy Thorn that blossomed each Christmas, as well as in the usual month of May. Though one of Cromwell's Roundheads hacked down the original, some off-shoots remain in the town, one in the abbey grounds, another at St John's church.

Before long, Glastonbury monks 'confirmed' this was Arthur and Guinevere's burial place by 'discovering' their bones and a lead cross conveniently inscribed in Latin: 'Here lies interred in the Isle of Avalon the renowned King Arthur.' Some say it mentioned Guinevere, but as it equally conveniently disappeared no one knows.

The bones were re-interred in their present grave near the high altar and the abbey grew to be one of the biggest and wealthiest, until it was reduced to ruins in the 16th century. As Henry James put it: 'Henry VIII, in the language of our day, came down so heavily. The ancient splendour of the architecture survives but in scattered and scanty fragments.'

James's compatriot John Steinbeck came to enjoy Glastonbury's 'ancient splendour' in 1959 while he scoured

Somerset for Arthurian sites and Camelot. Steinbeck had been fascinated by Malory's *Morte Darthur* all his life and he spent nine months researching his own version of the book, living in a medieval cottage at Bruton. It had been fixed for him by playwright Robert Bolt and Steinbeck sent him the 13-volume *Oxford English Dictionary* by way of thanks.

In 1961 Steinbeck was back at Glastonbury and Wells and went on to Cornwall and Northumberland, still following up Malory and Arthur. Years later in New York, he wrote of his 'curious kind

of longing' for Somerset, where he climbed Cadbury Hill at night on June 24 because, he wrote to a friend, 'The tradition, held very widely here is that Arthur rides that night'.

At Cadbury (in sight of Glastonbury Tor) stands Cadbury Castle, a Neolithic fort with strong claims to be Arthur's Camelot. Winchester and Caerleon contest it, but a modern excavation proved the hill-top earthworks, approached by a track from South Cadbury church, were the military HQ of a 6th-century chieftain at least as powerful as Arthur.

It was never, though, the 'many tower'd Camelot' of Lord Tennyson's poem *The Lady of Shalott*. Tennyson echoed Malory by picturing Arthur and his

knights as characters in a romantic 14th- or 15th-century landscape; and he, too, spent years following Malory's text, as well as Geoffrey of Monmouth's and the Welsh *Mabinogion*, to research his multi-volumed Arthurian poem, *Idylls of the King*.

Wandering through Cornwall in 1848 he came to Tintagel Head, where Geoffrey and Malory said Arthur was born at the castle and handed over to Merlin. In fact, Tintagel's crumbling castle, clinging dramatically to the cliffs, dates only from the 13th century, though it has signs of an earlier settlement.

No matter. The site suited Tennyson and his poem perfectly and it is a spectacular place for Arthur's mysterious conception (Malory is more graphic on this issue; Tennyson always had to remember Queen Victoria was in the audience). And Merlin's magic proved a magnet for others:

Tintagel Castle, named by ancient chroniclers as King Arthur's birthplace and the scene of Merlin's magic.

In Somerset, Steinbeck studied Malory's claim, 'King Arthur is not dead... men say he shall come again,' and found a local tradition that 'Arthur rides' on Cadbury Hill (left).

Swinburne, in 1864, followed Dickens and Lord Tennyson: 'To the wind-hollowed heights and gusty bays Of sheer Tintagel, fair with famous days.'

Charles Dickens, who beat Tennyson to it, Wilkie Collins soon after, and Swinburne.

Not far from the castle is Slaughter Bridge, near Camelford, said for centuries to be the site of Camlan, Arthur's 'last, dim, weird battle of the west' in which the king receives a mortal wound from Sir Mordred. But numerous places, including Queen Camel near Cadbury Castle, claim to be the place where 'all day long the noise of battle roll'd' and Slaughter Bridge's ancient inscribed stone probably doesn't refer to Camlan at all.

Yet Dozmary Pool, a lonely moorland lake a few miles from Camelford, near Bolventor, is still said to be the lake in which Sir Bedivere flung Arthur's sword, Excalibur. Three times, according to Lord Tennyson, the dying king insisted his knight must throw the massive sword into the 'wild water lapping on the crag'. When at last Sir Bedivere obeyed, he watched as an arm rose out of the water,

Clothed in white samite,
mystic, wonderful
And caught him by the hilt,
and brandish'd him
Three times, and drew him
under in the mere.

From the pool high up on Bodmin Moor, the River Fowey runs south to the sea passing more Arthurian sites. Castle Dor earthworks, on the west bank above Golant, are traditionally the stronghold of King Mark of Cornwall. And outside Fowey stands an ancient burial stone at Four Turnings inscribed in Latin 'Here lies Tristram...'

Matthew Arnold, Tennyson and Swinburne all made poetry out of the tangled love-story of Tristram, Iseult and King Mark. Swinburne named his version *Tristram of Lyonesse* and said, like Malory, that Tristram came from 'The lost land of Lyonesse' which once lay beyond Land's End. It was a place of fine cities and 140 churches, so the local story goes, until the great

*L*ord Tennyson's Idylls of the King *tell how Arthur, watched by Merlin and the Lady of the Lake, finds Excalibur –*
'...the sword that rose from out the bosom of the lake,
And Arthur row'd across and took it – rich
With jewels...'

storm of 1099, when the sea swept over it leaving the church bells ringing below the waves.

Thomas Hardy helped keep alive the idea of Lyonesse as a land of strange romance and beauty when he used the name for north Cornwall. To him Lyonesse conjured up the magic of his first meetings with Emma Gifford in 1870.

Later that year, writing *When I set out for Lyonnesse*, he admitted he had no idea he would return to his native Dorset

> With magic in my eyes,
> All marked with mute
>   surmise
> My radiance rare and
>   fathomless,
> When I came back from
>   Lyonnesse
> With magic in my eyes!

Emma was the sister-in-law of the rector of St Juliot, near Boscastle, when Hardy came as the young architect responsible for rebuilding the church. Hardy was captivated

by Cornwall's air of 'drama and mystery', the sheer, rugged grey-black cliffs, 'the eternal soliloquy of the water' - and by Emma.

Rebuilding the church (Hardy later regretted it was so draconian) took several years and return visits. With Emma he would walk the cliffs above Pentargon Bay, or the footpath down Valency valley from St Juliot to the sea at Boscastle harbour. They went for riverside picnics, explored other villages, paid a visit to Tintagel. She became his 'West of Wessex girl' (though they were both in their early 30s). In 1873 he published his third novel, *A Pair of Blue Eyes*, based on St Juliot and their happy expeditions. The following year they were married.

Long before Emma's death in 1912 their affection had turned to loathing and his great love lyrics, *Poems 1912-1913*, were written out of bitter remorse. It seemed to set in the minute Emma died and ruined his relationship with the second Mrs Hardy.

In 1913 he made a pilgrimage back to St Juliot and erected a plaque to Emma in the church. Revisiting the haunts where he had walked beside her on her pony, he pictured her as *The Phantom Horsewoman*. He wrote the sad-sweet poems that catalogue the Cornish places where they fell in love *At Castle Boterel, Where the Picnic Was* and *Beeny Cliff*:

> What if still in chasmal beauty
>   looms that wild weird
>   western shore,
> The woman now is - elsewhere -
>   whom the ambling pony bore,
> And nor knows nor cares for
>   Beeny, and will laugh there
>   never-more.

When Thomas Hardy came to Cornwall he had, Emma Gifford noticed, a pocketful of poems as well as his architectural drawings.

Cottages beside Boscastle harbour – Hardy's 'Castle Boterel'.

At St Juliot's church, Hardy met his first wife, Emma. He returned after her death in 1912 and again in 1916, writing The Marble Tablet *and 'I chiselled her monument'.*

Hawker's Hut beside the foot-path on Vicarage Cliff, his retreat for smoking and composing poetry.

CORNISH COASTS

During Lord Tennyson's tour of north Cornwall in 1848, researching the legends of King Arthur, he paid a visit to a writer who was a legend in his own time, the eccentric poet-parson Robert Stephen Hawker. They seem to have got on famously, walking the cliffs at Morwenstow, Hawker's remote cliff-top parish, swapping smuggling stories, legends and poems.

Hawker was appointed vicar of Morwenstow in 1834 and spent the next 40 years rescuing shipwrecked sailors, bribing the locals with gin to help him bury the dead ones. He was generally seen wearing a fisherman's jersey and seaboots under his clerical garb, except on the day he sat on a rock festooned in seaweed, apparently to prove that mermaids exist.

He rebuilt Morwenstow vic-

The Rev. Robert Hawker (1803-1875) at the door of Morwenstow vicarage, 1864.

A figurehead in St Morwenna's churchyard marks the graves of shipwrecked sailors buried by Parson Hawker and his flock.

arage, modelling the chimneys on elaborate church or college towers; restored St Morwenna's Norman church; and founded a local school. Alone on the cliffs he also built himself a hut out of drift-wood (now preserved beside the cliff path) where he sat meditating, smoking - some say opium - and writing poetry. His most famous piece *The Song of the Western Men*, known as the Cornish Anthem, has the rousing chorus:

And shall Trelawny die?
Here's twenty-thousand
*   Cornishmen*
Will know the reason why!

A mermaid at Zennor
Climbed out of the sea
By the seething Zennor shore.
Her gown was silver,
Her gown was gold
And a crown of pearl she
*   wore,*
She wore,
A crown of pearl she wore.

Charles Causley, Cornwall's popular poet and children's author, lives in Launceston.

Sir John Betjeman slips in several references to Hawker - 'The same Atlantic surges roll for me As rolled for Parson Hawker...' - among the many thousands of lines he wrote and broadcast about his adopted county, Cornwall.

Betjeman's life-long love of the

Those golden and unpeopled bays,
The shadowy cliffs and sheep-
worn ways,
The white unpopulated surf,
The thyme- and mushroom-
scented turf,
The slate-hung farms, the
oil-lit chapels,
Thin elms and lemon-scented
apples

John Betjeman, *Delectable Duchy.*

architecture, old churches, topo-
graphy, railway journeys, history,
almost anything truly English and
eccentric.

He would bicycle for miles
'church crawling' round St Protus
and St Hyacinth at Blisland, St
Endelienta's at St Endellion, and
St Petroc at Padstow.

It is fitting that the old
Wadebridge-Padstow railway line
has been turned into the Camel
Trail cycle route (licensed hirers at
both ends). From Wadebridge, he
wrote, the 'five and a half miles
beside the broadening Camel to
Padstow was the most beautiful
train journey I knew. See it on a
fine evening at high tide with
golden light on the low hills, the
heron-haunted mud coves flooded
over...'

By the time he died in 1984 at
his second home at Trebetherick,
Betjeman had become Sir John,
Poet Laureate - the most popular
since Tennyson - and a national
treasure. Yet he chose to be buried
at the sand-swept little church of
St Enodoc, hedged by tamarisk on

Sir John Betjeman,
pictured in 1972,
'monarch of miles of
sand' on the Cornish
beaches he grew to love
on boyhood holidays.

'St Enodoc's – Among
grassy hillocks on the
golf course...dark and
ancient': Betjeman
included it in Collins
Guide to English
Parish Churches *near-*
ly 30 years before he
was buried there.

Across the Camel
estuary,
Betjeman recalled com-
ing home by Padstow
ferry 'on a fine, still
evening, laden with
the week's shopping'.

place began on childhood holidays
with his parents, spent near
Padstow on the River Camel.
Every year they came from
London 'To far Trebetherick by
the sounding sea'.

Fond memories of those early
years take up two chapters of
Betjeman's verse-autobiography,
Summoned by Bells. With his ever-
potent mixture of whimsy and
nostalgia he recalls arriving by
train at Wadebridge, climbing
rocks, playing on the beaches of
Daymer Bay with other children,
treasure hunts, listening to the
roar of Atlantic rollers and wild
September gales.

Over the years his affection for
the county deepened. From the
1934 *Shell Guide to Cornwall,*
first of the famous county guides
he edited, to *First and Last Loves,*
published nearly 20 years later, he
made it clear 'Cornwall is another
country'. It was a place where he
could indulge all his great passions:

Trerice is the 16th-century house Winston Graham used in the Poldark stories as Trenwith, home of Ross's first sweetheart Elizabeth and her husband Francis.

Cornish Engines, typical of tall beam engine houses that worked Poldark's mine, preserved near Redruth, once the heart of Cornwall's tin and copper-mining country.

the edge of the golf course, beneath a Cornish slate headstone.

South of Padstow at Newquay begins the coastline Winston Graham turned into 'Poldark' country. From West Pentire past Perranporth to Porthtowan, inland around Redruth and over the moors, he unfolds the stories of Ross and Demelza and the history of 18th-century Cornish mines and shipwrecks.

Born in Manchester, Graham moved into the area in the early 1930s, living at a house named Treberran (now a small private hotel, Nampara Lodge) at Perranporth. He married and stayed there while he wrote the early Poldark books, *Ross Poldark, Demelza, Jeremy Poldark* and *Warleggan*, published 1945 to 1953.

Later volumes range further afield until the eleventh, *The Twisted Sword*, ends the saga in 1815 with the Battle of Waterloo. But its heart and hearth are still on the north coast of Cornwall.

Nampara cove, Graham says, is a mix of West Pentire, Porth Joke and neighbouring beaches and hamlets. The Poldark villages of St Ann's and Sawle are partly based on St Agnes and the valley winding down to Trevaunance Cove. Trenwith, home of Ross's cousin Francis, was modelled on Trerice, a lovely grey-stone Elizabethan manor down narrow lanes near Newquay, where Ross brings Demelza for Christmas just after their marriage.

Demelza's name was taken from a Cornish village; so was Warleggan, the newly-rich family that separates Francis from his fortune and plots against Ross. Other places appear as themselves: the towns of Truro and Redruth; beauty spots such as Bedruthan Steps and Trelissick gardens, overlooking Falmouth harbour. And, most graphically, the old tin and copper mines, now preserved as museums and amusement centres: Poldark Mine outside Helston and the tall beam-engine towers of Cornish Engines near Redruth.

Between Nampara's coast and the pretty little bay of St Ives, stands a lighthouse, Godrevy. To Virginia Woolf, it was a beacon on an island, the focal point outside the fishing village of St Ives, a place to be reached by boat, as the Ramsays plan in her novel *To the Lighthouse*.

She placed the action of the book in Scotland, on the Isle of Skye, where the Ramsays holiday as usual with their guests. Yet the scenery and sunlight on a mid-September evening, and the flowers in Mrs Ramsay's garden, are memories of Virginia's childhood at St Ives.

Each summer from 1882 her father, editor and critic Sir Leslie Stephen, brought his family from London to Talland House (since converted to holiday flats). High

up behind the village it looks down over a maze of steep streets and white-washed houses; and out across St Ives Harbour to Godrevy Island and the lighthouse.

To the Stephens children - Thoby, Vanessa, Adrian and Virginia - St Ives meant rock climbing, cricket (Virginia was a demon bowler), games on the sands at Porthmeor and Porthminster, mackerel fishing expeditions, and boat trips to Godrevy.

They were probably the happiest days of Virginia's childhood, 13 summers until her mother died in 1895 and her father sank into a state of melancholic bereavement. But after Sir Leslie's death in 1904 holidays in Cornwall resumed, with visits to St Ives and along the coast towards Zennor.

Writing to Vanessa years later, Virginia explained how whenever

Godrevy Island and Virginia Woolf's lighthouse.

We are on the cliffs quite by ourselves, nothing but gorse between us and the sea, and when I have done this letter we are going to take our books and roll up in a hollow over the sea and there watch the spray and the bees and the peacock butterflies.
Virginia Woolf, *Letters*.

Bedruthan Steps, beauty spot on the Cornish coast, where Francis Kilvert's Diary, 1870, records summer visits to the 'broken shattered tumbled cliffs ...not a voice or sound was to be heard except the boom of the sea and the crying of the white-winged gulls'.

she returned to Cornwall, 'I find that one lapses into a particular mood of absolute enjoyment which takes me back into my childhood.'

She drew on childhood holidays for *some* of the impressions in *Jacob's Room*, an early experimental novel. Published in 1922, it gradually builds into a portrait of a young man based on her brother Thoby who had died in 1906.

To the Lighthouse, published five years later, relies almost entirely on recollections of her family and Cornish holidays, as she anatomises the Ramsays and their symbolic trip across the bay through the minds of her characters. In gloomy philosopher Mr Ramsay and serene Mrs Ramsay, Virginia mirrors her parents' relationship. She pictures her mother meditating as the beam of the lighthouse streams through the windows at night: 'watching it with fascination, hypnotised, as if it were

stroking with its silver fingers some sealed vessel in her brain whose bursting would flood her with delight...'

It is the same lighthouse beam that finds its way into Penelope Keeling's dreams in Rosamunde Pilcher's novel *The Shell Seekers*:

'the sound of waves breaking on the beach far below and the curtains stirring at the open windows and the beams of the lighthouse swinging their way across the white-painted walls.'

Rosamunde Pilcher was born at Lelant on the edge of St Ives in 1924 and went to school in Penzance. She had moved away long before she published *The Day of the Storm* and *The Shell Seekers*, which came out in 1987, but both have Cornish settings, and she has returned to Cornwall with *Coming Home*, published in 1995.

In *The Shell Seekers*, Penelope's artist father moves his family to a village already 'discovered by painters from all over the country'. Though it is named Porthkerris it bears the strongest resemblance to St Ives, even mentioning Trevose Head away to the north. Among the steep streets and alleyways of Porthkerris, Penelope spends the war years with her father, and the brief winter months of her affair with Richard.

It is 40 years on when she presents her father's priceless painting, 'The Shell Seekers', to the local art gallery. Returning to the village she finds: 'nothing could ever alter that marvellous blue, silken sweep of the bay, nor the curve of the headland, nor the baf-

fling muddle of streets and slate-roofed houses tumbling down the hill to the water's edge.'

A few miles west of St Ives on the coast at Zennor, D. H. Lawrence tried to set up a farming-cum-literary commune he planned to call Rananim. With his German wife Frieda he left London at the end of 1915 and moved to Cornwall, where he soon decided 'one is much nearer to freedom - the freedom to love and be completely happy'.

After a spell near Padstow they found a group of cottages to rent cheaply at Higher Tregerthen, a mile from the centre of Zennor,

and wrote urging Katherine Mansfield and John Middleton Murry to join them.

Katherine and Jack had been witnesses at the Lawrences' wedding in 1914 and the four had stayed together several times, not entirely successfully. Katherine had her doubts about the experiment and thought it might just last 'the whole summer'. It lasted two months.

Lawrence loved the rough and remote beauty of the coast with its constantly crashing waves and the stony moorland behind. Frieda thought 'his very soul seemed to have sunk into that Cornwall, that

wild place under the moors'. And when they were forced out of the county - ludicrously suspected of spying for Germany - Lawrence had to 'tear himself out'.

They had been under police surveillance since 1915 when Lawrence's *The Rainbow* was suppressed. As World War I progressed the observation continued. At Zennor his pacifist views, her German connections (her cousin was the air-ace 'the Red Baron'), their unmarried visitors and irregular life-style heaped up local antagonism.

In spite of his obvious ill-health, Lawrence was twice sent for army medicals at Bodmin - the 'Nightmare' he described in *Kangaroo*. In October 1917 after police ransacked their cottage they were officially 'moved on', Lawrence's faith in Britain broken for good.

W hen Katherine and Murry arrived in April 1916 they moved into The Tower next to the Lawrences' cottage. At first Katherine enjoyed it, remembering afterwards: 'I had a whole spring full of blue-bells one year with Lawrence. I shall never forget it. And it was warm, not very sunny, the shadows raced over the silky grass and the cuckoos sang.'

But she found it too lonely. More important, she loathed Lawrence and Frieda's violent quarrels. Jack, meanwhile, found himself the object of affection from Lawrence, who made no secret that he thought Jack and Katherine's relationship seriously flawed.

K atherine Mansfield (1888-1923).

I n March 1916, D. H. Lawrence (below) wrote telling Bertrand Russell about his cottage on the moors near Zennor (left), 'just under the wild hills with their great grey boulders of gran-ite, and above the big sea, it is beautiful enough and free enough. I think we can be obscure and happy...'

In June Katherine and Jack left. Lawrence, however, working on one of his best books, *Women in Love,* had already decided to preserve the whole episode - casting them as Gudrun and Gerald, himself and Frieda as Birkin and Ursula. When they read it they were furious; though not so outraged as literary hostess Lady Ottoline Morrell, who could hardly forgive Lawrence for turning her into Hermione.

Katherine had used her health as an excuse to move to a more sheltered place, a cottage by an

*M*ousehole, 'really the loveliest village in England', wrote Dylan Thomas, who spent his honeymoon there in July 1937.

inlet at Mylor Creek on the south coast, where she and Jack stayed till the autumn.

Two years later they were back in south Cornwall, this time at Looe. They had married in London on May 3, but Katherine was now seriously ill with tuberculosis. Instead of a honeymoon, she needed rest and comfort while Jack sorted out their London home.

On May 17 she arrived on the coast and wrote happily to him, 'The approach to Looe is amazing ...We drove through lanes like great flowering loops with sea below and huge gulls sailing over...'

Most of her letters are more despairing as she struggled to accept that her illness was incur-

*W*riting to her husband from Looe, Katherine Mansfield promises: 'You shall have strawberries, love in this happy land, three times a day... Picnics! We shall have almost perpetual picnics.'

able. In June, Jack joined her for a while and she looked forward to him taking her to the local pub and beauty spots. But Katherine was anxious to be back in London for several reasons.

She had struck up a fragile friendship, more a rivalry, with Virginia Woolf and had stayed with her in Sussex. Katherine envied her the relative calm of her marriage and country home, which provided the peace Katherine also needed to write in. Now the Woolfs' Hogarth Press was about to publish her first novel, *Prelude,* and in July Katherine left Looe for London.

It had been a brief period of pleasant air and good food. She had carried on writing: *Bliss and Other Stories* appeared the next year, *The Garden Party* in 1920. But it was only a respite, and she died in France five years later at the age of 34.

*D*ylan Thomas *did* have a honeymoon on the south coast of Cornwall, at Mousehole, the same place Winston Graham chose.

Writing to his parents in Swansea, on June 10, 1937, Dylan explained he was staying with Caitlin Macnamara in a cottage he had borrowed 'in Lamorna Cove, a beautiful little place'.

Lamorna, made famous by the 19th-century Newlyn School of artists, lies at the bottom of a narrow, wooded valley that twists and

Lamorna Cove, on the coast path from Penzance to Land's End.

turns down to the cove. Dylan knew it from a visit the previous year, staying nearby with an old friend, Mrs Henderson, and no doubt he refreshed his memory at The Wink pub, just above his cottage.

'I suppose that I'm piling on the shocks and surprises in this very late letter,' Dylan wrote, 'but I must tell you too that Caitlin and I are going to be married next week by special licence...' Since he hadn't enough money to get the few miles to Penzance and phone them, he knew it wouldn't go down too well.

Mrs Henderson came up trumps again. She paid the £3 for the licence so the wedding could go ahead at Penzance register office; and put them up for the start of their honeymoon at the Lobster Pot in Mousehole, which she was running as a guest-house.

The rest of the honeymoon they spent in a former artist's studio overlooking the fish market at Newlyn harbour - and in the pubs at Mousehole, Newlyn and Penzance.

Penzance is the place where Calypso, Walter and Polly arrive by the London train at the start of each summer's visit to *The Camomile Lawn*. In Mary Wesley's most famous novel (written from her home in Totnes and published in 1984) it is August 1939 when they arrive. For 10 years the cousins have been coming to Aunt Helena's house, 'square and ugly but in a marvellous position' a short drive from the station, up the steep hill to the cliffs.

After dinner by candlelight on the lawn, they make their annual 'Terror Run' along the coast path, 'with the moon rising over the sea'. But Oliver, lying beside Calypso on the scented lawn in the warmth of the late summer night, decides he must join up and fight in the war. With Helena he makes the dawn drive to London via Truro, Bodmin Moor, past Jamaica Inn, with a stop at Launceston.

Forty-five years later, Helena returns by the same road for Max's funeral, while Sophy, already at the house and filling in

Looking across to St Michael's Mount, George Eliot and G. H. Lewes spent a week 'exploring charming walks round Penzance' in March 1857, before sailing to the Isles of Scilly. In lodgings in Marine Parade, Lewes noted: 'Teapot with wobbley top; fender without rests; chairs with yielding backs...'

time, walks along the cliffs following the Terror Run. It is now, Sophy discovers, the South West Coast Path, 'neatly signposted by the National Trust' and well known to Mary Wesley from many visits to the coast around Lamorna.

DAPHNE DU MAURIER'S CORNWALL

The beauty and the mystery beckon still.

Daphne du Maurier, *Vanishing Cornwall.*

From each of Daphne du Maurier's three Cornish homes she could see the waves beating along the south coast into Fowey Haven. She could walk above the cove where *Rebecca* drowned and hear the cry of the seagulls, as powerful and strange as her story *The Birds*.

Du Maurier's fame is often tied to the grim uplands of Bodmin Moor and *Jamaica Inn*. Her ride through the mists to this smugglers' hideout has taken on folkloric status and the inn, near Bolventor, celebrates her and the book with a den of blood-thirsty bars, themed restaurants and museums.

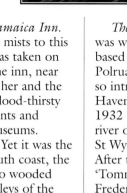

Yet it was the south coast, the two wooded valleys of the Fowey and Helford rivers, where she found most inspiration,

Daphne du Maurier, born in London in 1907, spent most of her life living in Cornwall, researching local history and writing best-sellers, until she died in 1989.

Jamaica Inn near Bolventor, popular with travellers ever since du Maurier's story of smuggling and murder was published in 1936.

wrote world best-sellers, and made her home for over 60 years.

She was 19, holiday-home-hunting with her mother and sisters, when she first came to Bodinnick-by-Fowey.

The hired car swept round the curve of the hill, and suddenly the full expanse of Fowey harbour was spread beneath us...the nearby jetties, the moored ships, the grey roofs of Fowey across the way, the clustering cottages of Polruan on the opposite hill by the harbour mouth...My spirits soared.

Her parents bought the chalet-style boathouse beside Bodinnick ferry and the following year, 1927, Daphne came for the first of many writing visits. She often stayed on when the family went back to London. She would sail up river and wander the cliffs west of Fowey, where she discovered a near-derelict house named Menabilly.

The Loving Spirit, her first book, was written at Bodinnick and based on a boat-building family at Polruan. One of her readers was so intrigued he sailed into Fowey Haven to find the author. In July 1932 she married him, sailing up river on the early-morning tide to St Wyllow's church at Lanteglos. After the ceremony, Daphne and 'Tommy', later General Sir Frederick Browning, sailed west along the coast to honeymoon in the quiet reaches of the Helford river and Frenchman's Creek, a tiny inlet half-hidden by trees and best explored by water.

Their boat, *Ygdrasil*, ended its days as a study in the garden of Menabilly, the house Daphne had dreamed of since 1927. In 1943 she learnt that she and Tommy could lease it from the Rashleigh family who had owned it for 400 years. Apart from periods working away and living in London, it would remain her home - Rebecca's Manderley, the setting for *My Cousin Rachel* and *The King's General* - until 1967. When the lease ended she moved to Kilmarth above Polkerris, another house with a past that merges into the present in *The*

House on the Strand. Published in 1969, she researched it, as always, combing Cornish records for details of the medieval priory at Tywardreath and the powerful families who once ruled Cornwall.

At Fowey, surrounded by centuries of Rashleighs - some buried in the dimly-lit church of St Fimbarrus, others recorded in the oak-panelled rooms of their townhouse, now the Ship Inn - Daphne had become absorbed by Cornish history.

Like the lone yachtsman in *Frenchman's Creek*, puzzling over an old parchment map of Cornwall, who sleeps while 'the past becomes the present', it is easy for du Maurier's readers to imagine time does not exist.

Rebecca still sails below the footpath from Fowey to Pridmouth. Philip Rashleigh's treasure ship is riding at anchor in Fowey Harbour. Lady St Columb waits on the rocks at Readymoney

R uined mine engine houses are part of Bodmin Moor's bleak landscape.

P olkerris, the tiny harbour where The King's General *escapes from the Roundhead soldiers.*

M enabilly, the ivy-covered house (private) that du Maurier discovered in 1927 and made into Rebecca's mysterious Manderley in 1938, became Daphne's own home with her husband and three children.

In Frenchman's Creek, near Helford, Dona St Columb found her pirate lover.

Polruan, the 'clustering cottages' opposite Fowey, is the home of the Slade family in du Maurier's first novel The Loving Spirit.

Cornishman Sir Arthur Quiller-Couch called his Astonishing History of Troy Town, *an 'indiscretion of my youth...' A tale that 'pokes fun at a town which I...loved at first sight'. It was Fowey and it stayed his favourite home till he died in 1944.*

Cove below St Catherine's Castle. Lord Robartes is dining at Lanhydrock House, near Lostwithiel. His Roundheads are gathered above Polkerris to sack Menabilly, not knowing Sir Richard Grenville, *The King's General,* is in hiding on the beach about to sail to safety on the Isles of Scilly.

Castle Dor, based on the Arthurian love-story of Tristram and Iseult and set around the fort and inscribed stone at Four Turnings, was a story Daphne completed when Sir Arthur Quiller-Couch died. He was still working on the manuscript at his Fowey home, The Haven, in 1944, and the story was entrusted to Daphne; just as Sir Arthur had been asked to finish Robert Louis Stevenson's story *St Ives,* (named for a Frenchman, not the town).

Quiller-Couch, his wife and daughter, Foy, were among

Daphne's earliest and firmest friends in Fowey. They supplied tea, supper and local history at their harbourside home, and Foy was her companion on rides over Bodmin.

Scholar-author-critic 'Q', whose memorial stone stands on the headland overlooking the harbour, is remembered chiefly as the first, possibly best, editor of the *Oxford Book of English Verse,* published 1900. But he also wrote stories about Fowey society, *Troy Town;* such gentle, sepia-toned satires that no one minded much, and he was elected mayor of Fowey in 1937.

Q was born in Bodmin, married in 1889 and settled soon afterwards at The Haven, where his literary visitors included J.M.Barrie once or twice, and Kenneth Grahame too often to count.

In July 1899, Grahame was married at St Fimbarrus with Q as his witness. But he only managed to tear himself away from messing about in boats with Q for a three-day honeymoon with Elspeth in St Ives, before hurrying her back for more boating at Fowey.

It was a pattern that went on for years. It gave Elspeth a dim view of marriage, yet it gave Grahame untold material for *The Wind in the Willows.* In May 1907, as well as Fowey, Kenneth and Elspeth spent a few days in Falmouth. From their hotel (since named Greenbank) by the packet-boat quay for Flushing, Grahame wrote to their son, in Sussex with his governess, a series of letter-stories, about a Rat, a Mole and a Toad.

Over the weeks at Fowey, which became 'the little grey sea town' of the Sea Rat's story, Grahame made friends with an American family, Austin Purves and his boys. They were certain, years later, that Mole and Rat's riverside picnic was based on a trip they made with him up the Fowey to Golant.

The 'river bank' stories continued through the autumn and were published 12 months later as *The Wind in the Willows*. Visits to Fowey and Q continued for years, long after Q was knighted in 1910 and made professor of English at Cambridge in 1912.

TORQUAY, DARTMOOR & SOUTH DEVON

Agatha Christie had to admit *The Mystery of the Plymouth Express* was 'easily the worst book I ever wrote'. It's a pity, because it begins with a scene close to her heart for more than 80 years. When the Plymouth Express pulls into Newton Abbot station, doors bang, a stentorian voice shouts 'Plymouth only. Change for Torquay' - and Alec Simpson, RN, finds he is sharing his first-class compartment with a corpse.

Torquay was Agatha Mary Clarissa Miller's birthplace in 1890 and her home until after her first, famously failed marriage in 1914. She returned to the town countless times till her family home in Ashfield Road (demolished) was sold, and in 1938 she bought her own country home, Greenway, a few miles south overlooking the lovely River Dart.

In 1916, living in Torquay while her husband, Archie - later Colonel - Christie, was on active service, she began her first crime novel. Four years and half a dozen publishers' refusals later, Agatha Christie and Hercule Poirot made their detective debut in *The Mysterious Affair at Styles*.

Short stories and at least a book a year followed until *The Murder of Roger Ackroyd* made her name in 1926. It caused a furore with what some critics called a 'rotten' cheat ending. But it was nothing to the fuss that followed her own

Torquay, where Agatha Christie spent a quiet, middle-class childhood and began her career as the 'Queen of Crime Writers'.

Dame Agatha Christie (1890-1976).

Starting high up on Dartmoor, the River Dart widens steadily on its way to the sea, running between Greenway, Dame Agatha's ancient manor house, and Dittisham, the setting for her Ordeal by Innocence.

mysterious disappearance to Harrogate a few months later, allegedly due to loss of memory and a nervous breakdown.

She went on to marry again, become Dame Agatha, universally acknowledged Queen of Crime, author of 80 detective novels and

The Agatha Christie Room in a 13th-century tower at Torre Abbey explains her links with Torquay and South Devon.

Elizabeth Barrett (1806–1861) stayed several years in Devon, first at Sidmouth and later Torquay.

19 plays, plus children's books and romances written under the pseudonym Mary Westmacott.

In the end she grew tired of Poirot, the little Belgian detective with a passion for order and grey cells. But she never went off her other leading character, Miss Marple, the deceptively sweet spinster who solved her first full-length case, *Murder at the Vicarage*, in the deceptively quiet village of St Mary Mead, in 1930.

Poirot tended to get the glamorous locations, like Burgh Island Hotel just off the coast west of Salcombe. It was built in 1929, Art Deco style, and became a favourite with the 'fast set' of the 1930s and 40s: Noel Coward, Mountbatten, King Edward and Mrs Simpson. Agatha Christie was writing while she stayed, and using island settings for two of her most celebrated cases, *Ten Little Niggers*

(retitled *And Then There Were None*) and *Evil Under the Sun*.

She typed most of her books, using three fingers she said, not two, straight on to the 1937 Remington typewriter now kept in a memorial room to her in Torre Abbey, on Torquay seafront. Among the Christie manuscripts, letters and portraits is a 1973 photo of her, hands clasped with glee, beside a giant birthday cake baked for the 21st anniversary of her play *The Mousetrap*, still running in London.

Torquay has more Agatha Christie exhibitions and film-set material in the town museum and a bronze bust of her in Palk Gardens, near the seafront.

The resort was growing increasingly popular as a watering-place when Lord Tennyson and Elizabeth Barrett arrived, separately, in 1838. He called it 'the loveliest sea village in England'. She thought it so improved her health that she stayed three years.

Elizabeth's life and letters have overshadowed her poetry. Her journal records life among 'The Barretts of Wimpole Street'. Her letters were to poet Robert Browning before their runaway marriage in London. But at the time her poetry was rated so highly that she was seriously considered (in 1850) as Wordsworth's successor as Poet Laureate; though her verse-novel *Aurora Leigh* wouldn't appear until later, in 1857.

In 1832 the Barretts settled at Sidmouth, further east on the Devon coast, and over the next three years Elizabeth's health - always a problem - seemed to improve.

Sidmouth, according to Austen family tradition, was the resort where Jane Austen (on holiday from Bath in 1801) fell in love with a young clergyman and might well have married him, if he had not 'died', or otherwise disappeared, soon after.

It may also be the town Jane satirised as a budding resort in her unfinished book, *Sanditon*. But Weymouth, Bognor Regis and Seaford all make similar claims.

Sidmouth obviously had an active social life when the Barretts came, first to a house in Fortfield Terrace. Elizabeth's letters noted 'much quadrilling and cricketing',

donkey rides on the sands, shrimping and boat trips to Dawlish.

Some of the family moved on but Elizabeth stayed, writing and recuperating till late in 1835, before she rejoined them in their new home in London.

Thackeray knew Sidmouth around the same time and used it, renamed Baymouth, in his semi-autobiographical story, *Pendennis,* published 1848. And it was still in its hey-day when Beatrix Potter came, at least three times between 1901 and 1910, and made sketches that ended up in *Little Pig Robinson* alongside scenes of Lyme Regis.

But when Elizabeth Barrett needed Devon air again, after

three years in London, she decided to try Torquay. Staying in Beacon Terrace at Bath House (now the Hotel Regina, marked with a plaque) she recorded: 'Here we are immediately upon the lovely bay - a few paces dividing our door from its waves.'

At first she grew stronger but in 1840 her much-loved brother, Edward, who had come with her against their father's wishes, was drowned while sailing nearby in Babbacombe Bay. Grief and guilt overwhelmed her and she was still an invalid when she returned to London the following year.

*N*o letters remain *from Jane Austen's visit to Sidmouth (above and left) and her holiday romance. There is only the word of her sister, who destroyed Jane's papers, that the man she met had won her heart and was 'worthy' of her.*

*W*illiam Makepeace *Thackeray (1811–1863) had just finished* Vanity Fair *when he wrote* Pendennis, *bringing his love-sick hero 'Pen' to Sidmouth to discover more about a beautiful, but unsuitable, young actress.*

Dartington Hall, restored in the 1920s by Dorothy and Leonard Elmhirst, greatly influenced by Indian poet and guru Rabindranath Tagore, who received the Nobel prize in 1913.

Robert Herrick (1591–1674), one of the Cavalier poets who made up 'the tribe of Ben', or 'sons' of Ben Jonson. He wrote most of his pastoral poems at Dean Prior (right) and named them Hesperides *on account of their western origin.*

East of Torquay, the River Dart - so thickly wooded around Agatha Christie's house Greenway that only her boathouse is visible - flows through Dartington and Totnes, one of the oldest boroughs in Devon.

Totnes has a literary tradition that begins with 12th-century chronicler Geoffrey of Monmouth. In his fanciful *History of the Kings of Britain* he declares it was founded by Brutus the Trojan. Now it's known for Dartington's arts centre and for novelist Mary Wesley, who wrote her first book, *Jumping the Queue* from her Totnes home, and went on using West Country scenes in *The Camomile Lawn* and *Harnessing Peacocks.*

Irish playwright Sean O'Casey left London for the country, just as he had left Dublin for London, at odds with theatres and audiences. He lived more than 15 years near the Dartington estate so his children could attend the progressive school set up in the cultural community that Leonard and Dorothy Elmhirst founded in the 1920s.

The school has closed but the arts centre flourishes. There are summer festivals of music and literature around the medieval Great Hall; and High Cross House has the Elmhirsts' contemporary arts and crafts collection. It includes first editions and correspondence with T. E. Lawrence 'of Arabia', Bertrand Russell, Agatha Christie and others.

Dean Prior, a small village near Dartington, on the edge of Dartmoor, would have suited Agatha Christie's Miss Marple very well. It didn't suit 17th-century poet and cleric Robert Herrick at all. Or so he said. His poems, of which he wrote hundreds including some of

the finest lyrics in English, are packed with pastoral images: *Corinna's Going a-Maying, Cherry Ripe* and his advice *To Virgins,* 'Gather ye rosebuds while ye may'.

Herrick came to Dean Prior as

vicar of St Mary's in 1630 when he was 39. He had already acquired a taste for London's Royalist and literary circles and went straight back to them when Parliament expelled him from his church in 1647. With the Restoration of the king, the Dean Prior living became his again in 1662 and he stayed till he died 12 years later.

His grave in St Mary's is uncertain, though a stone has been placed in the graveyard. More recently he was honoured with an

inscription in a church window; and in the 1960s he suddenly reached new readers when the Pirelli tyre company used a Herrick quote on one of its collectors-piece calendars:

> Whenas in silks my Julia
>   goes,
> Then, then (methinks) how
>   sweetly flows
> That liquefaction of her
>   clothes.

Behind Dean Prior, where Dartmoor rises rough and remote around Princetown, Sherlock Holmes rules. Ever since Sir Arthur Conan Doyle published the spine-chilling case of *The Hound of the Baskervilles* in 1902, the granite-strewn moorland has been Holmes's special patch.

Conan Doyle was inspired by stories of a spectral hound haunting the moor, which he heard while visiting the Duchy Hotel in Princetown (now Dartmoor National Park's High Moorland Visitor Centre). The local tales are based, some say, on Squire Cabell of Brook, near Buckfastleigh - a man so evil that, on his death in 1677, a pack of fire-breathing hounds emerged from the moor to carry his soul down to hell.

In 1900, when Sir Arthur came to Dartmoor, Sherlock Holmes was already 'dead', deliberately done away with by his author and Professor Moriarty at the Reichenbach Falls. Doyle had lost interest in his pipe-smoking sleuth and he took a considerable chance in reviving him.

He also took considerable licence with Dartmoor. Writing from his Surrey home, Undershaw (now a hotel) near Hindhead, Doyle made the moor bigger and wilder. He exaggerated the bogs, turning Grimspound into the

*S*ir Arthur Conan Doyle, caricatured in 1926 still shackled to his hero Sherlock Holmes. Doyle had tried to kill off Holmes more than 30 years before to allow him to write historical novels. But he brought him back to solve the case of The Hound of the Baskervilles, *said to haunt Dartmoor (left).*

*S*herlock Holmes, brought 'to life' again, at Dartmoor's High Moorland Visitor Centre.

Exmoor, the country-side of R. F. Delderfield's school-story To Serve Them All My Days *and the trilogy* A Horseman Riding By.

Grimpen Mire, and he shifted Princetown. But the book was a triumph and the Moorland Visitor Centre pays due tribute to Holmes and the Hound. It also has extracts and displays about other local writers, like Eden Phillpotts, who wrote dozens of Dartmoor novels including *Children in the Mist* and *Widecombe Fair*, published 1913.

R. D. Blackmore (1825–1900):'In everything, except the accident of birth, I am Devonian; my ancestry were all Devonians.'

St Mary the Virgin, Oare parish church for over 800 years.

NORTH DEVON AND SOMERSET

'A shot rang through the church' - and Lorna Doone lies wounded in her wedding dress. It is not unusual to find readers of R. D. Blackmore's *Lorna Doone* studying the altar steps of Oare church, between Lynton and Porlock, and roaming Exmoor book in hand.

Blackmore based his 'Romance of Exmoor' on legends of the Doone family, outlawed from

Scotland in 1620, who led a reign of cruelty over the remote moorlands for nearly 70 years.

Richard Doddridge Blackmore lived in Devon from the age of six, when his father became curate at Culmstock and then Ashford near Barnstaple. He attended Old Blundell's School at Tiverton, like his hero John Ridd. He spent holidays at the village of Charles with a clerical uncle, and toured the Devon-Somerset border with his grandfather, another vicar, whose livings included the parish of Oare.

Lorna Doone was mostly written from memory, in London, though Blackmore did pay a refresher visit, staying at Winsford. He confessed after the book was published in 1869 he would have made the sites more factual if he had realised so many readers would search them out.

Still, some of the descriptions are unmistakable and he gave his blessing to Oare as the setting for Carver Doone's attempted murder in the church (it has a Blackmore memorial).

South of Malmsmead, Badgworthy Water leads past a Blackmore memorial stone to the cascading stream John Ridd calls 'a long pale slide of water'; and on to Doone Valley, the 'deep green valley, carved from the mountains in a perfect oval', generally agreed to be Lank Combe.

Porlock is the town where John goes to buy gunpowder and lead, and Watchet is the scene of Lorna's kidnap.

Blackmore followed the Doones with *Christowell*, a Dartmoor story, but it never caught on like *Lorna Doone*. The Exmoor story became so popular that Ordnance Survey maps name the area Doone Country; Exeter Cathedral has a Blackmore memorial; and at Dulverton, Exmoor National Park office has a statue of Lorna.

Dulverton is also the town where David Powlett-Jones arrives and falls asleep at the station on his way to a public school on Exmoor, in *To Serve Them All My Days*. R. F. Delderfield grew up on the edge of Exmoor and used Devon backgrounds both for the story of David's teaching days at Bamfylde, published 1972; and for *A Horseman Riding By*, the trilogy that begins when Paul Craddock moves into the Sorrel Valley.

Beside Exeter Cathedral sits a statue of theological writer Richard Hooker. Born in the city in 1554, his Lawes of Ecclesiastical Politie *marked him out as the Elizabethans' finest exponent of the Anglican church-state relationship.*

Following Samuel Taylor Coleridge through north Devon and Somerset would mean walking up to 40 miles a day - along the coast, through Exmoor, over the Quantocks and the Blackdown hills.

From his 'hovel' at Nether Stowey, now named Coleridge Cottage, he would walk to Bristol, Bridgwater and Taunton. With essayist William Hazlitt he walked to Lynton, talking all the way.

In 1796 he strode south to Racedown in Dorset to see William Wordsworth and his sister Dorothy. The following year, once the Wordsworths had moved nearer Nether Stowey, they walked with him to Watchet one November afternoon and listened, according to Dorothy's letters, while he began *The Rime of the Ancient Marriner*.

Most famous of all his walks is the one along the coast when he paused near Porlock to write down what he could remember of an opium-dream; until 'a person on business from Porlock' interrupted, the dream vanished and with it most of the poem *Kubla Khan*.

By birth Coleridge was a Devon man, from Ottery St Mary, where his father was headmaster of the grammar school and rector of St Mary's. Samuel, born in 1772, was the youngest of 10, petted at home till his father died in 1781 and he was sent away to school.

Samuel Taylor Coleridge (1772–1834).

'*Coleridge came in the morning,*' Dorothy Wordsworth wrote in her journal, February 26, 1798. *Walking back with him over the Quantocks (above) to Stowey, 'We lay sidelong upon the turf, and gazed on the landscape till it melted into more than natural loveliness.'*

During Coleridge's stay in the cottage at Nether Stowey (centre) he wrote The Rime of the Ancient Mariner *and the fragmentary poem:*
'In Xanadu did
Kubla Khan
A stately pleasure-
dome decree;
Where Alph, the
sacred river, ran
Through caverns
measureless to man
Down to a sunless
sea.'

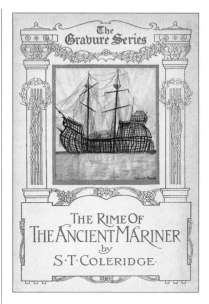

The Gravure Series

THE RIME OF
THE ANCIENT MARINER
by
S·T·COLERIDGE·

As Inspector Morse discovers on his Coleridge pilgrimage to Ottery St Mary, in *The Way Through the Woods*, Coleridge's rectory, school and schoolhouse have gone. Only the splendid 14th-century, collegiate church of St Mary remains, with 'a low-relief bust of the poet beneath the outspread wings of an albatross.'

Distinctly disappointed, Morse moves on to Somerset, Nether Stowey and the cottage where the poet lived barely two years. Here in the Quantocks Coleridge found his poetic kingdom and wrote most of his best verses.

Coleridge's first walks in Somerset were with Robert Southey, in August 1794, and Southey's prosaically named dog, Rover. Starting from Southey's birthplace in Bristol (the cathedral has a bust), they con-

St Mary Redcliffe, Bristol.

tinued to plan the 'Pantisocratic' community they had dreamed up in Southey's rooms at Oxford.

In Bristol over the next few months, Coleridge met Southey's friends the Fricker sisters and, though Coleridge left no mention of it, William Wordsworth.

Wordsworth did record it: 'Coleridge was at Bristol...I saw but little of him. I wished indeed to have seen more - his talent appears to me very great.'

In October 1795, Coleridge and Sara Fricker were married (Southey and Sara's sister Edith followed suit in November) at St Mary Redcliffe church. It was, Coleridge noted, the same fine

church where the 'marvellous boy' poet, Thomas Chatterton, claimed he had found some poems by a medieval monk, Thomas Rowley. Chatterton had, in fact, written them himself, forged the manuscripts and committed suicide in London, in 1770, when he was still aged only 17.

From Bristol, Coleridge and Sara went to Clevedon, on the coast, for a six-week honeymoon. Clevedon Court, an ancient manor house nearby, was the family home of the Eltons, whose daughter, Mrs Brookfield, William Thackeray fell in love with after his wife was certified 'insane'.

Thackeray spent some time at the house, seeing Mrs Brookfield, writing parts of *Vanity Fair* and gathering material for *Henry Esmond*, in which Clevedon becomes Castlewood.

Lord Tennyson's student friend Arthur Hallam, who had showed great promise as a poet, was another of the Elton family. When Arthur died abroad in 1833 he was brought back and buried with the Eltons in St Andrew's church. Tennyson never got over Hallam's early death and insisted on visiting the grave during his honeymoon in 1850; the same year his poem *In Memoriam, A. H. H.* was eventually published.

Once Coleridge and Sara's first child was born in 1796, Coleridge decided his sort of writing would not support them in Bristol. He imagined a 'rustic scheme' of self-sufficiency, surrounded by the glorious Quantock countryside, and moved them to the 'hovel' at Nether Stowey. In reality, the tiny primitive house (since enlarged), plagued with mice and damp, was not likely to suit him for long. Nor were Sara and his dreams of 'Pantisocracy' - already shelved indefinitely.

But for a while he was inspired. He wrote *Frost at Midnight* and the first part of *Christabel*. While Sara was out walking with writer Charles Lamb and the Wordsworths (William and Dorothy had moved to Alfoxden, now Alfoxton Hotel, in July 1797, to be near them) he wrote *This Lime-Tree Bower My Prison*.

In *Lyrical Ballads* he and Wordsworth published the extraordinarily rich collection of poems they had worked on and discussed

together in Somerset. William's included *Lines Composed a Few Miles above Tintern Abbey* and *The Idiot Boy*. Coleridge put in only four of the 23 poems (more in later editions), but one was his great, ballad-style *Rime of the Ancient Mariner.*

By the time they appeared in 1798, the Stowey period was almost over. Coleridge's opium addiction and splintering marriage were not the only problems. Local suspicion was mounting that the two poets were French spies (shades of D. H. Lawrence at Zennor in Cornwall a century later) and the Wordsworths' lease was brought to an end. When they left for a visit to Germany, Coleridge went too. He returned to Somerset only briefly before they all set up home again in the Lake Distict.

Charles Kingsley based *Westward Ho!*, a swash-buckling, Elizabethan story, on 'the little white town of Bideford'. There, he wrote, the River Torridge 'joins her sister Taw and both together flow quietly toward...the everlasting thunder

*R*obert Southey, born in Bristol 1774, Poet Laureate from 1813 until his death in 1843, first met Coleridge in Oxford.

*C*harles Kingsley's statue on Bideford quay carries a copy of Westward Ho!

*K*ingsley, born in Devon in 1819, spent most of his life in Hampshire, wrote The Water Babies *about Yorkshire and* Hereward the Wake *about the Fens. But he remained in spirit a Devon man.*

of the long Atlantic swell'.

Kingsley was born at Holne on the edge of Dartmoor in 1819 while his father was curate (the church has a memorial window). Almost immediately they moved to East Anglia and he was 12 before they returned to Devon. This time they lived five years at picturesque Clovelly, and again the church records Kingsley's presence. Most of his adult life was lived in Hampshire and Cambridge, yet Kingsley had seen enough of Devon to feel he had roots there.

In 1849 he was in Clovelly again and persistent local tradition says his long stay at Bideford, begun in 1854, was spent in an old merchant's house (now part of The Royal Hotel) writing *Westward Ho!*

Bideford, once the home port of Sir Richard Grenville, the seafarer hero of Tennyson's poem The Revenge, *who refused to leave his 'Men of Bideford in Devon' at 'Flores in the Azores'.*

Charles Kingsley and his wife at Eversley, Hampshire, where he was curate and rector from 1842 till his death in 1875.

His research for the book, the adventures of Sir Amyas Leigh and the Spanish Armada, had taken him south to Kilkhampton church to see the monuments of the seafaring Grenville family. From there he went to Stowe Barton, site of the Grenvilles'

mansion and later home to Sir Richard Grenville, Daphne du Maurier's Civil War hero in *The King's General*.

When *Westward Ho!* was published in 1855 it caught the rising tide of Victorian patriotism brought on by the Crimean War. By the 1870s, Kingsley was so popular - thanks partly to his book *The Water Babies* - that a modern resort close by was named Westward Ho! and a Kingsley statue stands on Bideford quay.

Rudyard Kipling knew Westward Ho! when he was a boarder at the United Services College, opened in 1874 as a school for future soldiers of the Empire. He was sent there, aged 12, from the 'House of Desolation' in Southsea, where he had spent an appalling childhood with foster parents while his own were in India. It was good preparation.

At school Kipling was nicknamed 'Gigger' on account of his exceptionally thick spectacles, and he described his first term as 'horrible'. But he was encouraged to write and when his schoolboy stories, *Stalky & Co*, were published in 1899, in which he and two friends are Beetle, Stalky and M'Turk respectively, he dedicated the book to his old headmaster.

After his death the Kipling Memorial Fund bought the 'furze-hill' behind the college, an open space renamed Kipling Tors, and gave it to the National Trust.

K ingsley's countryside is the same 'Land of the Two Rivers', the Taw and Torridge, that Henry Williamson made the territory of *Tarka the Otter*.

Williamson's unsentimental, ultimately tragic story of Tarka was written over several years while he lived at Georgeham in the 1920s. It begins where Tarka was born at Owlery Holt, by Canal Bridge over the Torridge near Weare Giffard village.

Williamson said Tarka was old Celtic for 'little water wanderer' and the otter's wanderings take him down river under Bideford bridge to the marshes and the

open sea. Travelling back up river he comes on to Dartmoor, near Okehampton; then down the Taw, passing Eggesford, until he is wounded by otter hunters and drifts with the river into Barnstaple (the branch line from Exeter, served by sprinter trains, follows the riverside all the way).

Crossing Exmoor, Tarka meets hunters again, slips in and out of the rivers above Lynton and Lynmouth, reaches the safety of the sea and swims westwards along the north Devon coast. The long journey back to the Taw-Torridge estuary takes him past Ilfracombe, where Williamson later lived near the harbour; and on to Woolacombe Sands, below the author's 'Writing Hut' at Georgeham.

But Tarka's happy reunion with his mate White-tip ends when he is pursued up the Torridge again by the terrifying hunt and his old hound enemy, Deadlock. In the pools below Great Torrington Common they catch up with him and Tarka is finally trapped when a dragonfly settles on his nose and makes him sneeze.

Henry Williamson's meticulous wildlife detail owed a lot to 19th-century Wiltshire writer Richard Jefferies, author of *Bevis, the Story of a Boy*. But Williamson's tales of Tarka, published in 1927, and *Salar the Salmon*, now draw a wider readership than Jefferies'; especially since a Tarka trail has been signposted, with displays at information centres and an exhibition in the North Devon Museum at Barnstaple.

C anal Bridge near Great Torrington, where:
'The river walks in the valley singing Letting her veils blow'
Torridge by Ted Hughes.

T he Long Bridge at Barnstaple dates from 1437.

W oolacombe's three-mile beach near the villages of Georgeham and Croyde, re-named Ham and Cryde in Henry Williamson's novels.

John Gay, author of 'How happy could I be with either, Were t'other dear charmer away', was buried in Westminster Abbey in 1732 with his own epitaph: 'Life is a jest; and all things show it. I thought so once; but now I know it.'

The old market town of Barnstaple is generally claimed as the birthplace of playwright and satirist John Gay, author of *The Beggar's Opera* - 'A Newgate Pastoral'.

Some say he was born at Frithelstock, south of Bideford. But everyone agrees the date was 1685; he grew up in Barnstaple; his father died when he was about six; and he went to the local grammar school.

In Gay's day the school was in St Anne's chapel, near the parish church. Built as a medieval bone house, it has been restored as a school-museum and includes a desk carved with Gay's name. His portraits hang in the Guildhall, close to the

The Pannier Market, Barnstaple, near the site of Gay's home.

Pannier Market and the tiny old shops in Butchers Row, and in Barnstaple museum.

From school Gay was sent to London, apprenticed to a silk dealer, where he made friends with Alexander Pope and Jonathan Swift. They seem to have suspended their savage wit where he was concerned, disarmed by Gay's amiable nature and talent; though Swift always made digs at him for being a duchess's lapdog, idling his time with wealthy patrons.

Yet it was Swift who suggested that a ballad-play based on Newgate jail 'might make an odd pretty sort of thing'. It did. When *The Beggar's Opera* was staged in 1728 it took London by storm. Gay's good-natured story of

Gay's gambling, drinking and socialising, sometimes at Bath (right) struck friends as a waste of talent. 'I find by the whole cast of your letter, that you are as giddy and volatile as ever,' wrote Swift, shortly before Gay died.

Macheath the highwayman and pretty Polly Peachum, with its underlying pathos and string of popular songs - 'Over the Hills and Far Away', 'Love's the Season Made for Joy' - played for an unprecedented seven weeks, with four nights as author's benefits.

FASHIONABLE BATH

Few cities have had so many and so mixed write-ups as Bath received in the 17th and 18th centuries. Some writers loved it, others loathed it. No one stayed indifferent - and no one of note stayed away.

After its first royal visitors came in 1615, Bath developed into the most popular spa in the country. It was planned to perfection as the leisure centre of the Age of Reason: *the* place to bathe and drink the water, to see and be

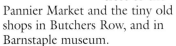

seen. But it also gained a reputation as the raciest place in Britain.

Pepys was intrigued. Smollett was appalled. Sheridan, on the make, made off with a lady. Fanny Burney thought it beautiful. Jane Austen thought it all right until she had to live there. Mrs Thrale settled in to enjoy widowhood, twice. Fielding came to stay with worthy Ralph Allen and turned him into Tom Jones's fairy godfather. Oliver Goldsmith came to write a life of Beau Nash. Charles Dickens came and met a man named Mr Pickwick. Wordsworth lodged in a house on North Parade; Walter Scott chose one on South Parade (now Pratt's Hotel).

So much of their city remains unspoilt that it is a first-rate place to 'watch' writers and characters sauntering along the wide parades, shopping on Pulteney Bridge, attending service in the Abbey Church. The Assembly Rooms where they danced now contain a costume museum that has the sort of bonnets Jane Austen bought. The Pump Room where they gathered still serves refreshments with a dash of chamber music among the potted plants.

Here is Pepys bathing in the Cross Bath in June 1668, one eye on 'very fine ladies', the other on hygiene: 'methinks it cannot be clean to go so many bodies in the same water.'

There sits Tobias Smollett's cantankerous character Matthew Bramble in *Humphrey Clinker*, declaring in the 1760s:

'You must know, I find nothing but disappointment at Bath, which is so altered, that I can scarcely believe it is the same place that I frequented about thirty years ago... [it is] become the very centre of racket and dissipation.'
Oliver Goldsmith, staying on North Parade

at much the same time, writing *The Life of Richard Nash, Esq,* records the rules Nash laid down as Master of Ceremonies and the daily social routine. Early morning meant visits to the baths followed by the Pump Room, the coffee-houses and breakfast parties. Afternoons were for walks, rides and carriage drives. At night there was the theatre, cards or concerts, plus a ball every Tuesday and Friday.

The 'racket and dissipation' is exactly what attracted bright young, and not-so-young, things like Fanny Burney; Lydia Languish in Sheridan's *The Rivals;* and Catherine Morland in Jane Austen's *Northanger Abbey*, full of 'eager delight' in the city and her

*B*ath's Museum of Costume is housed in the Assembly Rooms, the 'Upper Rooms' opened 1771, where Catherine Morland spends happy evenings dancing with Henry Tilney before visiting his family at Northanger Abbey.

*S*amuel Pepys in Bath: 'I staying above two hours in the water, home to bed... and by and by, comes musick to play to me, extraordinary good as ever I heard.'

The Circus at Bath, from a water-colour dated 1784, 30 years after it was laid out by John Wood.

The Royal Crescent, Bath's finest 18th-century landmark, is said to include the home of Sir Percy Blakeney, Baroness Orczy's original for The Scarlet Pimpernel, *published 1905. No.1 is now a Georgian House Museum.*

fashionable new friends.

Here is Miss Burney arriving in April 1780 with Dr Johnson's friends Mr and Mrs Thrale: 'Tuesday morning we spent in walking all over the town, viewing the beautiful Circus, the company-crowded Pump-room, and the exquisite Crescent...'

Fanny was here again, summer 1791, having just resigned after five years as Second Keeper of the Robes to Queen Charlotte. And again, staying in Queen Square, she writes long sisterly letters recounting her regular social round and an acutely embarrassing encounter with the famously-unfaithful Lady Duncannon: 'This was the last thing I could have wished.'

Jane Austen is far less squeamish. Writing to her sister the morning after a ball in 1801, she boasts, 'I am proud to say that I have a very good eye at an Adulteress, for tho' repeatedly assured that another in the same party was the *She*, I fixed upon the right one from the first.'

The tone is playful, but Jane hated being in Bath that year - and for the next five. Her parents had suddenly retired from the family's Hampshire home, selling the furniture including Jane's books and piano (it fetched eight guineas), in order to live in lodgings in Bath.

Jane had tolerated the place on previous visits in her early twenties, in November 1797 and May 1799. But living here - chiefly at 4 Sydney Place - was different. For one thing her aunt and uncle lived in Paragon Buildings and Jane could rarely resist a chance to be caustic about Aunt Leigh-Perrot.

By this time Bath was increasingly a place to retrench or retire to. Fanny Burney would come back in 1814 with her husband, General d'Arblay, and stay till she buried him four years later at St Swithin's (where she and their son are also buried).

Hester Thrale Piozzi came back to live in Russell Street after Mr Thrale died in 1781 and left when she married Mr Piozzi here three years later. Widowed again in 1809, she returned, took up residence in Gay Street and carried on dancing till her eightieth year, in 1820.

Jane danced too, went to concerts and parties. But like Anne Elliot, heroine of her last book *Persuasion* (written years after she had left the city) Jane 'persisted in a very determined, though very silent disinclination for Bath...anticipating an imprisonment of many months.'

Jane's 'imprisonment' lasted until June 1806, 18 months after her father died and was buried in St Swithin's, where he had married Jane's mother in 1764. Yet while she was irritated by 'another stupid party last night' and the 'common-place nonsense talked, but scarcely any wit', Jane reproduced them to a nicety in *Northanger Abbey*.

Probably her first complete mature novel, she uses it to burlesque Bath society and the current vogue for Gothic novels. *Northanger Abbey* sees Jane in high summer, satirising Mrs Radcliffe's sort of novels, notably *The Mysteries of Udolpho*, and taking a few swipes at Fanny Burney's *Evelina*.

Persuasion is Jane's autumn story, written only months before she died in 1817. Looking back over her life and loves she recasts them as Anne Elliot's. Anne comes to Bath at 27, past her best, still regretting she gave in to persuasion and didn't marry Captain Wentworth years ago. But for Jane there was never the happy reunion with her first serious suitor (Tom Lefroy, who eventually became Lord Chief Justice of Ireland) that Anne and Wentworth enjoy 'as they slowly paced the gradual ascent' - often assumed to mean the terraces beneath the Royal Crescent.

Near the middle of the crescent, in No 11, lived a young lady who Richard Brinsley Sheridan 'escorted' to France in 1772, to get her away from a rival suitor.

Sheridan was born in Dublin in 1751, went to school at Harrow, and arrived in Bath with his parents in 1770, where they lived in New King Street. He was supposed to be reading for the law

Beau Nash laid down rules for polite society – 'That the elder ladies and children be content with a second bench at the ball', and 'That ladies coming to the ball appoint a time for their footmen to wait on them home'. But the city drew so many less-than-polite visitors it was easy to satirise the 'Comforts of Bath' in 1798.

Henry Fielding, born at Sharpham Park near Glastonbury, 1707, stayed several times in and around Bath, at Charlecombe, where he was married in 1734, Twerton and Widcombe.

Tobias Smollett, born in Scotland, 1721, died in Italy 1771, sick, morose and unkindly caricatured by Sterne as 'the learned Smellfungus', in A Sentimental Journey.

At the Abbey Church, in Bath's Parade Gardens, Pepys noted: 'Here a good organ; but a vain, pragmatical fellow preached a ridiculous, affected sermon, that made me angry.'

but he fell in love with a beautiful singer, Elizabeth Linley.

When the young couple returned from France, Sheridan found his rival still fuming, fought two duels with him (in spite of Bath's no-duelling rule) and finally went off with Elizabeth to London to get married.

Once in London, Sheridan soon turned their adventures into his first play, *The Rivals*, set on the streets of Bath and full of young lovers and duels - but really starring Mrs Malaprop.

Charles Dickens used the Royal Crescent as the scene of the 'extraordinary calamity' suffered by Mr Nathaniel Winkle in *The Posthumous Papers of the Pickwick Club*.

Issued in cheap instalments, starting April 1836, Dickens's first novel reached a vast new audience. Everyone could read or hear about the Pickwickians and their jaunts round the country to Ipswich, Tewkesbury and Bath - the places Dickens had visited as a journalist working on the London-based *Morning Chronicle*.

At Bath the previous year, Dickens had met one Moses Pickwick, a foundling, named after the hamlet he came from, five miles away at Corsham. Moses had worked his way up in the world to become manager of Bath's White Hart coaching inn (demolished) and owner of the Bath-to-London coach service. As usual, once Dickens had hit on the name of a character he was away.

In Bath, Dickens also heard about Sally Lunn, who invented Bath's famous tea-cakes at the bow-windowed bakery where they are still served warm with melted butter (various flavours but somehow cinnamon seems best with Dickens).

In 1840, coming back to Bath

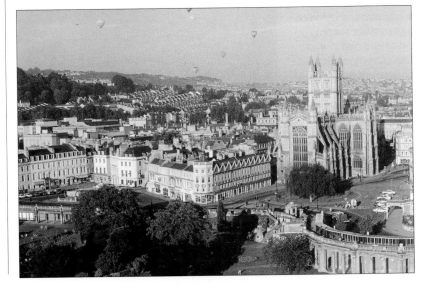

Prior Park (now a school), designed 1735, where Ralph Allen kept open house . to Henry Fielding, but Mrs Allen refused to see Alexander Pope's friend Martha Blount.

as a famous novelist, Dickens stayed with poet and essayist Walter Savage Landor in St James's Square. Landor was delighted that his house was the place where Dickens thought up Little Nell, the tear-jerking heroine of *The Old Curiosity Shop*. He wasn't at all pleased that he himself turned up as Lawrence Boythorn, the kindly old man with an explosive temper in *Bleak House*.

One of Bath's most famously kind men was local benefactor Ralph Allen. He made a fortune pioneering a postal service and spent it supporting good causes; befriending writers and artists; and building Prior Park, a magnificent Palladian mansion on the edge of the city.

Alexander Pope came a number of times around 1740 to advise on the design of Allen's estate, where the large garden is being restored with grottos, bridges, cascades and temples.

Samuel Richardson, 'father of the novel', who wrote *Pamela or Virtue Rewarded* and *Clarissa*, was a visitor rather than a regular. That may be because his rival Henry

Fielding was a favourite with Allen, and Richardson never forgave Fielding for parodying his work in *Shamela* and *Joseph Andrews*.

Fielding knew the area well and often stayed with Allen in and around Bath in the 1740s while he worked on *Tom Jones*. There was approval all round when Fielding identified

Mr Pickwick and his club took their name from the owner of a hostelry at Bath in Stall Street, one Moses (or Eleazear) Pickwick.

Ralph Allen as the original for Tom's wise and generous guardian, Squire Allworthy.

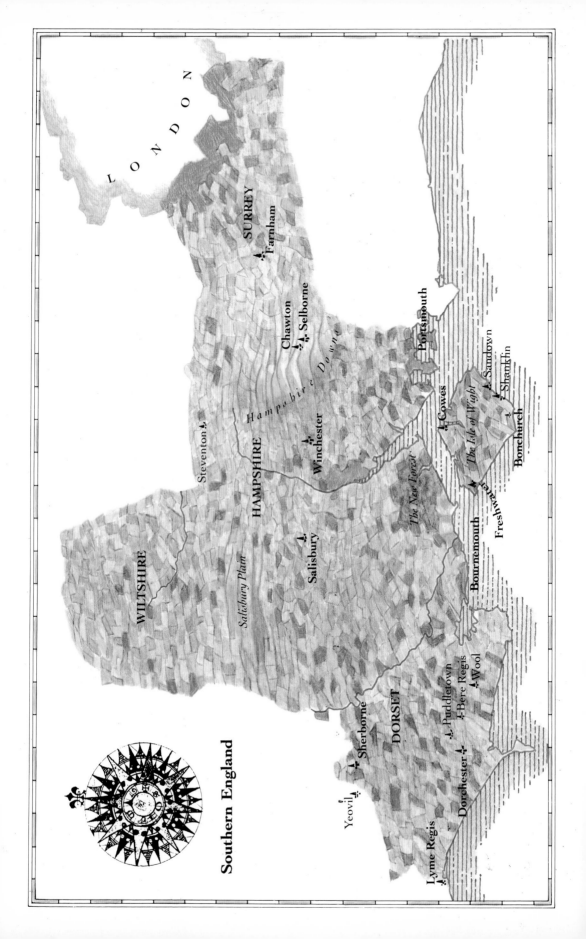

Southern England

CHAPTER 2

SOUTHERN ENGLAND

CATHEDRALS AND CLASSICS

Anthony Trollope began his Barsetshire novels by hiding Barchester somewhere in southern England:'The Rev. Septimus Harding was, a few years since, a beneficed clergyman residing in the cathedral town of -; let us call it Barchester. Were we to name Wells or Salisbury, Exeter, Hereford or Gloucester, it might be presumed that something personal was intended.'

Years later, in his autobiography, he did name Salisbury as the original (though strictly speaking Winchester was involved too). He recalled a visit there in May 1852 when 'wandering one midsummer evening round the purlieus of the cathedral I conceived *The Warden* – from whence came that series of novels of which Barchester, with its bishops, deans and archdeacon, was the central site.'

Trollope was then still working full-time for the post office, so *The Warden* took a couple of years

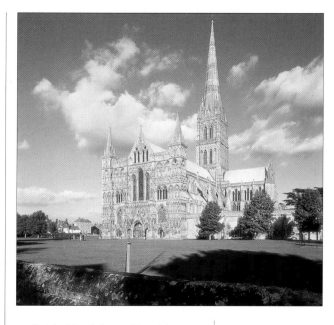

to finish. He followed it with *Barchester Towers, Dr Thorne, Framley Parsonage* and *The Small House at Allington*, unrolling the map of Barsetshire bit by bit and filling it with kind old Mr Harding, grandiose Dr Grantly, insufferable Mrs Proudie, slimy Mr Slope; not to mention pretty Lucy Robarts and Lord Lufton, jilted Lily Dale and faithful Johnny Eames.

By 1867 when he reached *The Last Chronicle of Barset*, Trollope had already launched a new, London-based series: the political world of the Pallisers and the romantic intrigues of Lady Glencora and Phineas Finn. It

Salisbury Cathedral inspired Dickens, Trollope, Hardy, and Nobel Prize winner William Golding, whose story of Dean Jocelin, driven by a vision to build The Spire, *was published 1964.*

Anthony Trollope (1815–1882) caricatured in Vanity Fair *magazine, 1873.*

never quite matched the charm and popularity of the Barsetshire Chronicles, which began when Trollope 'stood for an hour on the little bridge in Salisbury', enjoying the lovely cathedral and its quiet close.

Charles Dickens had already put Salisbury scenes in *Martin Chuzzlewit*; though the city and Martin are both thoroughly upstaged by two of Dickens's greatest comic characters, Mr Pecksniff and Mrs Gamp. And by saintly Tom Pinch, who had 'a shrewd notion that Salisbury was a very desperate sort of place: an exceeding wild and dissipated city'.

Thomas Hardy, on the other hand, thought: 'Upon the whole the Close of Salisbury under the full summer moon on a windless night, is as beautiful a scene as any I know in England.'

In the Wessex novels, Hardy renamed it Melchester and used it in *Jude the Obscure*. When Jude follows Sue Bridehead to her training school he finds himself by the cathedral, 'standing under the walls of the most graceful architec-

tural pile in England'.

Jude admits to Sue, as they wander by the market, that he is already married, and before long she marries Mr Phillotson in Salisbury's medieval church of St Thomas, asking Jude to give her away.

More recently, William Golding's *The Spire* and Edward Rutherfurd's *Sarum* have re-told

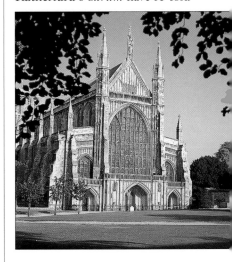

the story of the cathedral. Rutherfurd charts the entire history of the city from pre-historic life on Salisbury Plain to present-day efforts to save the cathedral and its spire from collapsing. 'No place in England, I believe, has a longer visible history of building and occupation than the Sarum region,' he explains.

The Henge in *Sarum* is the same 'heathen temple' that Thomas Hardy describes in *Tess of the d'Urbervilles*, as Tess, fleeing from the scene of Alec d'Urberville's murder, rests among the stones with Angel on the grass beside her. While they listen 'a long time to the wind among the pillars', dawn breaks and Tess's captors close in.

The city of Winchester certainly had played a part in the birth of Trollope's Barchester, even if with hindsight he decided it was subsidiary. It supplied the story line – the dispute over the wardenship of Hiram's Hospital.

At school in Winchester, Trollope knew the medieval almshouse at St Cross; the oldest place in Britain to keep up the custom of the Wayfarer's Dole, handing out bread and ale to travellers. He also knew of the scandal about the almshouses' wealth, which blew up in 1808 and took 50 years to settle.

John Keats had heard it, too, when he came to Winchester late in the summer of 1819. He described St Cross as 'a very inter-

esting old place, both for its Gothic tower and alms-square and for the appropriation of its rich rents', which went to a relation of the Bishop of Winchester, not the 13 poor inmates.

Keats arrived in the city on August 12 and spent two months in lodgings near the cathedral, walking every day through the

cathedral and College Street to St Cross Meadows and the river.

It wasn't the happiest period for him. He was short of money,

ill and wretchedly in love with Fanny Brawne. Writing to her in London on August 17 he complained, 'I am not happy enough for silken Phrases, and silver sentences. ...it seems to me that a few more moments thought of you would uncrystallize and dissolve me. I must not give way to it – but turn to my writing again – if I fail I shall die hard. O my love, your lips are growing sweet again to my fancy – I must forget them.'

When he did turn to his poetry again, one September day after walking through the watermeadows by the Itchen, Keats wrote the ode *To Autumn*:

> *Season of mists and mellow*
>   *fruitfulness,*
> *Close bosom-friend of the*
>   *maturing sun;*
> *Conspiring with him how to*
>   *load and bless*
> *With fruit the vines that*
>   *round the thatch-eves run.*

Izaak Walton also enjoyed the watermeadows and fishing in the River Itchen. He came to Winchester in 1662 as steward to the bishop. A few years later a revised edition of Walton's *Compleat Angler* was published. It is the only one of numerous books

'I take a walk every day for an hour before dinner...under the trees, past the beautiful front of the Cathedral' – John Keats in lodgings at Winchester, autumn 1819. There is a trail through the Close (above) following his route to the river.

St Cross Hospital – the model for Hiram's Hospital, where Septimus Harding is The Warden *in the first of Anthony Trollope's Barsetshire novels.*

When Walton died in Winchester, during 'the great frost' of December 1683, he was in his 90th year, still writing, editing and publishing. He was buried in Winchester cathedral, where this memorial window has been installed above his grave.

he wrote that now, as Wordsworth put it, preserves 'meek Walton's heavenly memory'.

Jane Austen spent her last days in Winchester, and was buried at the cathedral. She had known for some months before she came here to get medical help that she was seriously ill. In May 1817, with her sister Cassandra, she took lodgings in College Street (a plaque marks the house) but she died a few weeks later, in Cassandra's arms. It was a quiet end to a life that is often portrayed as uneventful and retiring – yet it was far from boring.

In less than 42 years Jane had permanent homes in four places: the Hampshire village of Steventon; Bath; Southampton; and Chawton in Hampshire again. She went to school, albeit briefly, in Oxford, Southampton and Reading. In Kent, she stayed in so many places so often that it became her second home county – never quite so well loved as Hampshire. She had summer holidays at half a dozen Dorset and Devon resorts. And she was no stranger to London.

When she moved out of Bath in 1806 with her mother and Cassandra, they went to Clifton, Cheltenham and Stoneleigh Abbey in Warwickshire. They toured Staffordshire and Derbyshire and visited Chatsworth House, said to be her model for Mr Darcy's Pemberley in *Pride and Prejudice*.

Jane also had at least four 'attachments', including a Sidmouth summer romance 'whose charm of person, mind and manners', Cassandra thought, might have won her if he hadn't disappeared, possibly died, soon afterwards.

Admittedly daily life was quiet and orderly in the rectory at Steventon, where she was born in 1775 and lived until 1801. But with six brothers and a sister, life was never dull and it was frequently interrupted with pleasant diversions.

The Austens were great ones for excursions, often visiting beauty spots described by William Gilpin and his fellow Picturesque theorists. They took

'I must write to you today. I want to tell you that I have got my own darling child from London. On Wednesday I received one copy...' Jane Austen, writing to her sister, January 29, 1813, announcing the arrival of Pride and Prejudice *in print.*

Jane Austen (1775–1817) from a sketch by Cassandra.

countless trips to friends and relatives, went to assemblies at Basingstoke and Newbury, and dances at great country houses. Steventon rectory, where Jane somehow found time to write as well, was demolished after her father retired and moved to Bath in 1801, but the church has a memorial.

At Bath and (after her father died) Southampton, life was too unsettled for Jane to write much. But from 1809, when she moved with Cassandra and Mrs Austen back to Hampshire to live at Chawton, there was less of the social quadrille she had danced in

Steventon Church.

her teens and twenties: more time to write.

At their Chawton home – renamed Jane Austen's House and kept as a museum with relics, first editions and her donkey carriage – Mrs Austen did the garden. Cassandra kept house. Jane's job was to get breakfast. Then she was free to work.

She revised earlier stories, re-naming them *Sense and Sensibility*, *Pride and Prejudice* and *Northanger Abbey*. She wrote three more, *Mansfield Park*, *Emma* and *Persuasion*, and started *Sanditon*, putting it aside as her health failed and she prepared to go to Winchester.

Their house is a comfortable

brick-built place, neither so small as Elinor and Marianne's cottage in *Sense and Sensibility*, nor so grand as many that Jane knew. What it notably lacks is a study. Jane wrote in the drawing-room, slipping her papers out of sight when the now-legendary creaking door warned her of visitors. Her immediate family were well aware of what she was doing. There was no reason to keep it secret. The Austens were, Jane said, 'great novel-readers and not ashamed of being so'.

Her father and brother Henry handled all her dealings with publishers. Brother Edward had a set of first editions at Godmersham in Kent (now part of the Chawton collection). And younger Austens

knew, when they stayed at Chawton and heard Aunt Jane giggling behind closed doors, that she was reading her latest chapter to Aunt Cassandra.

'*Our Chawton home, how much we find Already in it, to our mind...*' Jane Austen, July 26, 1809, soon after moving to her last home, now a museum (left).

St Nicholas, Steventon, where Jane's father was rector. She was baptised here and worshipped in the church until he retired to Bath in 1801.

Jane Austen's House museum, has memorabilia, furniture and books.

William Cobbett (1763–1835).

Cobbett's birthplace (right) in Bridge Square, Farnham, before it was restored and re-named after him.

William Cobbett's 19th-century *Rural Rides* took him miles and months through England. He travelled to France and America as well. Yet he remained at heart a southern counties man and the Jolly Farmer Inn at Farnham, where he was born in 1763, has been re-named after him. It was his home for 20 years while he worked on nearby farms and gardens, including Farnham Castle and Kew Gardens. He had returned to farm only a few miles away when he died in 1835 and was buried in Farnham churchyard.

During the 50-odd years in between he became a leading radical, a political writer passionately concerned for the state of working people, the countryside he loved, and the work of fellow writers like Tom Paine.

Passing ruined Waverley Abbey near Farnham, and Moor Park (now a college) Cobbett comments that it was 'the seat of Sir William Temple, when Swift was

Hampshire in November 1822, Cobbett is 'put in mind of a book, which was once recommended to me, but which I never saw, entitled The History and Antiquities of Selborne (or something of that sort) written, I think, by a parson of the name of White...'

It is a shame Cobbett missed White's book. The Reverend Gilbert White shared all Cobbett's joy in the same stretch of country and *The Natural History of Selborne* is a loving account of his endless observations in the area.

Born in Selbourne in 1720, he moved into The Wakes (now a museum) aged nine and soon became fascinated by the garden and the great beech woods, 'the most lovely of all forest trees'. After he inherited the house and settled there he constructed the Zig Zag Path (cared for by the National Trust) that leads through the steep woods to 'the vast hill of chalk rising three hundred feet above the village'.

He also began the letters which eventually appeared in 1789 as *The Natural History of Selborne* and led one friend to comment: 'No man communicates the pleasure of his excursions, or makes the world partake of them, in a more useful manner than you do.'

But his fondness for wildlife

'We came hither by the way of Waverley Abbey...I found the ruins not very greatly diminished' – Cobbett revisiting places he had known as a boy, Rural Rides, October 1825.

residing with him'. Jonathan Swift, author of *Gulliver's Travels*, had spent nearly a decade as Temple's secretary in the 1690s and his satirical book *A Tale of A Tub* was the first that Cobbett could remember buying, as a lad of 14.

On another ride through

didn't stop him experimenting. In 1780 he inherited his aunt's 30-year-old tortoise, Timothy, and conveyed it to Selborne: 'I dug it out of its winter dormitory in March last, when it was enough awakened to express its resentments by hissing; and, packing it in a box with earth, carried it eighty miles in post-chaises.'

Timothy wasn't always so tenderly treated. He was weighed, dunked in water – 'quite out of his element and much dismayed'. And he prompted the unsentimental thought, 'it is a matter of wonder to find that Providence should bestow such a profusion of days, such a seeming waste of longevity, on a reptile that appears to relish it so little as to squander more than two-thirds of its existence in a joyless stupor.'

Wilton House, on the edge of Salisbury, became a powerhouse of Elizabethan patronage under Mary Sidney, sister of poet Sir Philip, who lived here after her marriage to the Earl of Pembroke.

Sir Philip, during one of his many visits to Wilton, began writing *The Arcadia*, a

pastoral romance dedicated to her. After his death in battle, in 1586, Mary edited and published the work, along with much of the rest of his writing. She also continued to befriend and patronise his friends and fellow-poets, including Edmund Spenser, author of *The Faerie Queene* and *The Shepheardes Calender.*

Strong tradition says Shakespeare came to Wilton in 1603 and acted in his own *As You Like It*, put on to entertain King James while he stayed here escaping the plague in London.

By then dramatist Philip Massinger, who grew up in the Wilton household (baptised at Salisbury in 1583) had begun studying at Oxford. Massinger had a hand in 53 plays, often collaborating with Shakespeare's successor John Fletcher, but writing *A New Way to Pay Old Debts* on his own. One of the most popular 17th-century social comedies, it introduces young Welborne, fore-runner of Charles Surface in Sheridan's play *The School for Scandal.*

Gilbert White's House, The Wakes, where he died in 1793 after a lifetime observing The Natural History and Antiquities of Selborne.

In Mary Sidney's time, 'Wilton House was like a college, there were so many learned and ingeniouse persons', John Aubrey, Brief Lives, *written c.1690.*

*W*atership Down takes place on the Hampshire hills between Winchester and Newbury. Novelist Richard Adams has named the places where Hazel 'set out alone to face

*O*n the Hampshire Downs near Winchester, Hazel and Fiver sense 'bad danger' coming to the rabbits who live on Watership Down.

General Woundwort and try to save his friends against all odds'.

Near Whitchurch the rabbits cross the railway line. By Overton is the spot on the River Test where the punt was lying. East of Sydmonton is Watership Down itself. There the strange rabbit with ears 'shining with a faint, silver light' finds Hazel dozing in his burrow one blustery morning and helps him slip away, after his adventures are over, 'running easily down through the wood, where the first primroses were beginning to bloom'.

Adams wrote the story while living in London. But it 'was really a book about the beautiful country in which I was born and grew up,' he said.

EMINENT VICTORIANS ON THE ISLE OF WIGHT

*O*sborne, built for Queen Victoria as 'a place of one's own, quiet and retired'.

*A*lfred Tennyson made Farringford house near Freshwater his home for almost 40 years. Only his popularity would force him to flee the island's summer visitors and

*A*lfred, Lord Tennyson (1809–1892), a familiar figure striding along the clifftops in flowing cape and wide-awake hat.

retreat to a second home in Surrey, from 1869 onwards.

When he came to Farringford (now a hotel) in 1853, he had been Poet Laureate for three years. He was Queen Victoria's favourite writer and she and Prince Albert had recently built their own 'little paradise' on the island at Osborne.

Osborne became a Royal family retreat. It had views to the sea, open downland all round, and life there was relatively relaxed and secluded. To Alfred and his wife Emily, Farringford held just the same attractions and, between them, Queen and 'court poet' welcomed dozens of writers to the island.

Farringford was rented at first, but by 1858 his poem *Maud*

made Tennyson enough money to buy it. He added a library (now with a case of memorabilia); a spiral staircase to the garden so he could escape unnoticed from the house; and a wooden bridge from the garden to the clifftops.

Tennyson loved it and urged friends to join him. To F. D. Maurice, the Christian Socialist leader, he wrote,

...Come to the Isle of Wight;
Where far from noise and
*   smoke of town,*
I watch the twilight falling
*   brown*
All round a careless order'd
*   garden*
Close to the ridge of a noble
*   down.*

They accepted gladly. 'Mr Longfellow came with a party of 10,' Emily wrote in her journal for July 1868. 'Very English he is, we thought. A [Alfred] considered his *Hiawatha* his most original poem.'

Longfellow's travels round the island took in Shanklin Old Village, where he put up at the Crab Inn. He followed the path through the huge cleft in the cliffs, known as the Chine, past a fountain and wrote,

O Traveller, stay thy weary
*   feet*
Drink of this fountain pure
*   and sweet...*

The poem remains inscribed on the pub wall, though the fountain has been replaced by an unpoetic tap.

Lewis Carroll came to Farringford in 1859 hoping to hear some of the *Idylls*. But Tennyson wouldn't oblige, possibly, his grandson thought, because he remembered too clearly Carroll's parodies of his earlier poems.

Carroll couldn't resist sending Longfellow up either, in *Hiawatha Photographing*:

From his shoulder Hiawatha
Took the camera of rosewood,
Made of sliding, folding
*   rosewood;*
Neatly put it all together...
Said, 'Be motionless, I beg
*   you!'*
Mystic, awful was the process...

Edward Lear was always welcome once the Tennysons were settled at Farringford. He had been to the island before, summoned to old Osborne House in July 1846 to help Queen Victoria with her painting. 'Had a drawing lesson from Mr Lear, who sketched before me and teaches remarkably well,' she wrote in her diary.

A granite memorial stands on Tennyson Down above Freshwater Bay.

Farringford, Tennyson's home while he wrote The Charge of the Light Brigade *in 1854. The following year a thousand copies were handed out to the troops in the Crimea.*

In 1819 John Keats wished he had a penny for every visitor who passed his lodgings at Shanklin Old Village, heading for the Chine (left) in the cliffs.

At Farringford it was Lear's singing that was in demand. He didn't have a brilliant voice but Tennyson liked its sincerity. He also liked the drawings and travelogues Lear produced from his journeys, and Emily and Lear grew to be firm friends and correspondents when Lear was abroad.

In 1886, Oliver Wendell Holmes (joint founder of *The Atlantic Monthly* with James Russell Lowell) called at Farringford with his daughter. He describes in *A Hundred Days in Europe* seeing 'the poet to the best advantage under his own trees and walking over his own domain'.

Young Algernon Swinburne came to Farringford from his family home on the island at Bonchurch, where he grew up. He was already something of a pleasure-loving rebel, yet he made a reasonable impression on Tennyson, possibly by not retaliating with his own poems after enduring the obligatory reading of *Maud*.

Swinburne's life-style and views on politics and religion became so scandalous that his burial at St Boniface 'new' church caused outrage in Bonchurch in 1909. Teenage Edith Sitwell was banned by her mother from reading his poems, but that didn't stop her making a solo pilgrimage (with her maid) all the way from Bournemouth to place flowers and pour a libation on his grave.

Bonchurch locals found Swinburne especially shocking because his father was an admiral and his mother, Lady Swinburne, had taken tea with Charles Dickens.

Dickens rented a house almost next to the Swinburnes and their 'golden-haired lad' for the summer of 1849. Winterbourne (now another hotel) is 'the prettiest place I ever saw', Dickens wrote to his wife, Kate, describing its gardens and waterfall running down to the beach. Within days, Kate, her sister, the children and the servants left the mainland and came by steamboat to the island.

Dickens spent each morning writing episodes of *David Copperfield*. Afternoons were for walks, climbing the steep sides of

see nesting in the castle ruins. Following a few years after Wordsworth, he came in 1817, called it a 'Primrose Island' and stayed near the castle, writing his longest poem, *Endymion*.

Two years later he was back, this time by the sea at Shanklin Old Village. From his boarding house in the High Street he watched the visitors strolling to the Chine and worked on several major poems, including *Lamia* and *Hyperion*, perhaps guessing that his illness meant time was running out.

St Boniface Down, playing rounders, games on the beach – and tea with Lady Swinburne.

Tennyson's predecessor as Poet Laureate, William Wordsworth, had been to the island, too. In 1793 he spent 'a whole month of calm and glassy days, In that delightful island'. He went to Carisbrooke Castle where King Charles I had been held prisoner. But he was less interested in England's 17th-century conflicts than the current revolution in France, where he had not long left Annette Vallon alone with their love-child.

Keats, on the other hand, was intrigued by the idea that King Charles might have watched ancestors of the jackdaws he could

During the 1914-18 war, several writers came to the island in order to recuperate at Osborne house. Queen Victoria had spent months there after Prince Albert's death and died at the house in 1901. It then

*N*umber 393 Old Commercial Road, Portsmouth, Charles Dickens's birthplace on February 7, 1812, is now a museum.

*W*interbourne (left), Dickens's summer home, 1849. Looking out over the garden, he worked on David Copperfield and came up with the idea of Mr Dick being haunted by the head of King Charles I – once a prisoner on the island at Carisbrooke Castle (below).

At Osborne 'we patients could take all Queen Victoria's favourite walks...play billiards in the royal billiard–room' (right) – Robert Graves.

John Boynton Priestley, born in Bradford 1894, author of The Good Companions, When We Are Married, *and in 1947* An Inspector Calls. *The following year he moved to Brook Hill, looking towards Farringford and Freshwater Bay (below).*

became a convalescent home for officers, among them A. A. Milne and Robert Graves.

In *Goodbye to All That*, Graves remembers sleeping in the royal night-nursery, playing billiards in the room where Victoria learnt to play, and enjoying the gardens. Though Osborne remains partly a convalescent home, the nursery, billiard-room and gardens are all open.

Graves's stay at Osborne ended when he insisted on being passed fit in order to help Siegfried Sassoon, who had published *A Soldier's Declaration* against the war. Graves was anxious that Sassoon should get to a shell-shock hospital rather than face court-martial.

J. B. Priestley became almost as famous as Tennyson and Dickens for hospitality and long daily walks on the island. He lived there 'off and on for over a quarter of a century'. After World War II and his popular broadcasts (published as

Britain Speaks and *All England Listened*) Priestley moved to a 'kind of Edwardian folly', a mansion high on Brook Hill overlooking the bay towards Farringford.

'All my happiest memories cluster round that house,' he wrote. 'On fine Sunday mornings we used to march our guests over heath and downland towards Freshwater Bay.' The path that links Brook Hill and Tennyson's Farringford is marked as the Tennyson Trail and has superb views over the island.

HARDY'S WESSEX

Thomas Hardy's Wessex reaches right across south-west England. At its heart is Dorset's county town Dorchester, where Michael Henchard becomes *The Mayor of Casterbridge*. To the north it touches Oxford, spiritual home of *Jude the Obscure*. Eastwards it stretches beyond Stonehenge, the prehistoric stone circle that *Tess of*

the d'Urbervilles stumbles into in the dark with Angel. And in the west, Wessex comes to the coast of Cornwall where, working as a young architect, Hardy fell in love with his first wife Emma, and wrote *A Pair of Blue Eyes*.

He was already well into *Far From the Madding Crowd* when he revived the old regional title Wessex, to name the country round Bathsheba Everdene's farm. Over the next 40 years he made it the setting for hundreds of stories and poems. But though he helped write one of the rash of Wessex guidebooks that soon appeared, Hardy never accepted the idea that each fictional place had a single real-life counterpart.

His landscape was, he pointed out, a place from the past, a dream of a rural community whose way of life and customs were fading into folk memory. The Mellstock musicians playing in church; Giles Winterbourne the wandering cider-maker; Gabriel Oak waiting to be hired in the market; the sheep-shearings and haymakings – these were scenes of his boyhood and stories heard from his grandmother.

Much had changed before he began Bathsheba's story and has altered far more since his death in 1928. Yet there is still a core of countryside and places Hardy and his characters knew that is easily recognised and reached from Dorchester.

Thomas was born outside the town at Higher Bockhampton and lived there till he went to work in an architect's office in London in 1862. For the rest of his life he was drawn back to the 'long low cottage with a hipped roof of thatch'. Here the Dewys live in *Under the Greenwood Tree* and the Mellstock musicians gather by the fire before they set off carolling around the village – pausing by the schoolhouse till Fancy Day comes to the window with her candle.

Like Tranter Dewy and his son Dick, Hardy's grandfather and father played cello and fiddle in the 'choir' at St Michael's church,

Thomas Hardy outside Max Gate near Dorchester, his home from 1885 until he died there, January 11, 1928.

Hardy's Cottage, Higher Bockhampton, his birthplace in 1840 and still surrounded by trees which would supply the Mellstock men with a barrel of 'cordial from the best picked apples' before they set off into the night.

49

At Stinsford church, Hardy's heart is buried among his family's graves. Poet Laureate Cecil Day Lewis was buried near by, in 1972, because of his admiration for Hardy.

Stinsford, until they and the Mellstock men, were 'done away wi' for a new-fangled organ.

Hardy wanted to be buried at Stinsford beside them, but his status as the Grand Old Man of English literature meant his ashes were placed at Westminster Abbey. Only his heart and a memorial window are at Stinsford.

Between Stinsford and Hardy's Cottage lie Thorncombe Wood and the ancient Rainbarrows, on the edge of Egdon Heath, which Hardy used as the sombre setting for *The Return of the Native*. By the road to Puddletown is the site of Keeper Day's cottage, where Fancy's father lives. It is known as Yellowham Wood nowadays, though in springtime it's a deep sapphire sea of bluebells.

North of the wood the River Piddle runs by Waterston Manor, the 'solid stone' farmhouse with 'fluted pilasters' that Hardy pictured as Bathsheba's home in *Far from the Madding Crowd*. She rejects both Gabriel, her shepherd, and Farmer Boldwood for Sergeant Troy, only to discover

St Mary's, Puddletown, has a 17th–century 'minstrels' ' gallery, like the Mellstock choir's in Under the Greenwood Tree.

The 'Turberville' window in Bere Regis church, above the family tombs: 'canopied, altar–shaped, and plain, their carvings being defaced and broken; their brasses torn...'

her servant Fanny has died bearing Troy's child.

At Puddletown, the original of Weatherbury, poor Fanny's coffin is left in the rain and Troy spends the night in the porch of St Mary's, the church with 'horrible stone' gargoyles, after covering Fanny's grave with flowers and a headstone.

St Mary's has managed to keep its beautiful wooden 'minstrels' ' gallery where Hardy's grandfather played in the choir. It also has memorials to the owners of Athelhampton, a medieval manor on the edge of Puddletown that Hardy knew well and used in several stories.

At Bere Regis, Hardy's Kingsbere, is the church with d'Urberville memorials (and brilliantly coloured carved apostles in the roof) where Tess's homeless

*M*ax Gate. While it was being built, 1884–5, Hardy lived in Dorchester writing The Mayor of Casterbridge.

mother instructs the carter to off-load their 'old four-poster bed-stead' and erects it 'under the south wall of the church', claiming shelter in the d'Urberville Aisle.

Tess, Jude and *The Woodlanders*, Hardy's favourite, were written at

his last home, Max Gate. A charm-less place – he designed it himself – it is made even worse by the Dorchester ring road, and thoughts of the silent hostility that he and Emma were reduced to by the time they moved there in 1885.

It didn't prevent him receiving homage from almost every writer of the day and, when Emma died in 1912, he was overcome by such

remorse he wrote her his finest love poems. As a result, Max Gate seems like a shrine to his poetry and visitors: Robert Louis Stevenson (one of the first), J. M. Barrie, W. B. Yeats, A. E. Housman, John Cowper Powys, Siegfried Sassoon, Virginia Woolf (her father had been a good friend), and Hardy's near neigh-bour T. E. Lawrence.

After Hardy's own death, the contents of his study at Max Gate were installed at the centre of a Hardy exhibition – don't miss the music his father wrote for Stinsford choir – at Dorset County Museum: an excellent place to begin both a walk of Henchard's Casterbridge and a tour of Wessex.

*H*ardy's study, re–built at the county museum in Dorchester (left).

*D*orchester has a statue of Hardy (below) and another of Dorset dialect poet William Barnes.

T. E. Lawrence, 'Colonel Lawrence of Arabia', also known as John Hume Ross and Thomas Edward Shaw, was born in North Wales, 1888, the illegitimate son of Anglo–Irish parents.

T. E. Lawrence's cottage, Clouds Hill, stands on the edge of Hardy's Egdon Heath, near Wool. Hemmed in by high hedges and rhododendrons, it is an angular, uninteresting little place. It was scruffy, too, when he moved in, ideal for a national hero performing his second vanishing act.

As Lawrence of Arabia, leading Arab troops right up to Damascus in 1918, he was a legend by the age of 30. The following year he returned to Oxford. He had gained a 'first' in History in 1910; now he took up a fellowship and began writing his Arabian adventures, *The Seven Pillars of Wisdom*.

In 1921 he was called in as official adviser on Middle East affairs for the post-war peace negotiations. But believing the Arabs had been

Clouds Hill, the hideaway Lawrence discovered and began renting in 1923 for two shillings and sixpence a week.

betrayed, he staged his first disappearance and joined the ranks of the Royal Air Force as J. H. Ross.

Within a few months Lawrence was discovered and forced to leave. He tried again. He enlisted in the army in 1923 as Private T. E. Shaw and joined a training camp at Bovington.

He loathed the army and – with John Buchan and George Bernard Shaw pulling strings – managed a transfer back to the RAF. From Bovington, however, he had discovered his bolt-hole, Clouds Hill, and he made it his home until his death in 1935.

When his friend and biographer Robert Graves introduced him to Thomas Hardy at Max Gate, Lawrence soon became a favourite visitor. And Lawrence in turn introduced Hardy to guests at Clouds Hill: G. B. Shaw and E. M. Forster.

Forster was one of the first to come, in 1924, and to find the primitive little house curiously welcoming, with its log fires and 'windy gramophone'. Forster had read the first version of *Seven Pillars*, thought it a masterpiece and acknowledged its impact on the last few chapters of his own novel *A Passage to India*. He was captivated by Lawrence, too.

A slight figure, with vivid pale blue eyes, Thomas Edward Lawrence was deeply enigmatic: a

fantasist, escapist, brilliant scholar and capable of amazing bravery. His passion for speeding round Dorset on one of his beloved Brough motor-cycles was part of the legend; and his death in a road accident was as mysterious as his life.

Forster was too upset to attend the funeral, though Sassoon did. So did Sir Winston Churchill, who wrote of *Seven Pillars*: 'As a narrative of war and adventure it is

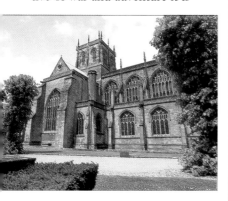

unsurpassable.' Lawrence was buried in the new cemetery at Moreton. An effigy of him in Arab robes was placed in St Martin's church, Wareham, and a bust in St Paul's Cathedral.

In Hardy's Wessex the age-old town of Sherborne – unspoilt, mellow and once famed for its magnificent abbey and two castles – becomes Sherton Abbas, where Grace and Giles, in *The Woodlanders*, sit talking among the tombs in the abbey church. In 1550, part of the abbey buildings became a boys' school, known for James Hilton's 1930s sentimental school story *Goodbye, Mr Chips*. But it has more solid literary links. Novelist brothers John Cowper and Llewelyn Powys were educated there 100 years ago, followed by Poet Laureate Cecil Day Lewis, his friend Louis

MacNeice, and novelist David Cornwell.

Three years Cecil's junior, MacNeice was at Sherborne 'prep' before going on to Marlborough School in 1921, and then Oxford, where they met again as students. After Oxford, Day Lewis started teaching and when he gave it up to write full-time he recycled Sherborne into his first pot-boiler detective book *A Question of Proof*.

David Cornwell did much the same, drawing on schooldays at Sherborne and teaching at Eton. In *A Murder of Quality*, he renamed the school Carne and adopted for himself the name John le Carré.

Le Carré's thoroughly English espionage epics involve a network of agents infiltrating the furthest corners of the world. Yet their code of ethics and spy-speak is essentially English public-school, and home base in his fifteenth novel, *Our Game*, is still rural southern England.

C. Day Lewis used the pen-name Nicholas Blake for his crime stories and W. H. Auden as his model for detective Nigel Strangeways.

Sherborne Abbey, burial place of courtier-poet Sir Thomas Wyatt in 1542.

Sherborne's Old Castle, on the edge of the town, is one of a pair that belonged to Sir Walter Ralegh. He acquired the 12th-century ruin from Queen Elizabeth. The other he began building himself in 1594, having given up trying to cure the earlier one of damp; though he spent more time living, and writing, in the Tower of London than he did in Sherborne.

A lum Chine, part of Bournemouth's wooded coast.

As *Our Game* kicks off, Tim Cranmer is enjoying life as a wine-grower in Somerset, lavishing gifts on his young lover, Emma, which he buys at a rather 'nice jeweller's shop in Wells'. When he is recalled to London 'office' because his former agent seems to have siphoned off a fortune from the Russians and gone AWOL from Bath University, Tim would no doubt prefer to stay put in Somerset – except that Emma has gone too.

R obert Louis Stevenson, born 1850, died in Samoa 1894.

At Alum Chine in Bournemouth there is a memorial garden to Edinburgh-born Robert Louis Stevenson, who lived here with his wife, Fanny, from 1884 to 1887. Though 'R. L. S.' was already suffer-ing seriously with consumption and came for the mild climate, he carried on writing and publishing.

Before they left to live abroad, he published *The Strange Case of Dr Jekyll and Mr Hyde*, wrote *A Child's Garden of Verses* and *More Arabian Nights*. He also found time to make friends with the son of Percy Bysshe Shelley and Mary Shelley.

M ary Shelley (1797–1851) began Frankenstein, or the Modern Prometheus staying with Shelley and Lord Byron by Lake Geneva in 1816 and finished it by the Thames after she and Shelley returned to London and married.

The poet's son, later Sir Percy, was liv-ing at Boscombe Manor with his wife, Jane, and a collection of family relics housed in a spe-cial Sanctum. They had amassed memorabilia not only of the poet and Sir Percy's mother, Mary Shelley, author of the cult novel *Frankenstein*, but fellow-writers and family as well.

Shelley and Mary had left England in 1818 (after selling their home at Marlow on the Thames) for Italy, where Lord Byron, already in exile, joined them at Pisa in 1821. These were Shelley's best years. He had just written *Ozymandias, King of Kings*, now came *Ode to the West Wind*, his essay *Defence of Poetry* and *To a Skylark*:

Hail to thee, blithe Spirit!
Bird thou never wert.

In 1822, however, while sail-ing in the Gulf of Spezia, Shelley was drowned. He was cremated on the beach – Byron and other friends were present – and Mary returned to England bringing what was said to be his heart, snatched from the flames of his funeral pyre.

After Mary's death in 1851, her son arranged that she (and her parents) should be buried at St Peter's, Bournemouth and Sir Percy and Shelley's 'heart' subsequently joined them.

The grand memorial sculpture

he commissioned for his parents was rejected by the vicar of St Peter's for fear of notoriety; so it ended up in Christchurch Priory instead, east of Boscombe.

His home, Boscombe Manor, is now an art college with a small library and collection about the Shelleys and their circle. In West Sussex, close to the Shelley family home, Field Place, there are more memorials at Warnham church, near Horsham.

The New Forest, decreed a Royal hunting forest by William the Conqueror in 1079, is the scene of Captain Frederick Marryat's Civil War story Children of the New Forest. *Marryat stayed several times at Chewton Glen (his brother's home, now a hotel) and wrote a string of popular sea adventures, from* Mr Midshipman Easy *to* Masterman Ready *and his children's tale of Cavaliers and Roundheads, his last book, published in 1847.*

Towards the end of the 17th century, T. S. Eliot's ancestors left East Coker, near Yeovil, for America. Thomas Stearns Eliot had visited the village in 1937 and though he died in London in 1965 his ashes were interred there.

St Michael's has a classic country churchyard, sloping down to the fields his family once knew, and inside the simple village church there is an oval plaque inscribed with lines from Eliot's poem *East Coker*, the second of his *Four Quartets*:

> *In my beginning is my end...*
> *...In my end is my beginning.*

There can hardly be a better place to catch the liturgical lilt of the lines which sprang from Eliot's visit to East Coker.

By the time Eliot wrote *East Coker*, late in 1939, Europe was at war. His recent play *The Family Reunion* had not been a success and his first marriage was over. Fearing his poetic power was passed, he turned back to an earlier, Cotswold-inspired poem and continued the spiritual journey he had begun in *Burnt Norton*.

*F*rederick Marryat *became a midshipman at 14 and used his seafaring exploits in dozens of stories after he left the navy in 1830.*

*C*hristchurch Priory *has the Shelley Memorial intended for St Peter's, Bournemouth, where Shelley's 'heart' is buried alongside Mary and her parents, radical writer William Godwin and pioneer feminist Mary Wollstonecraft.*

When *East Coker* appeared the
following Easter it suited the
nation's mood exactly. It re-
affirmed national spirit and
endurance; and it ensured his reputation as a mandarin among writers, winner-to-be of the Nobel
Prize and the Order of Merit.

LYME REGIS

'The first thing any stranger
to Lyme must realise is that
the Cobb is not only a harbour; it is just as importantly a
gigantic breakwater protecting the
town from the great storms out of
the south-west,' explains novelist
John Fowles in *A Short History of
Lyme Regis.*

John Fowles has become a fix-
ture – local historian, town centre
resident, even museum curator –
in the small Dorset resort where
he based *The French Lieutenant's
Woman.*

His story of Sarah Woodruff,
the strange figure staring seawards
from the end of the Cobb, and
her encounters on the Undercliff
(now a nature reserve) with fossil-

John Fowles followed
The French
Lieutenant's Woman
*with more West
Country scenes in*
Daniel Martin, *based
on his childhood at
Ipplepen in Devon.*

hunting hero Charles Smithson
became a best-seller almost as
soon as it appeared in 1969.

Until then Lyme Regis and its
Cobb had been Jane Austen's
patch: the place where, in
Persuasion, Louisa Musgrove

'must be jumped down' the steps
by Captain Wentworth, until 'she
fell on the pavement of the Lower
Cobb, and was taken up lifeless!'
The rest of the book takes place in
Bath and various country houses,
but it made Lyme famous as the
setting for the single most dramatic
event in the entire Austen canon.

Sidmouth, 1802 Dawlish. Then came Lyme and evidently Jane loved it. If her letter – caustic about her aunt, concerned for her father, cutting about her dance partners – gives the facts; her book spells out her fondness for the

Jane's first visit to Lyme is recorded by her reference years later to a fire in the town one November night in 1803. The following year she came again with her parents, her sister Cassandra, brother Henry and sister-in-law Eliza. Early in September the latter three moved to Weymouth, leaving Jane to look after their parents and, as always, to write chatty letters to Cassandra.

Jane's from 'Lyme Friday Sept 14' is the only letter that survives from the family's holidays in Devon and Dorset during the five years they lived in Bath. Holidays by the sea were the pay-off, as far as Jane was concerned, for putting up with Bath (she hated living in the city quite as heartily as her heroine Anne Elliot).

In 1801 the Austens tried

place. She describes in detail its 'principal street almost hurrying into the water, the walk to the Cobb, skirting round the pleasant little bay, which, in the season, is animated with bathing machines and company...the very beautiful line of cliffs, stretching out to the east of the town...'

Social life centred on the Assembly Rooms that stood on the seafront at the foot of Broad Street. It held assemblies on Tuesdays, card parties on Wednesdays (Mrs Austen attended) and a ball on Thursdays: Jane and her mother stayed till 10.30, while Mr Austen left early and walked to their lodgings with the help of a manservant 'and a lanthorn'.

The Cobb had almost a separate hamlet at the end of the breakwater, not easy to reach after

Daniel Defoe's Tour Through... Great Britain *(1724) reported that Lyme, where the Monmouth rebellion started in 1685, was now 'entirely united and all the churchmen moderate and well affected'.*

Cruikshank's 1819 cartoon, 'Hydromania! or a touch of the Sub-Lyme and Beautiful*'.*

'*And a very strange stranger it must be who does not see charms in the immediate environs of Lyme*' – Jane Austen, Persuasion.

a ball, even using the sedan chairs which the Assembly Rooms advertised. Yet one local tradition says they lodged there at 'Wings' house on Marine Parade (a small memorial garden marks the site) and the house opposite (now Jane's Café) is the model for Captain Harville's.

Others, however, say that the Harvilles' home, where Louisa recuperates, is the pink, thatched cottage on the front; and that the Austens stayed at 10-11 Broad Street.

As for the spot on the Cobb where Louisa fell, the favoured flight is the jagged steps called Granny's Teeth. It is not clear which site Lord Tennyson was shown when he uttered the now-legendary cry: 'Don't talk to me of the Duke of Monmouth. Show me the steps from which Louisa Musgrove fell.'

Versions of Tennyson's visit vary, but he was certainly drawn to Lyme by Jane Austen's writing. He arrived on foot from Bridport in 1867 and joined his friend and fellow-poet Francis Palgrave, who had known Lyme for years and would soon buy his own country house here, in 1872.

With Tennyson's advice,

Palgrave produced *The Golden Treasury,* the most popular anthology of English poetry ever published, and probably thanks to Tennyson it had more entries by Shelley than anyone except Wordsworth and Shakespeare.

Beatrix Potter's parents, like Jane Austen's exactly a century before, tried several Devon and Dorset resorts. For the Potters, main summer holidays meant Scotland or the Lake District: two or three months renting grand country houses.

It was generally spring when they went to the coast, relatively minor trips yet still with a baggage-load of cameras, paints and

place'. The following year Norman died, a few weeks after they had secretly become engaged. That may be why she wrote wistfully, when the book was published, 'Lyme Regis – lovely backgrounds to which I should have liked to do better justice.'

*G*ranny's Teeth – 'Louisa's steps' – on Lyme Regis Cobb.

pets. After Ilfracombe in 1883, they tried Falmouth, Folkestone, Hastings, Teignmouth and Sidmouth.

In April 1904, as Beatrix's letters and *The Tale of Little Pig Robinson* prove, they spent a fortnight at Lyme Regis.

Years later, sifting through her old seaside sketchbooks for a subject that would suit both her new American publisher and her original company, Frederick Warne, she decided to use a story she made up for her governess's children. It tells of a little pig who goes on board ship and narrowly escapes a dinner date with the crew.

To turn it into a book (the American edition needed many more pictures than Warne's small format) she added drawings from several holidays. She used the tall net sheds at Hastings, the harbours at Teignmouth and Sidmouth and 'the market streets at Lyme Regis' – steep Silver Street, Broad Street and the riverside path to Uplyme, passing the ancient thatched watermill.

Writing happily to Norman Warne in 1904, she had noted 'There is a splendid view from this little house [off Silver Street] ... I think this is a delightful

The year after Beatrix's visit, J. R. R. Tolkien and his brother came from Birmingham for the first of several summer holidays with their guardian, Father Morgan, staying at the Three Cups Hotel in Broad Street.

Once Tolkien's own children were growing up in the 1920s and 30s there were more family holidays here at Lyme – and at Sidmouth nearby. He was working then on *The Lord of the Rings* and notes that would become *The Silmarillion*, and he was fascinated

*F*or her last book, The Tale of Little Pig Robinson *(1930),* Beatrix Potter turned back to pictures she had painted of Lyme Regis in 1904: the main street, the Philpot sisters' house (now the Mariners Hotel) and other views nearby.

Lyme's Town Hall, beside the Philpot Museum, has the court-room where Fielding's valet was had up for breach of the peace.

by Lyme's constantly shifting fossil-rich coast. Each landslip shows millions of years' history and Tolkien's sketches of 'The Elder Days' are said to be based on the local landscape.

Lyme Regis Museum (where John Fowles was curator for 10 years) is world famous for fossils, but not – yet – for its engagingly odd writers' relics. Upstairs hangs a series of engravings by George Cruikshank – caricaturist and Dickens's illustrator – made from local sketches by Captain Marryat and including a perfect twin-satire on Picturesque theory and seabathing, titled 'Hydromania! or a touch of the Sub-Lyme *and* Beautiful'.

Downstairs are the 18th-century fire engine used when Jane Austen watched Lyme burning; the only fragments that remain from the Assembly Rooms where she danced; and Henry Fielding's earliest manuscript. Fielding's *Riposte*

Gilbert Keith Chesterton (1874 – 1936) was one of the first to bring Jane Austen's early work to a wider audience.

is a small placard that reads: 'Nov 15 1725 – This is to give notice to all the world that Andrew Tucker and his son John Tucker are Clowns, and Cowards. Witness my hand – Henry Fielding.'

He was 18 and had just failed

to abduct his 15-year-old heiress cousin, Sarah, from her uncle, Andrew Tucker. It was an escapade that has all the hallmarks of *Tom Jones*.

Fielding, fresh from Eton, was madly in love with Sarah (his first model for Sophia Western) and knew his best chance of gaining a fortune was to marry one. He holed up in Lyme for several weeks waiting to kidnap her as she walked from the house (now the Tudor House Hotel) to church. But Andrew Tucker had her closely guarded, probably intending to marry her to his son, and the attempt was foiled.

Fielding's manservant was bound over to keep the peace and they both left Lyme in a hurry, pausing only to pin up the *Riposte* for everyone to see.

Like Lord Tennyson, G. K. Chesterton – prolific essayist, biographer, author of *The Napoleon of Notting Hill, The Man Who Was Thursday* and *The*

Innocence of Father Brown – first came to Lyme chiefly because of Jane Austen.

In 1922, he had issued some of her previously unpublished work with a preface explaining, 'These pages betray her secret; which is that she was naturally exuberant.'

In 1928, motoring in the West Country, Chesterton and his wife looked in at Lyme and liked it so much they returned several times, always putting up at the Three Cups (now closed) where Tolkien had stayed with Father Morgan.

Chesterton's much-loved character Father Brown, the divinely comic detective with 'a face as round and dull as a Norfolk dumpling', couldn't be more different from Colin Dexter's Chief Inspector Morse.

Morse comes to Lyme for a 'holiday away from Oxford': only *The Way Through the Woods* doesn't work out like that. After he checks in to 'the only hotel on the Marine Parade' (the Bay Hotel) Morse finds he is sharing a table with a woman who resolutely reads *The Times* at dinner.

The clues to each day's crossword, and why Mrs Hardinge 'might earlier have been weeping a little', lead him back to Oxford. But not before he has made a

'Coleridge pilgrimage' to Ottery St Mary and Nether Stowey; explored Hardy's Dorchester; and decided he would like to introduce Mrs Hardinge to Mozart's 'Requiem', K626.

The harbour, Lyme Regis, where Kenneth Grahame paused in 1912, en route as usual for Cornwall; E. M. Forster enjoyed the 'peace and pearly greyness' in February 1921; and C. Day Lewis described the bay in the best of his detective books, The Beast Must Die, *while living here in the 1930s.*

View of Lyme Regis in 1844.

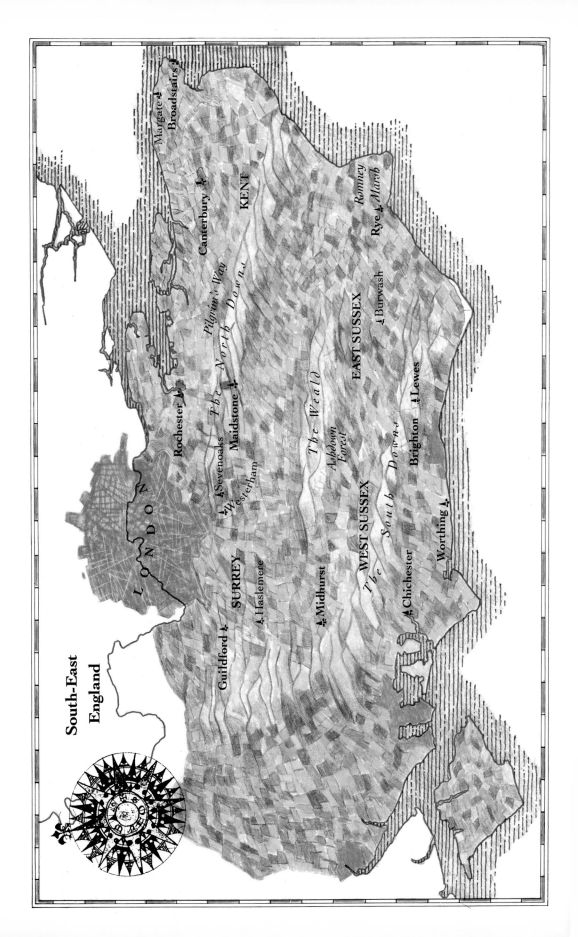

CHAPTER 3

South-East England

LONDON

SURREY

KENT

Margate
Broadstairs
Canterbury
Pilgrims' Way
The North Downs
Rochester
Sevenoaks
Maidstone
Westerham
Guildford
Haslemere
Midhurst
The Weald
Ashdown Forest
Romney
Rye Marsh
Burwash
EAST SUSSEX
The South Downs
Brighton
Lewes
WEST SUSSEX
Chichester
Worthing

SOUTH-EAST ENGLAND

CHARLES DICKENS'S KENT

'**M**agnificent ruin!' said Mr Snodgrass. 'Glorious Pile!' echoed Mr Jingle, as the members of the Pickwick Club crossed Rochester Bridge and came in sight of the fine old castle.

From his earliest novel, *The Pickwick Papers*, to his last, the unfinished *Mystery of Edwin Drood*, Charles Dickens made Rochester a setting for his stories. In *Edwin Drood* he called it Cloisterham. In *The Uncommercial Traveller* it becomes Dullborough. In *Great Expectations* it is Pip's home town.

Dickens, born in Portsmouth in 1812, came to Rochester and Chatham as 'a queer small boy' in 1817. He would move on to London, tour America and become the most popular writer of the English-speaking world. Yet north Kent was the area that drew him back again and again, till he died at home on Rochester's Gad's Hill. Dickens's life, G. K. Chesterton said, 'moves like a Canterbury pilgrimage along the great roads of Kent', between Rochester, Broadstairs and Canterbury.

Old Rochester begins on the bridge across the River Medway beside the ruins of the great Norman keep where Mr Pickwick 'leant over the balustrades... con-

*R*ochester Castle. 'A brilliant morning shines on the old city. Its antiquities and ruins are surprisingly beautiful' – The Mystery of Edwin of Drood.

*C*harles Dickens (1812-1870). 'I had my eye on a piece of Kentish road...it lies high and airy, with a distant river stealing away to the ocean, like a man's life' – The Uncommercial Traveller.

*A*round Rochester lies 'the marsh country, down by the river', where Pip encounters the escaped convict in Great Expectations.

The Artful Dodger shows Oliver Twist how to pick a pocket in Fagin's Den. Charles Dickens Centre, Rochester.

'*The upper room will make a charming study*', Dickens decided, when his chalet (now in Rochester) was assembled in the garden of Gad's Hill Place.

The Corn Exchange clock still looks 'as if Time carried on business there, and hung out his sign' – The Seven Poor Travellers, *Dickens's Christmas story for 1854.*

templating nature and waiting for breakfast' - at the Royal Victoria and Bull Inn. Pickwick Club meetings took place there and still do during the Dickens Festival in June.

Climb up Rochester Castle, look down and the streets below could well be Cloisterham and Dullborough. There is the cathedral, the graveyard and the huddle of old houses in Cathedral Close. Perhaps that is Edwin Drood strolling in the garden by the cathedral, or the sinister figure of John Jasper, muffled against the mist, hurrying along Minor Canon Row.

Scenes from the books string out along Dickens's 'silent High Street...full of gables, with old beams'. There is Eastgate House Museum, alias Miss Twinkleton's Seminary for Young Ladies, attended by Edwin's 'dear little Rosa Bud'. Next door is the Charles Dickens Centre, packed with displays on Dickens's life and times. In a series of tear-jerking tableaux are disgraced Lady

Dedlock beside her lover's grave; Little Nell tugging Grandfather past the puppet-makers in the churchyard; ghastly Quilp cradled in his hammock.

Further down the High Street are Uncle Pumblechook's house, the Corn Exchange with the 'queer old clock that projects over

the pavement' and the Guildhall where Pip is formally apprenticed to 'dear, good, noble Joe' Gargery. Just off the High Street stands Restoration House, the original of Miss Havisham's Satis House, where Pip plays round the cobwebbed wedding-breakfast and falls hopelessly in love with Estella.

Along the river lies Chatham dockyard. Dickens's father worked there in the Navy Pay Office, while the family lived in Ordnance Terrace and then St Mary's Place. The old docks, full of Georgian buildings, have recently been 'recalled to life' as a working museum.

Dickens never tired of telling how as a child, walking out from Rochester with his father, he would stop and admire Gad's Hill Place, determined he would one day return and buy it. The fact that Shakespeare brings Gad's Hill into *Henry IV, Part 1* (the scene of Prince Hal and Falstaff's attempted robbery) appealed to him greatly. And in 1858, at the height of his fame it became his final home, the only one he owned rather than rented.

Life at Gad's Hill meant entertaining friends and fellow-authors, long daily walks and writing. Hans Christian Andersen stayed five weeks. Wilkie Collins, founder of English detective fiction, came frequently as well as joining Dickens on journeys round Britain.

Dickens's walks took him back to the desolate marshes between the Medway and the Thames that he had explored with his father. He would stride out to Chalk past two separate cottages that each claim to have been his honeymoon home in 1836, and the forge he is thought to have used as Joe Gargery's. Other walks took him to Cooling churchyard and the strange 'little stone lozenges', the gravestones Pip believed 'were sacred to the memory of five little brothers of mine'; and to Cobham, scene of several Pickwickian adventures at the Leather Bottle Inn, the church and Cobham Hall.

He was working in the Swiss Chalet in the garden at Gad's Hill until his death in June, 1870. The sofa he died on is in the Birthplace Museum at Portsmouth. The chalet, a present that particularly

pleased him by arriving as a flat-pack in 58 boxes, is in the garden at Eastgate House, Rochester.

Broadstairs on the Kent coast, Dickens declared, was his favourite seaside holiday town. He wrote an affectionate account of it, *Our English Watering Place,* and Broadstairs repays the compliment with a Dickens Festival every summer.

The first year he came, 1837, he took lodgings in the High Street and finished off *Pickwick.* Over the next 15 years he came frequently, staying in various houses (including part of the present Royal Albion Hotel) while he finished *Nicholas Nickleby,* began *The Old Curiosity Shop* and worked on *Barnaby Rudge* and *Martin Chuzzlewit.*

He liked Broadstairs so much he urged friends, notably Andersen and Collins again, to join him: 'You cannot think how delightful and fresh the place is and how good the walks.'

In August 1850 he leased Bleak House (then Fort House), a sombre building high on the cliffs, and stayed till he finished *David Copperfield,* working in a study overlooking the sea. On the seafront below is Dickens House Museum. It is the house he described as Miss Betsey Trotwood's 'neat little cottage with cheerful bow-windows' in *David Copperfield,* where Aunt Trotwood sat in the parlour, ready to rush out at any donkey that dared stray into her garden.

Dickens House Museum, Broadstairs. Dickens's son confirmed it was the model for Aunt Betsey Trotwood's cottage, where David Copperfield *finds a haven from the Murdstones.*

In his study at Bleak House (now a museum) in the summer of 1851, Dickens could relax away from London and enjoy the 'larks singing, garden full of flowers, fresh air on the sea'.

Christina Rossetti (1830-1894)

'*Where is Becket, the traitor to the King?'- T. S. Eliot's verse drama gives a modern account of the medieval 'Martyrdom of St Thomas', pictured (right) in Canterbury Cathedral.*

Canterbury Cathedral – journey's end for Geoffrey Chaucer's pilgrims.

At Bleak House Dickens wrote his Broadstairs essay, praising the 'pretty little semi-circular sweep of houses' and 'first-rate bathing machines' - and planning his next novel, *Bleak House*. But he made the place so popular he decided to go elsewhere for future holidays.

Around the headland from Broadstairs, Dante Gabriel Rossetti, poet, painter and founder of the Pre-Raphaelite Brotherhood, spent his final months at Birchington, near Margate. The last decade of his life was clouded by chloral sedatives and ill health and he eventually moved from London to live by the sea.

When he died in 1882, aged 53, he was buried in Birchington churchyard. Fellow artist Ford Madox Brown carved his cross and Rossetti's sister, Christina, wrote a poem.

Christina was already suffering from increasing depression when she came for the funeral, with their mother and brother William, and her poem *Birchington Churchyard* is not so fine as *In the bleak mid-winter*, or her haunting lines:

When I am dead, my dearest,
Sing no sad songs for me;
Plant thou no roses at my head,
Nor shady cypress tree:
Be the green grass above me
With showers and dewdrops wet:
And if thou wilt, remember,
And if thou wilt, forget.

CANTERBURY TALES

The shrine of St Thomas à Becket, the 'holy blisful martir' murdered by four knights in Canterbury Cathedral in 1170, became the richest in Britain, covered in gold and jewels. By the time Geoffrey Chaucer began *The Canterbury Tales*, two centuries later, Canterbury was second only to Jerusalem and Rome as a place of pilgrimage.

They came in thousands, some on foot, some riding from London like the characters in Chaucer's poem, treating it more as a social event than a penance.

Chaucer had probably made the journey at least once and passed through the city on trips to the Continent as a king's messenger. He held several royal posts and his wife's sister, Catherine Swynford, married King Edward III's son, John of Gaunt - after some years as his mistress.

Chaucer intended to include 30 pilgrims in the poem - the Knight, Miller, Pardoner, Wife of Bath, 'Yong Squyer, a lusty bachelor' and so on. After they meet at the Tabard Inn in Southwark one evening, they agree to ride together telling stories all the way to Canterbury.

He never finished it. But there are enough tales to make it the first great poem in a language recognisable as English. Some of them are narrated in the Canterbury Tales Visitor Centre, with walk-through sets, sights-and-smells and life-size models of the pilgrims.

Archbishop Becket's story was re-told by T. S. Eliot in a verse drama, *Murder in the Cathedral*, commissioned for the 1935

Cathedral Festival and performed in the Chapter House within yards of the spot where Becket was murdered.

Eliot, who had been interested in the subject since his days at Harvard, treated the story as a latter-day morality play, introducing Four Tempters who challenge Becket's motives, as well as the Four Knights who kill him. It was

so well received it went straight on to London and helped Eliot towards winning the 1948 Nobel Prize for Literature.

Two years later Dorothy L. Sayers was invited to write a play for the festival (now an annual event in October involving the whole city). Sayers had just put the hero of her detective stories, Lord Peter Wimsey, on stage for the first time. But her cathedral play, *The Zeal of Thy House* was such a success that she wrote more religious works, including *The Man Born to be King,* and she gave up detective fiction.

Charles Dickens used Canterbury scenes in *David Copperfield*. 'Of all my books I like this the best,' he said and he made the city the setting for David's meeting with Agnes and Mr Wickfield, and for Doctor Strong's school: 'a grave building in a courtyard, with a learned air about it that seemed very well suited to the stray rooks and jackdaws who came down from the Cathedral towers.'

The school is King's, the oldest in Britain, whose roll-call runs from John Lyly in the 1560s to Hugh Walpole and Somerset Maugham in the 1890s. Maugham, who used to spend holidays with an uncle at Whitstable a few miles away on the coast, later endowed King's

Thomas Hoccleve's early 15th-century poem, De Regemine Principum, has one of the earliest portraits of Geoffrey Chaucer, who died in 1400.

The Wife of Bath, 'gat-toothed, y-wimpled wel, and on hir heed an hat', tells her own story at the Canterbury Tales centre.

In the Memorial Court of King's School the garden gate near the Maugham Library bears the emblem that Somerset Maugham used on his books.

with a new library, even though he said he hated the school as a boy.

But the school's most enigmatic old boy is Elizabethan dramatist Christopher Marlowe, author of *Tamburlaine the Great, Dr Faustus* and *Edward II.*

Christopher Marlowe (1564-1593) – to his fellow-poets and playwrights 'Kind Kit', 'the Muses' Darling', revered for his 'rare art and wit'.

Marlowe's mysterious life began in Canterbury in 1564 where he was born in George Street, the son of a shoe-maker, and baptised at St George's church (only the tower remains). It ended 29 years later when he was stabbed to death in a tavern brawl.

What happened in between has puzzled writers ever since. Anthony Burgess, author of *A Clockwork Orange*, made Marlowe the theme of his novel, *A Dead Man in Deptford*. He had been fascinated by the subject ever since he was a student and he finished the book only months before he died in 1993.

Down House, Charles Darwin's home from 1842 until his death in 1882, preserves the study where he wrote his sensational new theory of evolution.

Burgess's account follows 'Kind Kit' from his Canterbury home to college at Cambridge, the London theatres where he wrote and acted, and the underworld of Elizabethan espionage. Seduced into a spy-ring run by Lord Walsingham, Queen Elizabeth's 'M', Kit is compromised when he joins Walter Ralegh's atheistic 'School of Night', and is lured to his death in Deptford by Lord Walsingham's hirelings.

Polish-born Joseph Conrad was buried in Canterbury cemetery, after making his home in Kent for many years. His chair and the table he always wrote on are kept at Canterbury Heritage Museum, at the medieval Poor Priests' Hospital (more Conrad material and books can be seen on request).

A touch more colourful are the museum's exhibits about local artist Mary Tourtel and her cartoon character, Rupert Bear - the oldest children's cartoon in British newspapers.

When Rupert made his debut in the *Daily Express* on November 8, 1920, he was part of a circulation war between Fleet Street papers. The *Daily Mail* already had Teddy Tail, the *Mirror* Pip Squeak and Wilfred, and the *Daily News* Arkubs. Mary's husband (a night editor on the *Express*) suggested she invent a rival and he would write the captions.

The result was Rupert and his

pals Algy Pug and Bill Badger. Mary (a city trail links her birthplace and grave) drew the bear, now famous for his red jersey, yellow check trousers and muffler, for an unbroken run of 15 years' daily appearances.

ALONG THE PILGRIMS' WAY

Devoted medieval pilgrims, making the journey a penance not a social occasion, would tramp the North Downs on foot, more or less along the modern Long Distance Footpath but keeping below the ridge of the downs for shelter.

Ironically, present-day pilgrims joining the path in Kent begin near Downe, north of Westerham, where Charles Darwin wrote his godless theory of evolution, *On the Origin of Species*. In the

ordered calm of his study at Down House, Darwin lived the life of a wealthy Victorian (his wife was a Wedgwood). He was a pillar of local society, enjoying his garden and quietly writing the most subversive book of the century.

At Chartwell, south of Westerham, Winston Churchill spent his out-of-

office years gardening, painting, bricklaying, entertaining and, above all, writing: *The World Crisis; Marlborough*, a life of his ancestor the Duke; and *The History of the English-Speaking Peoples*, each running to four volumes and all best-sellers.

South of Sevenoaks, surrounded by a deer park, sprawls Knole house, so big it is more a stately hamlet than a home. Since the 16th century it has been the seat of the Sackville family and the Earls of Dorset, who supplied a succession of writers and patrons. Sir Thomas, the first earl, was a courtier-poet, joint author of one of the earliest English dramas, *Gorboduc*.

Under following owners Knole welcomed John Dryden, who became the first official Poet Laureate in 1668; and metaphysical poet John Donne, who

Chartwell, Winston Churchill's country home. Mornings were spent in bed dictating, afternoons were for enjoying the gardens sloping down to the Weald of Kent.

From the rooftops of Knole (left) young Duke Sebastian looks down 'on a lawn of brilliant green', sees his mother's guests and hears 'laughter and the tap of the croquet mallets' – Orlando, Virginia Woolf.

*Whan that Aprille with his shoures sote
The droghte of Marche hath perced to the rote,
And bathed every veyne in swich licour...
Than longen folk to goon on pilgrimages*

Geoffrey Chaucer, *The Canterbury Tales*

The Great Staircase, Knole. 'Then one moonlit evening they went up to the state-rooms together...' – Pepita, Vita Sackville-West's story of her grandmother.

cially *Knole and the Sackvilles, Pepita* and *The Edwardians,* would be witness enough to her love of the place. But after Virginia Woolf came to stay she too celebrated Knole in the fantastic world of *Orlando,* her most successful novel. Virginia called the book a 'biography' and based the hero-cum-heroine on Vita as a tribute to their ardent relationship.

Pop Larkin would probably have thought an 'official' exhibition on *The Darling Buds of May* just as funny as 'the National Elf lark' and living off 'the welfare'. But, in the midst of perfectly serious collections on Kentish farming at the Museum of Kent Life at Maidstone, there are exhibitions on author H. E. Bates

preached at Knole while visiting the church of St Nicholas in Sevenoaks, one of several livings he held from 1616 until his death in 1631.

But the Sackville family's most famous writer was one who, being a woman, could not inherit the house. Victoria Sackville-West was born at Knole in 1892 and grew up there. Her own books, espe-

H. E. Bates (1905-1974) spent most of his life in Kent among the 'miles of pink apple orchards' he described in The Darling Buds of May.

and several reconstructions: Ma's kitchen, Pop's strawberry shed and the lounge where Charley learns to play crib, drunk on Pop's cocktails and Mariette's warm presence. H. E. Bates based the Larkins books on the 'perfick world' of Kentish villages around Ashford, like Little Chart where he lived for 40 years. The 'darling buds' are lifted from Shakespeare's sonnet 'Shall I compare thee to a summer's day?': 'Rough winds do shake the darling buds of May, And summer's lease hath all too short a date.'

Ightham Mote, half a dozen miles from Sevenoaks at Ivy Hatch, is the moated Tudor manor-house Anya Seton used for the climax of her historical romance Green Darkness. *Here Celia de Bohun comes from Cowdray House, at Midhurst in West Sussex, following her priestly lover, only to be walled up in 'the lovely and mysterious' manor. When Anya Seton came to the house in the 1960s, it had just been rescued from ruin by new American owner C. Henry Robinson, who presented it to the National Trust.*

*U*nder the table in *Ma Larkin's kitchen (above), recreated at the Museum of Kent Life (left), Charley feels the soft touch of the goose on his leg – or is it Mariette?*

Boxley church as the place where maidens 'pelt us in the porch with flowers'.

The adventures of Mrs Aphra Behn begin with her baptism in 1640 at St Gregory and St Martin in the village of Wye. She certainly went to South America with her parents; probably to Holland as a spy for Charles II; and possibly became the first Englishwoman one could call a professional writer. When her plays - *The Rover, The City Heiress, The Lucky Chance* - were criticised for being too erotic, she defended them stoutly, saying they were certainly no worse than the plays men wrote. Evidently she made her point, as she was buried in Westminster Abbey in 1689.

When Jane Austen's brother Edward became heir to a wealthy cousin at Godmersham near Canterbury, Jane's visits to Kent became long and frequent. She had been used to staying with Austen relatives in grand homes at Sevenoaks, Tonbridge and Westerham; now she came to know the historic houses of east Kent as well.

'Edward excels in doing the honours to his visitors, and

Allington Castle, almost engulfed by Maidstone, was the home of Sir Thomas Wyatt, one of several men thought (unfortunately by Henry VIII) to be a lover of Anne Boleyn. He was also one of the 'silver poets' of the 16th century, author of 'They flee from me that sometime did me seek'. He shares with the Earl of Surrey the credit for introducing into English poetry the sonnet form which the Italian poet Petrarch had popularised, and which Shakespeare would go on to perfect in English.

Three centuries later Lord Tennyson stayed nearby at Boxley (his sister was marrying into a local family). *In Memoriam*, the poem Tennyson wrote afer the death of his intimate friend Arthur Hallam in 1833, describes

*A*llington Castle, home of Sir Thomas Wyatt (1503-1542). His poems, 'And wilt thou leave me thus?' and 'My lute awake!' were not printed until Tottel's Miscellany *appeared in 1557.*

A. A. Milne's son identified Winnie the Pooh's favourite places in Ashdown Forest (right). '...by-and-by they came to an enchanted place on the very top of the Forest'.

Goodnestone Park (above), family home of Jane Austen's sister-in-law, Elizabeth Bridges. Jane's letters report many meetings with 'Sir Brook and Lady B.'

A. A. Milne (1882-1956) and his son Christopher Robin, aged six.

providing for their amusement,' Jane confided in one of dozens of letters home to her sister Cassandra. He took her to all the houses where he and his wife dined - Chilham Castle, Sandling Park, Goodnestone Park (his in-laws' home) and, of course, to Canterbury.

Somehow, between social calls, playing with Edward's children, and attending Godmersham church, surely one of the coldest she ever sat in (it has memorials to Edward and his family), she found time to write. *First Impressions,* written in Kent in 1796, would be revised years later as *Pride and Prejudice.*

Pilgrims traditionally got their first sight of Canterbury from Harbledown. Now they must stand on a footbridge over a motorway that carves through the crest of the hill. It just misses the Norman church of St Nicholas, where Erasmus - Dutch humanist author of *In Praise of Folly* - visited the hospice around 1510.

Erasmus's letters record his meetings in London with Sir Thomas More, the author of *Utopia,* though often remembered now as the hero of Robert Bolt's play *A Man for All Seasons.* After More's execution, his eldest daughter, Margaret Roper, begged to be allowed to bring his head in a casket back to Canterbury. Here it was eventually placed in St Dunstan's church, opposite her home.

ASHDOWN FOREST AND THE WEALD

If Christopher Robin and Winnie the Pooh are inseparable, so are A. A. Milne's books and Ashdown Forest. 'Pooh's forest and Ashdown Forest are identical', the real Christopher (Milne's son) wrote later in *The Enchanted Places* - pinpointing Galleon's Lap and the Hundred Acre Wood.

Pooh took his first public bow in a poem, 'A bear, however hard he tries, Grows tubby without exercise', published in *Punch* magazine. In 1924 it appeared again in Milne's volume of verses for children, *When We Were Very Young,* along with 'Halfway down the stairs Is a stair Where I sit' and

'Vespers': 'Little Boy kneels at the foot of the bed, Droops on the little hands little gold head.'

Later that year Alan Alexander Milne and his wife discovered Cotchford Farm near Hartfield in Ashdown Forest, and immediately Milne had the background to the bear stories he had been toying with for some time.

In quick succession he produced *Winnie the Pooh, Now We are Six* and *The House at Pooh Corner*. Over the next three years they were published with equally popular illustrations, drawn by

E. H. Shepard in the same Forest. The Six Pine Trees next to the heffalump trap; the oak tree where Pooh sails up among the bees on the end of a balloon; Piglet's house in the middle of a beech tree; the spinney of larch trees where one Woozle's tracks suddenly turn into two - are all unmistakably part of Ashdown Forest, where the original Poohsticks Bridge is now signposted from a car-park.

At Hartfield, Pooh Corner shop stocks every Pooh book, map and calendar in print, including the Latin version, *Winnie ille Pu,*

the first book in a foreign language ever to reach the bestseller list in New York, when it came out in 1960.

Rudyard Kipling's study in his house, Bateman's, near Burwash, has been kept exactly as he used it for over 30 years. In front of the window, the table where he worked is laid out with his pens and paper-weights. Beside it stands his chair raised on blocks to the correct height. Near the fire is his oak day-bed. Every wall is lined with his books.

In 1902 when Kipling bought the house - a mellow, 17th-century manor - he had just published

*God gives all men an earth to love,
But since man's heart is small,
Ordains for each one spot shall prove
Beloved over all;
Each to his choice, and I rejoice
The lot has fallen to me
In a fair ground - in a fair ground -
Yea, Sussex by the sea!*

Rudyard Kipling, *Sussex.*

Bateman's at Burwash, Rudyard Kipling's home from 1902 until his death in 1936.

E. H. Shepard's drawing shows the bridge in the forest (now signposted) where Pooh and Christopher Robin invented the Poohsticks game.

Kim. It was his last book to draw entirely on his background in India, where he was born in 1865. He had been sent back to England as a child, and worked in India, London and America. In Sussex he found an English countryside he could settle in: at Bateman's a much-needed home, where he lived until his death in 1936.

Here Kipling wrote *Puck of Pook's Hill*, the story of two children who make Puck appear by acting out *A Midsummer Night's Dream* on midsummer's eve in the meadow beside Bateman's garden. It is a mixture of magic and myth and contains perhaps the most popular of all English poems,

> *If you can fill the unforgiving*
> *minute*
> *With sixty seconds' worth of*
> *distance run,*
> *Yours is the Earth and every*
> *thing that's in it,*
> *And - which is more - you'll*
> *be a Man, my son!*

Kipling used the water-mill at Bateman's (which now grinds flour) to install a turbine to supply the house with electricity. In the barns he garaged his much-prized motor cars (one remains on show).

He also began an autobiography, *Something of Myself*, explaining how he and his American-born wife, Carrie, came across Bateman's in 1902, house-hunting round Sussex in their new Lanchester car (later it would be a Rolls Royce): 'we reached her down an enlarged rabbit-hole of a lane...At very first sight, we said: "That's her! The Only She!"'

The village they had travelled from was Rottingdean, near Brighton. After four years in America, they had returned to England, moved in with Kipling's aunt, Georgiana, wife of the painter Sir Edward Burne-Jones, and then taken The Elms nearby (there is a plaque and walled garden open) for five years.

'Aunt Georgie and Uncle Ned' had been providing occasional refuge for 'Ruddy' at their London and Rottingdean homes ever since his parents brought him from India, still aged five, to live with foster parents at Portsmouth.

Through Uncle Ned, Kipling also acquired an honorary 'Uncle Topsy', the charismatic writer, painter and designer William Morris. As Burne-Jones's close friend and business partner, and an ardent admirer of Aunt Georgie (Morris often wished he had married her

instead of his wife, Jane), 'Uncle Topsy' was another frequent guest at Rottingdean, until 1895, when he paid his last visit. Morris was still working on 'the perfect book' and he arrived anxious to see

Burne-Jones's illustrations for his Kelmscott edition of Chaucer; but it was obvious to Georgie that Morris's health was failing and the following year he died.

When Kipling settled into

Rottingdean he was writing at his best. He had already published *The Jungle Book* stories of Mowgli the wolf-cub boy, old Baloo the bear, Bagheera the black panther, Kaa the python and Akela the 'leader of the wolf pack'. Now, he wrote *Recessional*, for Queen Victoria's diamond jubilee. He finished *Stalky & Co*, based on his schooldays in Devon; *Kim*, about an orphan boy working for the Secret Service in India; and the *Just So Stories for Little Children*, explaining 'How the Leopard Got its Spots' and 'How the Camel got his Hump'.

Rottingdean's Grange Museum and Art Gallery, a short walk from The Elms, has an exhibition about Kipling's Rottingdean years and a reconstruction of the study he used at The Elms.

Burne-Jones's house later became the home of Sir Roderick Jones, head of Reuters news agency in London. His wife, bet-

ter known as Enid Bagnold, based her novel *National Velvet*, (the story that gave Elizabeth Taylor her first major screen role) beside the Sussex coast at Worthing. Bagnold used Sussex again in *The Chalk Garden*, her popular play about a downland garden that defeats all Mrs St Maugham's efforts; until it gets the Miss Madrigal touch.

It is an open and shut case as to where Sir Arthur Conan Doyle sent Sherlock Holmes to solve the mystery of *The Valley of Fear*. Dr Watson's account supplies all the evidence and it points straight to Groombridge Place.

Sir Arthur knew the house well. When he wrote the book he was living not far away on the edge of Crowborough in a large house by the golf course, looking across the Weald.

The scene of the murder in *The Valley of Fear* is a 'Jacobean brick house', which 'rose upon the ruins of the feudal castle', surrounded by 'an old-fashioned garden of cut yews', on the 'fringe of the great Weald Forest'.

What clinches it for Groombridge Place is 'a fact which had a very direct bearing on the mystery':

'*The Cat that Walked by Himself*', Kipling's own illustration for one of his *Just So Stories*.

Sir Arthur Conan Doyle, 1892, the year after The Strand Magazine *began publishing monthly Sherlock Holmes stories.*

Groombridge Place, Kent, scene of the murder in The Valley of Fear, *1915.*

'the only approach to the house was over a drawbridge' across a 'beautiful broad moat, as still and luminous as quicksilver in the cold winter sunshine'.

While Watson strolls in the large gardens (recently re-established around the moat) Holmes muses over the body. Is it John Douglas or 'the bicyclist from Tunbridge Wells'?

Centuries earlier, Groombridge Place had been the home of the Waller family, where poet Edmund Waller stayed while he paid his addresses, unsuccessfully, to Lady

'*Now, Penshurst, they that will proportion thee With other edifices... May say, their lords have built, but thy lord dwells.'* Ben Jonson, 'To Penshurst', 1616, from The Forest. Jonson is better remembered for his sublime lyric 'Drink to me only with thine eyes'.

Dorothy Sidney at Penshurst Place.

Sir Philip Sidney's death in Holland in 1586, fighting at the Battle of Zutphen, robbed Elizabethan England of a leading courtier and poet, though it probably ensured his place in history as the romantic hero of the age, the perfect Renaissance figure.

He was born at Penshurst Place into one of England's most powerful families: King Philip of Spain was his godfather. He was also brave, handsome, generous, charming and one

W. B. Yeats c. 1907. The etching by Augustus John is now part of the Garman Ryman collection at Walsall Museum.

of a circle of gifted, aristocratic writers.

His love poems to his adored Stella (in real life Penelope Devereux, married - much against her will - to the roué Lord Rich) are the first great sonnet sequence in English. His prose romance *Arcadia* (written for his sister Mary Herbert at her home, Wilton) includes the lines 'My true love hath my heart, and I have his'.

After his death, Ben Jonson paid a poetic tribute to his birthplace and Mary rose to fame by managing his literary estate and continuing to patronise the arts at Wilton.

Sir Philip's great niece, Lady Dorothy Sidney, grew up at Penshurst to become the amour of Edmund Waller, who parked himself on his relatives at Groombridge specially to be near her. He courted her with dozens of poems, addressed to fair 'Sacharissa'. But his best, *Go, lovely Rose* wasn't one of them, which perhaps explains why he failed to win her. In 1639 she married Lord Spencer and went to live at Althorp.

W. B. Yeats and Ezra Pound spent three winters sharing a cottage at Coleman's Hatch on Ashdown Forest. Pound, who was acting as Yeats's secretary, thought he would hate it: 'I detest the country.' But he found 'Sussex quite agrees with me'. The three winters from 1913 to 1916 came towards the end of each poet's London period. Yeats would move on to Oxford and then back to Ireland. Pound, who put his London days into the poem *Hugh Selwyn Mauberley,* would go to Paris and then Italy. In the meantime Pound introduced Yeats to the classical traditions of Japanese Noh theatre, which would be a major influence on Yeats's work. And Yeats introduced Pound to James Joyce and D. H. Lawrence, who - along with T. S. Eliot, Robert Frost and others - gained invaluable help and encouragement from Pound.

RESIDENTS IN RYE

'Rye and its rock and its church are a miniature Mont-Saint-Michel,' wrote American-born writer Henry James.

James had settled into Lamb House near the church in 1898 and the charm of the place never wore off. He liked it best at evening, 'covered by the westering sun', when 'huddled, church-crowned Rye' - once almost an island in the sea - 'gives out the full measure of its old browns that turn to red and its old reds that turn to purple'.

If James regarded Rye as a 'haven on the hill-top' it was partly because he was in retreat from London. He had been living in

England for some 20 years and made his reputation with *The Europeans, The Portrait of a Lady* and *Washington Square.* But with *The Bostonians* his following began to falter.

When his play *Guy Domville* was booed off the London stage in 1895, James fled to the country. He was acutely sensitive to criticism. His visit to George Eliot, when her partner G. H. Lewes asked him to take away his novel *The Europeans* unread, scarred him for life.

In Rye he stayed first at the Old Vicarage (now a guest house) while he looked for a permanent home and wrote *The Spoils of Poynton.* By 1898 he was happily settled in Lamb House, a fine red-brick Queen Anne building, one of the best in Rye (though he returned to London often, particularly in winter).

In the Garden Room, 'the little old glass-fronted, panelled pavilion' that looked out on to Rye's cobbled streets, James wrote most of his last three major novels, *The Wings of the Dove, The Ambassadors* and *The Golden Bowl.*

He was hardly a popular story-teller, even in the eyes of close friends and guests, Joseph Conrad and Edith Wharton. Wharton made no secret of her debt to James and the books she wrote under his influence, like *The Age of*

*H*enry James (1843-1916) made his home for nearly 18 years at Rye (left) – 'the little old cobble-stoned, grass-grown, red-roofed town, on the summit of its mildly pyramidal hill' – rising out of Romney Marsh.

*A*t Lamb House, the 'bump of luggage has been frequent on my stair', Henry James wrote to H. G. Wells, commenting on his stream of visitors.

Innocence, added vastly to her wealth. But she had to admit she found the Master's later novels unreadable. The extra clauses he added, even to earlier works, at proof stage – witness the copies from *The American* on show at Lamb House – were a printer's nightmare.

James the host, though, was hugely popular. E. M. Forster, Rudyard Kipling (ruining a brand new car in Rye's little streets), Hugh Walpole, Hilaire Belloc, Rupert Brooke, Ford Madox Ford, Stephen Crane, Logan Pearsall Smith were among dozens who called and stayed. H. G. Wells came often until he wrote, shortly before James died, a violent attack on everything James stood for as a writer.

In James's work the Garden Room stayed in the background except in an essay on *Winchelsea, Rye and 'Denis Duval'*, when he imagined Thackeray working in the Garden Room on his unfinished novel *Denis Duval* set in the Two Ancient Towns that are attached to the historic Cinque Ports.

E. F. Benson's satirical stories *Miss Mapp, Mapp and Lucia, Lucia's Progress* and *Trouble for Lucia*, set in Rye in the 1930s,

E. F. Benson, son of a melancholic Archbishop of Canterbury and a mother who found more fun with women. One of them was Dame Ethel Smyth, who Benson caricatured in Dodo *as Edith, composer of symphonies over breakfast kedgeree.*

Edward Frederick Benson writing at Lamb House in the garden he described as Lucia's 'giardino segreto'.

invest the Garden Room at Lamb House with strategic importance.

Miss Elizabeth Mapp and Mrs Emmeline 'Lucia' Lucas are consecutive owners of Mallards (aka Lamb House) and in turn they use the Garden Room window to spy on Tilling (Rye) society in general and each other in particular.

Benson took over Lamb House a couple of years after James's death. He had been introduced to both by his brother A. C. Benson, biographer, hymn writer and poet, whose lines *Land of Hope and Glory* turned Elgar's 'Pomp and Circumstance March Number 1' into a second national anthem.

After Benson moved to Lamb House he imported *Queen Lucia* from her social triumphs in the Cotswolds, his earlier setting for her, to confront Miss Mapp in a stiletto battle for social supremacy in Rye. His Rye satires were, in fact, less pointed than his previous hit *Dodo*, based on socialite Margot Tennant and others in the Balfour and Asquith circle.

When *Dodo* appeared in 1893 and sold out in a month, Benson escaped the flak by being in Egypt, making friends with Lord Alfred Douglas. But he was respected enough in Rye to become mayor of the town. He lived there till he died in 1940 and there are family memorial windows in Rye church.

Some years later Lamb House became the home of Rumer Godden, author of *The Greengage Summer* and *Black Narcissus*, who moved in with her second husband. She was convinced the

Rye's famous smugglers' den, the Mermaid Inn, a few yards from Conrad Aiken's home, Jeake's House.

house had poltergeists (James and Benson said they had seen them) so she called in a priest who blessed everything including the fridge.

During Benson's time in Lamb House another American writer, Conrad Aiken, followed James's lead in moving to Rye. In 1924, the year he published an introduction to Emily Dickinson's poems, Aiken bought the former Quaker meeting-house in Mermaid Street, Jeake's House (now another guest house). Smaller but just as old as Lamb House, it has tilting floors and low-beamed rooms, where he wrote in a study overlooking 'a mile of green Romney Marsh and the blue edge of the Channel'.

For 23 years he made it his home, where he entertained old friends like T. S. Eliot. They had been contemporaries and colleagues at Harvard and they kept up regular, if occasionally scratchy, visits and letters when they both moved to Britain.

'Rye has Fletcher the dramatist, the Fletcher of Beaumont, whom it brought to birth,' Henry James wrote in his essay. John Fletcher was born in 1579 at Fletcher's House, then the vicarage (now a teashop). He collaborated with

Francis Beaumont in the most successful playwrighting partnership of Elizabethan drama. *The Maid's Tragedy,* written 1610, was one of their joint efforts; the entertaining *Knight of the Burning Pestle* is now thought to be a solo number by Beaumont.

AROUND ROMNEY MARSH

At Rye, Henry James was surrounded - partly by chance, partly by choice - with an extraordinary concentration of new-wave novelists, all living in and around the strange, lonely expanse of Romney Marsh.

Noel Coward's long love of Romney Marsh began in 1926 when he took a house at Aldington, where he wrote Present Laughter and based Blithe Spirit.

79

On Romney Marsh, around St Thomas à Becket's, Fairfield and neighbouring parishes, the Rev.Richard Barham, rector of Snargate, set some of his mock-medieval Ingoldsby Legends, *1840.*

Joseph Conrad (1857-1924).

The Marsh, strictly speaking several marshes, is a remote and secretive landscape, drained by ancient dykes and walls, often deserted save for the sheep that feed in thousands on fields that were first reclaimed from the sea by the Romans.

As James was moving into Lamb House, Joseph Conrad was arriving at Postling to take over Ford Madox Ford's farmhouse. Ford (formerly Madox Hueffer) was a great admirer of both men; he thought *The Spoils of Poynton* the 'technical highwater mark' of James's writing. When Conrad needed a home, he invited the Polish-born novelist to move in.

Conrad, like Ford, had established a reputation as one of the best 'younger generation' novelists. He gave up his career at sea in 1894 and by 1898 had published *Almayer's Folly, The Nigger of the 'Narcissus'* and *An Outcast of the Islands. Lord Jim, Heart of Darkness* and *The Secret Agent* would follow before he gave up the Postling farmhouse in 1907. After that there were three more homes in the area: at Orlestone, Wye and finally Bishopsbourne. At each one Conrad entertained friends like Henry James, H. G. Wells and John Galsworthy.

Stephen Crane, young American author of *The Red Badge of Courage*, was remembered by Conrad's son Borys as 'a very close friend of my father's up till the time of his premature death'.

> God, to be in Romney Marsh
> And see the ships above the
>   wall -
> For just an hour of storm
>   and shower
> And just a glimpse of Lydd
>   church tower,
> And just to hear the wind in
>   the thorns...
> But just to mark the tide
>   come in,
> Dear God by Romney Wall.
>
> Ford Madox Ford

Crane was also the donor of Borys's first pet dog.

Crane had visited Conrad at his Essex home and they had both been taken up by the influential *Blackwood's* magazine. Now Crane was spending the last months of his brief life at Brede Place, a run-down medieval manor a few miles westwards, where he was trying to stave off his debts.

His curiously Bohemian household was completely at odds with Henry James's devotion to the

proprieties of life. Yet James (as well as Conrad and H. G. Wells) thought highly of the young American and often cycled over to see him. Crane's American civil war novels were selling well and he was writing regular stories for *Harpers* magazine, but he was also seriously ill with tuberculosis. At a lavish and typically outlandish house party at Brede over Christmas 1899 (H. G. Wells left an account), Crane collapsed. His companion, Cora, had him carried to Germany in search of a cure, but he died there the following June.

In 1898 H. G. Wells arrived at Sandgate, between Hythe and Folkestone, aged 32, with four major novels behind him: *The Time Machine*, *The Island of Dr Moreau*, *The Invisible Man* and *The War of the Worlds*. By 1900 Wells could afford to move into a home designed for him by C. F. Voysey, Spade House at Sandgate (the house is not open but Folkestone Library has an archive on Wells). Much of his time went on visiting his author friends around the Marsh and entertaining them at Spade House. Yet he still produced a stream of articles, papers and lectures calling for social and political change - often working closely with Arnold Bennett - and many of his best books.

In *Kipps: the Story of a Simple Soul*, shop-assistant Arthur Kipps, Wells voiced the problems of 'lower class' young men trying desperately to rise. With *The First Men in the Moon* and *The War in the Air* he continued his science fiction. But by 1909 he had publicly quarrelled with Henry James and when he finished *Tono-Bungay* he left Folkestone for London.

For centuries Romney Marsh had been profiting from smuggling, known locally as 'owling'. Rudyard Kipling paints a charmingly romantic picture:

> *Five and twenty ponies,*
> *Trotting through the dark -*
> *Brandy for the Parson,*
> *'Baccy for the Clerk;*
> *Laces for a lady, letters for*
> *   a spy,*
> *And watch the wall, my*
> *   darling, while the*
> *   Gentlemen go by!*

Russell Thorndyke tells the rougher side of the business in a series of murderous adventures, written chiefly for children while he lived in Dymchurch. *Dr Syn*, published 1915, is set on Romney Marsh in the 18th century when 'owling' was a major industry. Killing excise men, fighting pitched battles with the militia, storing contraband in the Marsh churches - Brenzett, Appledore and Snargate - were all in a night's work.

Dr Syn leads a double life as the vicar of Dymchurch by day and the Scarecrow leader of the smugglers by night. He is a man with a genius for daring raids, like the one on Lympne Castle, and a stylish way of dealing with informers - one suffers a sickening death from an overdose of cock-

Herbert George Wells made Kent the setting for Kipps: The Story of a Simple Soul *who is brought up in New Romney and apprenticed to a draper in Folkestone.*

Lympne Castle on the edge of the Marsh is the scene of a raid by Dr Syn and his gang of smugglers.

Edith Nesbit (1858-1924), author of The Railway Children, *published 1906.*

roaches. Fortunately only some of the Scarecrow's exploits are re-enacted at Dymchurch each August on the annual 'Day of Syn'.

Dymchurch was also the adopted home of Edith Nesbit - always E. Nesbit on her books: *The Railway Children, The Treasure Seekers,* and *The Wouldbegoods.* She married young and badly, and turned to writing to support her husband, Hubert Bland and his various offspring. Their main home was near London but from the 1890s onwards (when she produced her most popular books) she looked to Dymchurch for 'working holidays'.

Edith was intrigued by the wide skies and quiet open spaces of the Marsh. Though she began holidaying elsewhere in 1911, she came back frequently, exploring the isolated churches by bike, and later in a dog cart. One of her best ghost stories, *Man-Size in Marble,* occurs on Hallowe'en at Brenzett church.

After Hubert's death and her second, possibly worse, marriage, she retired to Romney Marsh to spend her last years at Jesson St Mary.

During her Dymchurch years, Edith had been writing *The Wonderful Garden.* The year it appeared, 1911, Frances Hodgson Burnett published her children's classic *The Secret Garden,* inspired by a walled garden a few miles across the Marsh. Frances (who lived much of her life in America) leased Great Maytham Hall, Rolvenden, from 1898 to 1907 and fell in love with its 'beautiful old walled kitchen garden'. It had a rose garden, too, remodelled later by Sir Edwin Lutyens, where

Little Lord Fauntleroy, serialised in the American children's magazine St Nicholas in 1885, was an immediate best-seller in book form in 1886, and successfully dramatised two years later.

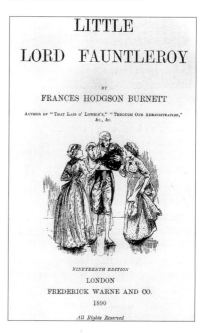

Frances Hodgson Burnett was born in Manchester in 1849. She emigrated to Tennessee in 1865, then returned to live in Kent for a number of years.

she would sit writing.

Frances described herself as 'a kind of pen-driving machine' but she made a fortune from *Little Lord Fauntleroy.* Both Frances and Edith died in 1924: Edith at Jesson, buried at St Mary's church, Frances in America, with a memorial in Rolvenden church.

LITTLE LORD FAUNTLEROY

BY

FRANCES HODGSON BURNETT

AUTHOR OF "THAT LASS O' LOWRIE'S," "THROUGH ONE ADMINISTRATION," &c., &c.

NINETEENTH EDITION

LONDON

FREDERICK WARNE AND CO.

1890

All Rights Reserved

BLOOMSBURY IN THE COUNTRY

Virginia Woolf started the so-called Bloomsbury Group's migrations to Sussex in 1911, when she rented a house at West Firle, near the old county town of Lewes. She was well into her second Sussex home before her sister, Vanessa Bell, took Charleston farmhouse in 1916 as a temporary wartime home. And by the time Charleston was fixed as the Bloomsbury artists' country retreat, Virginia

A gathering of 'Bloomsberries' at Charleston, 1930 (left to right): Angus Davidson, Duncan Grant, Julian Bell, Leonard and Virginia Woolf, Margaret Duckworth, Clive and Vanessa Bell.

had found her final Sussex home, Monk's House at Rodmell, tragically near the River Ouse.

Almost everyone who might be one of the 'Bloomsberries' (the name coined by Molly MacCarthy, wife of literary critic Desmond) managed to drift, at one time or another, out of London squares into this circle of Sussex houses and triangular relationships.

Virginia's first Sussex home was a modern semi-detached 'eyesore' - her description - at West Firle, which she rented in order to revise, yet again, her novel, *The Voyage Out.*

Number two she found while walking on the Downs: Asheham House near the River Ouse, now engulfed in cement workings. After her marriage to writer Leonard Woolf in May 1912, they used it as a country home for seven years; while their London homes were the base for their publishing business, the Hogarth Press.

Asheham was Virginia's *Haunted House.* Only the expiry of the lease made them search for another and eventually they bought Monk's House, again within walking or cycling distance of Lewes - and of Charleston. For in the meantime, Virginia and Leonard had discovered the isolated 18th-century farm which they thought would suit Vanessa.

It was 'all now rather wild, but you could make it lovely,' Virginia wrote to her sister, describing

Virginia Woolf, a bust by Stephen Tomlin at Monk's House.

M onk's House 'contains a large room where we sit, eat, play the gramophone, prop our feet up on the side of the fire and read endless books' – Virginia Woolf, writing to Ethel Smyth, April 22, 1930.

Clive Bell's bed-room at Charleston from 1939, previously Vanessa's studio and her children's nursery, decorated by Vanessa Bell and Duncan Grant.

Vanessa Bell designed book jackets and covers for many of Virginia Woolf's first editions, including her early essays, The Common Reader, *published 1925.*

Charleston farmhouse, its orchard, pond and flint-walled garden. She can hardly have guessed how 'lovely' Vanessa and her partner Duncan Grant would make it.

They covered the interior with bright colours and bold Post-Impressionist patterns that are the hallmark of Bloomsbury style (and of their friend Roger Fry's Omega Workshop). They also found time to cover the interior of nearby Berwick church with murals, after they received an understandably-controversial commission to decorate the church in 1941.

When Vanessa moved into Charleston with Duncan and her children in the autumn of 1916, it was the start of one of the oddest country-house parties on record. Lytton Strachey author of *Eminent Victorians,* came with artist (Dora) Carrington. Maynard Keynes stayed while he worked on *The Economic Consequences of the Peace* and was joined by Russian ballerina Lydia Lopokova. Desmond and Molly MacCarthy paid numerous visits, Molly commenting the first time that Charleston in the rain looked the nearest thing to Wuthering

Heights. Art-critic Clive Bell (Vanessa's husband), and artist Roger Fry also joined the household at times.

The comings and goings between Asheham and Charleston naturally continued after Leonard and Virginia bought Monk's House - for £700 at an auction in the White Hart Hotel, Lewes on July 1, 1919.

Monk's House is another modest 18th-century house, low and rambling, surrounded by a pretty garden where Virginia worked in a studio summer-house. At first it was minus mains water, gas and electricity. As Virginia's books and the Hogarth Press made money, they made improvements. They added more rooms so that friends and writers they published could stay: E. M. Forster, Strachey, Elizabeth Bowen, T. S. Eliot and Vita Sackville-West.

With 'Tom' (T. S.) Eliot, Virginia shared a correspondence that lasted 20 years. Despite his reputation as cold, aloof and reserved, with Virginia he could be confiding and playful, signing his letters - like his nonsense poems of *Practical Cats* - from 'Possum', sometimes 'Your devoted Possum'. Eliot first met Leonard and Virginia in 1918. In 1923 they published his most influential poem, *The Waste Land,* in book form. It was not an entirely easy relationship. Virginia felt he could be vain and difficult, and accused him of poaching Hogarth authors once he went to work for rival publisher Faber. But he was a frequent visitor

at Rodmell and she his frequent supporter - financially and during his difficult separation from his first wife.

With Vita Sackville-West, Virginia enjoyed a more passionate relationship and an affair that began in the mid-1920s.

Vita's first visit to Rodmell in 1924 left Virginia musing: 'I rather marvel at her skill, & sensibility; for is she not mother, wife, great lady, hostess, as well as scribbling?...Oh yes, I like her...this might be a friendship of a sort.'

It was certainly a profitable partnership for the Hogarth Press. Vita's work was at first more popular than Virginia's, until Virginia wrote a fantasy, time-travelling biography of Vita and her ancestral home Knole in Kent. When *Orlando* was published in 1928 it brought Virginia her biggest readership. Vita loved *Orlando* because it linked her forever with Knole. But she would shortly move into another house, Sissinghurst Castle in Kent, to which she became equally attached.

Vita first saw Sissinghurst's high, pink-brick Tudor towers standing in the remnants of a moat and walled gardens, on an April day in 1930. It 'caught instantly at my heart and my imagination', she wrote. With her husband Harold Nicolson she turned the 'truly appalling mess of rubbish...old bedsteads, old ploughshares...' into an exquisitely romantic garden.

They restored what was left of the castle, but its remaining rooms were so few and scattered that each member of the family had separate quarters dotted around the garden. In the tower where Vita had her sitting room and study is a small exhibition that includes the printing press the Woolfs initially used at the Hogarth Press.

In *Orlando* Virginia celebrated Knole; in *Mrs Dalloway* she covered one London day; *To the Lighthouse* and *Jacob's Room* capture her Cornish memories. Her Sussex story *Between the Acts* - a parody of every village pageant of English history -was to be her last. In 1941, fearing yet another mental breakdown, she walked into the River Ouse and drowned.

Leonard lived on at Monk's House till 1969, still writing on politics, international affairs and a five-volume autobiography. When he died Monk's House was handed over to Sussex University and for a decade was let to visiting professors from America. One of them was novelist Saul Bellow.

*V*ictoria, 'Vita', Sackville-West. *'I feel like one of those wax figures in a shop window, on which you have hung a robe stitched with jewels,'* she wrote after reading Virginia Woolf's Orlando.

*A*t Sissinghurst Castle, Vita Sackville-West's home *from 1930 to 1962, she wrote one of her best novels,* All Passion Spent, *as well as poetry and gardening articles for the* Observer.

Nearly two centuries earlier, in the same old coaching inn where Leonard made his bid for Monk's House - the White Hart in the centre of Lewes - radical Tom Paine, author of *The Rights of Man*, used to attend meetings of the Headstrong Club. Rebellion was in the air when Paine was born in 1737, son of a Thetford corset-maker. He became the most outspoken rapporteur and leader of the revolutionary times he lived in. For six years before he went to America he lived in Lewes at Bull House (it has a plaque and is now HQ of the Sussex Archaeological Society) and walked along the High Street to join the debating group in the upstairs room at the White Hart.

At the foot of Lewes's steep cobbled Keere Street, Pepys's contemporary and fellow-diarist John Evelyn spent part of his childhood with his grandmother at Southover Grange. The grey-stone Elizabethan house (the gardens are open) would later appear as Mock-Beggar Hall in *Ovingdean Grange - A Tale of the South Downs*, one of William Harrison Ainsworth's popular historical novels, written during his 15 years in Brighton.

Saturday, February 22, 1913 was an eventful day for Eric Gill. The engraver-sculptor-calligrapher, whose Gill typeface is one of the classics of

printed literature, spent his 31st birthday in Brighton being received into the Roman Catholic Church. After tea, back in Ditchling at his arts-and-crafts

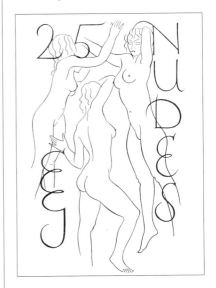

commune, the Guild of St Joseph and St Dominic, Leonard and Virginia Woolf arrived from the other side of Lewes to spend the weekend. The following morning, after Gill went to mass and took his first communion, he went for a walk with 'the Wolves' over the hills. D. H. Lawrence also tramped miles along the Downs to visit Gill; and given the two men's determined challenge to sexual conventions, the conversation must have flowed a little easier than it did with 'the Wolves'. Ditchling has the only permanent collection of Gill's calligraphy, designs, woodcuts and books, in a small museum in the former village school.

SUSSEX BY THE SEA

At the time Graham Greene was writing *Brighton Rock* in 1936/7, no other city 'not London, Paris or Oxford, had such a hold on my affections'.

He had known Brighton since 1910, when he was six. He came again in 1926 and stayed opposite the West Pier, working on his first published novel, a historical thriller, *The Man Within*. Two years later he was back preparing a piece for *The Times*, 'A Walk on the Sussex Downs'.

Now in 1936, he returned to research a thriller of the turf based

on Brighton's downland race-course, high above the sea. But a real-life local murder case soon absorbed him and *Brighton Rock* moved into the seedy landscape of the town's underworld.

The opening line says it all: 'Hale knew, before he had been three hours in Brighton, that they

meant to murder him.' There is no hiding for Hale among the trippers streaming down to the front from the station, sauntering along Madeira Drive, enjoying the Palace Pier. He is caught in the battle between the razor-slashing gangs and murdered on the pier by the teenage thug Pinkie.

Nearly 30 years later Greene used Brighton again, and his favourite pub, The Cricketers, in *Travels with my Aunt*. As Henry Pulling soon discovers though, Brighton proved only 'a bizarre foretaste of much that was to follow'. Aunt Augusta liked '"to be at the centre of all the devilry... with the buses going off to all those places." She spoke as though their destinations were Sodom and Gomorrah rather than Lewes and Patcham and Littlehampton and Shoreham.'

It is unlike Greene's darker crime and cold-war books, and more like the breezy Brighton most writers present: a fashionable place with a permanent smile on its face, put there, some say, by the Prince Regent when he secretly married Mrs Fitzherbert in 1785

Graham Greene's 'entertainment' Brighton Rock, *scripted by Greene and Terence Rattigan for filming in 1947, was released in the US as* Young Scarface.

Graham Greene at 50 in 1954. Ten years later his play, Carving a Statue, *was premiered at Brighton's Theatre Royal, starring Ralph Richardson.*

Hale's advertised route – 'eleven to twelve the Aquarium and Palace Pier, twelve till one the front' – makes him an easy target for his murderer in Brighton Rock.

Brighton's Royal Pavilion. 'Prinny', later King George IV, spent 35 years and a fortune transforming it from the 'superior farmhouse' he first rented in 1786.

and built the Eastern-style Royal Pavilion.

Several authors made 'Prinny' a character in their books. Conan Doyle, for one, involves him and the Pavilion in *Rodney Stone*, a Sussex adventure story about 'The Fancy'- the prize-fighting world of the Regency period.

Although the prince is credited with turning the little fishing town of Brighthelmstone into the most fashionable seaside resort in Europe, its fame began when Dr Richard Russell moved there in 1753 to set up a 'health clinic' advocating sea-bathing as a cure-all. So Brighton already had a social season before Prinny arrived in 1783.

Mrs Hester Thrale and her hus-

band had a house in West Street for years before she began bringing Fanny Burney here in 1779, fresh from Miss Burney's London triumphs as the author of *Evelina* and, later, *Cecilia*.

Dr Johnson came several times with the Thrales, attending St Nicholas church (it has a Thrale memorial) and the usual round of card parties and asssemblies. He didn't really enjoy Brighton, but he was devoted to his protégé 'young Burney' so he came again when she was invited.

Fanny found it delightful, even bathing in November:

We rose at six o'clock in the morn and by the pale blink o'the moon went to the seaside where we had bespoken the bathing-woman to be ready for us, and into the ocean we plunged. It was cold but pleasant. I have bathed so often as to lose my dread of the operation.

Writing to her sister Susanna the same month, after the last ball of the season, Fanny (not as young as Johnson implied, having turned 30) reports, tongue firmly in cheek, 'the grand moment! - the height - the zenith of my glory in the ton meridian!...this most flashy young officer (for whom all the belles here are sighing)...came forward, and desired to be introduced to me'.

Once war was declared on Bonaparte in 1793, Brighton 'bristled' with

'Bathing at Brighton', the fashionable new pastime as seen by cartoonist and illustrator George Cruikshank (1792-1878).

AUGUST.— Bathing at Brighton.

flashy young officers, as Osbert Sitwell put it in his book *Brighton*.

Jane Austen had the full measure of the place when she made it the scene of Lydia's downfall, running off with Wickham, in *Pride and Prejudice*. 'In Lydia's imagination a visit to Brighton comprised every possibility of earthly happiness. She saw... the streets of that gay bathing-place covered with officers. She saw herself the object of attention ... seated beneath a tent, tenderly flirting with at least six officers at once.'

In *Vanity Fair*, William Makepeace Thackeray describes it on the eve of the Battle of Waterloo: 'Brighton, that always looks brisk, gay, and gaudy, like a harlequin's jacket'. Here sweet Amelia and George Osborne come for their honeymoon, only to bump into unscrupulous Becky Sharp and Rawdon Crawley, also married and staying at the Ship Inn (now named the Old Ship Hotel, where Thackeray himself was a guest).

While Becky ruins Amelia's honeymoon and Rawdon fleeces George at cards and billiards, honest Captain Dobbin joins them at the Ship to let George know he has been disinherited.

In 1847-1848, when *Vanity Fair* was first published in monthly instalments, it was battling for readers against *Dombey and Son*, in which Charles Dickens followed the fad for Brighton.

Like Thackeray, Dickens had patronised the Old Ship, but while working on *Dombey and Son* he stayed at the Bedford Hotel (there is a modern replacement). He set Dombey Senior there when he comes to see his small son Paul, who is struggling to grow up at Mrs Pipchin's 'infantine Boarding-House' and Dr Blimber's 'hothouse', probably in Chichester Terrace.

But Paul is obviously dying as he lies on Brighton beach beside his devoted sister Florence, wondering what the waves are saying: 'I know that they are always saying something. Always the same thing.'

William Makepeace Thackeray (1811-1863), sketch for a self-portrait.

Fanny Burney (left) found everyone at Brighton's Assembly Rooms in October 1782 whispering, 'That's she! That's the famous Miss Burney!' and vowed, 'I shall certainly escape going any more ...'

Esplanade & Beach, Kemp Town, Brighton.

ALONG THE SOUTH DOWNS

Uppark, the house that changed H. G. Wells's life, stands alone on Harting Down, near Chichester, all square and stately, solid and red-brick.

'Above stairs' it has perfectly

Kemp Town Esplanade, Brighton, around the time that Harrison Ainsworth lived close by in Arundel Terrace and Lewis Carroll lodged in Sussex Square.

Uppark became Bladesover in H. G. Wells's Tono-Bungay, *the novel that satirised the 'Bladesover System' for maintaining 'the great house... and the servants in their stations'.*

Herbert George Wells, author of The War of the Worlds, The Time Machine *and* The First Men in the Moon, *admired by G. K. Chesterton as 'adventure stories in the new world the men of science had discovered'.*

Midhurst – its rambling old coaching inn, The Spread Eagle, was a favourite with Hilaire Belloc.

proportioned drawing-rooms, saloons and dining rooms, their 17th and 18th-century interiors painstakingly repaired after fire gutted the house in 1989.

'Below stairs' are servants' quarters, basements, tunnels and storerooms. Here Wells's mother, Sarah, came to preside as housekeeper in 1880 and Herbert George, aged 14, came for Christmas.

Snowed in for a fortnight, he passed the time in Sarah's subterranean sitting room writing, as he put it, 'a daily newspaper of a facetious character - *The Uppark Alarmist* - on what was properly kitchen paper'.

Years later, as a famous novelist, friend of G. B. Shaw, Henry James, Arnold Bennett and many others, Wells would describe Uppark as the doorway to his new life. Permission to use the library meant 'I had been able to do all sorts of things'.

But Wells's son Anthony (by writer, later Dame, Rebecca West) believed his father was appalled by the contrast between the servants' and the owners' quarters; and Wells certainly reflects the division in *The Time Machine*, the first popular science fiction novel from an English author.

Sarah originally worked at Uppark as a lady's maid, then married one of the gardeners, Joseph Wells, and moved away with him. When his shop-keeping efforts failed she left him, returned to Uppark and struggled to settle their son, Herbert George, into life as a draper's assistant. H.G. struggled equally hard to avoid it, inflicting it later on his hapless hero in *The History of Mr Polly*.

At Midhurst, the market town near Uppark, he spent a while at the Grammar School and worked at the chemist's shop, Morton Hickson's in Church Hill. He lodged over the 'tuck shop' next to the Angel Hotel while he crammed for exams to win a college place in London.

Midhurst, the apothecary's shop and Uppark (renamed

Bladesover) all appear in *Tono-Bungay*. Written at Folkstone and published in 1909, it is classic Wells, mocking the Edwardian social system that preserved Uppark and made progress impossible.

ilaire Belloc's poem *The South Country* is a hymn to Sussex.

> I will hold my house in the
>   high wood
> Within a walk of the sea,
> And the men that were boys
>   when I was a boy
> Shall sit and drink with
>   me.

In 1906 Belloc, who was born in France, returned to the Sussex Downs where he had spent his boyhood in the 1870s and 80s. The following year he produced the hilarious *Cautionary Tales for Children* - including 'Henry King, Who chewed bits of String'; 'Mattilda, Who told Lies, and was Burned to Death'; and 'Lord Lundy, Who was too Freely Moved to Tears'.

Belloc also continued his stream of poems, biographies and essays.

The house he made his home until he died in 1953, King's Land near Shipley, has the largest 'smock' windmill in Sussex (preserved as a memorial to him, with a small museum). It dominates the landscape Belloc loved as the epitome of rural England. His poems are a litany of Sussex places and pubs he would visit on foot, bike and boat: 'The River Arun, a valley of sacred water; the Amberley Wild brook which is lonely with reeds at evening'; Petworth, Duncton Hill, the Spread Eagle at Midhurst, the White Horse at Steyning and the Tabby Cat Inn at West Grinstead, where he was buried in the Catholic churchyard.

xactly where Stella Gibbons imagined *Cold Comfort Farm* on the South Downs is uncertain, but the landscape round Devil's Dyke and the villages of Fulking and Poynings are a close match with the Starkadders' farm and the village of Howling. Gibbons had been a journalist in London for 10 years when she produced her parody of earthy, melodramatic novels such as Mary Webb's Shropshire sagas. Stella was working for *The Lady* magazine in the early 1930s and allegedly wrote the story while she commuted to work on the tube.

Upstairs at Cold Comfort, Great Aunt Ada Doom tries to remember what she saw that was 'something nasty in the woodshed'. In the tumbledown cowsheds

Shipley windmill towers over the Sussex Downs beside Belloc's home.

Hilaire Belloc (1870-1953) was born in France, Joseph Hilary Pierre Belloc.

'*The Reviewer, reviewing my book, At which he had barely intended to look.*' Original illustration for Belloc's *A Moral Alphabet,* drawn by his friend B.T.B., Lord Basil Blackwood. B.T.B. produced all the pictures for the Book of Beasts and Cautionary Tales, matching H. B.'s words with his lively, loony style.

Graceless, Pointless, Feckless and Aimless wait patiently to be milked. And once 'the sukebind is in flower', the time is just ripe for orphaned Flora Poste, expensively and lengthily educated, to descend on Sussex and bring order to her relatives' rural chaos.

John Keats had recently had a couple of weeks in Chichester and Hampshire when he wrote to his brother in February 1819: 'Nothing worth speaking of happened in either place.' As an afterthought he adds: 'I took down some of the thin paper and wrote on it a little poem call'd "St Agnes Eve".' He promises to send it with his next letter, 'and if I should have finished it a little thing call'd the "eve of St Mark"...'

During his stay in Chichester (the house in Eastgate Square has a plaque) Keats had visited the cathedral and Vicars Close. Their medieval settings seeped into the poems, and perhaps the 'bitter chill' did too, as it numbed 'the Beadsman's fingers, while he told his rosary'.

In Hampshire, Keats mentions in his letter, he attended the consecration of the Gothic-style chapel at Stansted Park. He didn't enjoy the ceremony but it gave him the image of the triple-arched

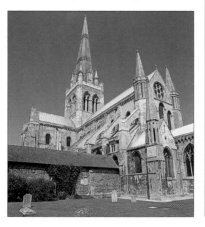

windows '...diamonded with panes of quaint device, Innumerable of stains and splendid dyes...' where 'shone the wintry moon' on St Agnes Eve.

A few years before Keats's visit William Blake was tried for treason in Chichester Greyfriars, used as the city's guildhall (now a museum). Blake had brought his family to live at Felpham in 1800, in a cottage (marked with a plaque) arranged for them by benevolent Chichester poet William Hayley.

In the following three years at 'lovely Felpham', Blake recovered the sense of joy and vision he feared he had lost in London. His 'three years' slumber on the banks of ocean' produced a tide of his best lyrical verses and the long, prophetic work *Milton*, which opens with the lines:

> *And did those feet in ancient time*
> *Walk upon England's mountains green?*
> *And was the holy Lamb of God*
> *On England's pleasant pastures seen?*

But in 1803, after a heated argument with a soldier in his cottage garden, Blake bundled the man out and was soon arrested in revenge, charged with sedition and treasonable expressions in support of Bonaparte (then threatening to invade England). At the trial, in January 1804, Blake was found not guilty, but the experience had seriously disturbed him and he had already moved his family back to London.

Lady Bracknell may have thought 'The line is immaterial', but to Oscar Wilde the importance of being in Worthing was quite considerable. He was staying there in the summer of 1894 while he wrote *The Importance of Being Earnest* and it

supplied not only the hero's name, Jack Worthing, but part of the plot.

On Wednesday July 11, 1894, page six of the *Worthing Gazette* reported 'A baby in a hamper' had been found at King's Cross Station. Wilde amended the hamper to the immortal 'black leather hand-bag' and the station to Victoria, which serves 'the Brighton line'.

In the cloakroom at Victoria, Jack explains to the formidable Lady Bracknell, 'an old gentleman of a very charitable and kindly disposition, found me, and gave me the name of Worthing, because he happened to have a first-class ticket for Worthing in his pocket at the time. Worthing is a place in Sussex. It is a seaside resort.'

Wilde was already a celebrity when he brought his wife and two sons to the town, partly to avoid creditors in London. He took a furnished house on the Esplanade (the building has gone but a plaque marks the site) and wrote to Lord Alfred Douglas: 'I have been doing nothing but bathing and playwriting' - though he had, in fact, found time to present the prizes at the Pier Pavilion for the best boats in the water carnival.

When Wilde finished *The Importance of Being Earnest* - it only took 21 days - he decided it was 'the best I have ever written'.

William Blake (1757-1827), visionary poet and painter, wrote of his three-year stay in a cottage (below left) in Sussex:
'Away to sweet Felpham, for Heaven is there; The Ladder of Angels descends through the air.'

Oscar Wilde and his young friend Lord Alfred Douglas, pictured 1894, the year Wilde stayed in Sussex and wrote The Importance of Being Earnest.

THE SURREY HILLS

The ill-fated 'exploring party' in Jane Austen's *Emma* helped make Box Hill the most famous of all beauty spots along the Surrey stretch of the North Downs ridge.

The place is a revelation to Emma in several ways: insufferable Mrs Elton and irritating Miss Bates reduce her to such rudeness that Mr Knightly's just reproaches can only be off-set by the penance of a 'whole evening of backgammon with her father'. But to Jane Austen, Box Hill was familiar ground.

Jane Austen (1775-1817), from a sketch by her sister Cassandra.

'They had a very fine day for Box Hill', but after a while Jane Austen's Emma wishes she were sitting alone 'in tranquil observation of the beautiful views beneath her'.

At Polesden Lacey on October 10, 1802, according to the local paper, Mr Sheridan entertained his tenants to 'a grand harvest home...with true English cheer and ancient hospitality'.

In 1809 (probably earlier as well) she stayed a week at Great Bookham, near the foot of the hill, where her relations and god-father lived. And she was there again in 1814 while working on the book.

Meanwhile, on the other side of Box Hill, a small group of French émigrés, who had fled the Terror in Paris, was staying with Madame de Staël at Juniper Hall (now a Field Studies Council centre). Among them was General d'Arblay, who met and married novelist Fanny Burney - in Mickleham church in 1793 - and set up home with her at Great Bookham.

Jane certainly knew of the group and Fanny Burney's home in the neighbourhood. She had her own copy of Miss Burney's best-seller *Camilla* and refers to it in *Northanger Abbey* and *Sanditon*. But there is no record that she met the d'Arblays; only that she declined to meet Madame de Staël.

Here at Box Hill Jane's path also crosses (as it had at Bath) with play-wright Richard Brinsley Sheridan's.

In 1814 while Jane was researching and writing *Emma*, Sheridan was looking after an estate nearby, Polesden Lacey, that he had acquired in 1797 as part of the marriage settlement with his second wife.

'I have every hour some new reason to be pleased with our purchase...we shall have the nicest place, within a prudent distance of town, in England,' he wrote to her. Their house was replaced soon after Sheridan died in 1816, but his extension to the long-terrace walk remains one of the main features of the large gardens.

John Keats came to Box Hill as well, still a few years behind Jane Austen, as he was at Winchester.

On November 22, 1817 he arrived at the local inn (now the Burford Bridge Hotel) and recorded: 'I went up Box Hill this

evening after the Moon.' In a small back room overlooking the stable yard he finished book four of *Endymion* within the week. 'I like this place very much,' he decided, and stayed on to write *In drear-nighted December.*

In 1924, the year *Passage to India* was published, E. M. Forster inherited a house on the North Downs above the village of Abinger. It was his home for more than 20 years and he called his 1936 book of essays *Abinger Harvest*. The next volume, *Two Cheers for Democracy* (published 1951) contains 'The Last of Abinger' and notes from an 'Evening walk round by the yew-wood on the Pilgrims Way'.

'Left to itself, there is not a safer place in England than

Abinger,' Forster wrote. He was distraught when the lease on his house, at West Hackhurst, was terminated. He was still writing bitterly years later about his exile from it and from Piney Copse. But the four-acre copse was his, bought outright soon after he moved to Abinger, and he left it to the National Trust when he died, to preserve as open woodland.

Lord Tennyson became so popular among Victorian readers that he was forced to find a second, more secluded home than his Isle of Wight house. In 1868 building started on Aldworth, south of Haslemere on the slopes of Blackdown Hill. Tennyson spent every summer there for the rest of his life, striding miles across the hills. Tennyson's Lane to Aldworth and Blackdown, and part of the downs, are preserved by the National Trust.

'I am every morning at the top of Box Hill' – George Meredith, esteemed for his local novels The Egoist *and* Diana of the Crossways, *lived here 1867 to 1909, visited by R. L. Stevenson, J. M. Barrie, James Russell Lowell and Henry James.*

Abinger Hammer village sign. 'I have promised to write ... the Abinger Church Pageant,' E. M. Forster noted, April 1934. He made it a Pageant of Trees, *celebrating the Surrey woods and his Piney Copse, planted with chestnuts, crab apples and wild cherry.*

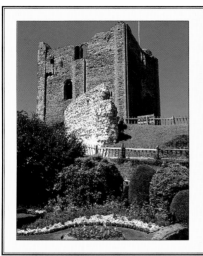

Guildford Museum has a Lewis Carroll collection - belongings, inventions, books and letters - recording Carroll's numerous visits to the town, where he died in 1898. His own bachelor quarters were in Oxford, but in the summer of 1868 he came house-hunting for his six unmarried sisters and an aunt. Before Christmas they were installed in a roomy house (marked with a plaque) near the museum and Carroll's diary shows he became a regular guest. He was here as usual for Christmas in 1897 shortly before he died, and was buried in the cemetery on The Mount. Castle Gardens, nearby, have a statue of Alice and there is another by the river.

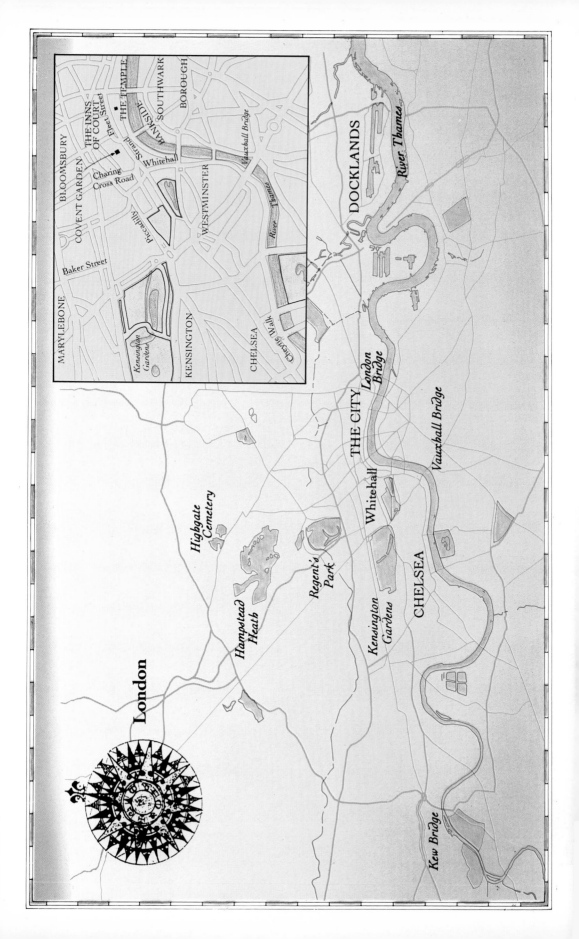

CHAPTER 4

LONDON

◆

WESTMINSTER AND WHITEHALL

In Westminster Abbey, scene of coronations and royal burials for centuries, the Elizabethans set a precedent in 1599 when they decided Edmund Spenser must be buried near Geoffrey Chaucer's new tomb.

Chaucer's remains had been brought to the abbey's south transept in 1556 (he died in 1400) and it seemed fitting that Spenser,

adored for his poem about Elizabeth, *The Faerie Queene*, should lie near by. Then came Michael Drayton, author of the topographical poem *Poly-Olbion*. In 1637 Ben Jonson was buried in the north aisle with the simple, spare but misspelt inscription 'O rare Ben Johnson'.

Most writers, though, were honoured near Chaucer in Poets' Corner, and now it is crammed with statues, busts, tablets and monuments (only a few tombs) for everyone from Mrs Aphra Behn to Lewis Carroll and Dylan Thomas.

John Dryden, first official Poet Laureate, was brought in with some pomp as soon as he died in 1700. Others arrived more quietly or waited decades for a decent monument. Charles Dickens was entombed promptly but privately in 1870 to avoid the crowds.

Deciding 'who's in, who's out' is down to the Dean because the Abbey is a Royal Peculiar outside the jurisdiction of the Archbishop of Canterbury. The result is a haphazard collection, including many a misfit - like atheist Shelley, sharing a plaque with Keats. George Eliot took a century to get here, as did the Brontës, while Lord

John Dryden (1631 –1700). His poem Annus Mirabilis *described 'The Year of Wonders 1666'; his play* Secret Love *gave Nell Gwynn her most famous role – on stage.*

'*Think how many royal bones Sleep within these heaps of stones*' -
Ode on Westminster Abbey, *Francis Beaumont, buried in Poets' Corner, 1616.*

Sir Walter Ralegh, Queen Elizabeth I's favourite courtier (and possibly her lover), whiled away years in the Tower of London writing a History of the World *before he was executed at Westminster. His statue stands in Whitehall.*

Byron waited twice as long.

In 1476, nearly a century before the Corner took in its first poet, William Caxton had set up his printing press a few yards away beside the Chapter House. Seven years later he shifted his workshop within the precincts and advertised to anyone with anything to print, 'late hym come to Westmenester in to the almonelrye at the red pale and he shall have them good chepe'.

Caxton was buried in 1491 at St Margaret's, the parish church next to the Abbey. Tradition puts Sir Walter Ralegh there too, in 1618. Ralegh had stood trial for treason, beneath the huge hammer-beam roof of Westminster Hall, and was lodged before his execution in the old Abbey gatehouse – leaving behind in a Bible his best-known poem:

E'en such is time,
*   which takes in trust*
Our youth, our joys, and
*   all we have,*
And pays us but with age
*   and dust.*

The following morning he was beheaded in Old Palace Yard between the Abbey and the Palace of Westminster. The rebuilt palace and original Hall are now The Houses of Parliament, setting for MP Michael Dobbs's thriller *The House of Cards*. But for five centuries, from King Edward the Confessor to Henry VIII, they were the monarch's main residence.

Then in 1529 Henry seized Cardinal Wolsey's riverside home near Charing Cross and began developing it into Whitehall Palace, leaving Westminster for parliament and state occasions – like the coronation banquet of King Charles II, on April 23, 1661.

Samuel Pepys's *Diary* gives, as always, a vivid, compassionate, artless account. Pepys was up before dawn to get a place at the coronation in the Abbey, 'where with a great deal of patience I sat from past 4 till 11 before the King came in. And a pleasure it was to see the Abbey raised in the middle, all covered with red and a throne... But so great a noise I could make but little of the musique.'

After the coronation, Pepys watched the banquet in Westminster Hall and 'took a great deal of pleasure to go up and

Renowned Spenser, lie a thought more nigh
To learned Chaucer; and, rare Beaumont, lie
A little nearer Spenser, to make room
For Shakespeare in your threefold fourfold tomb.
17th-century inscription, Poets' Corner.

down and look upon the ladies'.

Pepys had opened his private, short-hand diary on January 1, 1660, a few months before the Restoration of the monarchy, and kept writing for a decade through the political excitement, pageantry and play-going of 'Good King Charles's Glorious Days'.

He was 26 and living in Axe Yard (demolished) near Whitehall with his wife, Elizabeth. She was 15 when they married at St Margaret's in 1655, and Samuel's frequent infidelities and long hours at the Navy Board often left her lonely and unhappy.

Pepys himself was usually a cheery optimist, visiting lords and ministers in Whitehall or loitering around Westminster Hall to persuade some woman or other to a tavern.

In August 1662, as the royal household arrived by river at Whitehall Palace, Pepys was watching from the 'new banqueting house' and saw 'the King and Queen in a barge under a canopy, with ten thousand barges and boats I think, for we could see no water'.

The Banqueting House now stands in a sea of government offices: the Whitehall of Dickens's Circumlocution Office in *Little Dorrit*, and C. P. Snow's *Corridors of Power* (1964), based on his years as a scientific adviser in Whitehall.

In Pepys's day it was still part of a royal palace (the rest was destroyed by fire in 1698), a glittering building created by classical designer Inigo Jones.

Jones collaborated for more than 20 years with dramatist Ben Jonson, creating stage-sets and machines for the spectacular masques that Jonson wrote as royal revels, and designed the Banqueting House as the perfect place to present them.

One ceremony it wasn't intended for was the execution of the king. Pepys could remember how Charles I had stepped from a window of the Banqueting House on to a scaffold in Whitehall to be beheaded in the wintry sunshine on January 30, 1649.

'*And so to bed*', the most famous line in the Diary of Samuel Pepys (left) is really one of his more innocent, marking the close of a long day as a civil servant. He closed his Diary *for ever in 1669, fearing he was going blind.*

The Banqueting House, designed by Inigo Jones, the man who wrote the style book for the 17th century. He also created the Queen's House at Greenwich and collaborated with dramatist Ben Jonson.

The Cenotaph – a pillar of
Portland stone, where the
dead of two World Wars are
remembered each November
with wreaths and silence
and a salute. It was
unveiled in Whitehall on
November 11, 1920, and is
inscribed with Laurence
Binyon's poem For the
Fallen:

'They shall grow not old, as
we that are left grow old:
Age shall not weary them,
nor the years condemn.
At the going down of the
sun and in the morning
We will remember them.'

*John Milton, scholar,
poet, defender of the
Commonwealth. Born
near Cheapside, 1608,
he was schooled at St
Paul's and buried at St
Giles, Cripplegate,
1674.*

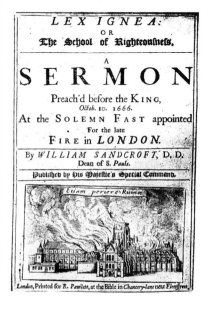

LEX IGNEA:
OR
The School of Righteousness.

A
SERMON
Preach'd before the KING,
Octob. 10. 1666.
At the SOLEMN FAST appointed
For the late
FIRE in LONDON.

By WILLIAM SANDCROFT, D.D.
Dean of S. Pauls.

Published by His Majestie's Special Command.

Etiam periere Ruinæ

London, Printed for R. Pawlett, at the Bible in Chancery-lane near Fleetstreet.

*The 'Fire Sermon'
preached before
King Charles II,
October 1666, was not
the only one that saw
divine retribution in
the crackling flames
of the Great Fire of
London.*

Later that year Puritan poet and
scholar John Milton was appointed
Latin Secretary to Oliver
Cromwell's new Council of State
and the Commonwealth. Like
Pepys, Milton lived only a short
distance from Whitehall, in Petty
France. Three years after Pepys's
wedding in St Margaret's, Milton
buried his second wife and their
child in the same church.

During the 1650s Milton
almost abandoned poetry to produce pamphlets arguing the
republican cause. Quite blind by
1652, he would draft Cromwell's
letters and diplomatic despatches
with the help of secretaries
(Andrew Marvell was one) until,
in 1659, the Commonwealth
began to crumble.

THE CITY
OF LONDON

By the time the Great Plague
gripped London in 1665,
John Milton and Samuel
Pepys both had lodgings in the
City and were there to hear the
first mournful cries of 'Bring out
your dead'.

Pepys, working for the Navy
Board, had rooms and offices in
Seething Lane and worshipped
at St Olave's, 'myne owne
church', where he was buried in
1703. He had known the City
as a child, born in Salisbury
Court off Fleet Street in 1633
and baptised in St Bride's
(Prince Henry's Room at the top of Fleet Street
has a Pepys collection).

Milton was living in Bunhill
Row, beside the Nonconformist
cemetery, Bunhill Fields (where
John Bunyan was buried in 1688,
Defoe in 1731 and William Blake
in 1827). But before long Milton
took his family to safety in the
country at Chalfont St Giles.

Pepys stayed, and witnessed not
only the plague but the next
tragedy, the Great Fire. Like his
friend John Evelyn, he recorded

both in his diary.

After the Restoration in 1660, King Charles II had lost little time in overturning the strict social code of the Puritans: playhouses re-opened, women appeared on the stage and the king kept a bevy of mistresses.

Charles was known, Pepys wrote, as 'a lazy prince...no counsel, no money and no reputation'. No wonder, some Puritans said, that the ancient City soon suffered its worst epidemic of bubonic plague and the most destructive fire it had ever seen.

'God preserve us all,' Pepys prayed in April. In August he noted: 'The people die so, that now it seems they are fain to carry the dead to be buried by daylight, the nights not sufficing to do it in.'

Twelve months later, in the early hours of Sunday morning, September 2, the Great Fire broke out in a bakehouse in Pudding Lane (the Monument stands near the spot). For five days it raged through the City's smelly streets and timber-framed houses.

'God grant mine eyes may never behold the like,' John Evelyn wrote, '...above ten thousand homes all in one flame, the noise and crackling and thunder of the impetuous flames, the shrieking of women and children, the hurry of people, the fall of towers, houses and churches was like an hideous storm.'

By the time it had burned out, nearly 90 churches, the Royal Exchange and the Guildhall were all gone. Old St Paul's was a smouldering ruin.

The 'stones of St Pauls flew like grenades, the lead melting down the streets in a stream', wrote Evelyn. As the cathedral's vast roof crashed down, one of few monuments to survive was the statue of 'metaphysical' poet John Donne, Dean of St Paul's from 1621 until his death in 1631.

Donne is remembered now for his despairing *Holy Sonnets* ('Batter my heart, three person'd God') and for his love lyrics ('Sweetest love, I do not goe, For wearinesse of thee' and 'Goe, and catche a falling starre').

But to Londoners standing in St Paul's, Donne was the greatest preacher of the age. Among his powerful sermons and *Devotions* is the meditation: 'Any man's death

diminishes me, because I am involved in Mankind; and therefore never send to know for whom the bell tolls; It tolls for Thee.'

Three days before it tolled for Donne on March 31, 1631, he received a visit from his friend and first biographer Izaak Walton, who had property nearby in Paternoster Row and Chancery Lane. Walton described how Donne had posed in a winding-sheet for the picture later used to create the statue saved from Old St Paul's, and still

*B*en Jonson (1572–1637) was born in London, went to school at Westminster and became one of the most biting poet-playwrights of the age. Like Shakespeare he was also an actor, noted for ranting around as Hieronimo in Thomas Kyd's Spanish Tragedy.

on show in Sir Christopher Wren's magnificent new cathedral.

Working on St Paul's as a pupil with Wren was a brilliant young architect named Nicholas Hawksmoor, whose own classically designed churches inspired Peter Ackroyd's puzzling novel *Hawksmoor*, published 1985.

Nicholas is not the hero of this time-travelling tale of occult forces. But it revolves around Hawksmoor's churches, chiefly St George-in-the-East at Wapping and St Anne's at Limehouse (two of Docklands' most distinctive landmarks), and Christ Church at Spitalfields, its tall spire and portico newly restored.

West of Spitalfields Market lies Smithfield Market, once the setting for open-air cattle markets, tournaments and pageants. Every August it held a massive fair on St Bartholomew's day, drawing traders from all over

*S*t Anne's, Limehouse, one of the Hawksmoor churches in Docklands that fascinate novelist Peter Ackroyd.

Europe as well as every cut-purse, ballad-monger, bawd and ginger-bread lady in London.

Ben Jonson turned it into 'a new sufficient play called *Barthol'mew Fair,* merry, and as full of noise as sport, made to delight all' at the Hope theatre on

Bankside on October 30, 1614: a satire, but not as savage as his earlier attacks on greed and avarice in the City, *Volpone* and *The Alchemist.*

To one side of the market stands the original Charterhouse School, where 18th-century essayists Joseph Addison and Richard Steele became friends, later collaborating on *The Tatler* and *The Spectator.*

On the other side are the remains of the priory of St Bartholomew the Great and 'Bart's' hospital, both founded in 1123. By Ben Jonson's day the priory's Lady Chapel (now the City's oldest church in use) was nearly all that was left, with the Elizabethan gateway that faces into Little Britain.

At the end of Little Britain, the Museum of London explains the history of the first playhouses, the Theatre and the Curtain, built in 1576/7 at Shoreditch and their successors on Bankside.

THE BOROUGH AND BANKSIDE

*U*ntil 1750, Old London Bridge was the only crossing place over the lower River Thames, and at its Southwark end dozens of inns and taverns grew up along Borough High Street to serve travellers and pilgrims.

Here in 'Southwerk at the Tabard as I lay ready to wenden on my pilgrimage,' Geoffrey Chaucer begins *The Canterbury Tales,* when 'nyne and twenty in a companye of sondry folk' gather one April night to ride to Canterbury.

The Tabard is long gone but the neighbouring George Inn remains, the only galleried inn left in London, where plays and entertainments still take place in the

open yard and low-ceilinged bars.

By Dickens's day the Borough inns were the starting place for stage coaches. Dickens made the White Hart (now just a street name close to the George) the inn where Mr Pickwick meets the inimitable Sam Weller.

Dickens knew the Borough well. As a child of 12 he began visiting the Marshalsea prison where his father was in jail for debt (it was the second Marshalsea in the High Street, both demolished, though a wall remains in Angel Place).

He recalled it with horror in *David Copperfield* and *Little Dorrit*, the story of Amy Dorrit, 'Child of the Marshalsea'. Locked out of the prison, Amy spends the night in the church of St George the Martyr, where she was supposed to have been baptised and married to her middle-aged hero Arthur Clennam (the church has a Little Dorrit window).

Amy's Iron Bridge, replaced by the present Southwark Bridge, was reached by a road that splits two of the most pregnant places in literary London: the sites of the Rose and the Globe theatres.

The golden age of Elizabethan playhouses began on Bankside when Philip Henslowe built the Rose in 1587 and presented, over the next five years, Christopher Marlowe's tragedies *Tamburlaine the Great, Dr Faustus*, and *Edward II*, starring Edward Alleyn.

In 1599 came the bigger, better Globe, with William Shakespeare as shareholder, playwright and actor, though Richard Burbage played the heroes and Will Kemp was Bottom.

Only a fraction of each site has been excavated. The Globe lies partly below a Park Street brewery once owned by Dr Johnson's friends the Thrales (they also had the Anchor tavern nearby). The Rose is almost covered by modern buildings.

But within yards of the Rose's

The George Inn, typical of the rambling medieval hostelries in the Borough, where travellers found shelter after Old London Bridge closed for the night.

The new Globe on the banks of the River Thames, a replica of the Burbage brothers' playhouse, is part of an International Shakespeare Globe Centre.

*J*ohn de Witt's
drawing of the
Swan playhouse, 1596,
gives a rough idea of
what Shakespeare
meant in Henry V by
'this wooden O'.

*C*hristopher
Marlowe, drama-
tist at the Rose theatre,
dedicated 'Come live
with me and be my
love' to Ralegh.

*S*outhwark Cathedral
has monuments to
Chaucer and fellow-
poet John Gower and
sees the start each
April of a 'pilgrimage'
to Canterbury.

foundations and the site of the old Bear Gardens, a new Globe Theatre has recently arisen, brain-child of American actor-director Sam Wanamaker.

It follows as closely as possible the original Globe design, timber-framed, open to the sky, thatch-roofed. It does, however, have a modern sprinkler system to prevent it burning down as the first Globe did in 1613, when a spark from a gunshot caught the thatch during Act I, scene iv of *Henry VIII*.

The new Globe and its exhibition are a monument to every theatre, actor and dramatist once seen here on Bankside, for by 1575 players were being forced out of City inn-yards, where they had long per-formed to the public, and into permanent theatres.

Bankside was perfect. It was already known for entertainments, bear-baiting pits,

taverns and stews (brothels). As well as the Rose and the Globe there was the Swan and later the Hope. There were plays by Ben Jonson, Beaumont and Fletcher, Massinger, Dekker, Heywood and Middleton – and old favourites from Shakespeare and Marlowe.

*A*udiences rose, playwrights thrived. Theatre managers made fortunes. Edward Alleyn made enough to found Dulwich College in south London, and an art collection (now in Dulwich Picture Gallery) that includes portraits of authors and colleagues on Bankside.

Tradition says many of them lived in Clink Street. Certainly Shakespeare's brother Edmund was buried in Southwark Cathedral in 1607, the same year that John Harvard, American uni-versity founder, was baptised there. John Fletcher and Philip Massinger were also buried there and the cathedral has memorials and windows to them all, and to Chaucer.

But in 1642 the Puritan parlia-ment closed the playhouses. When they reopened after Charles II was restored to the throne in 1660, tastes had changed and 'Restoration Drama' would develop in new ways – and in new theatres around Drury Lane.

BLOOMSBURY AND THE INNS OF COURT

Virginia and Vanessa Stephen were house hunting during December 1903 in a part of London then unfashionable and deliberately far from their very

respectable birthplace in Hyde Park Gate.

'We have been tramping Bloomsbury,' Virginia wrote to a friend. 'But Lord, how dreary!'

The following year, after the death of their father Sir Leslie Stephen (biographer and critic, son-in-law of Thackeray, friend of Tennyson and Thomas Hardy), they found a house that Virginia thought 'the most beautiful, the most exciting, the most romantic place in the world'.

Vanessa transformed 46 Gordon Square, Bloomsbury, into a modern, white-walled home for her sister and two brothers. Everyone had *A Room of One's Own* and on Thursday evenings they held regular 'at homes' for former friends from Cambridge.

It was the birth of the Bloomsbury Group: less a formal Group than a collection of individ-

ualists weaving tangled, triangular love-lives around Bloomsbury's many green squares.

Over 40 years, Virginia lived in five Squares – Fitzroy, Brunswick, Tavistock and Mecklenburgh as well as Gordon – and Bloomsbury became home at different times to her husband Leonard Woolf, Vanessa's husband Clive Bell, Duncan Grant, David Garnett, Desmond MacCarthy, John Maynard Keynes, Lytton Strachey, and Lytton's companion Dora Carrington.

E. M. Forster took a flat in Brunswick Square for a decade, starting 1929, and by that time Leonard and Virginia had returned to the area from Richmond to set up their Hogarth Press in Tavistock Square. Working for them was a young man named Richard Kennedy, who waited till 1972 before issuing his hilarious, alternative view of 'Bloomsbury', *A Boy at the Hogarth Press*.

At Richmond the Woolfs had already published T. S. Eliot's

poem *The Waste Land*, hailed as the voice of a despairing post-war generation. Eliot himself called it 'a piece of rhythmical grumbling'. It is dedicated to Ezra Pound and contains numerous references to European and Eastern culture. Yet it is essentially a London poem, echoing John Donne, Marvell,

Virginia Woolf describes London in the 17th century in Orlando, *during a frost fair, 'a carnival of the utmost brilliancy' on the frozen Thames; and again in the 20th, as* Mrs Dalloway *walks through St James's Park on the morning of her party.*

American-born poet and critic T. S. Eliot settled in London in 1915, published the Prufrock poems, Sweeney Agonistes *and* Old Possum's Book of Practical Cats, *known now for the musical* Cats.

Karl Marx lived in Dean Street, Soho, in the 1850s, preparing Das Kapital *and studying Thomas Carlyle's writings about the 'cash nexus'. Marx Memorial Library is at Clerkenwell Green, where Lenin edited the Bolshevik paper* Iskra, *1902–3.*

Shakespeare and Spenser, and drawing images from Eliot's early years working for Lloyd's Bank on Lombard Street, watching the daily crowds who

Flowed up the hill and down
 King William Street,
To where Saint Mary
 Woolnoth kept the hours
With a dead sound on the
 final stroke of nine.

In 1925 Eliot became an editor for Faber and Faber in Russell Square, one of many publishers' offices that had helped to create the bookish Bloomsbury atmosphere long before the Stephens and Stracheys moved in.

Thackeray had used Russell Square in *Vanity Fair*, placing the homes of sweet Amelia Sedley and dashing George Osborne on opposite sides of the square, which he knew well from living nearby in Coram Street in 1838.

Mary Russell Mitford, author of *Our Village*, was there too, hosting literary evenings: 'I like Mr Wordsworth, of all things...

The British Museum and Library gave Keats the inspiration for his Ode on a Grecian Urn *and G. B. Shaw a place to write his first play – a debt he repaid by endowing it with profits from* Pygmalion.

Also we had a Mr Browning, a young poet...'

In the 18th century, poets William Cowper and Thomas Gray lodged in Russell Square. Cowper was studying law. Gray was enjoying the incomparable calm of the British Museum library (later the British Library, moving presently to new premises near St Pancras Station).

Tales of who sat where in the domed Reading Room, writing, studying, sometimes sleeping, are

legion. Lenin, Marx and Engels were here, Marx working daily 'most often from 9 in the morning until 7 in the evening' on *Das Kapital.*

George Eliot, Robert Browning and Oscar Wilde were also Reading Room regulars. So were H. G. Wells and Bertrand Russell, winner of the Nobel Prize for literature in 1950 (there is a bronze of him in Red Lion Square, half a mile away).

George Gissing recalls the Reading Room in *The Private Papers of Henry Ryecroft* and *New Grub Street*. W. B. Yeats, living in Woburn Walk from 1895 to 1919, brings it into *The Trembling of the Veil*. And novelist Angus Wilson modelled several characters on British Museum users, including eccentric Rose Lorimer in *Anglo-Saxon Attitudes*.

Angus Wilson joined the museum staff in 1937, and two years later helped to evacuate the museum's treasures from threats of war damage, an episode he worked into *The Old Men at the Zoo* after he resigned in 1955.

Among the library's vast collection on show in the galleries surrounding the Reading Room are two original copies of *Magna Carta*, the *Lindisfarne Gospels*, *Beowulf*, the *Anglo-Saxon*

Chronicle, and holograph manuscripts by authors as different as Jane Austen and the Beatles.

Charles Dickens, determined to rise in the world (Jane Carlyle said he had 'a face made of steel') made good use of the museum and library as a young man. Clerking for a lawyers' office nearby in Gray's Inn at 15, he 'educated himself', according to his father. He learnt shorthand, became a law-court reporter, began covering House of Commons debates at 19, and was soon a well-established journalist, author of the London-life *Sketches by Boz*.

The same month that Dickens married Catherine Hogarth, April 1836, the first *Pickwick Papers* appeared. A year later he rented 48 Doughty Street, still within walking distance of the Inns of Court and the British Museum.

Tall, narrow, Georgian, it is the only one of Dickens's many London homes that survives and it is now Dickens House Museum, containing the most comprehensive Dickens library in the world, plus portraits, papers, relics and mementoes.

Here Dickens finished *The Pickwick Papers,* wrote *Oliver Twist* and *Nicholas Nickleby* and began *Barnaby Rudge*. But it was also the house where his adored young sister-in-law, Mary, died in his arms, so that within two years he felt compelled to move again, this time to Marylebone.

Dickens's novels, like his walks and work, spread all over London. *Barnaby Rudge* stretches from the

Maypole Inn at Chigwell to Dolly Varden's home in Clerkenwell and the riots in Gordon Square. *Oliver Twist* takes in Clerkenwell again and Nancy's Steps in Southwark. *David Copperfield* includes Hungerford Stairs, now covered by Charing Cross, where Dickens worked in the never-to-be-forgotten blacking factory.

Yet, again and again Dickens returned here to Bloomsbury. He had a house (demolished) in Tavistock Square from 1851 to 1860, while he began public readings and theatricals, fell in love with 17-year-old Ellen Ternan and separated from Catherine.

He brings the Inns of Court and Chancery into many of his novels. They were 'Curious little nooks in a great place like London,' he thought, and already centuries old.

Off Chancery Lane lies Lincoln's Inn Fields and the ancient chambers where Sir Thomas More, John Donne, Benjamin Disraeli and John Galsworthy were students.

Charles Dickens pictured in a window at his Doughty Street home. Writer and social reformer (Marx thought Little Dorrit *a seminal anti-capitalist book), Dickens was also an actor and showman. His dramatic readings made a fortune – and probably shortened his life.*

He installed Tommy Traddles at Gray's Inn in *David Copperfield*. Staple Inn became part of *The Mystery of Edwin Drood*. And Lincoln's Inn is the Court of Chancery where 'at the heart of the fog, sits the Lord High Chancellor', while the case of Jarndyce and Jarndyce drones on in *Bleak House*.

The 16th-century Old Curiosity Shop nearby probably has nothing to do with Dickens's novel and Little Nell. But 58 Lincoln's Inn Fields (then the home of Dickens's friend and biographer John Forster) is certainly the house where lawyers like Mr Tulkinghorn 'lie like maggots in nuts'.

FLEET STREET, THE TEMPLE AND COVENT GARDEN

Between the Inns of Court and the Temple – 'Legal London' – runs Fleet Street, traditional home of the Press ever since Wynkyn de Worde moved Caxton's printing business here, around 1500.

Every major newspaper had offices around Fleet Street until the migration to Wapping and Docklands in the 1980s. On the north side are the former homes of the *Daily Telegraph, Daily Express*, and *Evening Standard;* to the south the *News of the World* and *Sun*, Reuters news agency and the Press Association; near Blackfriars, *The Times* in Printing House Square.

For centuries the Press and the Law rubbed shoulders, sharing taverns and coffee houses – from the Wig and Pen Club and the Royal Courts of Justice at the western end, to the Cartoonist pub and the 'Old Bailey' at the other. When John Mortimer's belligerent barrister *Rumpole of the Bailey* appeared in 1978 he was just one in a long line of local characters.

Early on came Joseph Addison and Richard Steele, customers at the Devil's Tavern (it once stood at 1 Fleet Street) and creators of *The Tatler* and *The Spectator* periodicals. In April 1709, *The Tatler* promised to bring all the news, views and gossip from the coffee houses that had first sprung up in the City in 1652 and spread to Fleet Street and Covent Garden.

Soon after, in the 1720s, Samuel Richardson set up his printing business in Salisbury Square, before he wrote *Pamela* and *Clarissa*,

Samuel Richardson (1689–1761) author of Clarissa, *arguably the earliest 'bonk-buster' in English: it runs to more than a million words.*

The Old Bailey, spiritual home of novelist and playwright John Mortimer, best-known for Rumpole, Summer's Lease *and A Voyage Round My Father.*

'tall, stout, grand and authoritative'. James Boswell, Johnson's young friend and biographer-to-be, wrote in his *London Journal*: 'Mr Johnson is a man of a most dreadful appearance...very slovenly in his dress and speaks with a most uncouth voice.' The toga-clad statue of the Great Doctor in St Paul's Cathedral could hardly be more inappropriate.

No. 17 Gough Square, now Dr Johnson's House museum, is the only one of his London homes to survive and it is the most significant. On the top floor he produced most of his *Dictionary*, helped by six assistants. Here he also wrote over 200 essays for *The Rambler* in two years, and began *The Idler* series (less solemn and, Boswell thought, an easier read).

Despite the despondency Johnson felt as he struggled to earn a living, he found endless

Beneath the wedding-cake spire of St Bride's church is the burial place of several writers, including handsome cavalier Richard Lovelace, who wrote 'Stone walls do not a prison make', and 'I could not love thee (dear) so much, Lov'd I not honour more'.

the books that earned him the (disputed) title 'Father of the English Novel'. When he died in 1761 he was buried close by at Wren's pretty church of St Bride's, the 'parish church of the Press'.

In an earlier St Bride's, Wynkyn de Worde (1535) and poet Richard Lovelace (1658) had been interred and Pepys baptised (1633). The present church has a display of Fleet Street history – in which no one is more prominent than Dr Johnson.

When he published *A Dictionary of the English Language* in 1755, Johnson was already well known; by the time he died in 1784 he cut the most famous figure in Fleet Street. He had lived a decade in Gough Square from 1749, and in 1765 returned to live in Johnson's Court and Bolt Court for the rest of his life.

Fanny Burney, daughter of his friend Charles Burney, called him

SAMUEL JOHNSON,
BORN AT LICHFIELD, Sept. 18ᵗʰ 17⁣...

'When a man is tired of London, he is tired of life; for there is in London all that life can afford' – Dr Samuel Johnson, seen with his birthplace, Lichfield, in a window at his Gough Square house.

time to enjoy taverns and coffee houses with friends like Smollett, who named him 'The Great Cham of literature'.

Ye Olde Cheshire Cheese in Wine Office Court, most famous now of all Fleet Street pubs, is said to have been a favourite with Johnson, and with Oliver Goldsmith, who lodged in the court around 1761 writing *The Vicar of Wakefield*.

Goldsmith worked for a time at Richardson's printing press and eked out a living as a 'Grub Street hack'. When he wrote *She stoops to Conquer* Goldsmith was living in the Temple, where he was buried in 1774.

Boswell doesn't mention the Cheshire Cheese, though he is part of its 'literary tradition', along with Dickens, Tennyson, Carlyle, Thackeray, Mark Twain and Conan Doyle. In the 1890s it also became the home of the Rhymers' Club that gathered around Ernest Dowson and W. B. Yeats, who received the Nobel Prize in 1923.

By then the Cheshire Cheese and Fleet Street had a character large enough to rival Dr Johnson: the huge, friendly figure of Gilbert Keith Chesterton, creator of *Father Brown*, ceaseless writer of books and newspaper articles.

Chesterton and Hilaire Belloc made a famous and frequent sight around Fleet Street pubs and restaurants, and in the jolly controversy that Chesterton and G. B. Shaw conducted (largely through the *Daily News*), Shaw gave them their lasting nickname, the 'Chesterbelloc' pantomime elephant.

At the time Johnson and Boswell met in 1763, Johnson had rooms in the Temple. It was 'a pleasant academical retreat', Boswell decided, as Henry Fielding had already discovered during three years there, preparing his parodies on Richardson's *Pamela*.

The Temple, originally the headquarters of the Knights Templars, was absorbed into the Inns of Court by 1500. It remains a warren of legal chambers and lodgings, home of dozens of writers and characters, right up to John Mortimer and Rumpole.

From the Temple it was only a short walk for Johnson and Boswell past St Clement Danes (Johnson's parish church, with a statue and memorials) along the Strand, across the Aldwych to Covent Garden. Then, as now, it was filled with places to eat and drink, read papers, shop and gossip.

Soon after the Restoration, the Piazza and streets laid out by Inigo Jones beside St Paul's (now the 'actors' church') became

Ye Olde Cheshire Cheese pub, formerly the Cheshire Cheese tavern, has been a writers' haunt for centuries.

The Temple was a hot-bed of Elizabethan and Jacobean drama. Tradition says Shakespeare acted in Twelfth Night *at Middle Temple Hall, 1602. John Ford and John Marston had rooms here, and Marston, noted for black comedies,* The Malcontent *and* The Dutch Courtesan, *was buried at the Temple Church, 1634.*

famous for coffee houses and entertainment. By 1662 Pepys was pausing to watch 'a puppet play... and indeed it is very pleasant' (a plaque in the portico records it). In February 1664, Pepys notes 'In Covent Garden tonight...I stopped at the great coffee-house there, where I never was before' and bumped into 'Draydon the poet (I knew at Cambridge) and all the wits'.

Will's coffee house, where Dryden held court till he died in 1700, was at 1 Bow Street, patronised by Pope, Congreve and Wycherley as well. Its main rival, Button's, frequented by Addison and Steele, stood in Russell Street. So did Davies's bookshop (now a coffee shop) where, Boswell wrote in his journal, on May 16, 1763 at

'about seven came in the great Mr Samuel Johnson, whom I have so long wished to see'.

The Bedford coffee house in the corner of the square was the haunt of actors employed at the new theatres built nearby, starting in 1663 with The Theatre Royal, Drury Lane – now the oldest site in the world continuously used as a playhouse.

Here, so the story goes, King Charles II fell in love with Nell Gwynn. An illiterate Cockney, part-time actress and orange seller in Covent Garden, her most famous part (other than royal mistress) was Florimel in Dryden's play *Secret Love*.

Once actor-manager David Garrick joined Drury Lane in 1747, it became famous for his Shakespeare productions (Garrick in the lead); and in 1777, after Sheridan took over, it staged a triumphant première of his comedy *The School for Scandal*.

Sheridan's previous hit *The Rivals* was presented at Covent Garden, which opened in 1732 on the site of the present Royal Opera House. Under John Rich (the man who first staged John Gay's popular *Beggar's Opera* in 1728), it began with a revival of *The Way of the World*, William Congreve's last and best play, written 1700 – and went on competing with Drury Lane for years.

Only yards away, near the spot where Shaw's heroine Eliza Doolittle in *Pygmalion* (and *My Fair Lady*) sat selling flowers, is The Theatre Museum, in the old Flower Market.

The museum is an introduction to theatre history, but especially London's, with lots of gilt and red plush. It has costumes, models and playbills of historic productions, such as Agatha Christie's *The Mousetrap*, which opened at the Ambassador's in 1952 to become the longest-running play in history.

Theatre Royal, Drury Lane, c. 1800.

Covent Garden Piazza presents plenty of 'street theatre' and a festival of musical arts and entertainment each summer.

Richard Brinsley Sheridan, watching from a coffee house while his Theatre Royal burnt down in 1809, remarked: 'A man may surely take a glass of wine by his own fireside.'

Sir Noel Coward (1899–1973) produced a string of stylish comedies, Hay Fever, Blithe Spirit *and* Present Laughter, *and still more popular lyrics: 'The Stately Homes of England', 'Mad Dogs and Englishmen', 'I'll See You Again', and 'Some Day I'll Find You'.*

It also has (on loan) the Somerset Maugham collection of theatrical paintings from 1759 to 1846, and souvenirs of almost everyone who came later: 'Mrs Pat' Campbell and Dame Ellen Terry (both showered with love-letters by Shaw) and popular playwrights like Terence Rattigan and Noel Coward.

Coward's *Private Lives*, possibly the best play he wrote for himself and Gertrude Lawrence, was the opening production in 1930 at The Phoenix theatre which stands in Charing Cross Road – a street more famous for its bookshops.

At the southern end Charing Cross Road leads towards Trafalgar Square, known to George Orwell, when he was *Down and Out in Paris and London* as a place to sleep among the tramps and shave in the fountains (scenes he later used in *A Clergyman's Daughter*). At the northern end is Foyles. In between there are new and second-hand booksellers, art and antiquarian, paperback and political specialists.

Sadly the shop has gone from *84 Charing Cross Road* where Helene Hanff sent her shopping lists and letters; and few booksellers still hold meetings. In the 1920s, Chesterton could fill a basement to overflowing, and when he realised his listeners were lying on the pavement and calling questions down through the skylights, his grin was as wide as his girth.

FROM THE STRAND TO MARYLEBONE

'Portraits of Celebrities' in the Christmas edition of *The Strand Magazine*, 1891, carried a full page about one of its own authors.

'There are few better writers of short stories than Mr Conan Doyle,' the magazine reported, 'and it gives us great pleasure to announce that the extraordinary adventures of Sherlock Holmes, which have proved so popular with our readers during the past six months, will be continued in the new year.'

The six-penny illustrated magazine, launched in January by George Newnes in offices off the Strand, carried its first Holmes

Charing Cross Road in the 1930s, when George Orwell slept among the tramps in Trafalgar Square.

story, *A Scandal in Bohemia*, in July. *The Red-Headed League*, 'a three-pipe problem', followed in August. At Christmas came *The Man with the Twisted Lip*, set in an opium den near London Bridge.

The Strand and Arthur Conan Doyle helped make each other's fortune: the magazine was soon selling half a million copies. Holmes had, in fact, solved his first case, *A Study in Scarlet*, in 1887, when he sized up Dr Watson with the incomparable line, 'You have been in Afghanistan, I perceive.'

Their meeting (at St Bartholomew's Hospital) took place – like most of Holmes's adventures in London – amid swirling fog, gas lamps and hansom cabs. Even

The Hound of the Baskervilles, solved on Dartmoor, has Sir Henry Baskerville staying near the Strand in Northumberland Street, at a hotel since replaced by the Sherlock Holmes pub (it has a perfect reconstruction of Holmes's study).

In 1889, following dinner at the fashionable Langham Hotel with an American literary agent and Oscar Wilde, Conan Doyle wrote the hotel into his second Holmes book, *The Sign of Four*. It was a familiar landmark, the largest luxury hotel in London (restored in 1991), patronised by Wilkie Collins, one of Doyles's favourite authors, and later by Arnold Bennett – though his first choice was the Savoy and its omelettes.

But the centre of Sherlock Holmes's world is 221b Baker Street, the fictional address where he lodged and shared rooms for a while with Watson. The site is now occupied by the Abbey National bank, which cheerfully replies

Upstairs in the Sherlock Holmes pub is the super-sleuth's 'study', while the bar has mementoes and illustrations for his Strand Magazine adventures, drawn by Sidney Paget.

The Langham Hotel has been popular with American visitors from Longfellow and Mark Twain to Ed Murrow, who made his famous Blitz broadcasts from the roof of the BBC, across the road.

Elizabeth Barrett (1806–1861) lived with her family, The Barretts of Wimpole Street, *until she secretly married Robert Browning.*

to Holmes's post, while Number 239 has become a Sherlock Holmes House Museum.

Doyle wrote his first short stories for *The Strand* while waiting in vain for patients at his medical practice at 2 Devonshire Place, midway between Regent's Park and Wimpole Street.

In May, 1846, returning home from the park to 50 Wimpole Street, Elizabeth Barrett wrote to Robert Browning enclosing a stalk of laburnum flower: 'I gathered it for you when I was walking in the Regent's Park...Arabel and Flush were in the carriage and I wished so much to walk that we stopped the carriage and I put both my feet on the grass...'

'*I love your verses with all my heart, dear Miss Barrett,' wrote Robert Browning on January 10, 1845, after reading her volume of* Poems 1844.

Elizabeth was walking again after years as an invalid, twelve months on from Browning's first visit. Every week he had visited her and her dog Flush, helped by Arabella, her sister, to avoid their tyrannical father.

On September 12 Elizabeth was strong enough to slip out of

the house with her maid, Wilson, and marry Robert at St Marylebone church (it has Browning mementoes), returning to Wimpole Street as if nothing had happened.

Eight days later she left home again in secret with Wilson and Flush, and joined Robert to catch the night boat from Southampton to Italy.

Few of their poems are now as famous as their letters and love story (dramatised as *The Barretts of Wimpole Street*) except Elizabeth's sonnet 'How do I love thee? let me count the ways'; and Robert's *Pied Piper of Hamelin* and *Home-thoughts, from Abroad,* 'Oh, to be in England Now that April's there.'

Even Wilson and Flush have had their 'memoirs' written for them. Virginia Woolf recounted the adventures of *Flush*, who was repeatedly stolen and ransomed before leaving London with Elizabeth; and Margaret Forster gave 'Wilson's version' of the elopement in *Lady's Maid* (1990).

After Elizabeth's death in Italy in 1861, Robert returned to London and made his home in Warwick Crescent by Regent's Canal for more than 25 years. The house has gone but the pretty stretch of water at Little Venice is known as 'Browning's pool'. There is a memorial to him by Warwick Avenue station.

From Little Venice the canal swings one way into the basin by Paddington Station, one of Sir John Betjeman's Victorian treasures. He failed to save Euston Station from destruction, but his campaigning and poetry were instrumental in preserving St Pancras Station.

The main canal skirts Maida Vale, part of Martin Amis's territory in *London Fields*, published in 1989 and dedicated to his father, Kingsley. With *Money* , and *The Information* (in which failed-and-40 Richard Tull battles it out against successful rubbish-writer Gwyn Barry), it forms a London trilogy of violence and grotesquely funny relationships.

Where Regent's Canal reappears near leafy St John's Wood and Lord's Cricket Ground, it passes the site of George Eliot's most important London home, The Priory (demolished) in North Bank.

Eliot, Marian to her friends, had moved to Marylebone in 1860 soon after she published one of the best-sellers of the century, *Adam Bede*. Here, in the next three years (in two homes that have also gone), she produced *The Mill on the Floss, Silas Marner* and *Romola* – her least successful story, over-loaded with historical research (Trollope had warned her not to mention every door nail in Florence).

In 1863 she could afford to buy a house on the edge of Regent's Park and by Christmas

London Zoo had only been open five years when Edward Lear sat drawing its exotic birds in 1831. He was just 19 but his parrot pictures (on a par, experts say, with Audubon's) became the first luxury, coloured bird books in England and led him, via Liverpool, to a new career in limericks and comic animals.

she and G. H. Lewes were safely in The Priory. They had led an unsettled life since they began living openly together in July 1854: long trips abroad, homes on the fringe of London.

Now she was famous and to some extent socially acceptable. In The Priory period (from 1863 until the last year of her life) she was at her height with *Middlemarch* and *Daniel Deronda*, lunches and tea-parties with Tennyson and Turgenev, though some 'ladies' still wouldn't call. But less than two years after *Daniel Deronda*, G. H. Lewes died and was buried on December 4, 1878 in Highgate cemetery.

Eliot stayed in her room, reading Izaak Walton's *Life of Donne*, and Donne's poems, marking the lines:

For love, all love of other
sights controules,
And makes one little roome
an everywhere.

*G*eorge Eliot, born Mary Ann Evans, 1819, died Mrs John Cross, 1880, a few months after her surprise marriage at fashionable St George's church, Hanover Square.

*M*artin Amis, born 1949, son of Sir Kingsley, published his first novel, The Rachel Papers *in 1973.*

HIGHGATE AND HAMPSTEAD

Sir John Betjeman. His devotion to London, Victoriana and railways came together in his poem 'London Railway Stations', published in First and Last Loves, 1969.

Four months would pass after G. H. Lewes's death before George Eliot could arrange the gravestone. Then on several fine April days in 1879 the carriage would take her up Swain's Lane to Highgate's huge cemetery.

The granite slab she chose for Lewes's grave (in the public, east section) is one of the simplest among acres of ornate tombs and statues, obelisks and urns, draped with ivy and turned to crazy angles by overgrown trees and shrubs – a strange, shady, romantic place.

Within a few feet, Eliot herself was buried the following year. In the long procession that followed her from Chelsea on a biting December day were Browning, Millais, George du Maurier, Herbert Spencer, and Eliot's husband of a few months, John Cross.

Cross, and Spencer – one of Eliot's earlier passions – lie a few yards off. So does Karl Marx, buried in 1883 beneath the inscription 'Workers of the World Unite'.

Across Swain's Lane in the western section, shadier and more mysterious (guided tours only), is the Rossettis' tomb, excluding Dante Gabriel, who is buried in Kent, but including Christina, author of *Gobelin Market*.

It also contains D. G.'s wife Lizzie Siddal who died in 1862 of an overdose. In remorse he buried some unpublished poems with her – and exhumed them seven years later, deciding they were too good to waste.

While Highgate cemetery (right) has the graves of George Eliot and Karl Marx, its twin at Kensal Green (tours there as well), also founded in the 1830s, has Trollope, Thackeray, Wilkie Collins, Leigh Hunt and Terence Rattigan.

At the top of the lane, John Betjeman was born in West Hill and grew up, as he describes in *Summoned by Bells*, 'Safe, in a world of trains and buttered toast'. He knew the cemetery as the site of his family grave, a 'red granite obelisk'. Later he would think of it as a 'Victorian Valhalla', one of the sights that led him to a life-long love affair with Victoriana.

At the foot of Highgate Hill, near Archway station, the Whittington Stone marks the traditional place where (*c.* 1390) Dick paused with Puss and heard the peal of Bow bells that made him 'turn again' to the City to become Lord Mayor of London and marry Alice Warren.

Highgate Literary and Scientific Institute, in South Grove, contains a collection on Samuel Taylor Coleridge, who spent his last 18 years in Highgate and died in The Grove (he is buried in St Michael's).

When Coleridge came to live here in 1816, his health was in ruins. But his reputation was made – Carlyle christened him the 'Sage of Highgate' – and his astonishing conversation, as well as his poetry, drew a steady flow of visitors.

'I heard his voice as he came towards me – I heard it as he moved away – I heard it all the interval,' wrote John Keats in a letter to his brother in 1819. Walking on Highgate Hill, Coleridge had left Keats reeling: 'In those two miles he broached a thousand things – let me see if I can give you a list – Nightingales, Poetry, on Poetical Sensation – Metaphysics – Different genera and species of Dreams – Nightmare...'

It was their one meeting, a happy, chance encounter 'in the lane that winds by the side of Lord Mansfield's park', probably Millfield lane.

Keats was living close to Hampstead Ponds in part of Wentworth Place, now renamed Keats's House - to many the loveliest literary shrine in London. It could easily be a melancholy house: the brief home of a brilliant poet, who died at 25 and never sold more than a few hundred books in his lifetime.

Instead it is friendly, full of mementoes and Regency style and still has the pretty garden where Keats heard the 'light-winged Dryad of the trees' and wrote *Ode to a Nightingale*.

Keats first came to Hampstead and met Shelley through his friend and fellow-writer Leigh Hunt who

lived in the Vale of Health. He took lodgings in Well Walk in 1817, and turned to poetry.

In 1818 he moved to Wentworth Place and met Fanny Brawne, whose mother and sisters had rented part of the house and garden. At first Keats thought Fanny a 'Minx' and for months tried not to fall seriously in love. But by the end of 1819 they were engaged (the ring is among the relics in the house).

John Keats, drawn by his friend Joseph Severn. He was training at Guy's and St Thomas's hospitals in Southwark (the Old Operating Theatre is preserved near the cathedral) until he moved to Hampstead and abandoned medicine for poetry.

'*They say I must remain confined to this room for some time. The consciousness that you love me will make a pleasant prison of the house next to yours*' – Keats, writing to Fanny Brawne at Wentworth Place, February 1820.

To reach Kenwood (above; the library is one of Robert Adam's best interiors), Bill Sikes -'strode up the hill at Highgate, on which stands the stone in honour of Whittington'.

Wilkie Collins (1824–1889) lived much of his adult life in Marylebone. He was Dickens's favourite companion for night-time rambles through low-life London and Paris.

By February 1820 it was clear that Keats was seriously ill with tuberculosis, as he coughed and commented: 'That drop of blood is my death warrant.' Again he left the house but was back in August to be nursed by Fanny until he left with Joseph Severn in September to overwinter in Italy.

'Tell him – tell that great poet and noble-hearted man – that we shall all bear his memory in the most precious part of our hearts,' Leigh Hunt wrote to Severn in March 1821, not knowing that Keats had died in Rome on February 23.

Keats had dedicated to Leigh Hunt his 1817 volume of poems, including 'I stood tip-toe upon a little hill', which Hunt identified as Kenwood, at the top of the Heath.

Dickens described Kenwood as the place the Gordon rioters head for in *Barnaby Rudge*, 'bent upon destroying that house likewise' after burning several buildings in the City. In *Oliver Twist*, Bill Sikes skirted Kenwood and 'came out on Hampstead Heath' after murdering Nancy and making his getaway up Highgate Hill past the Whittington Stone. And one of the earliest *Pickwick Papers* considered by Mr Pickwick's club is 'Speculations on the Source of the Hampstead Ponds'.

Dickens loved the area, walking miles over the Heath. John Forster quotes as typical of Dickens's letters: 'You don't feel disposed, do you, to muffle yourself up and start off with me for a good brisk walk over Hampstead Heath?' The walk ended, Forster adds, at a

118

coaching inn, Jack Staw's Castle, 'memorable for many happy meetings', which often involved Wilkie Collins.

Collins grew up by the Heath (his father was a friend of Coleridge) and made his name as the master of sensational stories with a Hampstead-based story serialised in Dickens's magazine in 1859. *The Woman in White* begins as Walter Hartright walks back to London one night by way of Frognal Lane and Finchley Road and meets 'a solitary woman, dressed from head to foot in white garments'. This was, in fact, how Collins met Caroline Graves, who became his 'house-keeper' for most of his life.

B etween Jack Straw's Castle (rebuilt) and Frognal are Hampstead Grove and Admiral's Walk. In the Grove lived George du Maurier, *Punch* cartoonist and author of the Svengali novel *Trilby*. After George died in 1896, his son, matinee-idol Gerald, returned to live a few streets away, bringing his nine-year-old daughter Daphne to live at Cannon Hall for a decade, until she discovered Cornwall.

From 1918 until he died in 1933, John Galsworthy made his London home in Admiral's Walk where he wrote most of *The Forsyte Saga* and the subsequent Forsyte stories, ending with *Swan Song*.

Galsworthy, winner of the Nobel award in 1932, is one of dozens of writers who homed in on Hampstead in the early years of the 20th century: Edgar Wallace, Compton Mackenzie and D. H. Lawrence in the Vale of Health; J. B. Priestley, John Masefield and Lawrence again, in Well Walk. Katherine Mansfield lived for a time in East Heath Road and stayed in Pond Street with artist Dorothy Brett in 1922.

Others had family homes in Hampstead: the Huxleys, Waughs and Stracheys – Lytton dividing his time after Cambridge between friends and family, Bloomsbury and Hampstead. A committed hypochondriac, obviously unfit for war service, Lytton was summoned to Hampstead Town Hall in 1917 to explain his conscientious objections to war. There he gave the legendary reply that he would protect his sister from a soldier by endeavouring to interpose his body between them.

Evidently Lytton wasn't in Hampstead in February that year when Dora Carrington, his devoted companion, wrote to tell him: 'we went tobogganing on Parliament Hill by moonlight till nearly 12 o'clock. I am going skating this morning and tonight on Hampstead.'

G eorge Orwell thought he would enjoy working in a bookshop surrounded by bookish residents. He was especially fond of *A Shropshire Lad* (he knew all 63 poems by heart when he was 17) and A. E. Housman had lived up Highgate Hill at Byron Cottage in North Road,

J ohn Galsworthy, known now for The Forsyte Saga, *was popular in his day for dozens of plays. With G. B. Shaw and Somerset Maugham, he helped make Chelsea's Royal Court Theatre famous for modern drama – though not so forcefully as John Osborne and* Look Back in Anger, *premièred there in 1956.*

F lask Walk, Hampstead, part of the pretty 18th-century Spa known to Jonathan Swift, Addison and Steele: the 'Whiggish' Kit Kat Club, which also counted Congreve and Vanbrugh among its members.

from 1886 until 1905, while he wrote them.

So in 1934 Orwell took a part-time job at Booklovers' Corner (and lived over the shop, now a restaurant) in South End Green. In the mornings he worked on *A Clergyman's Daughter*; in the afternoons he sold books. When his own appeared the following spring he was living in Parliament Hill, writing *Keep the Aspidistra Flying*, based on the bookshop where he still worked mornings. When that was finished, in 1936, he left Hampstead for the long journey north that became *The Road to Wigan Pier*.

Bookselling had not been all he had hoped for: 'really bookish people' didn't often come in. And Hampstead – as D. H. Lawrence found, dining with H. G. Wells in a borrowed dinner jacket – was not entirely congenial.

PICCADILLY, CHELSEA, KENSINGTON AND WEST LONDON

D. H. Lawrence gave a dinner of his own at the Café Royal in Regent Street in March 1924 to persuade friends to join him in a new community in New Mexico.

Before it was over, Lawrence got drunk (on claret and port), and Frieda, his wife, got cross; only Dorothy Brett was so enthused that she set sail with them for America.

Few of the Café's countless literary gatherings can have been so doomed, though some were more outlandish. Opened in 1865 – rebuilt in the 1920s but with the same gilded figures and mirrors – it became a regular haunt of Aubrey Beardsley, Max Beerbohm, Oscar Wilde and Frank Harris; followed by Harris's 'journalists', H. G. Wells, Rebecca West and G. B. Shaw.

Oscar Wilde always called in for lunch when he was in town. Mayfair was his natural habitat, the setting for most of his work and his only novel *The Picture of Dorian Gray* (1890). As he strolled along Piccadilly (the lily in his hand was a comic invention by Gilbert and Sullivan, but it ensured their operetta *Patience* was a hit), he passed Albany, the exclusive address where Lord Byron, Arnold Bennett, J. B. Priestley and Graham Greene had rooms at various times.

On the opposite side are Hatchard's, booksellers here since the end of the 18th century, and the church of St James's, scene of William Blake's baptism in 1757.

In Pall Mall, Wilde would have seen the Athenaeum club, built in the 1820s for 'men of learning'. Anthony Trollope was never happier than sitting, working here. He was in the long drawing room one morning, writing *The Last Chronicle of Barset* (1867) when he overheard two members complain about Mrs Proudie, and promised them to 'kill her before the week is over'.

At the other end of Pall Mall in St James's Street are White's club, originally a chocolate house, known to Swift, Steele, Gay and Pope; and Byron House, on the site of Lord Byron's lodgings in 1812, where he 'awoke one morning and found myself famous' - thanks to the first cantos of *Childe Harold's Pilgrimage*.

Byron, like Wilde, was in his element in Piccadilly. In 1813 he was living in Bennet Street (the Blue Posts Inn, near the site, is said to be haunted by his lordship) and the following year he took rooms in Albany. After his wedding to Annabella Milbanke in 1815, he rented a house in Piccadilly (now absorbed by 139

Piccadilly) for their brief marriage, which had ended before he left England for ever in 1816.

Twenty years later, Lord and Lady Byron's former butler and maid, Mr and Mrs James Brown, set up a hotel in Dover Street. Brown's was a great success, became a favourite with British and American writers, and appears in a number of stories.

Agatha Christie made it the model for Bertram's. Rudyard Kipling made it his honeymoon hotel when he married Carrie Balestier in 1892. Henry James, another Brown's guest, gave her away, though he didn't like her at all. He did like Edith Wharton, and she too stayed at Brown's. So did Mark Twain and S. J. Perelman, who came so often, he said, 'even the hall porters ask me for directions!'

The Athenaeum, Trollope's 'second home'. He was miserable at Harrow School, while his mother, novelist Fanny Trollope, was abroad becoming a celebrity, but he enjoyed the conviviality of the club. When he retired to Sussex in 1880 he missed it so much he was soon back, living just yards away in Suffolk Street.

Oscar Wilde made a familiar figure around Piccadilly, when he wasn't 'Bunburying' in the country, or exporting dandyism on the lucrative lecture circuit in America.

Sir Thomas More had published his eloquent plea for communism, Utopia, *before he came to Chelsea. Here the king would arrive unannounced to 'be merry with him'. And here, after refusing to sanction Henry's divorce, More began his last journey by river – to the Tower. 'We may not look at our pleasure to go to Heaven in feather beds,' he wrote; 'farewell till God bring us together again,' and was executed in 1535.*

Scott and Zelda Fitzgerald, in London during June 1921, checked in at Claridges because they thought it the most fashionable and expensive, and dined with John Galsworthy, though without much joy.

That same month, Sinclair Lewis (Nobel award winner 1930) was staying at the Cadogan in Chelsea when he met Rebecca West and H. G. Wells, with similarly little pleasure. The Cadogan hotel had been the home of actress Lillie Langtry (mistress of King Edward VII, close friend of artist James McNeill Whistler and Oscar Wilde); and the scene of Wilde's arrest in April 1895.

Whistler and Wilde both had homes in Tite Street, in the close circle of Chelsea streets that Mark Twain called a 'village', full of artists and writers.

Wilde bought No. 16 (now 34) Tite Street in 1884 after his marriage and – though he had rooms elsewhere in London – it remained his home while he wrote all his major plays. In 1895, *An Ideal Husband* and *The Importance of Being Earnest* 'were both running at the time of their author's disappearance from English life' – as *The Times* wrote in one of its classic obituaries, published on December 1, 1900.

Wilde's sentence, two years' hard labour for 'indecent acts', had destroyed him, though he still managed to write the *Ballad of Reading Gaol*.

The imprisonment of another Chelsea resident, Sir Thomas More, in 1534, resulted in *A Dialogue of Comfort* and ended when Henry VIII had him beheaded. More's home in Chelsea and the orchard where he

Poet and painter Dante Gabriel Rossetti (1828–1882), author of The Blessed Damozel.

used to walk with the king are covered by Crosby Hall (More's former City home, re-erected here in 1910) and Roper's Gardens. Chelsea Old Church, rebuilt since More worshipped there, has a monument and statue to him.

The link with Sir Thomas was one of the attractions of Chelsea that Thomas Carlyle mentioned to his wife Jane in 1834, before they settled on a new home, now Carlyle's House in Cheyne Row.

They rented the small-ish red-brick house for the rest of their quarrelsome lives. Jane died there in 1866; Thomas lived on till 1882, and the house is kept more-or-less as he left it.

In the library and later the soundproof room built at the top

of the house, Thomas wrote weighty histories of *The French Revolution* and *Frederick the Great*. Less politically correct now, at the time they earned him a huge reputation, the title 'Sage of Chelsea', and a statue on the Embankment.

The Carlyles rarely entertained (Jane had a genius for managing on a small budget) but their fabled conversation drew a succession of callers: Browning, Dickens, John Stuart Mill, Ruskin, Tennyson and George Eliot, who became a near neighbour for the last few weeks of her life, in Cheyne Walk.

In May 1880, to the astonishment of her friends, George Eliot married Johnny Cross, at St George's, Hanover Square. It was only 18 months since the death of her long-term companion, writer G. H. Lewes, and Johnny was 20 years her junior.

Cross seems to have suffered mental derangement (possibly a suicide attempt) during their honeymoon in Venice. But on December 3 he supervised their move into 4 Cheyne Walk – where she died three weeks later.

At 16 Cheyne Walk, Dante Gabriel Rossetti had been living since 1862, at first accompanied by Swinburne and (very briefly) George Meredith. They made an incompatible and chaotic trio, thanks to Swinburne's drinking, Rossetti's drug-taking, and his menagerie. But the house, Henry James thought in 1869, was 'the most delicious melancholy old house at Chelsea'.

Henry James was 26, homesick for America and not very happy in London, until he began to visit writers like Rossetti and Ruskin (Ruskin also admired Rossetti's house, but wisely remained a visitor rather than a resident).

Hilaire Belloc's arrival at 104 in the Walk in 1900 ushered in a new era and new visitors – his children never forgot gargantuan 'Uncle Gilbert' (Chesterton) arriving with puppets and playing in the nursery.

And in the 1950s, both T. S. Eliot and Ian Fleming were living at Carlyle Mansions, where Henry James had had an apartment for three years before he died in 1916 (Chelsea Old Church has a memorial).

Fleming was tapping out his first block-buster novel, *Casino Royale*. James Bond's world of espionage is partly based on Fleming's wartime naval intelligence work, now revealed in 'secret war' exhibitions at the Imperial War Museum, south of Vauxhall Bridge.

Vauxhall had one of the grandest 18th-century pleasure gardens in London (Finchcocks Collection in Kent traces their history) where Jos and Becky, Amelia and George spend a happy evening in *Vanity Fair*.

When Thackeray wrote the last numbers of *Vanity Fair* in 1848, he was living in Young Street, near Kensington and Holland gardens. Two years later his house (it has a plaque) was the scene of a dinner party at which Charlotte Brontë, newly famous for *Jane Eyre*, proved

Ian Fleming (1908 –1964) was a Reuters correspondent in Moscow before he joined naval intelligence.

Cheyne Walk and its neighbour Cheyne Row were among the choicest addresses for 19th-century writers and artists. After the Carlyles moved in it became the conversational centre of London.

*S*ir James Matthew
*Barrie (1860–1937)
came to London after 18
months as a journalist in
Nottingham – like Rob
in Barrie's first novel,*
When a Man's Single
(1888).

a boring conversationalist.

Holland House welcomed more entertaining visitors while Joseph Addison lived there from his marriage in 1716 till he died three years later. Another century on, as the home of Lord Melbourne, leader of the Whigs and the Lamb family, it witnessed the most glittering gatherings in London.

At one of them, in 1812, Lord Byron probably met Lady Caroline Lamb, whose scandalous, unstable behaviour became too much even for his taste. Yet *she* managed to label *him* 'mad – bad – and dangerous to know'.

*T*he V & A in
*Kensington, the
national collection of
applied art and
design, was quick to
spot William Morris's
importance. Only five
years after he set up
the 'Firm' of Morris
and Co it commis-
sioned him to create
the perfect example of
a mid-Victorian,
medieval-inspired
dining room.*

The statue of Peter Pan in Kensington Gardens (near the Long Water) appeared overnight in 1912, because J. M. Barrie wanted children to believe it came by magic. Barrie's eternally popular hero, the boy who 'never grew up', appeared on stage in December 1904,

when Barrie was already a distinguished author.

He had lived in Kensington since 1895 and walked his dog through the gardens every day. By the Round Pond he met the young Llewelyn Davies boys, who inspired his tales of Peter Pan.

When they were orphaned in 1910, Barrie became their guardian. It was an arrangement that made neither the boys nor Barrie happy ever after. He had, though, an impressive circle of friends. When he lived in London's Adelphi Terrace, or rented Stanway House, Gloucestershire, in the 1920s and held summer weekend parties, he was generally joined by Conan Doyle, John Galsworthy, Walter De La Mare, L. P. Hartley, H. G. Wells and G. K. Chesterton.

While Barrie was entertaining the Llewelyn Davies boys in Kensington Gardens, Miss Beatrix Potter was sitting drawing in South Kensington, studying exhibits in the Natural History Museum.

Next door is the Victoria and Albert museum, 'her own' V & A, Beatrix called it. Among its textiles and costumes she found exactly the coat she wanted to paint for *The Tailor of Gloucester*. The coat

helped to design gardens for his friends' rural retreats, and created his own near Twickenham, where he is buried. His villa at Cross Deep has gone but his Grotto remains in the grounds of a school.

On the same side of the Thames at Strawberry Hill is Horace Walpole's 'little Gothic castle'. After buying it in 1749 as a coachman's cottage, Walpole spent 40 years converting it to a battlemented 'medieval' fantasy (now part of a college) where he sat writing another Gothic masterpiece, *The Castle of Otranto*.

On the opposite bank, up river from Kew, is Queen Anne's favourite summer palace, Hampton Court, the 'structure of majestic frame', where Pope mockingly pictures her in *The Rape of the Lock*.

> *Here thou, great Anna!*
> *whom three realms obey,*
> *Dost sometimes counsel take –*
> *and sometimes Tea.*

K elmscott House, by the Thames at Hammersmith, formerly owned by Scottish fantasy novelist George MacDonald. It became William Morris's last London home, where he died in 1896, and is now the William Morris Society headquarters, with exhibitions and memorabilia.

H ampton Court Palace was the scene of King James's conference, in 1604, which led to the Authorized Version of the Bible, perhaps the finest piece of all Elizabethan prose, in which 'the glory of the Lord shall be revealed'.

is still on view and the museum holds the biggest collection of her drawings and paintings.

The V & A is also the place to see some of William Morris's best manuscripts, books and designs, as well as the 'Green Dining Room' commissioned from his 'Firm', Morris and Co, in 1866. Morris's output, versatility and interests were vast: Shaw called him 'four men rolled into one'.

More of his work is preserved at the William Morris Gallery, his early home in Walthamstow, and at his last London house, Kelmscott in Hammersmith, near the Kelmscott Press he founded in order to produce 'the perfect book'.

When Morris set off from here in 1880 to travel up river to Kelmscott Manor, his Cotswold home, he followed an historic waterway between 18th-century gardens and Palladian mansions.

At Chiswick House and Marble Hill, Alexander Pope

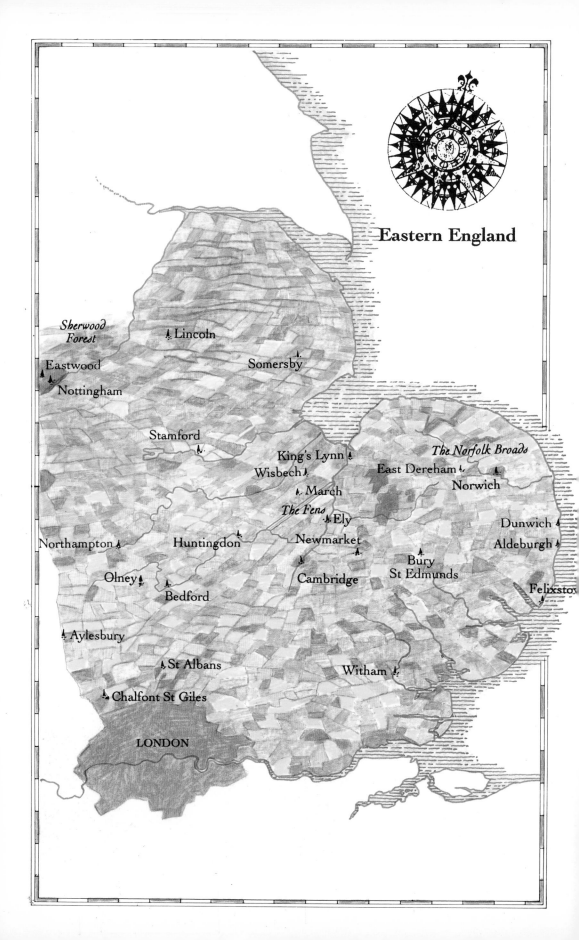

Eastern England

Sherwood Forest

Lincoln

Somersby

Eastwood

Nottingham

Stamford

King's Lynn

Wisbech

The Norfolk Broads

East Dereham

Norwich

March

The Fens

Ely

Northampton

Huntingdon

Newmarket

Dunwich

Aldeburgh

Olney

Bury St Edmunds

Bedford

Cambridge

Felixstow

Aylesbury

St Albans

Witham

Chalfont St Giles

LONDON

CHAPTER 5

EASTERN ENGLAND

♦

CAMBRIDGE

The university began, so tradition says, in 1209 when students fled from the riots around Oxford's monastic schools and came to peaceful Cambridge to set up a new school of learning.

Ironically, two years later 'Bad' King John granted a licence for Stourbridge Fair, on the edge of the city. It grew into the biggest, noisiest, most riotous market in Europe, partly the model for John Bunyan's 'Vanity Fair' in *Pilgrim's Progress*.

The exuberance remains - at college May Balls, in 'rag' week, and in the 'bumping' boat races on the River Cam. It's the spirit that Julian Slade caught in the 1950s in *Salad Days*, a nostalgic reprise on his own student life in Cambridge, in which a fresh crop of graduates bid farewell to 'the dons we've placated and lectures we've missed'.

E. M. Forster didn't see it quite like that. He thought his first year was a quiet, rather 'puddling' affair. He had come up to King's College for the Michaelmas Term 1897 as an 'immature, uninteresting, and unphilosophic' young man (his own typically self-effacing verdict).

His college is one of

Cambridge's finest, and its pale Gothic chapel easily the most beautiful building in the city. King's, like neighbouring Queens' and Clare, Trinity and St John's, stands between the main street and the river, with lawns – the Backs – leading down to the water and the open banks beyond.

The view from the river is sublime, and at its best when the lawns are carpeted with spring flowers. Boats can be hired from the Quayside in Bridge Street. Entry to gardens and chapels varies from college to college and through the year (most colleges close April to June for exams). Organised walking or punting-plus-walking tours are recommended.

The gatehouse to King's, one of the colleges Henry James described 'turning their backs to the river' and forming 'the loveliest confusion of Gothic windows and ancient trees, of grassy-banks and mossy balustrades'.

Edward Morgan Forster (1879–1970). 'Sad as ever,' D. H. Lawrence wrote to him after reading A Passage to India *(1924). 'But I prefer the sadness to the Stracheyism. To me you are the last Englishman.'*

127

Lytton Strachey – prim, short-sighted, with a high-pitched voice – was delighted to become a student at Trinity: '...the gown's blue! Lovely!' he wrote to his mother in 1899.

Trinity (below) was also alma mater to Francis Bacon, George Herbert, Andrew Marvell, John Dryden and A. A. Milne, who edited the university paper Granta.

The Dean of King's in Forster's day was Montague Rhodes James. Better known now as M. R. James, author of several volumes of vintage *Ghost Stories* (some with East Anglian settings), he was also director for a time of the Fitzwilliam Museum, and a liberal host to King's students.

Inspite of James's convivial evenings of whisky and cards, however, Forster didn't seem to make new friends — until his second year, when things improved. Lytton Strachey might have nicknamed him 'the Taupe' [mole], but Forster began to feel in his element. 'People and books reinforced one another, intelligence joined hands with affection,' he wrote later, and he was invited to join the famously secret society known as the Apostles.

Based at Trinity in the 1820s, the Apostles were Cambridge's elite intellectual circle. Forster describes a typical Apostles' meeting in the opening pages of *The Longest Journey*. It was his most autobiographical novel, his favourite, and he devoted the first

half of it to his student days at Cambridge.

Almost 40 years after *The Longest Journey* appeared in 1907, Forster returned to make his home at King's again. He lived in college, the 'Sage of King's', until his death in 1970, rarely missing the Christmas 'Festival of Nine Lessons and Carols' broadcast round the world from King's College Chapel.

On the War Memorial in the chapel, among the names of those killed during World War I, is Rupert Brooke, who died in the Dardanelles in 1915. The sidechapel has copies of his poems *The Dead* and *The Soldier*:

> *If I should die, think only this*
> *   of me:*
> *That there's some corner of a*
> *   foreign field*
> *That is forever England.*

Like Forster, Brooke didn't really enjoy his first year at King's in 1906 and moved to Grantchester outside the city when he began working for a fellowship.

essential image of an English village:

> ...I only know that you may lie
> Day-long and watch the
>   Cambridge sky,
> And, flower-lulled in sleepy
>   grass,
> Hear the cool lapse of hours
>   pass,
> Until the centuries blend and
>   blur
> In Grantchester, in
>   Grantchester...
> ...oh! yet
> Stands the Church clock at
>   ten to three?
> And is there honey still for tea.

One of Brooke's friends at King's was Geoffrey Keynes, whose brother, economist Maynard, entertained D. H. Lawrence to a bruising breakfast in Cambridge in 1915.

Keynes decided Lawrence was 'ignorant, jealous, hostile' to the Cambridge fraternity that was 'obviously uncomfortable and unattainable for him'.

The previous night, Lawrence had dined with Bertrand Russell at Trinity, the largest and grandest of all Cambridge colleges. At the turn of the century it was a hot-

The Old Vicarage, Grantchester, 'is a deserted, lonely, dank, ruined, overgrown, gloomy, lovely house: with a garden to match...It is a fit place to write my kind of poetry in,' wrote Rupert Brooke.

He had come to the village, three miles from Cambridge, in 1909. Over the next four years he became the idol of young Cambridge. He was gifted, golden-haired and good-looking (W. B. Yeats thought him the handsomest man in Europe) and the Old Vicarage, now the home of novelist Jeffrey Archer, was far from deserted once Brooke moved in.

His visitors, among them Virginia Woolf, Lytton Strachey and E. M. Forster, would join him in the garden or on night-time rambles to Trumpington, to swim in Byron's Pool, where 'his ghostly lordship' used to swim while at Cambridge.

Brooke's dreamy poem about the house and its surroundings, half sentimental, half satirical, was written in Berlin during a holiday in 1912 and has become the

King's College Chapel. Its Christmas carol service often includes While Shepherds Watched, *by 17th-century Poet Laureate Nahum Tate,* John Wesley's *Hark, the Herald Angels Sing and the American* O Little Town of Bethlehem. *But the service is always heavily over subscribed: try choral evensong on other winter afternoons.*

Rupert Brooke (1887–1915) had rooms in King's and soon became a friend and fellow-Apostle of Strachey, Keynes and Forster.

bed of young Bloomsburyites (as well as Apostles). Lytton Strachey, Thoby and Adrian Stephen, Clive Bell and Leonard Woolf (who would, respectively, marry the Stephens sisters Vanessa and Virginia) all studied there, under the historic influence of philosopher G. E. Moore. Strachey reckoned the publication of Moore's *Principia Ethica* in 1903 was the dawning of a new 'age of reason'.

En bloc, Bloomsbury echoed Maynard Keynes's opinion: whatever Lawrence's literary prowess, his Nottingham background put him on another planet. They were never too sure about E. M. Forster either, and when Clive Bell and T. S. Eliot wrote scathing obituaries of Lawrence in 1930, it was Forster who came to his defence.

In 1911, Bertrand Russell and G. E. Moore were joined at High Table in Trinity by A. E. Housman, newly appointed professor of Latin. Over the next 25 years,

living in dreary rooms in Whewell's Court, Housman became a legend for his lectures on Latin poetry.

He rarely referred to his own verses at all (though *A Shropshire Lad* had been in print since 1896) and he published only one more volume in his lifetime, *Last Poems*: 'We'll to the woods no more, The laurels all are cut.'

Housman seemed to spend more time on the college garden committee than writing poetry, and when he died in 1936 his coffin was 'Wearing white for Eastertide', shrouded in cherry blossom from the boughs of Trinity's trees. In the riverside Wren Library overlooking the garden there is an autographed copy of *A Shropshire Lad*.

Designed by Sir Christopher Wren and built 1676-1695, the library is Trinity's crowning glory, with manuscripts and memorials (more in the ante-chapel) to many of Trinity's long list of writers.

*I*n Trinity's beautiful, baroque Wren Library, Lord Byron's statue is flanked by rare books, manuscripts and letters – some from George Eliot, who paid several visits to Trinity. In May 1873, she was strolling in the Fellows' Garden with Virginia Woolf's father (among others); in 1877 she went on to call at newly-opened Girton.

Pepys's Library is housed in a 17th-century building at his old college, Magdalene, which also has his portrait. In 1667, hearing about 'old acquaintance of the College, concerning their various fortunes,' Pepys noted in his Diary, *'to my joy, I met not with any that have sped better then myself.'*

Between 1826 and 1828 Alfred Tennyson (an early Apostle), Arthur Hallam, Edward FitzGerald and W. M. Thackeray all arrived at the college and formed life-long friendships.

Preceding them by a few years was Lord Byron, whose statue (rejected by Westminster Abbey on account of his dubious morals) is in the library. Byron broke every rule in the book, bar the one about not keeping dogs in college. He kept a bear cub instead. Cambridge was notorious, he said, for 'din and drunkenness'.

Thomas Gray had found the 'din' and student pranks unbearable at Peterhouse. In 1734 he came up from Eton with his friend Horace Walpole, though Walpole, author of the Gothic novel *The Castle of Otranto*, went to his father's old college, King's. They stayed four years before setting off together on a lengthy tour of Europe.

When they quarrelled, Gray returned and by 1743 he was back at Peterhouse in top-floor rooms above Trumpington Street and Little St Mary's. Frightened of fire, he had his window (still visible) fitted with a rope ladder. But a group of college 'hearties', aiming to take a rise out of the retiring, melancholic poet (it was a bit of a pose: his letters are none too gentle about other writers) raised a false alarm. They were hoping, some say, to make Gray climb down the ladder into a barrel of water. Gray was so furious with the college for failing to discipline them that he moved across the road and lived in Pembroke College till he died in 1771.

Samuel Pepys was also 'scandalously overseen in drink' on one occasion, according to the only college record of his time at Magdalene (1651 to 1653). His diary, however, makes several happy allusions to his old college and the return visits he made, October 1667 and May 1668, en route to his family home near Huntingdon.

When Pepys died in 1703 he left his magnificent library to Magdalene with strict instructions that the 3,000 books should be kept as he had catalogued them, in the bookcases made for them at his London home.

Clive Staples Lewis, born Belfast 1898, finished his unbeaten history of English Literature in the Sixteenth Century at Oxford and moved to Cambridge, 1954. In the next two years he wrote a spiritual autobiography, Surprised by Joy, and married Joy Davidman. He returned to Oxford shortly before his death in 1963.

The Fitzwilliam Museum, one of Britain's oldest and best, owes much to the taste of its directors. After M. R. James came Sir Sydney Cockerell, who shared with G. B. Shaw an unlikely 50-year friendship and correspondence with the Abbess of Stanbrook (near Malvern), Dame Laurentia McLachlan, expert on Gregorian chant.

Pepys had made the collection his life's work and in 1724 the Bibliotheca Pepysiana, including his own shorthand diary, was finally installed in the handsome Pepys Building in Magdalene's Second Court.

C. S. Lewis was a fellow of Madgalene and professor of medieval and Renaissance English literature when he married Joy Davidman in 1956. Their strange courtship – the *Shadowlands* love story of William Nicholson's play – began with a letter to Lewis from Joy in America.

Joy 'stood out from the ruck' of his usual Narnia fans, Lewis thought, because of 'her amusing and well-written letters'. He had arrived at Cambridge in 1954, after 30 years as a bachelor in Oxford, leaving behind his academic friends and the first few *Chronicles of Narnia*.

At Cambridge he closed the chronicles with *The Last Battle*, and to the amazement of friends married Joy. She died just four years later.

In all Lewis's teaching his aim was to bridge the gap between classical and modern culture. Cambridge's world-famous Fitzwilliam Museum does just the same. Among the rare books and

manuscripts are letters of Tennyson, Housman and Brooke; a first edition of Milton's *Paradise Lost*; a Second Folio of Shakespeare; and Keats's *Ode to a Nightingale*.

Milton, Shakespeare and Keats were three of the great writers that Virginia Woolf commended to students when she lectured on English literature in Cambridge in the 1920s.

At the start of the century, after visiting her brothers and friends at Trinity, Virginia railed against the 'bloodless' brains of Cambridge dons. Yet underneath, her lack of a university education bothered her.

Now, with the literary status she won with *Jacob's Ladder* in 1922, she had the confidence, and the invitations, to address the university's first two colleges for women: Girton, opened in 1873, and Newnham, two years later.

The papers Virginia read to them in 1928, published the following year as *A Room of One's Own*, have become a feminist classic and, together with other essays, they contain insights into her own literary taste: slating the Edwardian

> *Ring out, ye crystal spheres,*
> *Once bless our human ears*
> *(If ye have power to touch our*
>   *senses so)*
> *And let your silver chime*
> *Move in melodious time.*
>
> John Milton, *On the*
> *Morning of Christ's Nativity.*

novels of Galsworthy, Bennett and Wells; lauding the 'melodious days' of Milton.

John Milton wrote his first major poem, *On the Morning of Christ's Nativity,* while he was at Christ's College. He spent seven studious years there, starting in 1625, and earned himself the nickname 'The Lady' among his contemporaries.

Later generations paid more respect, though Wordsworth (a student at St John's) had to admit that he got drunk toasting the poet's memory when he visited Milton's rooms in 1787.

The mulberry tree in the Fellows' Garden probably isn't really Milton's; the portrait and bust in the hall are. Another portrait in the hall is of Charles Darwin, who entered Christ's in 1828 and left in 1831 to embark on his epic voyage in the 'Beagle' that would lead to *The Origin of Species.*

Three of Darwin's sons fol-lowed him into science and academic life and established a Darwin dynasty in Cambridge. His granddaughter, Gwen Raverat, born 1885, grew up at Newnham Grange (now Darwin College) and gives an irresistible glimpse of life among the Darwins in *Period Piece – A Cambridge Childhood,* published 1952. She's especially good on Darwinian health – 'in my grandparents' house it was a distinction and a mournful pleasure to be ill'.

The Fellows' Garden at Christ's has a memorial to another literary scientist, C. P. (Charles Percy) Snow. Later Lord Snow, he was made a fellow in 1930 and in 1940 published *Strangers and Brothers,* the first of a 30-year sequence of Cambridge novels including *The Masters* – the power struggle for mastership of a college. For his first book, though, in 1932, he tried a popular detective story, *Death Under Sail* on the Norfolk Broads.

MURDER AND MYSTERY IN EAST ANGLIA

Under a cloudless sky, a yacht glides smoothly along the Norfolk Broads. Slowly it turns out of the tall reeds in Salhouse Broad into a straight stretch of the River Bure and heads towards Horning – until the crew discover 'we were being sailed by a dead man'.

C. P. Snow's *Death Under Sail* charts a chilling course (sketch map included)

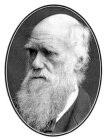

Charles Darwin (1809–1882). His theories might remove God from the Victorian world but his family faithfully observed Cambridge dinner party rules. 'The guests were seated according to the Protocol...After the Masters came the Regius Professors in the order of their subjects, Divinity first...'

George Borrow returned to East Anglia and the Broads (left) to live near Oulton (1840–1866) and write Lavengro *and* The Romany Rye. *He claimed he was born at East Dereham, 'pretty, quiet D – ', where the 'venerable church' had received the 'mortal remains of England's sweetest and most pious bard' – William Cowper.*

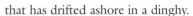

C. P. Snow was a fellow of Christ's when he married novelist Pamela Hansford Johnson, author of Next to the Hatter's, in the college chapel in 1950.

P. D. James finds inspiration in East Anglia, the same region that Ruth Rendell has made her home, drawing on local landscapes in her psychological thrillers by 'Barbara Vine'.

through the waterways from Wroxham to Potter Heigham. He based it on a boating holiday with friends in 1931, which he nearly refused to join. He loathed sailing and complained loudly about the discomforts. But when he succumbed to 'the thin hoot of an owl' and the 'reedy wastes of Heigham Sound', he became yet another author to turn to crime in East Anglia's eerie landscape.

From Wilkie Collins in the 1860s to P. D. James a century later, at least a dozen leading crime writers have littered the region with dropped clues and dead bodies – and their thrillers double as guidebooks.

This is, P. D. James says, a suitable site for murder. *Unnatural Causes*, one of her earliest Adam Dalgliesh books, takes place on the coast of Suffolk, where Adam's aunt has a house (like James herself) overlooking the sea near Dunwich Beach, the site of a medieval town that was swallowed by the sea.

On his way from London to stay with the aunt, Adam pays a visit to Blythburgh church, one of East Anglia's superbly carved 'angel roof' churches. He drives on to the coast but instead of an autumn holiday – long walks on the beach, bracing air and tea by the fire – he finds himself pursuing the case of the handless corpse

that has drifted ashore in a dinghy.

With the *Death of an Expert Witness* P. D. James shifts the scene to the coast of north Norfolk, and sends Dalgliesh over the desolate dykes to a disused 17th-century chapel, its lights streaming into the night (the original is the little Wren Chapel at Pembroke College, Cambridge), to find another body.

By the time Dalgliesh comes back to the Norfolk coast in *Devices and Desires* (1989), his aunt has died at her last home, on a headland near a Sizewell looka-like, 'Larksoken Power Station'. His visit coincides with the latest serial killing by the 'Norfolk Whistler', but as the mystery moves along the coast to Wells-next-the-Sea, Adam heads inland to carry out Aunt Jane's last wishes.

At Norwich he revisits the cathedral and at Salle he scatters his aunt's ashes by the wonderful soaring 15th-century church that dominates the empty Norfolk countryside.

The church that makes Lord Peter Wimsey, Dorothy L. Sayers's detective, look up 'entranced with wonder', owes its roof of flying angels with 'gilded

Elm Hill, Norwich, well known to the Paston family, authors of the most famous 15th-century 'Letters' in English; and to Sir Thomas - Urn Burial- Browne, whose statue is beside St Peter Mancroft church.

outspread wings' to St Wendreda's at March.

In the most famous of all

Fenland murder stories, *The Nine Taylors,* published 1934, Sayers sent her aristocratic sleuth back to the watery region where she had grown up.

Having crashed his car at a humpback bridge, on the B1098 beside the Drain east of March, on a snowy New Year's Eve, Wimsey is stuck overnight at a rectory. And when he helps ring in the New Year on the church bells (a marathon change of 15,840 Kent Treble Bob Majors peeling out over the flat white Fens) he learns about the mystery of 'the Thorpe necklace'.

Sayers invented the village and church of Fenchurch St Paul from several originals dotted among the drains and ditches between Huntingdon and King's Lynn: Upwell, Walpole St Andrew and Terrington St Clement.

Dorothy lived at Bluntisham-cum-Earith in the old rectory (marked with a plaque) from the age of four till she was 15 and went away to school, in 1909. Later she studied at Oxford and worked abroad. But she often returned to Bluntisham and Christchurch, near March, her

father's last parish, until he died in 1928.

Wimsey, hero of 14 volumes, first appeared in *Whose Body*, in 1923, written when Dorothy was working in London. By the time *The Nine Taylors* came out, she was writing full-time at Witham, near Chelmsford in Essex. She died there in 1957 and the town has a statue facing the house, and a Dorothy L. Sayers centre at the library.

Wimsey made Sayers as popular as Agatha Christie during the 1930s and 40s, the 'golden age' of detective writing when another Essex writer, Margery Allingham, completed a triumvirate of 'crime queens'.

Curiously, Margery Allingham was born and died (1904–1966) within 10 miles of Witham, and her detective, Albert Campion, was a cross between Wimsey and P. G. Wodehouse's Bertie Wooster.

*D*orothy Leigh Sayers (born 1893) made her amateur sleuth, Peter Wimsey, a rich aristocrat so that she might have the fun of spending his fortune.

*A*t Blythburgh, Commander Adam Dalgliesh admires the 15th-century church (left) before he is caught up in death from Unnatural Causes.

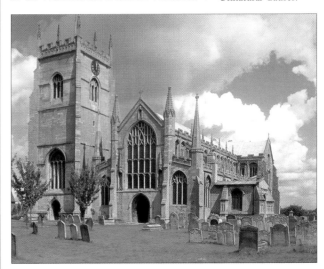

She described Campion as 'a silly ass' with pale-blue eyes and glasses, yet somehow he manages to solve *The Crime at Black Dudley* and *Mystery Mile*, both based here near the sea on the Essex-Suffolk borders.

*T*errington St Clement, 'the Cathedral of the Marshes', has the original of the bell tower where Lord Peter Wimsey helps ring The Nine Taylors.

*S*taying at Aldeburgh (right), Thomas Hardy paid a visit to Boulge, near Woodbridge, to the grave of Edward FitzGerald (1809–1883), translator of the 11th-century Persian poem The Rubaiyat of Omar Khayyam: 'A Jug of Wine, a Loaf of Bread – and Thou Beside me singing in the Wilderness...'

A few miles north on the Suffolk coast is the small fishing town of Aldeburgh, now famous for its annual music festival. Composer Benjamin Britten began the festival in 1948, not long after completing his opera *Peter Grimes*, a character created by local poet George Crabbe.

The son of an Aldeburgh salt-tax collector, Crabbe grew up in the town, and returned briefly in 1781. Soon afterwards he wrote a lengthy poem, *The Village*, describing the grim realities of local life. In *The Borough*, published 1810, Crabbe again pictured life in Aldeburgh, and told the tale of 'Peter Grimes' and other characters – 'whom I endeavoured to paint as nearly as I could'.

Through Aldeburgh Festival, Britten brought to Suffolk a number of writers as well as musicians, including E. M. Forster who wrote the libretto for Britten's opera, *Billy Budd*, based on Herman Melville's novella.

In the 1960s a young novelist named Susan Hill was also drawn to Aldeburgh. Starting with *The Albatross*, she set a number of

*M*ontague Rhodes James (1862–1936).

*F*elixstowe, the setting for M. R. James's vintage ghost story Oh, Whistle, and I'll Come to You.

stories among the villages here, matching her isolated, wounded characters with the loneliness of the landscape and the sea.

Her ghost story, *The Woman in Black*, which takes place on the haunting East Anglian marshes, is in the classic tradition of suspense stories started by Wilkie Collins, who visited Aldeburgh in 1862.

Two years earlier Collins had published *The Woman in White* in his friend Charles Dickens's magazine. It was hugely successful and began a decade of great Victorian sensation novels in contemporary settings (the heroine, Marion Halcombe, was a portrait of George Eliot). At Aldeburgh Collins found the scenery for his next, *No Name*, and a few years later he wrote *The Moonstone*, which T. S. Eliot called 'the first and greatest English detective novel'.

M. R. James, ghost-story writer and scholar, knew Aldeburgh from childhood visits to his grandfather's house beside the church. He returned almost every spring for 15 years until he died in 1936, and he used the beach near Aldeburgh's Martello tower in

A Warning to the Curious.

James grew up in Suffolk at the old rectory in Great Livermere, near Bury St Edmunds, and some of his sinister stories were placed in the flattened countryside and seashore of Suffolk.

The strangely carved figures in *The Stalls of Barchester Cathedral,* which come alive under the evil archdeacon's hand, are said to be in Livermere church. *Rats,* James wrote, 'happened in Suffolk, near the coast'. *The Tractate Middoth* took place in a library in Cambridge, and *A School Story* was one of his Christmas tales, told to the boys of King's College Choir.

Most hair-raising of all James's mysteries is *Oh, Whistle, and I'll Come to You.* It begins in Cambridge and moves to the coast at Felixstowe, where Professor Parkins finds himself running for his life through the shingle, scrambling over the 'black wooden groynings' by 'the dim and murmuring sea'.

Inland from Felixstowe, along the River Orwell, Arthur Ransome sat writing *Coot Club.* He had moved to a home near Pin Mill overlooking the river in 1935. On holiday in the Norfolk Broads in 1931, with his wife, Evgenia, he had hired a cabin yacht at Potter Heigham and promptly decided the Broads were 'the finest nursery for sailors in the world'. Once *Coot Club*, based on the Broads, was finished, he turned to the river he could see from his new home and wrote *We Didn't Mean to Go to Sea.*

Early morning on Newmarket Heath, and out of the mist a string of horses comes thudding over the turf. This is the world of Dick Francis's thrillers and his ex-jockey turned private detective, Sid Halley.

Former National Hunt jockey Francis has harnessed violence, doping, swindlers and bookies into more than 30 best-selling books. From *Nerve* and *Dead Cert*, published in the 1960s, to *Risk* and *Whip Hand*, one of the best, he recreates the thrill of 'the sport of kings' centred here in Newmarket.

The National Horseracing Museum in the High Street has nearly 400 years of racing history, tours to see horses exercising on the gallops, and visits to the National Stud.

Newmarket, centre of horse-racing since King James I set up a hunting lodge around 1610, is the spiritual home of champion jockey Dick Francis (photographed in 1967), who has a winner every time with crime readers.

PASSION AND POETRY IN THE SHIRES

Robin Hood occupies a sun-lit glade in English story telling – some say in Sherwood Forest, not far from the wicked Sheriff of Nottingham.

There may well have been a people's hero with a band of Merry Men (probably not wearing Lincoln green) who lived rough in the forest in the days of King Richard I. But Robin was soon confused with the Green Man of folk stories and May Day revels, as well as with other outlaws who took to the woods of Yorkshire and Derbyshire to avoid Norman oppression.

During the 14th century he became a fully-grown legend, hero of the minstrels' ballads that were gathered together early in the 15th century as 'The Geste of Robin Hood'. By 1500 they had been printed by Wynkyn de Worde (Caxton's successor) as a *Lytil Geste*, and would one day reappear in Sir Walter Scott's *Ivanhoe*.

Around the remains of Sherwood Forest lie villages linked to the Merry Men, including Papplewick, Fountaindale – with a footpath to Friar Tuck's Well – and Edwinstowe, where Robin and Maid Marian were married in St Mary's, and the forest now has a visitor centre.

Lord Byron was 10 when he inherited Newstead Abbey, arriving with his mother to find the estate penniless and the house too dilapidated to live in.

The 12th-century abbey, owned by the Byrons since 1540, had been run down by his grand-father and now, in 1798, was so much in need of repair that they were forced to take lodgings in Nottingham, 10 miles south.

Lord Byron (1788–1824), from a portrait at Newstead Abbey. Replying to Shelley about Keats's death, Byron wrote: 'I am very sorry to hear what you say...Poor fellow! though with such inordinate self-love he would probably have not been very happy.'

Sherwood Forest has a visitor centre near Robin Hood's oak tree and a week-long Robin Hood festival each summer. Nottingham has Robin's statue near the castle and a colourful 'recreation' of the legends at The Tales of Robin Hood centre.

After school and university at Harrow and Cambridge, then travels abroad, Byron took up residence at Newstead, made a few improvements, and threw the first of his legendary parties. It was, some said, little short of a satanic orgy, with guests in clerical gear (hired) chasing serving maids through the cloisters.

The skull-goblet that they drank from is still on show at the house, along with Byron's great gilded bed, the chapel where he kept his menagerie, and the pistols he used for target practice in the great hall.

There were quieter times here among the Gothic ruins, too, with his half-sister, Augusta Leigh, his 'dear goose', the greatest and saddest of his many passions. Compared with her, the others – Lady Caroline Lamb, Lady Oxford, his wife Annabella – were passing affairs.

Augusta was the one woman who could tease him from his melancholy moods. They were snowed up together for nearly a fortnight at Newstead and he visited her several times at her home, Swynford Paddocks (now a hotel) near Newmarket. When her daughter Medora was born, rumour spread rapidly that the child was his.

Byron had been feted in London for his poetry after the first cantos of *Childe Harold's Pilgrimage* appeared in 1812. Later came *The Corsair* and shorter verses: 'She walks in beauty, like the night' and 'So We'll Go No More a Roving':

> *Though the night was made*
> *for loving,*
> *And the day returns too soon,*
> *Yet we'll go no more a roving*
> *By the light of the moon.*

Women adored him. He was as beautiful as a young Apollo despite his club foot, and he was passionate, romantic and reckless. But his revolutionary politics and scandalous affairs, most publicly with Lady Caroline, ostracised him from society, and in 1816, after his marriage failed and his debts mounted, he left England never to return.

Living in Italy, though, he continued to write about England and Newstead. In the unfinished epic *Don Juan* (a self-portrait), he brings the hero to join a party in his own 'mansion of a rich and rare mixed Gothic', by a 'lucid lake, broad as transparent, deep, and freshly fed'.

Byron's death in 1824, on his way to join the Greek freedom fighters, was a third disastrous blow to English poetry. In three years, three brilliant young poets had died abroad: Keats, Shelley and now Byron at Missolonghi. He was brought back to England,

Newstead Abbey, family home of Lord Byron, who entertained his half-sister here, and wrote When We Two Parted -
'They know not I knew thee,
Who knew thee too well: -
Long, long shall I rue thee,
Too deeply to tell...

If I should meet thee
After long years,
How should I greet thee? -
With silence and tears.'

D. H. Lawrence died in France, 1930. His headstone is part of Eastwood Library's collection.

Footpaths around Felly Mill farm, Underwood, lead to Moorgreen Reservoir, the lake 'all grey and visionary, stretching into the mist' in Women in Love.

At 8A Victoria Street, Eastwood, Lawrence was born on September 11, 1885.

and was buried in the family vault at St Mary Magdalen's church just south of Newstead, at Hucknall.

Nottinghamshire was 'the country of my heart', wrote D. H. Lawrence. He revealed it – too frankly for local liking – in *The White Peacock, The Rainbow, Sons and Lovers* and *Lady Chatterley's Lover.*

Lawrence was born in 1885 in a small mining town, Eastwood, surrounded by 'an extremely beautiful countryside, just between the red sandstone and the oak trees of Nottingham, and the cold limestone, the ash trees, the stone fences of Derbyshire'.

His birthplace, 8A Victoria Street (now a museum), is a typical terrace house – 'two up, two down', an attic where the boys slept and a bit of a yard at the back. Small and crammed with brass bedsteads, kitchen range, patterned cloths and rag-rugs, it seems to have no room for a family of five children.

His father was a coal-miner; his mother, Lydia, a teacher who married beneath her class. She was determined that her adored son, David Herbert, 'Bert', a sickly child, should not follow his father into Brinsley colliery.

Her social climbing took the family to a new home at 28 Garden Road ('less common' than Victoria Street) in an area known as The Breach, re-named The Bottoms in Lawrence's autobiographical *Sons*

and Lovers. Two more Eastwood homes followed and, true son of an upwardly mobile mother, Lawrence noted the neighbourhood niceties of each one, parading the class distinctions of the day through his novels. It didn't make him popular.

Lawrence's own story was bad enough - running off to Germany in 1912 with Frieda, wife of a uni-

versity professor in Nottingham where 'Bert' had been educated and trained as a teacher. But the novels were worse. The town couldn't forgive his portrait of his father as a coarse, uncaring drunk in *Sons and Lovers*, and too many other people and places in his 'shockingly' explicit stories were recognisable.

Eastwood library has a room of Lawrence material and trails around every one of his settings in the town and the villages and farms nearby. He loved the countryside, 'the old England of the forest and the agricultural past... and Robin Hood and his merry men were not very far away'.

Past Brinsley colliery (now a picnic site) is Haggs Farm, home of Lawrence's first love, Jessie

Chambers, immortalised as Miriam in *Sons and Lovers*. The farm is private but from footpaths through Felley Mill farm you can see 'Miriam's farm – where I got my first incentive to write'.

In Cossall village – Cossethay in *The Rainbow* – the house beside the church (home of one of Lawrence's several fiancées) becomes the honeymoon cottage of Will and Anna Brangwen. Here the 'faint firelight glowered on the blinds' as the newlyweds lie in bed listening to the carollers outside, 'all the men singing their best' and 'two violins and a piccolo shrilling on the frosty air'.

Though Lawrence and Frieda left England in 1919, a decade later, shortly before he died in the South of France, he (like Byron) was still thinking of Nottinghamshire: 'I shall never forget the Haggs... Oh, I'd love to be nineteeen again, and coming up through the Warren.'

Alfred Tennyson's favourite among all his poems was:

Come into the garden, Maud,
For the black bat, night, has
*   flown,*
Come into the garden, Maud,
I am here at the gate alone.

Maud is traditionally linked to the gardens at Harrington Hall, in the Lincolnshire Wolds near Tennyson's home at Somersby. There is no real proof that he was seriously in love with Rose (or Rosa) Baring who came to live at the hall in 1831. He may have been, and he wrote a number of poems for her – 'Rose of roses, bliss of blisses, Rosebud-lips for honey-kisses'. But if he was in love, he knew it was hopeless by 1836. Anyway, he fell in love with

Emily Sellwood that year, though it took him another 14 years to marry her.

Tennyson, later Lord Tennyson and Poet Laureate, was born at Somersby rectory, one of 12 children, half of whom wrote poetry. Alfred began at the age of eight, wrote presentable stanzas at 12, and his first volume came out in 1827, the year he went to Cambridge.

Inevitably, with a house so full, the young Tennysons spent hours out of doors, reading and reciting poetry as they wandered the lanes and fields. At Mablethorpe, on the coast a dozen miles to the east, they loved the space and loneliness of the sand-dunes and the sea.

In Memoriam, Tennyson's elegiac poem to his dead friend Arthur Hallam, is as much a lament for Lincolnshire, which the family left in 1837. The wych-elms where 'My Arthur found your shadows fair', and 'the well-beloved place, Where first we gazed upon the sky' are at Somersby.

Years later, on the Isle of Wight, still thinking of the Wolds, Tennyson

'Maud's garden' – Harrington Hall near Spilsby.

Alfred, Lord Tennyson, caricatured in Vanity Fair *magazine, 1871.*

Somersby church, opposite the rectory where Tennyson was born.

wrote *Maud* (a huge success, selling 10,000 in a year) and *The Brook*, one of his English idylls:

> I come from haunts of coot
>   and hern,
> I make a sudden sally...
> Till last by Philip's farm I
>   flow
> To join the brimming river,
> For men may come and men
>   may go,
> But I go on for ever.

The original of Philip's farm is said to be Stockwith Mill, between Harrington and Spilsby. It has a Tennyson exhibition and both his father's churches, Somersby and Bag Enderby, have small collections.

But the best place for Tennyson material is the city of Lincoln, where his statue stands outside the cathedral. Called by Ruskin 'out and out the most precious piece of architecture in the British Isles', the cathedral can be seen for miles, rising above Steep Hill.

The Usher Gallery has a Tennyson Room with relics (hat and cloak), photographs and so on; and Lincoln Castle has a superb collection of manuscripts, letters, documents, books and more possessions (seen by appointment) in the Tennyson Research Centre.

'*Willows whiten, aspens quiver, Little breezes dusk and shiver...*'
The Lady of Shalott, *Alfred Tennyson.*

Tennyson's statue at Lincoln Cathedral. Inside is the tomb of Chaucer's sister-in-law Catherine Swynford, heroine of Anya Seton's romance Katherine.

On the green at Helpston, five miles east of Stamford, stands a memorial to the poet John Clare, who was born in the village in 1793 and buried

here 71 years later after a life of poverty, poetry and madness.

Son of an illiterate labourer and with little education himself, Clare poured into hundreds of un-romanticised rural poems his mystic passion for the countryside.

He spent his first 38 years in the thatched cottages beside the Blue Bell Inn, and came to know every wild flower, bird and animal on Helpston Heath and Emmonsale Common. But the traditional rural life that he knew was changing fast, and the hard-

ship forced on the poor by whole-sale enclosure of common lands caused him bitter sorrow.

Clare's first volume, published 1820, earned instant attention, as though he were a fashionable 'peasant poet'. But Clare followed no pretty pastoral path or Picturesque conventions. His dislike of 'enclosing' landlords and his earthy, unpunctuated, dialect didn't suit drawing-room tastes for long:

> The fields grow old and
>   common things
> The grass the sky the winds
>   ablowing
> And spots where still a beauty
>   clings
> Are sighing 'going all a
>   going'.

Clare's fame was short lived in London. Charles Lamb had warned him that the poems were 'too profuse' with 'rustic Cockneyism', yet Clare persisted, producing The Shepherd's Calendar (1827) and The Rural Muse (1835).

Moving in 1832 to a 'foreign' village, Northborough, only three miles away, compounded his sense of dislocation from a world which was rejecting his work and his values. In 1837 he started his first confinement in a mental asylum. The second, at Northampton, began in 1841. It lasted until his death 23 years later, though he was allowed out to sit under the portico of All Saint's; and he wrote another 850 verses, despite greiving that:

> My heart has left its
>   dwelling-place
> And can return no more.

POLITICS AND RELIGION

George Bernard Shaw's home in the village of Ayot St Lawrence is, like everything about him, a perfect paradox and a brilliantly successful anti-climax: an unremarkable, suburban-style house in a rural setting north of St Albans. Nothing less would suit such an eccentric, flamboyant genius.

Shaw's Corner, his home for 44 years, still has his curious collection of hats and his pens on the desk. It smacks of Ruskin and Brantwood house in Cumbria, but Shaw is Ruskin with a wicked sense of humour and a twinkling Irish eye: 'all genuinely intellectual work is humorous,' he insisted.

G. B. Shaw was born in Dublin in 1856, came to London 20 years later and was working as journalist, novelist, music and drama critic when Arms and the Man opened on a public stage in 1894.

In 1905, a few months before Shaw and his wife, Charlotte, came to Ayot St Lawrence, Major Barbara started its London run, with Shaw's portrait of Gilbert Murray as the character Adolphus Cusins.

In the garden at Shaw's Corner, he would write in a hut that revolved to catch the sun. Charlotte organised his teetotal, vegetarian regime and limited the

Shaw's Corner, Ayot St Lawrence: a respectable house for a red-bearded, rationalist, revolutionary – Irish-born playwright 'G.B.S.'

John Clare (centre) – ploughboy, soldier, labourer, called himself 'A peasant in his daily cares, a poet in his joy'. As a boy he climbed over the park wall of Burghley House to sit reading James Thomson's landscape poem The Seasons; published 1726–30 it was still a major influence on other poets 100 years later.

*I*n his study at Chalfont St Giles, John Milton (1608–1674) completed his 12-volume epic 'Of Man's first disobedience', Paradise Lost.

G. B. Shaw (1856–1950), a 1911 cartoon. His Intelligent Woman's Guide to Socialism (1928) was so influential it was re-issued as the first 'Pelican', to launch Penguin Books' mould-breaking, non-fiction paperback series in 1937.

number of visitors so that Shaw could work (T. E. Lawrence was always welcome; they looked on him almost as a son). 1913 saw the first performances of *Androcles and the Lion* and *Pygmalion* (source of the hit musical *My Fair Lady*), then came *Heartbreak House*, and in 1924, the year before he was awarded the Nobel Prize, *St Joan*.

In a single speech Shaw could play prophet, poet, pundit, clown and comic, and he kept on writing all his life. *The Millionairess* appeared shortly before he was 70, soon followed by *In Good King Charles's Glorious Days*. *Buoyant Billions* was published in 1948 when he was 92, and he continued his colossal output of socialist, Fabian and rationalist material almost to his death two years later.

The Great Plague that brought blind John Milton to a 'pretty box' of a cottage in Chalfont St Giles in 1665 was the last epidemic to sweep England, and the most terrible since the Black Death of 1348. It hit London in the spring and sent thousands fleeing for their lives.

Milton was 57 when he arrived at Chalfont St Giles, south-west of St Albans. He had not yet completed his great epic poem *Paradise Lost*, where:

High on a throne of royal
state, which far
Outshone the wealth of
Ormus and of Ind...
Satan exalted sat, by merit
raised
To that bad eminence...

For nearly 15 years Milton had suffered the blindness that would later make his *Samson Agonistes* cry 'O dark, dark, dark, amid the blaze of noon...Without all hope of day!'

He came to the village with his third wife, and with three daughters by the first (a young girl half his age who had died after a miserable marriage). The small Tudor house, now Milton's Cottage, was theirs for little more than a year before they returned to London. But it is Milton's only surviving home and the sole shrine to one of the most revered English poets: a small museum with a pretty cottage garden of herbs and flowers.

In his twenties, Milton lived in west London and Horton, near Windsor, where his parents retired. Milton had joined them after Cambridge and devoted his days to more classical studies and writing: *L'Allegro, Il Penseroso,*

Lycidas, Comus. His mother is buried at Horton and the church there has a window to him.

An ardent Nonconformist and anti-royalist, Milton's great classical learning drew him into the service of the Commonwealth. It wasn't until 1658 that he began seriously dictating *Paradise Lost.* Now, at Chalfont St Giles, probably already planning *Paradise Regained,* he finished it, as Adam and Eve,

> *...hand in hand, with*
> *wandering steps and slow,*
> *Through Eden took their*
> *solitary way.*

Hughenden Manor, home of Prime Minister Benjamin Disraeli. Accepting a copy of Queen Victoria's Highland journal in return for his novels (Coningsby, Sybil, etc) he is said to have murmured, 'We authors, Ma'am.'

Bedford has been named as John Bunyan's 'Town of Carnal Policy, a very great Town, and also hard by from whence Christian came'. Others say it is the original 'City of Destruction' in *The Pilgrim's Progress.* Either way, Bunyan

hardly flatters Bedford, but he was, after all, writing in gaol (probably the county gaol whose site is marked at the corner of Silver Street and High Street, some yards south of Bunyan's statue).

After he was arrested in 1660 for illegal preaching and non-attendance at his parish church, Bunyan spent 12 years in the prison and in 1675/6 he was

there again. At some point during the two periods he produced part one of *The Pilgrim's Progress,* the allegorical story of Christian's journey 'from this World to That which is to Come'.

It begins, Bunyan explains, when he 'lighted on a certain place where was a den' (often identified as Bedford's smaller town gaol which once stood on the old bridge) 'and as I slept I dreamed a dream...'

Beyond the bridge stands St John's Rectory, the 'House of the Interpreter' at which Christian calls and asks to be told such things 'as would be a help to me on my journey'.

In Mill Street is the Bunyan Meeting house, built 1849, with its famous memorial windows, and beside it the Bunyan Museum which covers the site of the barn he bought to preach in. The museum contains his anvil, the flute he made from the leg of a stool, the jug and platter he ate from in prison, and endless translations of his works. (Bedford library and the Cecil Higgins Gallery have more copies and Bunyan material).

Like his great Nonconformist contemporary Milton, Bunyan waged a pamphlet war for religious

Milton's Cottage, Chalfont St Giles, has rare copies not only of his great poems and pamphlets defending liberty and Cromwell's Commonwealth, but his psalms and sonnets, such as 'Let us, with a gladsome mind', and the lines On his Blindness: 'they also serve who only stand and wait'.

Puritan preacher John Bunyan (1628–1688) found his life, like Milton's, bound up with the struggles between king, parliament and church. Both authors were in trouble after the Restoration of the king in 1660.

freedom. Yet their work is worlds apart. Milton was a scholar and a gentleman. Bunyan was a working man with little schooling, a rustic who followed his father as a wandering tinker, mending pots and pans at great houses and villages around the county – and preaching where anyone would listen.

He was born in 1628 near Elstow, a mile from the town (a stone in a field at Harrowden marks the site), and baptised in Elstow church, which now has windows showing scenes from Bunyan's books. On the village green as a youth he regularly broke the Sabbath playing games, and enjoyed the fun and bustle of the annual May fair. On the edge of the green is Elstow's splendid Moot Hall – a medieval market-place that has been restored as a museum of 17th-century life, with more Bunyan material.

Progress is still written in simple colloquial prose, vividly describing Bedfordshire scenes and characters.

Bunyan never identified the sites, yet centuries-old tradition links Pilgrim with certain places as he toils up and down the county. At Stevington Cross where Bunyan preached, Christian is supposed to have dropped his burden – the weight of his sin – and watched it roll down to the stream and the holy well.

On the winding slope of Ampthill 'he fell from running to going, and from going to clambering upon his hands and knees, because of the steepness of the place'.

At the top of Christian's 'Hill Difficulty' stood 'The House Beautiful' where he is welcomed in as 'the blessed of the Lord'. This is Houghton House, built in 1615 for Sir Philip Sidney's sister Mary, Countess of Pembroke. To

Bunyan Meeting house has windows showing Bunyan and Christian, who makes The Pilgrim's Progress with the help of Evangelist pointing the way to the Celestial City. Evangelist was based on Bunyan's friend John Gifford, who founded the meeting house and was presented with the living of St John's.

In Grace Abounding Bunyan tells of his 'wicked' childhood and abandoned youth at Elstow, playing on the Green by the Moot Hall (right), dancing, swearing and bell-ringing in the bell-tower of Elstow Church.

Still in his teens, Bunyan took up Parliamentary arms against King Charles, and his brief schooling in Elstow was rapidly augmented by the radical free-thinkers who joined the Nonconformist army. When he returned to Elstow around 1649, married, and set up as a tinker with his own anvil, he was well versed in theological argument. But his *Pilgrim's*

Bunyan it was a shining new mansion standing high on the ridge south of Bedford, looking over the county. Today it is an elegant, roofless shell and all that is left of its interior is the staircase now in Bedford's Swan Hotel.

Below Ampthill the valley of the Great Ouse stretches away north and west to the low-lying meadows of Olney and *The Poplar-Field*, where 18th-century poet William Cowper wrote sadly:

> *The poplars are fell'd,*
> *farewell to the shade*
> *And the whispering sound of*
> *the cool colonnade.*

Cowper was living in Olney with Mary Unwin at Orchard Side, a large red-brick house (now the Cowper and Newton Museum) in the Market Place. Mary and her husband had taken Cowper in as a lodger in Huntingdon after Cowper's attempted suicide in 1763. When the Rev. Unwin died in 1767, William and Mary – who never married – moved to Olney and made further kindly, if overbearing, Evangelical friends, including the Rev. John Newton.

Newton encouraged Cowper's poetry and co-wrote with him the 300-strong *Olney Hymns*, containing 'God moves in a mysterious way His wonders to perform'. The museum is a memorial to both these mild and pious men. Behind it are the garden and Cowper's summer house, 'not much bigger than a sedan chair' It was, though, large enough for him to sit writing *The Diverting History of John Gilpin*, 'a citizen of credit and renown', and the truly awful *Loss of the Royal George* – 'Toll for the brave, The Brave! that are no more'.

For Cowper, poetry was a diversion from the depressions and dreads that threatened his sanity. He wasn't even happy for long after writing about John Gilpin's wild ride (a forerunner of Burns's *Tam O'Shanter*). He admitted in a letter: 'the most ludicrous lines I ever wrote have been written in the saddest mood.'

Sir Francis Bacon (1561–1626) essayist and statesman, has sometimes been claimed the author of Shakespeare's plays. His library is at his family home, Gorhambury House, St Albans; his statue is at Gray's Inn, London, where he laid out the gardens in 1606.

William Cowper (1731–800), a gentle, friendly but depressive poet. He recorded his thoughts and daily life in The Task – 'God made the country, and man made the town'; and in dozens of letters, detailing the 'Escapade of Puss' and 'Arrival of the desk'.

Houghton House (above left) is Christian's House Beautiful – 'built by the Lord of the Hill on purpose to entertain such pilgrims in'.

The Peaks

DERBYSHIRE

Tunstall
Burslem
Stoke-on-Trent
Hanley
The
Potteries

R. Dove

Derby
R. Trent

STAFFORDSHIRE

Stafford

Lichfield

Walsall
WEST
Birmingham
MIDLANDS

Nuneaton

Coventry
Rugby

WARWICKSHIRE

Stratford·upon·Avon

Chipping
Campden

Banbury

Broadway

R. Severn

Gloucester

GLOUCESTERSHIRE

OXFORDSHIRE

Stroud
Slad
Cotswolds

Finstock

Woodstock

Swinbrook
Astall
Witney

Aylesbury

Wotton-
under-Edge
R. Thames

Kelmscott
Lechlade

Oxford

BUCKINGHAMSHIRE

Clifton
Hampden

Uffington

Henley
Stoke Poges
Eton

Pangbourne
Reading
Windsor

BERKSHIRE

The Midlands and Cotswolds

CHAPTER 6

THE MIDLANDS AND COTSWOLDS

◆

SWEET SWAN OF AVON

> *Stratford of course is a very sacred place.*
> Henry James 1877.

Stratford-upon-Avon started being sacred almost the day William Shakespeare died in 1616. To fellow dramatists he was, in Ben Jonson's words:

> *Soul of the Age!*
> *The applause! delight!*
>   *the wonder of our stage!*
> *My Shakespeare, arise; ...*
> *Sweet Swan of Avon!*
>   *what a sight it were*
> *To see thee in our waters*
>   *yet appear,*
> *And make those flights upon*
>   *the banks of Thames,*
> *That so did take Eliza, and*
>   *our James!*

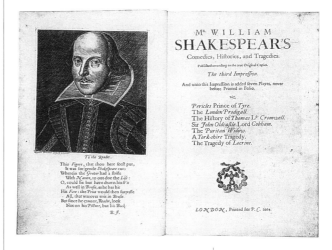

Before long, legions of literary pilgrims were descending on the Warwickshire market town. Shakespeare's plays and poems were written almost exclusively 'upon the banks of Thames'. Yet they wanted to see where he was born in 1564, grew up, attended the grammar school, married, set off for London (probably around 1585 to 1590), returned a prosperous playwright, bought the second-biggest house in town, New Place, and lived his last years.

By 1756 the owner of New Place was so irritated by demands to see the mulberry tree Shakespeare is said to have planted in the garden, that he axed it. A couple of years later he demolished the house. All that remains for visitors now are some foundations and the gardens, reached through neighbouring Nash's House

The Third Folio of Shakespeare's plays, (above) published 1664.

Soest's 17th-century portrait of Shakespeare hangs in the Shakespeare Centre in Henley Street.

An Elizabethan-style knot garden (left) covers the site of Shakespeare's last home, New Place in Stratford.

149

Shakespeare's birth-place in Henley Street.

In the Bard's birth-room (right), Sir Walter Scott and Thomas Carlyle recorded their visits by scratching their names in the window.

Mary Arden's house at Wilmcote, three miles north of Stratford.

Anne Hathaway's cottage at Shottery (right), where tradition says William wooed her on the oak settle in the parlour.

museum (once owned by Shakespeare's granddaughter).

In September 1769, actor-manager David Garrick helped revive Stratford's reputation by arranging a three-day festival, the Garrick Jubilee, in Shakespeare's honour. Thanks to the weather it was not a great success. But Garrick, never one to miss a curtain call, made good his losses with a repeat per-formance at his Drury Lane the-atre in London.

As Shakespeare's birth and death each came close to St George's Day, April 23, the patriotic notion developed that they had occurred that day - hence Stratford's Shakespeare ceremonies are held on the Saturday nearest St George's Day.

Inevitably, Stratford gets crowded and the much-needed pedestrian precinct round Shakespeare's birthplace has marooned it like a high altar in Henley Street. So the house gives little impression of family life when Will was born there, allegedly in the upstairs room where genera-

tions of writers - Sir Walter Scott, Thomas Carlyle and others - have left their mark on the window.

What the birthplace lacks in atmosphere is compensated for by quantities of information, displays and costumes at the Visitor Centre. In any case, other proper-ties managed by The Shakespeare Birthplace Trust - Mary Arden's House, Anne Hathaway's Cottage and Hall's Croft - have plenty of character, especially ' In the spring time, the only pretty ring time, When birds do sing, hey ding a ding, ding', before the peak summer season.

Mary Arden's House at Wilmcote, three miles north of Stratford, is a grand stone-and-timber house generally agreed to be William's mother's home before her marriage. It is the house of a land-owning farmer of some rank, as the impressive stone dovecote proves, and both the house and extensive farm buildings are fitted with Tudor furniture and farm history.

Anne Hathaway's Cottage at Shottery, once a village outside the town, was the family home of William's in-laws. It is more a sub-stantial farmhouse than a 'cottage'. Under the thick thatch roof are a dozen different rooms, also furnished

as a traditional yeoman farmer's home. Here in the gardens and by the open fire, so the story goes, William came to woo Anne. When they married in 1582 he was 18; she was eight years older and expecting their first child, Susanna.

Susanna's house in Stratford is the one many would call most rewarding. Hall's Croft in Old Town, where she lived with her husband Dr John Hall, is the townhouse of a prosperous medical man, with furnishings and displays to match. It stands in a sleepy, secluded garden, somewhat out-of-the-rush of the town, with a tearoom, and seems purpose-made to sit in reading Shakespeare's sonnets.

Near the end of the street is Holy Trinity Church, where the Shakespeare family was baptised

and buried, and William lies in the chancel beneath a bust and monument. From the church a path leads back by the River Avon to the Royal Shakespeare Company's main, modern theatre.

Beside it, in what remains of an earlier theatre building, the RSC has a collection of theatrical relics and a second theatre, The Swan, shaped liked the 'wooden-O' stages that Shakespeare wrote for in London.

Still in Stratford, 'Shakespeare's London' is part of the tableaux-show at The World of Shakespeare. Queen Elizabeth's visit to

Kenilworth Castle, 10 miles to the north, also gets the sights-and-sounds treatment. In 1575 Elizabeth stayed nearly a fortnight at the castle - now preserved as a spectacular ruin - while her favourite, Robert Dudley, Earl of Leicester, entertained her with nightly revels, fireworks and jousts. Sir Walter Scott wrote it all - including the mysterious death of Dudley's wife, Amy Robsart - into his historical romance, *Kenilworth*.

Where the River Avon passes the tableaux and the theatre, once-popular romantic novelist Marie Corelli used to glide up and down in an imported Italian gondola. Daughter of a Scottish poet (her real name was Mary MacKay), she moved to Stratford in 1901 so that her literary talents should thrive under Shakespeare's influence. She is practically unheard of now. But she lives on, partly through E. F. Benson's characters (she was the model for the lady-novelist in *Secret Lives* and for Lucia's outrageous affectation), and in the preservation of one of Stratford's finest 16th-century buildings, Harvard House.

It was built by the grandfather of the founder of the university, John Harvard. In 1909, with Corelli as a prime mover, it was bought and presented to Harvard university by a Chicago benefactor, Edward Morris.

*H*oly Trinity church by the River Avon, where Shakespeare was christened and buried, has an effigy commissioned by his family within a few years of his death.

*T*he Swan (left), a modern reconstruction of an Elizabethan stage, is one of three theatres in Stratford.

*H*arvard House, built by the grandfather of John Harvard, founder of the American university, is among the finest townhouses in Stratford.

The Potteries then and now – coal-fired 'bottle' kilns (right) in use, and (far right) a Victorian pottery factory preserved at Gladstone Working Museum.

Enoch Arnold Bennett (1867-1931) – born in Hanley, buried in Burslem.

MIDLANDS MASTERS

Arnold Bennett called Stoke-on-Trent's six towns 'the Five Towns' simply because it sounded better. He left out Fenton and renamed Tunstall, Burslem, Hanley, Stoke and Longton, as Turnhill, Bursley, Hanbridge, Knype and Longshaw.

That apart, what Bennett wrote about the Potteries, especially their 'grim and original beauty', is exactly as he remembered from his childhood. He was born Enoch Arnold Bennett at Hanley in 1867 and lived in various parts of the district until he set off for London at the age of 22.

He was miles away (sometimes in Paris) when he wrote *Anna of the Five Towns, The Old Wives' Tale, Clayhanger, The Card* and *Hilda Lessways* (plus plenty of Five Towns short stories). Yet they give an extraordinarily vivid picture of life in the 'five contiguous towns' in the 1880s. And Bennett went to some lengths to explain both the 'vague picturesque mass of bricks through its heavy pall of

smoke' and the pottery industry that Josiah Wedgwood had revolutionised a century earlier.

Bennett's favourite view must have been from the bandstand on the top terrace of Burslem Park, high above 'the Indian-red architecture of Bursley - tall chimneys and rounded ovens'. It comes in his journals, in *Clayhanger* and in *Anna*, where 'the miser's daughter' strolls in the park with Henry Mynors not realising she is worth 'as near fifty thousand as makes no matter', though Henry has a shrewd idea.

'Look down,' Bennett urges, 'into the valley from this terrace-height where love is kindling, embrace the whole smoke-girt amphitheatre in a glance, and it may be that you will suddenly comprehend the secret and superb significance of the vast Doing which goes forward below.'

The smoke has gone and the coal-tips are grassed over but it is still possible to 'comprehend' the doing of the pottery business and visit places Bennett knew.

In Burslem itself, 'the mother town of the Potteries', there are plaques pin-pointing more than a

Nothing could be more prosaic than the huddled, red-brown streets; nothing more seemingly remote from romance. Yet be it said that romance is even here - the romance which, for those who have an eye to perceive it, ever dwells amid the seats of industrial manufacture...
Arnold Bennett, *Anna of the Five Towns.*

Surely, that the industry has ever made.

Longton is the place to see a typical 19th-century 'pot-bank'. Gladstone Working Pottery Museum has daily demos in the old workshops and rows of bottle-kilns around a cobbled yard. Stoke, meanwhile, has the oldest pottery, Spode, still on its original site and open for factory tours, museum and shop visits.

Keele University on the edge of Newcastle-under-Lyme (where Bennett went to school) has a Bennett Archive, available on request. There are minor gems (major ones are in America) about his schooldays; letters written once he joined the ranks of the highest-paid writers in the world, flagrantly

*C*aricature in the magazine Vanity Fair. *Bennett became one of the highest-paid writers in the world.*

dozen Bennett sites including the Town Hall with the gold angel where *The Card*, Denry Machin, dares to dance with the Countess. Bennett based her on the Duchess of Sutherland and felt obliged to write an apology after they met at a dinner. Another plaque marks the Wedgwood Institute where Denry goes to school, as Bennett did.

On the corner facing St James's Square is John Baines's draper's shop, the same that Bennett's grandfather had. At the top of the square is the bank in which Anna collects 'her cheque-book, a deposit-book, and a pass-book... in a whirl of uncertainty as to the uses of the three...'

Beyond Burslem is Bennett's birthplace in Hanley (best explored near the city centre on the regular China Link Bus) and the City Museum. The museum has only a small case of Bennett memorabilia (fountain pen, walking stick and a railway reading lamp), but a vast, world-famous china gallery; samples of everything,

THE SCHOOL OF ART
"The Old Wives' Tale"
ARNOLD BENNETT'S BURSLEM
ARNOLD BENNETT 1867-1931

enjoying his fortune; and correspondence from friends and fellow-writers. Here is George Bernard Shaw writing in 1911:

'Some months ago I went to your Five Towns...I spoke in a huge hall in Hanley. It was crowded...When I alluded to you, they cheered enthusiastically...'

And that was before Bennett published *Hilda Lessways, These Twain*, and *Riceyman Steps*, which raised his popularity and earnings still higher.

*B*urslem market place, earlier this century, and the Town Hall – scene of the countess's ball in The Card.

153

Outside Johnson's Birthplace Museum, Lichfield Cathedral choir takes part in the annual birthday celebrations.

Dr Samuel Johnson – writer, critic, lexicographer and conversationalist – a pastel portrait after Sir Joshua Reynolds.

A bound edition of The Rambler and the two-volume Dictionary of the English Language *lie by a bust of Dr Johnson at his birthplace in Lichfield.*

Dr Samuel Johnson declared, 'When a man is tired of London, he is tired of life.' His views on Lichfield, where he was born in 1709, are less well known. When his young friend and biographer James Boswell remarked that it was a sleepy little place that didn't seem to do much work, the Great Doctor replied that it was 'a city of philosophers; we work with our heads'. It was, Boswell recorded, the place where Johnson 'formed friendships whose influence lasted throughout his life', and thought the inhabitants 'the most sober, decent people in England'.

Daniel Defoe would have agreed. Writing when Johnson was 16 and still living in Lichfield, Defoe called it 'a place of good conversation and good company, above all the towns in this county or the next'.

It clearly had a strong cultural tradition (other Lichfordians included essayist Joseph Addison) and Johnson's father was by no means the only bookseller in town when he built the house-cum-book-shop where Samuel was born.

As a writer's museum, Samuel Johnson's Birthplace is everything one could wish for. It is a handsome 18th-century house, facing the marketplace of a graceful old city, with room above room of displays (some with special appeal to children); a second-hand book shop in the original groundfloor premises; even a place to sit and read his books.

The room Johnson was born in looks straight on to his statue (wreath-laying and civic ceremony in September) and another of Boswell nearby. Beyond lie the cathedral close; the Bishop's Palace, which Johnson often visited;

and the cathedral, which has memorials to him and his great friend, actor David Garrick.

Ten years Johnson's junior, Garrick followed him to Lichfield grammar school and then became a pupil at the school that Johnson and his wife Tetty tried to run for a few years, just outside the city. When it closed in 1737 Sam and David set off to London together to make their fortunes.

Johnson never did. His *Dictionary, Lives of the English Poets*, and twice-weekly *Rambler* essays made him famous and revered - not rich. So short of money was he when his mother died in 1759 that he quickly finished a novel, *Rasselas*, to cover her funeral expenses and some debts.

Only his state pension, £300 a year awarded in 1762 for services to language and literature, freed him from the daily drudgery of writing and selling his work, which had been his excuse for not coming back to see his mother for 20 years.

It enabled him to travel, most famously through Scotland but also to Wales with his friends the Thrales, and to return to the Midlands almost every year thereafter, enjoying his celebrity status to the full.

On one Midlands trip, still suffering guilt over relations with his family, Johnson went to Uttoxeter, 17 miles from Lichfield. There he stood in the rain for several hours to atone for refusing some 50 years earlier to take his sick father's

place selling books in the market.

Nathaniel Hawthorne, following Johnson's footsteps nearly a century later, stayed at the Swan Inn, Lichfield, just as Johnson had on the way to Wales. When he got to Uttoxeter Hawthorne was amazed to find nothing marking 'Johnson's Penance'. It was soon rectified by a plaque, copied from a panel on Johnson's statue in Lichfield, and each year the Great Doctor is remembered there a couple of days after Lichfield's ceremony.

The cathedral close in Lichfield is the setting for Lady Bountiful's House in George Farquhar's play *The Beaux-Stratagem*. In 1705 Farquhar stayed at the old George Inn at Lichfield (replaced by the present inn) while he worked, temporarily, as an army recruiting officer.

After more recruiting in Shrewsbury he went back to playwriting and divided his experiences into two Restoration comedies of

*J*ohnson's statue sits opposite the Birthplace Museum.

*L*ichfield Cathedral (left) has memorials to Dr Johnson and his friend and pupil, the actor David Garrick.

*E*dward Ward's painting of Johnson reading the manuscript of The Vicar of Wakefield by his friend Oliver Goldsmith, which Johnson managed to sell to a publisher to prevent Goldsmith being arrested for debt.

brilliant wit. Lichfield became the 'Scene' of his social comedy *The Beaux-Stratagem*, with the George

Izaak Walton's cottage, Shallowford – left to the town of Stafford in Walton's will.

Izaak Walton (1593-1683), author of The Compleat Angler, *was more esteemed in his day for his biographies of George Herbert, Richard Hooker and John Donne – who made Walton a present of the seal (centre) that Walton used on his will.*

as the model for Landlord Boniface's inn; while Shrewsbury and army life are the subject of *The Recruiting Officer.*

When Izaak Walton died, in 1683, his gentle discourse on *The Compleat Angler, or the Contemplative Man's Recreation* had already gone into several editions. His much-loved 'fishing tackle and lumber' were valued at £10 and his total wealth came to well over £2,225.

It was a sizeable amount for the son of a Stafford alehouse keeper and though he had moved on to London and Winchester, he still owned property, including a thatched, half-timbered cottage at Shallowford, a few miles from Stafford.

He left them in his will to his son, unless he 'shall not marry before he shall be of the age of forty and one years... then I give the said farme or land to the towne or corporation of Stafford, in which I was borne'.

They went to the corporation. The cottage, somewhat squeezed between the railway and the road, has become a museum to Izaak and to fishing: a collection as modest and beguiling as the book.

When and where Walton was born in Stafford is uncertain.

Tradition says August 9, 1593 in Eastgate Street, the site now covered by the police station. His baptism, in the curious Norman font in St Mary's Church, is recorded and honoured with a bust.

By the time he was 20 he was in London making his fortune and friends among writers and clerics. But once Oliver Cromwell made the City of London uncomfortable for a staunch royalist and Anglican, Walton spent much of his time back in the comparative calm of Staffordshire, fishing the 'silver streams' and the River Dove with his friend Charles Cotton.

He published the first edition of *The Compleat Angler* in 1653 and enlarged it two years later, adding more fishing lore and legend, poems and songs to the anthology. In 1676 it was revised again, this time with Cotton's text on fly-fishing. But by then Walton had moved to Winchester, where he died, still writing at the age of 90.

Furnished as a typical 17th-century farmhouse, Walton's cottage also has a museum of angling: four centuries of 'the contemplative man's recreation'.

SCENES OF PROVINCIAL LIFE

Living openly with a married man meant that Mary Ann Evans - novelist George Eliot - became an outcast from Nuneaton and Coventry where she had spent the first 30 years of her life.

She became the foremost woman writer of the age: after Dickens, the greatest novelist of the

changing world of 19th-century England. But for her, unlike Dr Johnson, there could be no triumphal return to the Midlands once she decided to live openly with the writer George Lewes.

Her brother Isaac, still living at Griff House, their family home on the edge of Nuneaton, refused all contact for more than two decades. He only saw fit to resume correspondence after her brief, curious but formal marriage to Johnny Cross. He was 20 years her junior and she married him less than 18 months after Lewes died (barely seven before her own death in 1880), yet Isaac was evidently pleased with the proprieties.

Even liberal-minded friends from her Coventry years, the Brays and Hennells, were uncertain about her liaison with George Lewes. (Coventry has a town-trail

around her school and home at Foleshill, though it admits she would find the area unrecognisable). Mary Ann after all, had had a few close encounters of the married kind already. One was with Rufa Hennell's father, said to be the model for Dr Casaubon, the ageing pedant in *Middlemarch* who marries ardent young Dorothea Brooke.

Mary Ann's relationship with Lewes, though, was a more serious matter and he was only prevented from divorcing his wife because he had supported her illegitimate children as his own.

If Mary Ann could not return to her native Warwickshire, she could still carry away deeply etched memories, and her earliest stories, the three *Scenes of Clerical Life*, are scenes from her childhood.

Arbury Hall and estate where her father was land agent, and Mary Ann was born in 1819, are the originals for Cheverel Manor. In the second tale, 'Mr Gilfil's Love-Story', Arbury is the 'castellated house of grey-tinted stone' whose glorious Gothic style 'impressed one with its architectural beauty like a cathedral', and whose creamy-white carved ceilings looked 'like petrified lace-work'.

Mr Gilfil's 'wonderful little church' with 'marble warriors and their wives without noses' and 'the twelve apostles holding didactic ribbons, painted in fresco on the wall', is the church at Astley. In fact it

George Lewes wrote for every issue of the Westminster Review *that Mary Ann Evans edited in London – and lived with her nearly 25 years until his death in 1878.*

Mary Ann Evans (1819-1880) adopted the pen-name George Eliot when Blackwood's Magazine *published her first stories,* Scenes of Clerical Life, *in 1857.*

The dining room at Arbury Hall – the model for Cheverel Manor in Eliot's Scenes of Clerical Life.

The medieval panels at Astley church, where Mr Gilfil always preached from one of his 'large heap of short sermons'.

Griff House (right) near Nuneaton; George Eliot's childhood home, and Maggie Tulliver's.

George Eliot's statue in the centre of Nuneaton.

has nine apostles facing nine prophets painted on medieval wooden panels above some splendid sets of misericords. The church key is kept at the studio of John Letts, sculptor of Nuneaton's George Eliot statue.

Nuneaton was her model for Milby, and a number of townspeople she knew while at boarding school and church there found their way into the 'Scenes'.

Nuneaton Museum and Art Gallery has a small George Eliot exhibition and a reconstruction of her London drawing room with the grand piano George Lewes gave her. It also has her silk dress and kid boots, surprisingly small when one remembers Henry James's description of her as a 'great horse-faced bluestocking'.

Nuneaton library has another collection - early editions, biographies, criticism and letters that can be seen on request; and the town holds twice yearly wreath-layings, in June at the

George Eliot Memorial Garden, in November at her statue.

A few months after Mary Ann was born at Arbury estate farmhouse, the family moved to Griff House, still in Chilvers Coton parish. In *Scenes of Clerical Life* it became the parish of Shepperton and the curate who baptised her was distressed to find his own unhappy history used as the life of the Rev Amos Barton.

Griff House has recently been re-styled as an inn (with a hotel extension) themed on George Eliot. It has numerous Victorian-pub-style bars and dining areas exuberantly decorated as Casaubon's Library, Rosamond's Parlour and so on.

But the great attic that was a 'favourite retreat' for Maggie Tulliver in *The Mill on the Floss* - and for Mary Ann - is still visible 'under the old high-pitched roof'. The inn garden preserves the Round Pond where Maggie

pushed 'pretty little Lucy' in the mud and went fishing with her adored brother Tom, Mary Ann's portrait of her own brother Isaac.

Most of the originals for *The Mill* however are further afield. She used Gainsborough in Lincolnshire as St Ogg's and the tidal Trent is recast as the Floss, the flooding river that finally re-unites Maggie and her estranged brother.

In *Adam Bede* she again went further afield, using Ashbourne in Derbyshire and Ellastone in Staffordshire. Yet in all her best-known work it is still the 19th-century Midlands she portrays, from the little village world of *Silas Marner - The Weaver of Raveloe* to the whole panorama of Midlands provincial life that makes up *Middlemarch*, where the coming of the railway, parliamentary reform and women's independence are all woven around the tangled loves of Dorothea Brooke and Rosamond Vincy.

Hobbit and *The Lord of the Rings* he created the fantasy world of Middle-Earth with its own language and landscape. Yet he knowingly drew on recollections of the Midlands. 'As an Englishman brought up in an "almost rural" village of Warwickshire,' he explained years later, 'I take my models - from such "life" as I know.' And he knew Sarehole and its watermill as the pleasantest part of his unsettled childhood.

He was three when his mother brought him from South Africa, where he was born in 1892, to visit relatives in England. His father died while they were away and Mrs Tolkien decided to stay put, renting a semi-detached house near the mill at Sarehole.

It was then a rural hamlet on the edge of the city. Young Ronald and his brother crossed fields and streams to play round the mill-pond ringed with willows and

John Ronald Reuel Tolkien (1892-1973) made Middle England the landscape for Middle-Earth, the fantasy world of The Hobbit *and* Lord of the Rings.

Sarehole Mill near Birmingham (left) was a dilapidated corn mill when Tolkien and his brother made it their playground.

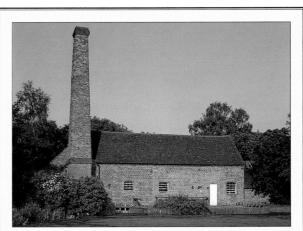

To the end of his days Bilbo could never remember how he found himself outside, without a hat, a walking stick or any money... and running as fast as his furry feet could carry him down the lane, past the great Mill, across The Water, and then on for a mile or more.

J.R.R. Tolkien, *The Hobbit*.

J. R. R. Tolkien could remember exactly how Bilbo Baggins reached the mill. He had led the hobbit back down the avenues of his own memory to Sarehole Mill and pond, 'a kind of lost paradise' from his childhood in Birmingham.

When Tolkien wrote *The*

explore the mill (later restored with Tolkien's support and preserved as the city's last working water mill).

They nicknamed the dust-covered miller's son who chased them away as the White Ogre. The local farmer, the Black Ogre, became another of Tolkien's characters.

Perrott's Folly, one of the images for The Two Towers of Gondor.

In 1927 Jerome K. Jerome received the freedom of the Borough of Walsall, outside Belsize House, his birthplace in 1859.

And The Shire, the pleasant hobbit country that Bilbo is press-ganged into leaving and where Frodo returns, owed much to the West Midlands countryside.

In 1900 the Tolkiens moved into Birmingham and though the next 11 years, until Ronald went to Oxford, were far less happy and settled (his mother died in 1904), the city continued to supply him with images for Middle-Earth. Going to school and church along the Hagley Road (Mrs Tolkien joined Cardinal Newman's Catholic community, then building its opulent great oratory) the tall twin towers of Perrott's Folly and the waterworks became familiar landmarks to young Ronald and are thought to have inspired the *The Two Towers* of Gondor, '...the hidden paths that run towards the Moon or to the Sun'.

Jerome K. Jerome was quite surprised by the success of *Three Men in a Boat*: 'I did not intend to write a funny book, at first. I did not know I was a humorist. I have never been sure about it.' How he came to write the story of Harris, George, Montmorency the dog and Jay (himself) holidaying on the Thames, is explained at his birthplace museum in Walsall.

The exhibition and a reconstruction of the Jeromes' parlour as it might have been when he was born at Belsize House on May 2, 1859, make up the small museum of his life and work. Of other work there was lots. But *Three Men in a Boat*, generally reckoned a masterpiece of 20th-century comedy, so upstaged everything else he wrote that his serious work was never taken seriously.

Jerome's parents were still comfortably off when they came to Walsall, until the failure of his father's latest business meant they must move on. By the time he was four they were in London. Nonetheless the town claims him. He was made a freeman in 1927 and his writing desk is proudly kept in the Mayor's Parlour (seen on request).

Walsall Museum and Art Gallery has a booklover's bonus. The little-known Garman Ryan art collection, left to the town by Sir

Every hour Three Men in a Boat *move gently along the Thames on the clock in Walsall shopping centre, within chiming distance of Jerome's birthplace museum.*

Merman, The Scholar-Gipsy and others, had a huge Victorian and Edwardian readership. After Hughes and Arnold came a succession of writers-to-be: Lewis Carroll, Rupert Brooke (born in the town, and son of a Rugby schoolmaster) and Salman Rushdie. There is a statue of Hughes outside the school library and a monument to Dr Arnold in the Chapel.

But the story of young Tom Brown and the boarding-school bully, Flashman, opens with chapters set in Uffington, the village where Hughes was born in Berkshire's beautiful Vale of White Horse. So Uffington has a Tom Brown's School Museum, set up in the former village schoolroom, with displays and memorabilia of Hughes; and its church, St Mary's, known as the Cathedral in the Vale has a brass tablet to Hughes. The little village museum also has items about Sir John Betjeman, recording the few, but happy, years he spent enjoying village life in Uffington.

Jacob Epstein's widow, includes Sir Jacob's beautiful bronze bust of T. S. Eliot - so lifelike he still seems to be thinking - and numerous literary portraits. There is Sir Walter Scott, John Keats by Joseph Severn (the friend who took Keats off to Rome in the vain hope of a cure), W. B. Yeats by Augustus John, Thackeray by himself, and pictures by John Ruskin and William Blake's disciple, the visionary Samuel Palmer.

Thomas Hughes based *Tom Brown's Schooldays* on his own boyhood at Rugby School, 1834 to 1841, when its legendary headmaster Dr Thomas Arnold made it a blueprint for the public school system. Hughes was a contemporary of Dr Arnold's son, Matthew, whose poems *The Forsaken*

Belsize House has a small museum of Jerome's life and work and a reconstruction of his parents' parlour.

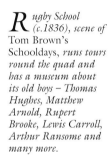

Rugby School (c.1836), scene of Tom Brown's Schooldays, runs tours round the quad and has a museum about its old boys – Thomas Hughes, Matthew Arnold, Rupert Brooke, Lewis Carroll, Arthur Ransome and many more.

COTSWOLD CHARACTERS

The slow-paced villages and valleys around Stroud and Painswick, in deepest Gloucestershire, are the land of Laurie Lee's *Cider with Rosie*. He grew up in Slad towards the close of World War I and his account of his Cotswold boyhood is a classic of village life before the invasion of motor-cars and farm machines.

He tells of the T-shaped house shared with two grannies, seven brothers and sisters; of life with little money and lots of laughter; and of the day 'Rosie Burdock decided to take me in hand' and gave him his first taste of cider:

> *Never to be forgotten, that first long secret drink of golden fire, juice of those valleys and of that time, wine of wild orchards, of russet summer, of plump red apples, and Rosie's burning cheeks...For a long time we sat with our mouths very close, breathing the same hot air. We kissed, once only, so dry and shy, it was like two leaves colliding in air. At last the cuckoos stopped singing and slid into the woods.*

At 19 he left Slad, walking away to London. His life as a young man there and his adventures in Spain are recounted in *As I Walked Out One Midsummer Morning*. But it was *Cider with Rosie* that made him enough money to return to Slad and, as he says, to 'Thank God that I live in Gloucestershire' - near the Woolpack Inn and the village school that caught fire on Armistice Night, 1918.

The 'House of the Tailor of Gloucester', near Gloucester Cathedral, is the house Beatrix Potter used to illustrate her picture-book story of a poor old tailor trying to finish clothes for the mayor's wedding 'on Christmas Day in the morning'.

'The queerest thing about it is,' Beatrix wrote in a letter, 'that I heard it in Gloucestershire, and that it is true'. She was staying near Stroud - one of many visits to a cousin who lived at Harescombe - when she learned about a local tailor who was so overworked he couldn't complete an order for the mayor. He left the waistcoat lying in his workroom and after the weekend found someone else had sewn it, all but one button-hole, and left it with a note explaining, 'No more twist!'.

Laurie Lee (right) photographed at his cottage in Slad, 1960.

Beatrix Potter, aged 26, shortly before her first visit to Gloucestershire.

Slad, the village where Laurie Lee was born, grew up, and discovered the joys of Cider with Rosie.

William Tyndale's Monument (far right), erected 1866, looks over the village of North Nibley.

The tailor, Mr Prichard, was so bemused that he put a notice outside: 'Come to Prichard where the waistcoats are finished at night by fairies.' Mrs Prichard more accurately attributed it to his assistants.

Beatrix more whimsically made it the mice; changed the period to 'the time of swords and periwigs', and the mayor's order to a cherry-coloured coat and 'an embroidered waistcoat - to be lined with yellow taffeta'.

The little house she painted as the tailor's premises has become a Beatrix Potter shop and museum, and her pictures of the tailor and Simpkin his cat stepping through

the snow are easily placed in College Court.

Popular novelist Joanna Trollope came to Gloucester to research *The Choir*, her 'Aga-saga' of sex and singing among the choirstalls. She renamed it Aldminster, but the debt to Gloucester's glorious Norman cathedral, the close and King's School is acknowledged at the start of the book.

T he 111-foot William Tyndale Monument at North Nibley, near Wotton-under-Edge, commemorates the 16th-century scholar who first translated the New Testament into English. The view of the Cotswolds from the top is magnificent, but Tyndale's tower is, in truth, more concrete than his Cotswolds connections. He may have been born at North Nibley, or Slimbridge, or Stinchcombe. All that is certain is that he was tutoring at Little Sodbury in 1522 and caused enormous controversy when his English New Testament was published in 1526: even the normally charitable Sir Thomas More called him 'a beast' and 'a hell hound'.

Tyndale spent most of the rest of his life in Antwerp, where he was arrested for heresy in 1535 and later burned at the stake. The

' *The sun was shining on the snow*' – when Beatrix Potter's *Tailor of Gloucester stepped out of his shop with Simpkin running before him, into College Court, the narrow lane leading to Gloucester Cathedral (left).*

William Tyndale (c.1494-1536), first translator of the New Testament into English.

first editions of his New Testament were also hunted down and burnt and only one complete copy is known to survive, in The British Library in London. But Tyndale's exquisite Elizabethan prose would reappear before too long, incorporated in the Authorized Version, the *King James Bible* of 1611.

Alexander Pope paid several visits to Cirencester Park and helped Lord Bathurst lay out the 3,000-acre estate. Despite the numerous gardens he worked on, and his prolific output as a poet, Pope was ever ready to help 'dear Bathurst' design Cirencester's woods and walks and neo-classical follies - one of which is named Pope's Seat. During his visit in 1726, Pope was accompanied by friend and fellow-satirist Jonathan Swift, allegedly carrying with him the manuscript of *Gulliver's Travels*.

Cirencester Park. Alexander Pope helped design the park, drawing up plans to 'open avenues, cut glades, plant firs, contrive water-works, all very fine and beautiful...'

The Fox Inn at Juniper Hill became Flora Thompson's Waggon and Horses at Lark Rise, where her father would drink, sing songs and 'wrangle' over politics.

Summer Sunday polo fixtures in Cirencester Park make this *the* place to read local novelist Jilly Cooper's blockbusting series on sex and steaming horse-flesh: *Polo, Riders* and *Rivals*. Their jumping-off point is Rutshire, theoretically fictional but not a million miles from Gloucestershire. Many of the scenes, Cooper says, are set among the wooded valleys and green rides of the Stroud countryside where she lives.

Banbury was the main model for Candleford in Flora Thompson's trilogy *Lark Rise to Candleford*, her gently nostalgic account of late-Victorian life among the poor villages of north Oxfordshire.

She was born Flora Jane Timms in the hamlet of Juniper Hill, the eldest of a stonemason's 10 children. She went to school at Cottisford (Fordlow in her books), worked at Fringford post office, moved away to Surrey in 1897, married and lived for a time in Devon. It was not until the 1930s that she began writing her recollections of life in and around Juniper Hill (Lark Rise):

> *The hamlet stood on a gentle rise in the flat, wheat-growing north-east corner of Oxfordshire. We will call it Lark Rise because of the great number of skylarks which made the surrounding fields their springboard and nested on the bare earth between the rows of green corn.*

The first volume *Lark Rise* appeared in 1939. *Over to Candleford* and *Candleford Green*

came at two-year intervals. In 1945 they were published together as *Lark Rise to Candleford*. Flora went on to write poetry and prose on other subjects. But in her last book, *Still Glides the Stream* (published posthumously in 1948) she returned to the scenes of her childhood, where 'Miss Finch remembers Restharrow', and where, sometimes - farming technology permitting - larks still rise over Oxfordshire fields.

Batsford Park near Chipping Campden is one of three Cotswold homes that Nancy Mitford rolled into one in her satirical semi-autobiography *The Pursuit of Love*. At Batsford her grandfather had created the garden and arboretum that are now open to visitors. In 1916 her father inherited it and the title Lord Redesdale, and moved in. Nancy was the eldest of his six daughters who made headlines in the 1920s and 30s as the 'Mitford Girls': Diana married Oswald Mosley, Unity became a Hitler supporter, Jessica wrote *Hons and Rebels* and *The American Way of Death*.

In spite of family efforts (Nancy kept goats) it proved impossible to make ends meet firmly enough to stay at Batsford and two years later it was sold. Lord and Lady Redesdale, immortalised by Nancy as the eccentric, irascible philistine Uncle Matthew, and gentle, eternally vague Aunt Sadie, decided to move house to Oxfordshire. First

they lived at Asthall, in the manor house beside the church, where her father (alias Uncle Matthew) and his family, real and fictional, fished and hunted around the Windrush Valley. In 1926 they moved again, a mile or so along the meanders of the Windrush to Swinbrook.

The girls didn't much like their new home but Nancy and Unity are both buried at Swinbrook, near the porch of St Mary's. Inside the church are memorials to their parents and brother, though it must be admitted they are thoroughly upstaged by the 17th-century Fettiplace figures lying stacked in 'bunks' beside the altar rails.

T. S. Eliot named the first of his *Four Quartets* for a house and garden near Chipping Campden in Gloucestershire. 'Burnt Norton', steadily decaying in its ornamental gardens, gave him the idea for 'The unheard music in the shrubbery', the image of the dry pool

At Batsford Park, one of the Mitford family homes, Nancy's grandfather laid out the arboretum, a huge collection of rare trees and bronze statues.

Nancy Mitford satirised her eccentric, upper-class childhood in the Cotswolds in The Pursuit of Love.

At 14 Flora Thompson (1876-1947) went to work at Fringford post office. She was in her sixties when Lark Rise to Candleford *was published.*

*T*homas Stearns
Eliot (1888-1965)
wrote the first of his
Four Quartets *after
visiting a Cotswold
garden. He was
received into the
Church of England at
Finstock, near Oxford.*

and 'the dead leaves, In the autumn heat'.

Eliot came across the house by chance in 1934 during one of several visits he made with an American friend, Emily Hale, to Charingworth Manor (now a hotel). He had known Emily before his first marriage, in England in 1915, and visited her in America during lecture tours. From 1934 onwards, the year Eliot separated from his first wife, Emily came to England a number of times to see him and her relatives.

Eliot's poem 'Burnt Norton' was first published separately and then appeared in 1943 with 'East Coker', 'The Dry Salvages' and 'Little Gidding' as the *Four Quartets*. Each one recorded a sort of pilgrimage to a place of some significance to Eliot, and for him the Cotswolds were important not just for the garden, but also for Finstock Church, a few miles north-west of Oxford.

At Finstock in 1927 Eliot was secretly baptised and received into the Church of England. Even close friends like Virginia Woolf knew nothing about it for months. To some it was a considerable shock that the author of *The Waste Land* (published 1922), the ultimate poem of spiritual decay and despair, should now turn into a heavily committed Christian.

OXFORD ACADEMICS

This Oxford, I have no doubt, is the finest City in the world.
John Keats.

This is surely the safest city on earth in which to arrive without a single book. It has the largest bookstore in Europe, Blackwell's; one of the oldest, grandest libraries, The Bodleian - 80 miles of shelves, 5 million books (no borrowing) and manuscripts (notably *The Wind in the Willows, The Seven Pillars of Wisdom*, Shelley's notebooks); and its own city-grown crop of classics.

Ever since scholars first came to study at the monasteries 800 years ago, dons and students have been writing books and best-sellers. Even off-duty, dons have been the brains behind some of the best children's books in the world: *Alice in Wonderland, The Lord of the Rings* and the *Chronicles of Narnia*.

Matthew Arnold's description of the 'sweet City with her dreaming spires' was based on the view from Boar's Hill south of the city. But there are handier and more central views to be had from Carfax Tower or the University Church, St Mary's, which also has an audio-visual introduction to the

Beautiful city! so venerable, so lovely...whispering from her towers the last enchantments of the Middle Age...Home of lost causes, and forsaken beliefs, and unpopular names, and impossible loyalties.

Matthew Arnold describing Oxford.

city. The 'alternative version' is The Oxford Story, a series of time-travelling tableaux with all the sights-smells-and-sounds of college life through the centuries.

One of the latest additions to Oxford's local fiction list is Chief Inspector Morse, Colin Dexter's middle-aged detective, devoted to best bitter, Mozart and Oxford's academic atmosphere.

'Oxford makes a very gentle background to all the murders,' Dexter says; 'I couldn't write the stories the same way if I didn't know the geography of the city intimately.'

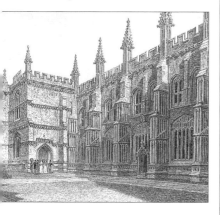

Dexter and Morse know the River Thames (called the Isis at Oxford) and the Cherwell (its tributary) as a place for concealing corpses. Suspected drugs-dealer Edward Brooks in *The Daughters of Cain* is just one of the bodies that turns up, neatly wrapped and skewered with a strange hunting knife.

In *The Jewel that Was Ours* the body is in Room 310 at the Randolph Hotel, a regular case study for Morse and one of the best hotels in Oxford (Henry James's choice).

One of Dexter's predecessors writing Oxford detective fiction was Dorothy L. Sayers, a student

at Somerville from 1912. Her amateur sleuth Lord Peter Wimsey, mostly case-solving in the Fens, made her such a celebrity she was invited to propose the college toast at Somerville's annual Gaudy dinner. It gave her the idea for *Gaudy Night*, a scholarly mystery surrounding Harriet Vane at Shrewsbury College. The name change didn't fool anyone and Somerville's High Table was hardly ecstatic.

When Wimsey wades in to Harriet's rescue (he was a Balliol man himself and modelled on one of Sayers's student romances) he falls more madly in love with Harriet than ever as they punt up river from Magdalen Bridge and stroll together through the quadrangles. Sayers was born in Oxford while her father was both head of the choir school and chaplain to Christ Church. It is one of the most notable of Oxford's 40-odd colleges and one

Magdalen Bridge over the Cherwell, where Lord Peter Wimsey takes Harriet Vane punting in Gaudy Night, and Inspector Morse knows he may find a body or two.

Oxford's Divinity Schools and Bodleian Library, c. 1836 (left). One of the oldest public libraries in Europe, the Bodleian dates from 1490 and was refounded by Thomas Bodley in 1602.

At All Souls College, T. E. Lawrence, a fellow from 1919 to 1926, introduced Robert Graves to Ezra Pound: 'Graves, Pound. Pound, Graves. You'll hate each other.' 'We did,' Graves confirmed later.

Lewis Carroll (right), born Charles Lutwidge Dodgson (1832-1898).

of many that admit visitors. Access to colleges varies considerably so details are essential, walking tours advisable, and both are available from the Tourist Information Centre in St Aldate's.

Sir John Tenniel studied the Oxford background carefully before illustrating the first edition of Alice's adventures.

It was at Christ Church, in the shadow of Christopher Wren's Tom Tower, that the young mathematics don Charles Lutwidge Dodgson turned to writing children's stories to entertain the Dean's daughter, Alice Liddell. Using the pen-name Lewis Carroll, he published *Alice's Adventures in Wonderland* in 1865 and *Through the Looking-glass* six years later.

The Rev Dodgson entered Christ Church in 1850, a shy but brilliant student, and stayed lecturing on geometry, algebra and symbolic logic for the rest of his life (though he died on a visit to his sisters in Guildford). When Queen Victoria expressed a wish to receive his next book after *Alice in Wonderland,* what she got, so the story goes, was *A Syllabus of Plain Algebraical Geometry.* Yet Dodgson's interest in logic and logical absurdity doesn't surprise anyone who has eavesdropped carefully on the mad Hatter's tea party.

How Dodgson recounted Alice's adventures to amuse Alice Liddell and her sisters as

'Oh my ears and whiskers, how late it's getting!' – Alice's White Rabbit is among the characters in The Oxford Story tableaux, in Broad Street.

they boated up river from Folly Bridge to picnic at Godstow one hot July afternoon, has been told times without number. Dodgson's version is in the Dedication of the book to Alice herself:

> All in the golden afternoon
> Full leisurely we glide,
> For both our oars, with little
>   skill,
> By little arms are plied,
> While little hands make vain
>   pretence
> Our wanderings to guide...
>
> Thus grew the tale of
>   Wonderland:
> Thus slowly, one by one,
> Its quaint events were
>   hammered out -
> And now the tale is done,
> And home we steer, a merry
>   crew,
> Beneath the setting sun.

Dodgson thought of illustrating the book himself until John Ruskin, the university's professor of fine art, advised against it and suggested *Punch* illustrator John Tenniel instead. Tenniel was given Carroll's original sketches and copious instructions as to characters and places the real Alice knew, many of them still in situ: the 'Old Sheep Shop' in St Aldate's (now 'Alice's Shop') where the Liddell girls bought barley-sugar; the University Museum where they would have seen the Dodo; the Botanical Garden; and the fawns in Magdalen College deer park.

John Ruskin, poet as well as art historian and doyen of Victorian taste, was 17 when he entered Christ Church; even so his mother took lodgings in the High Street to be near him. He went on to be first Slade Professor of Fine Art at the University and was largely responsible for the Gothic style of the University Museum, designed in 1855 in accordance with the architectural principles he had recently laid down in *The Stones of Venice*. His five-volume study of *Modern Painters* more-or-less resurrected Turner's reputation as an artist (his own collection of Turner watercolours is in Oxford's Ashmolean museum), and is per-haps better known now than his poetry. Not that Christ Church has been short on popular poets, from Sir Philip Sidney onwards.

W. H. Auden was at Christ Church when he began publishing his collections *Poems 1930* , *The Orators* and *Look Stranger*; and came together with the most important young, left-wing poets of the period: Louis MacNeice, Stephen Spender and Cecil Day-Lewis (he dropped the hyphen later).

Auden came back to Oxford, having moved to America with Christopher Isherwood at the end of the 1930s, became Professor of Poetry for a time, and spent many of his last years here. In Christ Church Cathedral there is a memorial to him in the floor, near the spot where he often sat for Sunday early Communion, wearing carpet slippers.

Stephen Spender was at University College, Day-Lewis at Wadham. MacNeice was at Merton - noted for the oldest quadrangle in the university, Mob Quad. T. S. Eliot was at Merton a few years earlier, having arrived from America in 1914 to do post-graduate research.

Whereas Auden headed west-wards to become a poet of the New World, Eliot was following the old American path eastwards in search of European culture. He didn't really enjoy Oxford though, and in June 1915 left to move to London and marry Vivienne, his first wife.

John Ruskin's disciple William Morris was at Exeter College, where he made life-long friends with artist Edward Burne-Jones. Their meeting proved cru-cial to the arts-and-crafts move-ment and to Dante Gabriel

William Morris's tapestries, books and personalia are part of the collection at Exeter College, where he was a stu-dent in the 1850s.

The Arthurian decorations in the Oxford Union Library were originally painted by William Morris, Edward Burne-Jones and Dante Gabriel Rossetti during the Long (summer) Vacation of 1857.

C. S. Lewis (above), J. R. R. Tolkien (right) and their Oxford literary cronies formed a group known as The Inklings, who met regularly in The Eagle and Child pub. A plaque in the back bar marks their meetings.

Rossetti and his Pre-Raphaelite Brotherhood; and the three men soon collaborated on the Arthurian decorations in the Oxford Union.

Morris's influence at Exeter and his interest in early English history, Icelandic sagas and the chivalric world of Thomas Malory's *Morte Darthur* had other consequences too.

John Ronald Reuel Tolkien came up to Exeter in 1911. Already fascinated by ancient mythology, he soon encountered Morris's imaginative writing as well as his translations from the Icelandic. Tolkien used a college-prize windfall to buy Morris's prose-and-poetry romance *The House of the Wolfings* and, following Morris's example, created the minutely detailed imaginary landscape of Middle-Earth, the world of *The Hobbit* and *The Lord of the Rings*.

They deal with elves and dwarves, ogres and shy little hairy-footed hobbits, but they are the work of a brilliant academic, steeped in European language and mythology. Tolkien spent 33 years teaching, researching and writing at the university; Auden, as a student, described his lectures on

Beowulf as unforgettable.

University life gave Tolkien the clubbable, chatty, masculine atmosphere he liked best, though he was married for 55 years. It also gave him the friendship of another famous children's writer, C. S. Lewis.

Before Clive Staples Lewis moved over to Cambridge in

1954, where he met and married Joy Davidman, he spent 30 years as a fellow in Oxford. He joined Tolkien's small club who met and read old Icelandic sagas aloud.

Through Tolkien's influence Lewis became a committed Christian and most of his work was divided between literary criticism (*The Allegory of Love*) and religious writing (*The Screwtape Letters*). But to millions of children he is above all the author of *The Chronicles of Narnia*, the land Lucy discovers through the wardrobe. Like Tolkien's Middle-Earth it is a world where good and evil are in conflict, in the guise of Aslan the Lion and the White Witch, and it owed its origin to Lewis's years in Oxford, at Magdalen.

Magdalen, with its riverside walks, deer park and tower where the choir sings at dawn each May Morning, became Oscar Wilde's college in 1874. He filled his rooms with exotic furnishings, professed 'Art for Art's Sake', cultivated a reputation for conspicuously exquisite taste, yet still found time to get a first and win the Newdigate prize for poetry.

John Betjeman followed suit - as far as the aesthetic and eccentric reputation went. He came up to Magdalen in 1925 with his teddy bear, Archibald; attended some, but by no means all, tutorials with C. S. Lewis; edited the university magazine *Cherwell*; but left in

1928 without a degree.

The most famous account of Oxford in the 1920s is easily Evelyn Waugh's novel *Brideshead Revisited*, based on his student days at Hertford College, though he cribbed both Betjeman's bear for Lord Sebastian *and* something

of Betjeman's wife, Penelope, for Lady Cordelia.

As a 'freshman' Waugh's shopping list of handmade shoes from Ducker and Son in the Turl - grey buckskins with silk laces, golfing brogues, patent dress shoes, yachting shoes - would have suited Sebastian down to the ground.

Brideshead is a lament for an Oxford and a world that Waugh knew was long gone: decadent, dandified, drunk and distinctly less funny than his earlier novels *Decline and Fall*, *Scoop* and *Put Out More Flags*. Before the book

Crowds gather early on Magdalen Bridge to hear the May Morning singers on Magdalen Tower. Beside the river is Addison's Walk, named after essayist Joseph Addison, fellow of Magdalen from 1678 to 1711.

> *My wide-sashed windows*
> *looked across the grass*
> *To tower and hall and lines*
> *of pinnacles.*
> *The wind among the elms,*
> *the echoing stairs,*
> *The quarters, chimed across*
> *the quiet quad*
> *From Magdalen tower and*
> *neighbouring turret-clocks,*
> *Gave eighteenth-century*
> *splendour to my state.*

John Betjeman,
Summoned by Bells.

The Sheldonian Theatre, designed by Christopher Wren in 1663.

The Bridge of Sighs at Hertford College, where Evelyn Waugh was an undergraduate.

The Shelley Memorial (right) at University College shows the drowned figure of Percy Bysshe Shelley. He spent only a year at Oxford in 1810 before he was sent down for circulating a pamphlet on atheism.

was published, American critic Edmund Wilson rated Waugh as 'the only first-class comic genius' Britain had produced since George Bernard Shaw. He was less glowing after Waugh, not noted for soft-pedalling on snubs, dismissed him as an 'insignificant Yank' (Waugh's own account).

Wilson retaliated when he reviewed *Brideshead* early in 1946, calling it a disaster of a novel and snobbish. It was, nonetheless, nearly as popular in America as in Britain where Waugh was soon to influence two rising young Oxford writers, Kingsley Amis and Philip Larkin, who were friends and fellow-students at St John's.

Kingsley Amis set the action of his 1950s 'campus novel', *Lucky Jim* in an anonymous 'redbrick', reaching an uproarious climax in Jim Dixon's drunken Merrie England lecture. Philip Larkin based his university story, *Jill*, back among the 'dreaming spires' of Oxford. Writing to Amis in 1943 from his home in Warwick, Larkin is - as so often - derogatory about his work, dismissing it as 'a lot of boring nonsense about a boy of 17 or 18 called John Kemp who does not get on very well at Oxford'.

Thomas Hardy's Jude did not

get on well at Oxford either. In *Jude the Obscure* Hardy renames the city Christminster and sends Jude here to find work. But Jude finds his fair cousin Sue Bridehead as well. Towards the end of their harrowing affair (and his hopes of ever improving himself) Jude decides they should return to the city 'to live there - perhaps to die there!'

'I don't think I like Christminster!' murmured little Time [Jude's son] mournfully,' as his father addresses the crowd outside the 'circular theatre with that well-known lantern above it' - the Sheldonian.

Henry James visited the Sheldonian and Oxford several times. In an 1877 essay, published later in *English Hours,* he describes attending a commemoration ceremony in the Sheldonian to watch

the awarding of honorary degrees, several decades before he received his own in 1910.

Mark Twain had his honorary Oxford degree three years earlier. Twain's *Adventures of Tom Sawyer* and *Huckleberry Finn* (published in the 1870s and 1880s) were so famous in Britain that when he came in 1907 he was feted, cheered and received by royalty.

Balliol College was the birthplace of Coleridge and Southey's dreams of an earthly paradise, living by a social system they labelled 'Pantisocracy'. En route to Wales for his epic walking tour, Coleridge paused at Oxford in June 1794 to meet Robert Southey, a 20-year-old Bristol-born rebel with a budding reputation for poetry and anarchy. Fired with a joint enthusiasm for Rousseau and the back-to-nature movement, they determined to set up a community of 'Pantisocrats' in some rural retreat, living by self-government, shared property and labour. Three weeks later, Coleridge set off for Wales, but not before he and Southey had pledged a reunion.

Gerard Manley Hopkins was also at Balliol, in the 1860s, when he wrote *Duns Scotus's Oxford* - 'Towery city and branchy between towers; Cuckoo-echoing, bell-swarmed, lark-charmed, rook-racked, river-rounded.' It was a contented period for Hopkins and an important one. He made friends with poet Robert Bridges who ensured after Hopkins's death that his poems were saved and published.

Robert Bridges (Poet Laureate 1913-1930) wrote a masque in 1904 for the official opening of Somerville College library. Its women students, though, were not formally recognised until 1910. By then Somerville's 'School of Novelists' had already begun with Rose Macaulay as an undergraduate, followed by Vera Brittain, Winifred Holtby, Dorothy L. Sayers, and later Iris Murdoch.

SLOWLY DOWN THE THAMES

Sweet Thames, run softly, till I end my song.
Edmund Spenser.

When Jerome K. Jerome turned a jaunt on the Thames with friends into a book, he had meant it to be a guide to the river with some light passages thrown in. His editor preferred the funny bits.

The result, *Three Men in a Boat - To say nothing of the Dog*, was book of the year 1889. It was so immediately popular that *Punch* in particular, felt threatened. The magazine slated 'the new

I knew the river well, its deep pools and hidden ways, its quiet backwaters, its sleepy towns, and ancient villages.
Jerome K. Jerome

Jerome K. Jerome made his home near the Thames after the success of Three Men in a Boat *and was buried at Ewelme.*

While Percy Bysshe Shelley (right) sat writing The Revolt of Islam *at Marlow, his wife Mary finished her Gothic horror story* Frankenstein.

humorist' with his suburban-style-comedy about clerks on holiday. But it couldn't sink Jerome's success.

He was one of the new career-novelists, writing to earn money, like Bennett and Wells, and catering for a new Edwardian audience. The boatloads of 'provincial 'Arrys and 'Arriets' the Three Men had met on the river were immediately hooked.

They followed the book and the route in their thousands, from London's Kingston Bridge and Hampton Court, where Harris nearly causes a riot in the maze, to Marlow - 'one of the pleasantest river centres I know of' and 'Cookham, past the Quarry Woods... Dear old Quarry Woods'.

At Clifton Hampden the trio put up at the Barley Mow, 'the quaintest, most old-world inn up the river', as Jerome had done, for the last night before Oxford.

Most of the book was written in London, though part was done right there at the Barley Mow. With the money and fame it earned him, he spent the rest of his life living near the Thames, at Marlow and Ewelme (where he was buried) and entertaining fellow members of the Authors' Club: Kipling, Wells, Bennett and Barrie.

Jerome may have been first to make it a best-seller, but he wasn't the first author to journey up river. Percy Bysshe Shelley and William Morris, had beaten him to it.

Shelley rowed up river to Lechlade from Old Windsor one August day in 1815 with novelist Thomas Love Peacock. They had thought to go on but stayed the night at the inn by the church. Shelley described the effect of the fading light on the church in *A Summer Evening Churchyard, Lechlade:*

Clothing in hues of heaven thy dim and distant spire Around whose lessening and invisible height Gather among the stars the clouds of night.

An extract is quoted on a plaque in the churchyard wall at the start of Shelley's Walk.

Staying near Windsor that summer with Mary Godwin, his mistress, Shelley's wanderings slowed a little. He took to writing under the trees in Windsor Great Park and boating with Peacock, who was living in West Street at Marlow and writing comical portraits of Shelley, Coleridge and Byron as Mr Scythrop Glowry, Mr Flosky and Mr Cypress in his send-up of the current literary fraternity, *Nightmare Abbey.*

The following year, when Shelley's first wife committed suicide, Shelley took Mary to visit Peacock and they soon followed his advice to get married. In February 1817 they bought their

Hampton Court, scene of Harris's wanderings in the maze, before Jerome's three clerks set off up the Thames.

sort of insane gondola' - and rowed up to Kelmscott with friends and family. It took six days from their London home, Kelmscott House at Hammersmith, to their country home on the riverside, Kelmscott Manor.

To Morris it was a sheer delight 'to see the landscape out of a square pane of glass, and sleep at nights with the stream rushing two inches past one's ear'. His wife, Janey, left the boat at Oxford and went ahead to open the manor and welcome them: just as Morris describes in *News from Nowhere*, his socialist 'dream' issued as a novel in 1891.

Morris first took a joint lease on

*W*illiam Morris *(1834-1896), writer, socialist, artist, craftsman and designer, aged about 50.*

own home in West Street (marked with a plaque). Shelley worked on his poem *The Revolt of Islam*, often writing 'in his boat', according to Mary, 'as it floated under the beech groves of Bisham'. Mary worked on a book she had started during a trip to Switzerland with Shelley and Byron, *Frankenstein, or the Modern Prometheus*. But Shelley was nomadic by nature, romantically as well as geographically. Pretty soon he brought Mary's step-sister 'Claire' and her daughter by Byron into the household but within a year he sold the house and they all left England; Shelley never to return.

William Morris twice made the journey up river. In August 1880 and again the following year he hired a houseboat, the Ark - his daughter May thought it resembled 'a

THIS IS THE PICTURE OF THE OLD HOUSE BY THE THAMES TO WHICH THE PEOPLE OF THIS STORY WENT; HEREAFTER FOLLOWS THE BOOK ITSELF WHICH IS CALLED NEWS FROM NOWHERE OR AN EPOCH OF REST & IS WRITTEN BY WILLIAM MORRIS.

*F*rontispiece of *Morris's utopian story* News from Nowhere, *printed 1892 by his Kelmscott Press.*

*K*elmscott Manor, the 16th-century Cotswold house Morris regarded as his Earthly Paradise.

*T*he grave of William Morris and his wife at Kelmscott church is marked with a 'rudely simple' coped stone designed by Morris's friend and partner Philip Webb.

Kelmscott Manor with Dante Gabriel Rossetti in 1871. It was a difficult arrangement given Gabriel's affair with Janey. Three years later Morris announced the joint arrangement was at an end and in 1874 Rossetti paid a last visit. For the rest of his life Morris could enjoy to the full the traditional grey-stone Elizabethan house he regarded as 'a heaven on earth'.

Today it houses a collection of his work as writer, thinker, artist and craftsman; possessions from his London home; items by the design company and workshops he set up in London; work by friends and contemporaries, including Rossetti and Burne-Jones - and the result is more furnished than Morris had it. When George Bernard Shaw and W. B. Yeats came to see him it was a rough-and-ready holiday home; Burne-Jones didn't care to stay too often, though he did come and visit Buscot Park and its art collection, a mile away.

Morris died in London in 1896 but he was buried here at Kelmscott church - one of several in the area with Pre-Raphaelite work and connections.

Several historic houses and gardens up and down the Thames were well-known to Alexander Pope, who is perhaps as easily appreciated now as a garden designer and grand-master of style as he is a poet.

Pope would have seen all three

There is no need now to sail or row up-river to enjoy the Thameside scenery and its writers' retreats. Plenty of boat-hire companies have cabin cruisers and narrow-boats to charter all the way in the wake of Jerome, Shelley or Morris. There are boats to be had for an hour or two from Oxford - and elsewhere - just to punt or paddle and picnic like Alice. And there are regular public passenger boats plying up and down, such as Salter's and French Brothers, so you can hop-on-and-off to explore.

roles as expressions of Classicism, the ordered, elegant style of the Augustan Age. His output of all three was colossal in spite of crippling ill-health from childhood that left him less than five feet tall and in spite of spending so much time dining and quarrelling with fellow-writers in London, and lodging with literary-minded lords

in their stately homes.

At Stanton Harcourt, Lord Harcourt lent him the top of the tower to work in while he translated the *Iliad*, converting the whole of Homer's epic into currently fashionable couplets.

The Harcourts had allowed the house, a 15th-century manor eight miles west of Oxford, to decay (only the kitchen, tower and gatehouse remain) and Pope was charmed by his medieval surroundings; which is odd, coming from the high priest of the Age of Reason. His *Iliad* was a triumph. It made Pope and the publisher a small fortune.

At Rousham House, north of Oxford, Pope came to admire the gardens William Kent had laid out round the 17th-century house. So did Pope's friends John Gay and Jonathan Swift, enjoying the temples and terraces running down to the river Cherwell. The house has

mementoes of all three. Kent's gardens here and at Chiswick in London are probably the best survivors of the sort of garden Pope designed for himself at Twickenham, and with Lord Bathurst for Cirencester Park.

Near Reading is Mapledurham House, home of Pope's friends Miss Mary and Miss Martha Blount. Pope paid them several visits at the Elizabethan manor on the riverside, until they moved to London. Miss Martha was a particular friend and correspondent and one of the few Pope kept till he died in 1744. He managed to polish up the art of the literary quarrel - as well as the heroic couplet - so highly that his satire on his 'enemies', *The Dunciad*, makes bickering over Booker prizes sound quite gentle.

At Garsington Manor, southeast of Oxford (now the scene of a summer opera festival), Lady Ottoline Morrell

Alexander Pope (1688-1744).

Rousham House (left) and gardens were greatly admired by Alexander Pope, John Gay, Jonathan Swift and Horace Walpole. The house has mementoes of their visits.

At Garsington Manor, Lady Ottoline Morrell played hostess to a constant stream of young writers and artists during the 1920s.

ran an 'alternative salon' to the Sussex HQ of the Bloomsbury Group.

From 1915 to 1927 she and husband Philip were constant and generous hosts to up-and-coming writers and artists, including many opposed to the 1914-18 war.

Aldous Huxley was a regular. He made his first visit, introduced by literary critic Desmond MacCarthy, in 1915 while still an Oxford undergraduate at Balliol, where he had made friends with novelist L. P. Hartley, author of *The Go-Between*, who also joined the Garsington guest-list.

Huxley thought Ottoline, 'arty beyond avarice' and left a satirical picture of her and the house in his first novel *Chrome Yellow*. Vanessa and Clive Bell's son Quentin once called her 'a wilderness of pearls, jewels and safety pins'. Others were more savage. Some thought her frankly ludicrous, but still came.

December 1916 saw a full turn-out. It was Katherine Mansfield's first Garsington Christmas with John Middleton Murry. She brought gifts (he didn't) for everyone: Bertrand Russell, Huxley, Clive Bell, Lytton Strachey and Carrington, and T. S. Eliot.

Eliot had been introduced the previous year by Russell and made frequent visits. In 1921 he brought

K enneth Grahame – born in Edinburgh 1859, buried in Oxford 1932.

B oats on the Thames at Cookham Dene, between Marlow and Maidenhead, where Grahame came to live with his grandmother.

his mother, over on a visit from America. Eliot relied a lot on Ottoline's sympathy, as he did on Virginia Woolf's. Yet Ottoline, in common with most of her guests, often found him chillingly distant.

At other times there was Rupert Brooke, W. B. Yeats, Frieda and D. H. Lawrence: Lawrence more at ease with the Morrells than with Bloomsbury's inner circle.

P angbourne near Goring and Cookham Dene, well down river towards Maidenhead, are the places most closely connected with Kenneth Grahame's *The Wind in the Willows*.

The Water Rat's reverie -

*Believe me, my young friend,
there is* nothing *- absolutely
nothing - half so much worth
doing as simply messing about
in boats -*

describes Kenneth Grahame's own
joy in boating on every river he
knew: the Thames, the Isis, the

Fowey and the Fal. Each one was
a tributary of the river that ran
past Pan Island and Rat's House,
on below the Wild Wood where
Badger lived, to Toad Hall.

Grahame came to live by the

Thames at Cookham Dene with
his grandmother after his mother
died when he was five. A couple of
years later they moved but it had
been long enough for Grahame
to learn to love and remember
Quarry Wood on the hill, and the
river below at Cookham.

At school in Oxford there was
the Isis (lack of money prevented
him becoming an undergraduate,
to his endless regret). Working in
London at the Bank of England
there was the Thames. On honeymoon and holidays he was by the
Fowey and the Fal in Cornwall.
And in 1906 he brought his family
back to live at Cookham Dene.

Two years later *The Wind in the
Willows* was published, gathering
together Grahame's letters and
stories for his son - which are not
so much about animals as they are
about a band of Edwardian gentle-
men leading the happy, boating,
bachelor life Grahame would
probably have preferred.

Not until E. H. Shepard's illustrations for a new edition, in

'*R ounding a bend
in the river,
they came in sight of a
handsome, dignified
old house of mellowed
red brick, with well-
kept lawns reaching
down to the water's
edge' – Mapledurham
House, drawn by E. H.
Shepard.*

*B y the Thames at
Pangbourne,
Kenneth Grahame
spent the last years of
his life, and showed
E. H. Shepard the
riverside settings to
illustrate* The Wind in
the Willows.

Thomas Gray's Elegy in a Country Churchyard is traditionally linked to the Buckinghamshire villages of Stoke Poges, where his mother retired after his father died in 1741.

1930, did the Thames become fixed as the setting for the book. By then Grahame was at his last home, at Pangbourne, and he pointed Shepard to the reaches round about as his models, with Mapledurham House on the opposite bank just begging to become Toad Hall. Grahame died at Pangbourne in 1932 and was buried, as he wished, in Oxford at Holywell Cemetery beside his son, who had died tragically many years before.

Thomas Gray, writing to Horace Walpole in 1737, describes where he is staying with an uncle in a house (now part of a Moat House hotel) overlooking the well-known beauty spot of Burnham Beeches:

AN ELEGY

WRITTEN IN

A COUNTRY CHURCHYARD

BY THOMAS GRAY.

LONDON:
SAMPSON LOW, MARSTON, SEARLE, & RIVINGTON,
CROWN BUILDINGS, 188, FLEET STREET.

Stoke Poges churchyard, last resting place of Thomas Gray and his mother, has memorials to them both.

I have at the distance of half a mile, through a green lane, a forest...Both vale and hill are covered with most venerable beeches...The timorous hare and sportive squirrel gambol round me like Adam in Paradise, before he had an Eve; but I think he did not use to read Virgil, as I commonly do here.

A few years later his mother came to live nearby in the village of Stoke Poges, where a strong local tradition says Gray produced his much-quoted *Elegy Written in a Country Churchyard*:

Now fades the glimmering
landscape on the sight,
And all the air a solemn
stillness holds,
Save where the beetle wheels
his droning flight,
And drowsy tinklings lull the
distant folds.

When he wasn't visiting mother, or 'doing' Europe with Walpole - that is until they quarrelled in Italy and Gray came home - or searching Scotland and the Lakes for 'sublime' and 'picturesque' views, Gray made his own home in his bachelor rooms at Cambridge University. But on his death in 1771 his body was brought to Stoke Poges to be buried with his mother, where he had placed a memorial and epitaph to her. Just to the north of the church is another large Thomas Gray monument, whose restoration was loudly applauded by Sir John Betjeman.

It was also on a visit to Stoke Poges that Gray is said to have written his *Ode on the Distant Prospect of Eton College*, his old school:

Thomas Gray (1716-1771).

Alas! regardless of their doom
*   The little victims play!*
No sense have they of ills to come,
*   Nor care beyond today...*
Thought would destroy their
*   paradise.*
No more; where ignorance is bliss
*   Tis folly to be wise.*

Eton College (parts are open to visitors at certain times) has educated any number of literary 'victims' since the school was founded in 1440. Shortly before Thomas Gray and Horace Walpole, Henry Fielding was here, already limbering up for a life like Tom Jones with his high spirits and amorous adventures. He had barely left school when he tried to abduct a young heiress in Dorset, failed, and was sent abroad.

Shelley's explosive schoolboy experiments and opinions quickly earned him the nicknames Mad Shelley and Shelley the Atheist. Swinburne arrived in 1849, also showing early signs of eccentricity. Aldous Huxley came for a few years and returned briefly from Oxford to teach in 1917. David Cornwell, aka John le Carre, taught for a time; and Ian Fleming and Eric Blair, better known later as George Orwell, were schoolboys here – though Blair said he didn't learn much.

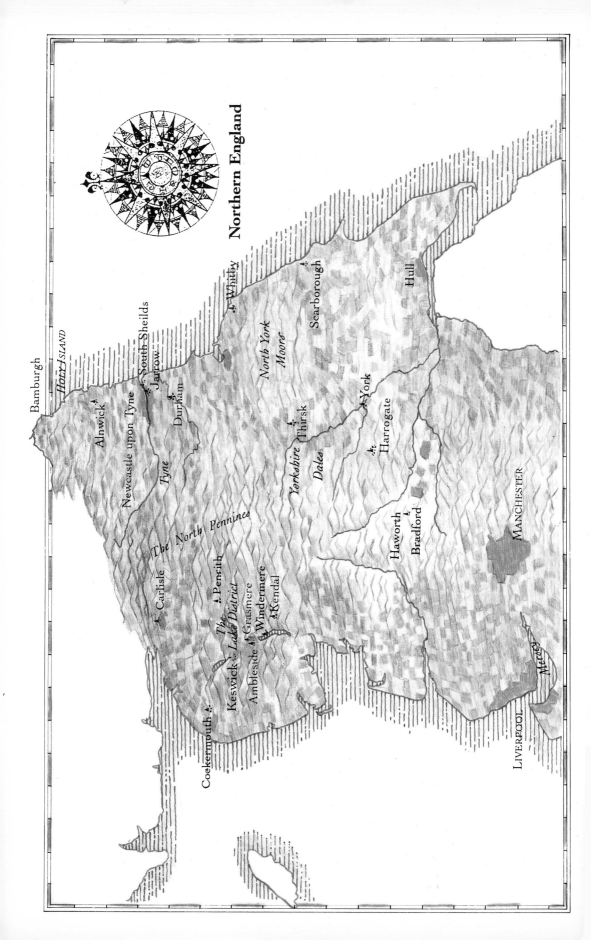

Northern England

Bamburgh

Holy Island

South Shields

Jarrow

Whitby

Alnwick

Newcastle upon Tyne

Durham

Scarborough

North York Moors

Tyne

Hull

The North Pennines

Thirsk

York

Yorkshire Dales

Harrogate

Carlisle

Penrith

Bradford

Haworth

The Lake District

Keswick

Grasmere

Ambleside

Windermere

Kendal

Cookermouth

MANCHESTER

Mersey

LIVERPOOL

CHAPTER 7

NORTHERN ENGLAND

❖

POETS' CORNER IN CUMBRIA

On New Year's Eve, 1802, a report by Samuel Taylor Coleridge on 'The Keswick Imposter' appeared in a Lake District newspaper. It was the latest episode in the life of Mary Robinson, the landlord's lovely daughter at the Fish Inn, Buttermere.

Mary was 'The Buttermere Beauty', whose story Melvyn Bragg turned into a best-selling novel in the 1980s. She became a celebrity after Joseph Budworth stayed at Buttermere in 1792 and wrote her up as a local attraction in *A Fortnight's Ramble to the Lakes*, one of the earliest Lake District guidebooks.

Unfortunately her new-found admirers included con-man and bigamist John Hatfield, 'The Keswick Imposter', who was hanged at Carlisle in 1803.

In *The Maid of Buttermere*, Bragg, himself a Cumbrian from Wigton near Carlisle, tells how Coleridge, William Wordsworth, Charles Lamb and Thomas De Quincey all became involved in the case.

Cumbria was the newly-fashionable place for travellers in search of sublime and beautiful scenery. Thomas Gray, author of the *Elegy in a Country Churchyard*, had written a journal and letters during his tour of the region in 1769, the year before Wordsworth was born. Three years later, William Gilpin (another Cumbrian, born at Scaleby in 1724) assessed the Lakes for their 'Picturesque potential'.

Gilpin's illustrated guidebooks gained avid readers, and after his *Observations on Cumberland and Westmoreland* appeared in 1786 sightseers began flooding in. By 1818 John Keats was complaining that London had invaded the district.

Gray's journal and Gilpin's guide weren't the only factors. The previous, Augustan age (Dryden, Pope, Swift, Dr Johnson) had done Classical style and reason

At Buttermere (below), Wordsworth and Coleridge stopped to see the famous 'Maid of Buttermere' in 1799. Years later, in The Prelude, *Wordsworth recalled their walking tour and their admiration for 'the artless daughter of the hills', with her 'unexampled grace'.*

Thomas De Quincey's friendship with Wordsworth began in 1807 when he finally found courage to call at Dove Cottage. But they had been estranged for years when he published Recollections of the Lakes and the Lake Poets, 1834, *including memories of Wordsworth cutting the pages of a book with a butter knife.*

William Wordsworth (1770-1850).

At Dove Cottage Wordsworth wrote Intimations of Immortality: 'The Rainbow comes and goes, And lovely is the Rose...'

to death: now was the age of the 'Romantics'. The industrial revolution had begun to reveal the value of beautiful landscapes. Getting around got easier; but revolution in France and the Napoleonic Wars put Continental touring off limits. Here in Cumbria was a substitute that matched the spirit of the age – revolutionary romanticism and the rights of the 'natural man'.

For Wordsworth, supreme poet of the Lakes, they had added charm: he was born here. At Cockermouth, William and his sister Dorothy grew up in a handsome town house backing on to the River Derwent (now Wordsworth House, furnished in 18th-century style, with some of the poet's possessions).

At Penrith, their mother's home town, they went to infant school with Mary Hutchinson, William's future wife.

At Hawkshead, William went to the grammar school (open to visitors in summer), began writing poetry, boarded in the village and explored as far as Furness Abbey. On the death of their parents, William and Dorothy went separate ways until they took a walking holiday around the Lakes in 1794 and decided to set up house together, in the West Country.

In 1799 William was wandering round Cumbria again, with Coleridge. He came across Dove Cottage, a modest, white-washed house at Grasmere and by Christmas William and Dorothy had settled in. For the next 50 years they lived within a few miles of Grasmere.

Nothing less than a year-long visit and Dorothy's *Grasmere*

Journal can really do justice to the places where they watched *The Redbreast Chasing the Butterfly* in spring; where they gathered wild strawberries and sailed the lakes in summer; saw *The Leech-gatherer* in autumn; and walked 'by moonlight to look at Langdale covered with snow' one December night. But if time is limited begin at Dove Cottage (museum and research centre next door).

Almost from the day William and Dorothy moved in, Coleridge would come and stay for weeks. Then Mary Hutchinson came for good when she married Wordsworth in October 1802, an event Dorothy found so disturbing she took to her bed with hysterics. After Mary came her sisters, Sarah and Joanna - lengthy visits to lend a hand with the house and children.

It is difficult to imagine where guests, Sir Walter Scott and De Quincey as well as Coleridge, found room to stay. It is almost impossible to imagine anyone finding enough peace to write laundry lists, let alone parts of *The Prelude, Michael, She was a Phantom of Delight, I wandered lonely as a cloud* and:

My heart leaps up when I behold
A rainbow in the sky.

Overcrowding may explain why Wordsworth composed so much outdoors, out loud; and why Walter Scott, tradition says, slipped out of the window for secret visits to the inn, re-named the White Swan. By 1807 Dove Cottage was definitely too small. The Wordsworths spent a couple of years at Allan Bank, a larger house nearby, and a couple more at Grasmere's old vicarage, beside St Oswald's church.

In 1813 they moved to their final home, Rydal Mount, near Ambleside, which is also preserved and furnished with family portraits and possessions. Close by is Dora's Field, the small meadow Wordsworth bought and named for his daughter, now filled with wild daffodils every spring.

Dorothy's journal for 1802 gives chapter and very nearly verse for the originals that were Words-worth's 'host of golden daffodils'. She and William had been walking by the lake at Ullswater on April 15 when she recorded, 'I never saw daffodils so beautiful...they looked so gay, ever glancing, ever changing.' Wordsworth did not write his own version until 1804.

That was the year Coleridge went abroad, leaving his wife, Sara, and children at Greta Hall,

Keswick. He had moved to the hall (now part of Keswick School) in 1800 and regularly tramped the dozen miles to Dove Cottage so that he and William could revise their joint volume of *Lyrical Ballads*.

In a new preface, Wordsworth explains how poetry 'takes its origin from emotion recollected in tranquillity'. He said later that he didn't give a fig for the theory, and Coleridge, in *Biographia Literaria*, attacked it roundly. But for the moment it was Coleridge's differences with his wife that showed, and his opium habit. At Christmas 1803 he walked out, spent several weeks with the Wordsworths at Dove Cottage and abandoned Greta Hall and his family to brother-in-law Robert Southey.

Thomas De Quincey shared both of Coleridge's addictions: staying with Wordsworth, and opium. After Wordsworth gave up Dove Cottage, De Quincey moved in and lived there until 1820 – shortly before finishing his *Confessions of an English Opium Eater* – when he moved to Foxghyll (now a guest-house) near Ambleside, still close to Wordsworth at Rydal Mount.

*R*ydal Mount, Wordsworth's home from 1813 until 1850, where he land-scaped part of the garden and used the terrace and shelter to compose the later Duddon Valley Sonnets, Evening Voluntaries *and* Surprised by Joy.

*A*n Evening Walk, Addressed to a Young Lady, *Wordsworth's first volume of verse, published 1793, is among the rare editions in the Wordsworth Museum, by Dove Cottage.*

'A host, of golden daffodils; Beside the lake, beneath the trees, Fluttering and dancing in the breeze'. Wordsworth's daffodils – pale, wild 'Lent lilies' – were seen on the banks by Ullswater. But they grow in drifts all round the lakes and in April the district has a daffodil-data phone line telling when and where to find them.

*A*t Crosthwaite church (centre) Robert Southey was buried on a rainy day in March 1843; Wordsworth attended and wrote the inscription for Southey's memorial.

*A*lfred Tennyson, sketched at Mirehouse by his host James Spedding. The 17th-century house has mementoes of Spedding's other guests as well: Carlyle, Wordsworth, Southey and Edward FitzGerald, translator of The Rubaiyat of Omar Khayyam.

D uring Wordsworth's long years at Rydal Mount and Southey's at Greta Hall, both men became Poet Laureate (Walter Scott nominated Southey after refusing it for himself in 1813); both wrote copiously, and both solidified into local society and conservative politics.

John Keats, during a walking tour of the Lakes in 1818 (his only visit) was appalled to find that Wordsworth, the greatest poet of the age, had not only turned High Tory but was away drumming up political support.

P. B. Shelley called on Southey at Greta Hall expressly to accuse

him of betraying the revolutionary ideals that had once made Southey even 'Mad' Shelley's hero. When Southey died in 1843 he had been Poet Laureate for 30 years, though hardly anything of his is remembered except the stirring ballad of *The Inchcape Rock* and his poem on the famous Lake District waterfall, *The Cataract of Lodore*. He was buried at Crosthwaite church, Keswick (the museum has letters and books).

Wordsworth held the laureateship for only seven years before he died in April 1850. He was buried at St Oswald's church, Grasmere. Dorothy, who had been ill for years, followed in 1855; Mary in 1859.

If Wordsworth and Southey retreated from their revolutionary ideals (some say they didn't) it never bothered Walter Scott, Tennyson, Dr Thomas Arnold or his son Matthew, who idolised Wordsworth almost all his life.

Scott paid several more visits to Wordsworth after his first stay at Dove Cottage in 1805. Tennyson called in 1835 while staying at Mirehouse, a large and pleasant place on the side of Bassenthwaite (it may be the setting for the closing scenes of his *Idylls of the King*).

Matthew Arnold was 11 when he first met Wordsworth. His father, Dr Thomas Arnold, headmaster of Rugby School, began

building a summer home, Fox How, near Ambleside in 1833. Until it was finished the Arnolds rented Allan Bank, Wordsworth's former home, and entertained him several times.

Algernon Charles Swinburne was 12 when he was taken to Rydal Mount by his parents in 1849 and made to listen while Wordsworth read Gray's *Elegy*. It was a grim foretaste of his visit to Tennyson on the Isle of Wight.

John Ruskin could remember seeing Wordsworth in Rydal church in 1830, during one of several visits to the Lakes with his parents. More than 40 years later, Ruskin returned to make his home at Brantwood, beside Coniston Water.

Brantwood has become a national centre to Ruskin, filled with his books, paintings and furniture. He was 53 when he bought it and he already had a phenomenal reputation as a poet, artist, critic, philosopher of

architecture, moralist and social reformer. He was Oxford's first Slade Professor of Art. He championed the new Pre-Raphaelite Brotherhood, and inspired William Morris as an arts-and-crafts Utopian.

Tolstoy called him 'one of the most remarkable of men, not only of England and our time but of all countries and all times. He was one of those rare men who think with their hearts'. Ruskin's wife, Effie, might have queried that. She divorced him in 1854 on the grounds of seven years' unconsummated marriage and went off with artist John Everett Millais (one of the Pre-Raphaelite Brotherhood whose cause Ruskin had supported).

Brantwood was a 'cottage' when Ruskin bought it unseen in 1871 on the strength of its position and views – probably the best in Lakeland. Yet despite his great studies on architecture - *The Stones of Venice* and *Seven Lamps of Architecture* - it is no architectural gem. His additions turned it into a rambling, muddled, country home, big enough for his relatives and his numerous visitors; among them were Holman Hunt, Sir Edward Burne-Jones and Kate Greenaway.

St Oswald's, Grasmere, has the graves of the Wordsworths and Coleridge's son, Hartley.

'*Morning breaks as I write, among those Coniston Fells, and the level mists... and the sleeping village, and the long lawns by the lake shore*' – *Ruskin describing the view from Brantwood (above), 1878.*

John Ruskin (1819-1900). His readers ranged from Tolstoy and Darwin to Mahatma Gandhi, who translated Ruskin's Unto This Last *into Gujurati. He is buried at Coniston where there is a small Ruskin Museum.*

Kate, the most popular children's illustrator of the day, was one of Ruskin's favourites, though she was nearly 30 years his junior. He greatly admired her little mob-capped figures, playing games in ribboned gowns, and even lectured on her work at Oxford.

In 1878 Greenaway's 'Pictures and Rhymes for Children', *Under the Window*, was a sensation. Over the next decade came *A Apple Pie*, her *Birthday Book for Children* and an illustrated edition of *The Pied Piper of Hamelin*.

'The Piper is sublime – and the children lovely', Ruskin wrote to her in February 1888, when she sent him her drawings for Robert Browning's poem. 'You really have got through your rats with credit.'

In 1897, three years before Ruskin died, Kate was writing to him about John Everett Millais's paintings, which they both admired. Millais was not, naturally, on the guest-list at Brantwood, but he had other places to stay.

In 1882 Millais's wealthy friend Rupert Potter brought his family to the Lake District, and Rupert's daughter Beatrix always welcomed Millais's advice.

Beatrix was 16 that first holiday. Until she married 31 years later she spent almost every summer here painting and studying plants and wildlife.

THE PIED PIPER OF HAMELIN

BY ROBERT BROWNING

ILLUSTRATED BY KATE GREENAWAY

LONDON
FREDERICK WARNE AND CO.
AND NEW YORK

Kate Greenaway's sadness at Ruskin's death and her own failing health meant she produced nothing more after 1900 and died the following year.

Beatrix Potter at Hill Top – 'It is as pretty a little place as ever I lived in.'

For the Potters, summer holidays meant several months in the country, renting houses big enough for family, friends, servants and a mountain of luggage. Mr Potter took all his photographic gear; Beatrix travelled with paints, pet mice and rabbits.

At first the family stayed by the southern lakes, where Beatrix would later make her home, and rented Wray Castle (the gardens are open) beside Windermere. Later they took Lakefield (now Ees Wycke hotel) overlooking Esthwaite Water. From there, Beatrix explored Near and Far Sawrey.

Once her royalties rolled in from *The Tale of Peter Rabbit* in 1902, Beatrix began buying fields and farms round Sawrey, including the simple, 17th-century house that has been preserved and filled with her furniture and china. Hill Top was her inspiration, a place to paint and write in.

Her house formed the backdrop to the illustrations for *The Tale of Tom Kitten*, and *The Tale of Samuel Whiskers*. Many other tales are set in and around the village of Sawrey. The local pub, The Tower Bank Arms, appears in *The*

Tale of Jemima Puddle-Duck, the shop owned by Ginger and Pickles used to be the village store, and Ribby's garden in *The Pie and the Patty Pan* belonged to one of the cottages in the village.

At first Beatrix used Hill Top as a bolt-hole from London and her parents. But when, in 1913, at the age of 47, she married her solicitor, William Heelis, they settled in Castle Cottage. She kept her beloved Hill Top, so she could have a place to write and draw, though she found her time increasingly taken up in managing her farmland and sheep, and only produced four more books.

The southern lakeland 'Potter sites' are fully signed and 'shrined'. But it is easy to miss the northern ones, where *Mrs Tiggy-Winkle*, *Squirrel Nutkin* and *Benjamin Bunny* lived.

Derwent Water, near Keswick, seems to have been the Potters' favourite and they frequently rented either Fawe Park or Lingholm. Each house has terraced gardens running down to the lake and Lingholm's are open.

'I think I have done every imaginable rabbit background, and miscellaneous sketches as well – about seventy!' Beatrix wrote to Norman Warne, in 1903.

On Derwent Water she pictured Squirrel Nutkin and friends, paddling across the water to St Herbert's Island. In Newlands Valley and Cat Bells mountains she based Mrs Tiggy-Winkle, the shy, dumpy hedgehog in cap and pinny, who admits, 'Oh, yes, if

you please'm, I'm an excellent clear-starcher.'

The town of Keswick has an exhibition about Beatrix Potter and the lakeland properties she gave to the National Trust. Hawkshead village has Mr Heelis's law office, now a Beatrix Potter Gallery. Bowness-on-Windermere has The World of Beatrix Potter tableaux and film-show; and a boat museum containing the flat-bottomed boat that Beatrix used on Moss Eccles Tarn – home of

O riginal drawings for Beatrix Potter's books are part of the collection at the Gallery in Hawkshead.

Mr Jeremy Fisher. In the same collection are Arthur Ransome's 'Amazon' and the houseboat he described as Captain Flint's.

A rthur Ransome's Swallows and Amazons, published 1930, began a series of ripping Lake District yarns in which everyone plays by the rules. Children are honour bound to be

D erwent Water, overlooked by Lingholm gardens, where Beatrix sat painting and watching the wildlife during holidays with her parents.

home by bedtime. Adults always pop up with steaming hot cocoa when the going gets rough. And when the Swallow's young crew, John, Susan, Titty and Roger, sail the high seas of lake Windermere, with the Amazon's crew, Nancy and Peggy, the weather turns rough indeed.

Ransome wrote the book at Low Ludderburn near Windermere after a visit from a group of children whose parents and grandparents had been his neighbours for years. But the story, soon followed by *Swallowdale, Peter Duck* and *Winter Holiday*, was as much about his own childhood as the children's adventures in 1928.

Though he was born in Leeds in 1884, his father's passion for the Lakes meant Arthur went to school in Windermere, and every holiday was spent around Nibthwaite, at the southern end of Coniston Water: sailing, swimming in the icy clear lake, fishing and picnicking on Peel Island.

He worked in London for a time before setting off to Russia, in 1913, where he became special correspondent for London papers during the Great War and Bolshevik revolution. Meeting Lenin and Trotsky, he fell in love with (and later married) Trotsky's

secretary, Evgenia, and travelled Eastern Europe with her before they returned to England and the Lake District in 1924.

At Low Ludderburn, over the next 10 years Ransome wrote the *Swallows and Amazons* series and (after spells in East Anglia and London) he had a succession of homes among the fells round the southern lakes. When he died in 1967, he was buried at Rusland church.

Some of his papers and possessions, his fishing rods, pipes, typewriter, Jolly Roger flag and chess set – he said he beat Lenin once – are now in an Arthur Ransome Room at Abbot Hall museum in Kendal.

Lake Windermere froze over in the Great Frost of January 1895. Arthur Ransome, at prep-school in Windermere, had lessons cancelled so that boys could learn to skate, as Wordsworth had: 'All shod with steel, We hissed along the polished ice in games' (The Prelude, Book I). Lake Coniston was still frozen over in February when John Ruskin's family gathered on the ice below Brantwood for a group photo to mark his 76th birthday.

The museum also has a room about local author John Cunliffe, creator of *Postman Pat.* Cunliffe was teaching in Kendal when he invented the bespectacled postman who drives his jolly red van round recognisably Cumbrian places.

Pat's town of Pencaster is Kendal, whose rooftops manage to rise over the snow in *Postman Pat's White Christmas*, and Greendale valley is based on Longsleddale. But Cunliffe has given his valley a lake that is more or less Grasmere, and added an imaginary canal to Kendal; which perhaps explains the puzzled expression of Pat's black-and-white cat.

ANCIENT AND MODERN NORTHUMBRIA

Catherine Cookson's 60 or more published novels, often set around her native Newcastle upon Tyne, have made her one of the most popular writers of the century.

Born out of wedlock and into the poverty and hardship of the South Tyneside dockyards in 1906, Catherine got a job at the workhouse laundry, educated herself, moved away, married and began writing.

Her first book, *Kate Hannigan*, appeared in 1948 and was soon followed by a procession of increasingly popular sagas, written from Hastings in East Sussex but vividly recreating life around Tyneside.

When Cookson decided to return to Northumbria she made her home inland along the River Tyne in Allendale – where she based the Mallen family trilogy – high up in the North Pennines, 'for the most part bare and barren and rising to miniature mountains'.

Allendale apart, 'Catherine Cookson Country' lies chiefly in South Tyneside and the places she knew have been carefully mapped, plaqued and trailed. Leam Lane is the site of her birthplace. The shipbuilding yards are the setting for *The Blind Miller*, *The Glass Virgin* and *Katie Mulholland*. Westoe village has more scenes from *Katie* and South Shields Museum has reconstructions and exhibitions about all of them.

A few yards but more than a thousand years separate Catherine Cookson's birthplace from the monastery that made Jarrow a literary centre of Western Europe in the 8th century.

Jarrow monastery (St Paul's Saxon church remains among the ruins) was the home of the Venerable Bede, author of *Historia Ecclesiastica*, the Ecclesiastical History of the English People. It is the best account we have

Helvellyn, part of Cumbria's mountain range, has 'the strongest effect on the imagination,' wrote William Gilpin, explaining their Picturesque effect in 1792. In 1805, William Wordsworth and Sir Walter Scott climbed Helvellyn together.

Tyne bridges span the river where Catherine Cookson grew up in Jarrow and South Shields, until she moved south to work in 1929.

St Cuthbert's window, Durham Cathedral.

The Lindisfarne Gospels, *created in Cuthbert's honour by the monks of Lindisfarne soon after his canonisation in 698, are on show at the British Museum.*

of events up to 731AD and it earned Bede the title 'Father of English history'.

In simple Latin, it explains that it was the work of 'Bede, servant of God, and priest of the monastery of the blessed apostles Peter and Paul, which is at Wearmouth and Jarrow...' How Bede arrived at the newly-founded monastery in 682 is explained at Bede Monastery Museum, Jarrow Hall, and at Bede's World, a recreation of his life-and-times with an 11-acre Anglo-Saxon farm.

How he spent his days until he died there in 735, Bede himself explains: 'I wholly applied myself to the study of Scripture; and, amidst the observance of regular discipline, and the daily care of singing in the church, I always took delight in learning, teaching and writing.'

Bede's delight in writing resulted in 40 major works, including the *Historia Ecclesiastica.* His *De Natura Rerum,* The Nature of Things, is a complete encyclopaedia of Anglo-Saxon knowledge, from astronomy and arithmetic to medicine, music and poetry.

Unlike other early 'chronicles', Bede's history owed nothing to imagination and everything to a painstaking search for truth using every written and first-hand source he could find. His life of St Cuthbert is almost a contempo-

rary record of the hermit who inspired one of the loveliest illuminated books in the world, *The Lindisfarne Gospels.*

Cuthbert's simple life was legendary even by the rigorous standards of the early Church. He was a shepherd boy in the Lammermuir Hills in Scotland before he became a monk and, in 664, joined the tiny community on the storm-swept Holy Island of Lindisfarne.

'As the tide ebbs and flows, this place is surrounded twice daily by the waves of the sea,' Bede explains. Sir Walter Scott paints the same picture in *Marmion* a millennium later, when untold pilgrims had made their way across the sands to Holy Island, guided by the staves in the causeway.

Infuriatingly, when Bede's history gets to King Arthur's day, the turbulent times around 500AD, the author promises 'more of this later' – and never returns to the subject.

It is Sir Thomas Malory (admittedly with another 700 years' hindsight) who claims for Northumbria a role in the Round

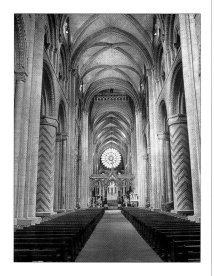

Table legends and Camelot. In *Le Morte Darthur* Malory describes Joyous Garde, the castle to which Sir Launcelot rides off with Queen Guinevere, and observes, 'Somme men say it was Anwyk and somme men say it was Bamborow'.

So Alnwick or Bamburgh – both eminently suitable strongholds – are the setting for the tragic end of Malory's tale, and Sir Ector's lament for Sir Launcelot, the greatest of all knightly lovers.

In 1964, American novelist John Steinbeck copied out Sir Ector's lament and sent it to Mrs John F. Kennedy, a few months after her husband was murdered in Dallas.

Jackie Kennedy had invited Steinbeck to write a book on the president's 'Camelot' years in the White House, turning to him as America's greatest living writer, author of *The Grapes of Wrath*, *Of Mice and Men*, *East of Eden*; winner of the 1962 Nobel Award.

She didn't realise Steinbeck had

been mesmerised by Arthurian tales since he was nine years old. He was already 'studying this recurring cycle', preparing a modern-English version of *Le Morte Darthur*. It is, he told her, 'the first and one of the greatest of novels in the English language'.

In 1959 he had explored the Arthurian sites in Somerset. In October 1961 he toured Northumbria, visited Hadrian's Wall and stayed at Chollerford. 'We are loving these few days of quiet. There's a great rain and wind and the Tyne is swollen with brown peat water,' he wrote.

In November 1965 he was back, at Alnwick Castle, with Arthurian expert Professor Eugene Vinaver of Manchester University. They had been invited by the Duke of Northumberland to inspect a manuscript in the Percy family's collection; and in his excitement, Steinbeck dashed off an incautious report of their 'discovery' to *Newsday*, his Long Island newspaper.

When the British press embellished it as a 'Malory' manuscript

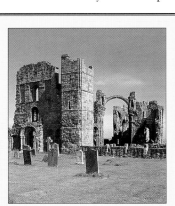

Dry shod, o'er sands, twice every day,
The pilgrims to the shrine find way;
Twice every day, the waves efface
Of staves and sandall'd feet the trace.

Sir Walter Scott, *Marmion*, Canto 2 - Holy Island, Northumbria.

The mortal remains of St Cuthbert and the Venerable Bede were both moved several times before they were enshrined at Durham, where a magnificent Norman cathedral rises above the city and the wooded banks of the River Wear.

Alnwick Castle, home of the Percy family and the Dukes of Northumberland since the beginning of the 14th century. In 1364 it was the birthplace of rebel Sir Henry Percy, Shakespeare's Harry Hotspur, killed in battle by Prince Hal in Henry IV part I.

find, Vinaver's academic standing and Steinbeck's confidence were both undermined, and he abandoned his research (and the Kennedy book) for good. The truth was that Steinbeck was afraid his project was as flawed as Sir Launcelot, the knight who betrayed his king and friend through his love for Guinevere.

Knowing how important the subject had been to Steinbeck, his widow agreed the research should be published and *The Acts of King Arthur and His Noble Knights* appeared posthumously in 1976.

John Ruskin's first visit to Wallington, the Northumbrian home of the Trevelyan family, north-west of Newcastle, made a lasting impact on Ruskin's life – and the house. In 1853 he arrived with his young wife Effie and the artist John Everett Millais to visit Pauline, Lady Trevelyan. Wallington is said to be the place where Effie and Millais

Sir Walter and Lady Pauline Trevelyan made Wallington (right) famous for the gardens, and for Lady Pauline's 'circle'. As well as Ruskin, her friends included Swinburne (grandson of a neighbouring landowner), biographer Augustus Hare, and Christina Rossetti, said to be in love with Bell Scott.

fell in love and certainly within a few weeks she had decided to divorce Ruskin and marry Millais.

The effect of their visit on the house was happier. Lady Pauline greatly admired Ruskin and followed his preference for the Pre-Raphaelite style as decoration for Wallington's huge hall. Most of the murals and designs were commissioned from William Bell Scott, but some were painted by Ruskin, Lady Pauline and her friends.

Morden Tower, part of the old city walls in Newcastle upon Tyne, has become an important place for modern poetry. Restored in the 1960s as a literature performance centre, it provides a platform for local writers like the late Basil Bunting, author of the Northumbrian poem *Briggflatts*, whose work owes much to Ezra Pound.

Allen Ginsberg and other 'Beat Generation' poets of the 1950s have made their way here, followed by Roger McGough and the 'Liverpool Poets' of the 1960s; and by Nobel Prize winner Seamus Heaney, whose first collection *Death of a Naturalist* appeared in 1966.

NORTH YORKSHIRE –
THE DALES TO
THE SEA

'Herriot Country' began to spread through North Yorkshire when Alf Wight, vet, went to work at Thirsk, an old market town that lies between the North York Moors and the Yorkshire Dales.

In 1970, using the pen-name James Herriot, Wight published his first story, *If Only They Could*

Talk, about a vet living in so-called Darrowby. Next came *All Creatures Great and Small*, the television series and a film version. Very soon fact, fiction and film were firmly fused into 'James Herriot's Yorkshire'.

Follow Alf and James from Thirsk, up the Hambleton Hills to Sutton Bank Top and there below is their favourite view: 'all things bright and beautiful' in the moors and dales, dotted with traditional villages and market towns that 'both' vets knew for almost half a century.

Thirsk has most claim to be Darrowby. Wight had his vet's surgery in Kirkgate, the museum has displays about him and one of his manuscripts, and his home was nearby at Thirlby. But imaginary Darrowby uses bits of Richmond, Leyburn and Middleham too, and Richmond museum has the film-set for the Farnon-Herriot surgery.

Deeper into Swaledale and Wensleydale are the villages and beauty spots picked out on local Herriot trails: Aysgarth waterfalls and Askrigg village, Wensley church, Reeth, and Hawes, where the old railway station has become the Dales Countryside Museum.

Harrogate, renamed Brawton, was the town James and Helen Herriot would make for when James had an afternoon 'off' to wander through the gardens and 19th-century streets, and sit over tea in Betty's café.

Built as a spa town, Harrogate made headlines in 1926 when Agatha Christie did her disappearing act - still as much a mystery as any of her books.

Knowing her husband was having an affair, Mrs Christie drove away from their Berkshire home one night in December and vanished. Her car was found abandoned, newpapers went into over-

drive and rewards were offered for information.

Nine days later she was 'found' in Harrogate. She had checked in to a hotel, now the Old Swan,

A 'missing person enquiry' at the Old Swan Hotel, Harrogate, ended when Agatha Christie was discovered staying there under an assumed name.

The North Yorkshire Dales (left) and Swaledale (below). Thomas Gray thought them perfectly Picturesque when he toured northern England in the 1760s. Two centuries later Alf Wight turned them into 'James Herriot Country'.

Coxwold village (right) where Laurence Sterne (below) was buried at St Michael's in 1768.

using the name of her husband's lover. She claimed loss of memory, though guests said she was perfectly normal and entertained them on the piano. How or why she managed to hide without leaving a single clue was never explained.

A few miles south-east of Thirsk, at Coxwold, 18th-century novelist Laurence Sterne made his home for the last eight years of his life. 'I am as happy as a prince at Coxwold,' he wrote. 'I sit down alone to venison, fish and wildfowl...and all the simple plenty which a rich valley under the Hambleton Hills can produce.'

Sterne became 'perpetual curate' of St Michael's, Coxwold, in 1760 and moved in to the medieval house now known as Shandy Hall. He had already published the opening chapters of *The Life and Opinions of Tristram Shandy, Gentleman* who was 'brought forth into this scurvy and disastrous world of ours' on 'the fifth day of November, 1718'.

Shandy Hall – the name was a joke, since it was far from a stately hall, though Sterne made many improvements – has a collection of mementoes and rare editions.

the widow Wadman. He went on to write Parson Yorick's *Sentimental Journey* through France and Italy.

Tristram Shandy was a sensation in London in the 1760s, not least because its outrageous humour came from a man in holy orders. Dr Johnson's ponderous pronouncement, 'Nothing odd will do long, *Tristram Shandy* did not last', was well wide of the mark. Its readers range from Jane Austen to Virginia Woolf.

The story is based in the North Riding and, as Sterne's fellow Yorkshire-born novelist Malcolm Bradbury points out, 'the region has much to do with his literary identity'.

Sterne had been vicar of Sutton-on-the-Forest since 1738 and lived for a time in Minster Yard, York. Coxwold seemed to him a 'delicious retreat'. He liked it even more after his wife moved out and he began making plans for his young lover, Eliza Draper, to come and join him.

She never did, but the house and garden have been restored as Sterne hoped she would find them, with the 'sweet sitting room' he prepared for her.

In the comfortable study at Shandy Hall, Sterne continued Tristram's bawdy, satirical, plot-less ramblings about his family and friends, most memorably Uncle Toby, Dr Slop, Parson Yorick and

Count Dracula's landing on the Yorkshire coast at Whitby one sultry August night is among the most spine-chilling storm scenes in fiction. As crowds gather to watch the sea crashing over the harbour, a strange schooner, with all sails set, is driven on to the shore.

Strangest of all, Bram Stoker goes on, 'the very instant the shore was touched, an immense dog...jumped from the bow on to

the sand'. The 'dog', Dracula, makes for the churchyard on the cliffs and waits to vampirise his victim, Lucy, before he leaves Whitby, 'un-dead' in a wooden box on a train bound for London.

Abraham Stoker began writing *Dracula* in 1895, staying on the coast of Scotland. But he knew Whitby from earlier visits to the little port, and his detailed, happy pictures of Whitby Abbey, Lucy in the Crescent, and Mina sitting in the sun in St Mary's churchyard, make Dracula's arrival all the more sinister.

In Mrs Gaskell's novel *Sylvia's Lovers*, St Mary's becomes St Nicholas, parish church of imaginary Monkshaven, and she describes its many memorials to

'mariners, shipowners, seamen' who conducted Whitby's whaling trade.

Published in 1863, Elizabeth Gaskell's story tells of the press-gangs who 'worked' their way through Whitby seizing sailors during the Napoleonic wars. She stayed a fortnight in a house on the corner of Abbey Terrace, researching it: her first full-length work after *The Life of Charlotte Brontë*.

The official biography of her dear friend Charlotte had been a painful business, though it took Mrs Gaskell to many of the North Country cities, beauty spots and spas that the Brontë sisters had known.

At Bridlington, holidaying with an old school friend, Ellen Nussey, Charlotte lodged on the Esplanade in September 1830, and had her first sight of the sea. Watching the waves she 'could not speak till she had shed some tears', Ellen recalled years later. In the 1850s, writing *Villette*, Charlotte returned to Bridlington and she is believed to have made it the model for the 'clean and ancient town of Bretton'.

Ellen was with Charlotte again in May 1849, bringing Anne Brontë to pass her last hours at Scarborough. Emily Brontë had died in December and Anne was clearly too ill to live long. She had to be carried for most of the journey, yet she was determined to see York Minster and hear once more the sound of the

*A*braham, 'Bram', Stoker (1847-1912) published Dracula in 1897.

*B*y St Mary's, Whitby (left), Mina joins the visitors who sit 'all day long looking at the beautiful view and enjoying the breeze', till nightfall, when Dracula claims his first victim.

*I*n 1859 Mrs Gaskell paid a visit to Whitby's ruined abbey, where (so the Venerable Bede said) a 7th-century cowherd, Caedmon, became the first recorded English poet when he was divinely inspired to interpret the Scriptures in verse.

York's ancient streets were the 'stage' for some of the earliest plays in English, the York Mystery Cycle, performed on Holy Days, generally the Feast of Corpus Christi, and popular in the 14th century. The York 'cycle', or sequence, contains 48 plays in rhyming verse, based on Bible stories and performed on 'pageant wagons' at different sites around the city. Though many towns possessed their own plays only four 'cycles' survive, from Chester, Wakefield, Coventry and York – where they are still re-enacted every four years.

When Matthew Bramble reaches Scarborough (right) in Smollett's Humphrey Clinker *(1771), he tries the new fad of sea-bathing and suffers an embarrassing rescue from the water.*

Edith Sitwell (1887-1964), modernist, style-setter and author of Façade, *poems she called 'patterns in sound', set to music by William Walton.*

sea at Scarborough, where she had stayed as a governess.

Charlotte took rooms for them at a lodging house (the site is covered by the Grand Hotel) and, with Ellen's help, carried Anne to the beach, and to church.

Three days after they arrived, Anne died. 'I did not think it would come so soon,' Charlotte wrote, and buried Anne at St Mary's, Scarborough – to spare her father yet another interment at the family vault in Haworth.

Brontë sisters apart, Scarborough's spirit is generally more entertaining, especially since it has become home base for prolific, present-day playwright Alan Ayckbourn.

In *How the Other Half Loves, Absurd Person Singular* and a stream of stage and television successes, Ayckbourn turns middle-class marital failure into endless comedy.

Most of his work is premièred at Scarborough's Stephen Joseph Theatre.

Edith Sitwell and her brothers, Osbert and Sacheverell, spent much of their aristocratic childhood at Scarborough, in grand houses in the Crescent area. Edith was born in 1887 at Wood End (now a natural history museum, with Sitwell books and pictures in the restored West Wing). Sacheverell was born a decade later in Belvoir Terrace. Osbert was born in between, but in London.

Their mother's family owned Londesborough Lodge, next-door-but-one to Wood End, and long periods were spent there as

well. It had a private bridge, Osbert recalled, where yards of red carpet were unrolled whenever their grandparents walked to the beach.

For sheer style and eccentricity, the Sitwells would sparkle even in a group graced by Anthony Powell, author of *A Dance to the Music of Time*, John Betjeman and Evelyn Waugh. They would live in more splendid houses: Renishaw Hall near Sheffield, as Osbert recounts in *Left Hand: Right Hand*; Weston Hall in

Northamptonshire; and in Italy and London. Yet judging by Edith's *Façade*, Osbert's *Before the Bombardment*, and Sacheverell's *The People's Palace*, Scarborough left lasting impressions.

A few miles north of York is Castle Howard, one of the grandest houses in the country, designed in 1699 by Sir John Vanbrugh.

He had made his name in London as a stylish, witty playwright, author of *The Relapse* and *The Provok'd Wife* but as an architect he was a complete novice. His design, nonetheless, was a triumph. He went on to create Blenheim Palace for the Duke of

Marlborough, Audley End, and Stowe (now a school). But thanks to television Vanbrugh's Castle Howard is for ever linked to novelist Evelyn Waugh and *Brideshead Revisited*, published 1945.

Waugh visited the house in 1937 and its baroque grandeur is a good match for his vision of England's aristocratic past. As his friends realised, though, Waugh's remorseless black comedy about bright-young-things was really based on the Lygon family, who lived at Madresfield in Worcestershire. And his old friend Nancy Mitford was soon writing to tell him that she'd guessed.

M alham Tarn, a large natural lake high up in the Dales National Park near Settle, gave Charles Kingsley the

setting for the story of young Tom and *The Water Babies*.

Kingsley was staying at Tarn House (now a field studies centre)

and it became his Harthover House, 'built at ninety different times and in nineteen different styles', where Tom arrives to clean the chimneys and runs away covered in soot.

'There has been a great black smudge all down the crag ever since,' Kingsley explains, describing Tom's journey over the fells and down the limestone cliffs near Malham.

At the bottom, Tom jumps into the cool, clear limestone stream. 'I will be a fish; I will swim in the water; I must be clean', he cries, entering the magic world of the

'Nobody informed me that at one view I should see a palace, a town, a fortified city, temples on high places' – Horace Walpole on first seeing Castle Howard, now known for its role in Brideshead Revisited.

York Minster has one of the finest cathedral libraries in the country, housed in a 13th-century chapel in a corner of the Minster Close. Among its treasures are prayer books, breviaries, manuscripts, and the beautiful York Missal with richly painted blue and gold letters glowing from the yellowing pages.

water babies and Mrs Doasyouwouldbedoneby.

It was published in 1863 – four years after Darwin's *Origin of Species* – as Kingsley's own version of evolution.

*M*alham Tarn in Yorkshire, where Charles Kingsley based his fairy-tale, The Water Babies, *intended to explain to children that survival depends on the state of their souls, not their bodies.* Westward Ho! *had already made him popular;* Hereward the Wake *would follow before he died in 1875.*

WEST YORKSHIRE MOORS

*F*rom the day the Rev. Patrick Brontë acquired the living and Parsonage of Haworth in 1820, his children were surrounded by a heady mixture of wild landscape, Romantic literature, and death – ever present in the family and in the graveyard beside their home.

Charlotte, Emily and Anne were free - unusually so for the age - to explore the remote and rugged moorland, while their minds roamed the works of Lord Byron and Sir Walter Scott.

They shared the sombre, windswept house (now enlarged and kept as a museum) with a brilliant, weak and drunken brother, Branwell; an authoritarian aunt; Emily's dog Keeper; and their increasingly blind, querulous father – who outlived them all.

It is little wonder that their first published novels, *Jane Eyre*, *Wuthering Heights* and *Agnes Grey*, were so spiked with raw emotion and realism that they raised Victorian eyebrows, at once scan-

'*W*here, behind Keighley...the church
Stands on the crest of the hill,
Lonely and bleak; – at its side
The parsonage-house and the graves.'
Haworth Churchyard, Matthew Arnold, 1855.

dalising and titillating their readers.

Thackeray's verdict on Charlotte, 'there's a fire raging in that little woman' could not have been more true. Critic G. H. Lewes, thinking of the thunder and lightning that crash across across the night sky as Mr Rochester asks Jane Eyre to marry him, suggested Charlotte should study Jane Austen and tone down the melodrama.

All three sisters wrote in the same house, absorbed the same moorland spirit and shared similar shyness. They adopted filial pseudonyms: Currer, Ellis and Acton Bell. Yet if the Parsonage Museum preserves anything among their possessions and portraits, it is the hints of their different characters.

Anne, the youngest, ringlets falling round an oval face, looks gentle, melancholic. She was bruised by Branwell's drinking, which she described in *The Tenant of Wildfell Hall*, and by years as a governess, recycled into *Agnes Grey*.

Emily – taller, angular, stoic, mystic – was homesick whenever she was uprooted and denied the freedom of the moors. Her favourite footpath (now marked) leads past the ruined building known as Top Withens, her *Wuthering Heights*, to Ponden Hall, claimed the original Thrushcross Grange.

Charlotte, the eldest, was smaller, dumpy, short-sighted. In her letters she comes and goes, one minute prim, blunt, bossy; the next struggling to be conventional, fighting down her desire for Monsieur Heger in Brussels. In *Villette* she made her feelings for him far too public for Madame Heger's liking. With *Jane Eyre* she caused uproar by revealing the savage regime at Cowan Bridge school in Lancashire which hastened the death of her two elder sisters.

Despite the Brontës' small output (one novel by Emily, two from Anne, four and a bit by Charlotte, and poems from all three) curiosity soon turned on them and their home. Readers refused to believe that the frankly passionate stories were written by three women. If so, they must be the work of brazen women, never the spinster daughters of a country parson.

Emily was spared much of the criticism of *Wuthering Heights* as violent and morbid: she died in December 1848, refusing all medicine and help.

'No need now to tremble for the hard frost and the keen wind. Emily does not feel them,' Charlotte wrote on December 21st. 'I now look at Anne, and wish she were well and strong; but she is neither.'

Emily was buried in the family vault at Haworth (there is a memorial, though the church has been rebuilt). Anne died the following summer, and in 1855 Charlotte died at Haworth Parsonage, soon after she married the Rev. Arthur Nicholls.

Newspaper reports of Charlotte's death and her 'official biography' by her friend Mrs Gaskell generated still more curiosity, more visitors to Haworth. Matthew Arnold was one of the first, recording his thoughts in *Haworth Churchyard*.

Since then every place the Brontës knew has been marked and mapped on a 40-mile Brontë Way. It takes in the Black Bull Hotel in Haworth, one of Branwell's drinking haunts; their birthplace at Thornton; and Wycoller Country Park with its ruined hall, said to be Ferndean Manor in *Jane Eyre*.

The Brontë sisters – Anne, Emily and Charlotte – painted c.1834 by their brother Branwell.

Pack Horse Bridge at Wycoller, an abandoned hamlet thought to have inspired Oliver Goldsmith's poem The Deserted Village *(1770).*

*The Red House,
home of Charlotte
Brontë's schoolfriends
Mary and Martha
Taylor, was the model
for Briarmains in her
novel* Shirley, *and its
owners were based on
the lively, liberal-
minded Taylors.*

South-east lies
'Shirley Country': the
Red House Museum
at Gomersal and
Oakwell Hall Country
Park have details of
their links with
Charlotte and her spir-
ited heroine Shirley
Keeldar. Closer to
Halifax stands Shibden
Hall (now a folk museum), another
claimant for Thrushcross Grange.
And surrounding them all lie the
Yorkshire moors and Calder Valley
that inspired Emily's poetry.

first volume, *The Hawk in the
Rain*, published 1957, had already
established him as a North
Country 'nature' poet.

His work, by turns tender and
brutal, still draws startling images
from the jagged Yorkshire landscape he described in his earlier
poems: *Bridestones Moor,
Hardcastle Crags* and the *Pennines
in April*.

In Devon Sylvia Plath published her first poems and a semi-
autobiographical novel, though
most of her work, *Ariel* and
Winter Trees, appeared after her
death.

In 1963, having previously suffered a nervous breakdown and
made suicide attempts, Plath took
her own life and was buried near
Hebden Bridge at Heptonstall
Cemetery – the subject of one of
Hughes's poems.

*Oakwell Hall at
Birstall, the origi-
nal for Shirley's own
home – known to
Charlotte Brontë from
visits to her friend Ellen
Nussey.*

'Moors are a stage for the
performance of heaven.
Any audience is inci-
dental,' wrote Ted Hughes (Poet
Laureate since 1984) in *Remains
of Elmet*. His Elmet was also
inspired by the Calder Valley, and
the book is a return to the countryside where he was born in
1930 at Mytholmroyd, just south
of Haworth.

As a student at Cambridge he
met American poet Sylvia Plath.
They married in 1956 and moved
to America for a couple of years.
When they returned to England in
1959 it was to settle in Devon
where Hughes still lives. But his

Phyllis Bentley, born in
Halifax in 1894, wrote more
than 20 books set in the
Calder and Colne valleys. She wit-

*Bridestones Moor,
Calderdale, the
rough, powerful
Pennine landscape of
Ted Hughes's poems:
'Hoisting heather and
stones to the sky'.*

nessed the growing dole-queues outside the textile mills in the 1930s and cast her best-known book, *Inheritance*, back into the days of Victorian industrial power.

'Real incidents, persons and places put me in mind to write this book,' she explained; only the name Ire Valley, and the mill-owning Oldroyds and Bamforths were invented. She was still publishing *Tales of the West Riding* in 1974, three years before she died.

Bentley was encouraged to write by two fellow-writers from the region: Winifred Holtby and Vera Brittain.

Winifred Holtby was born at Rudston in the East Riding of Yorkshire in 1898 and buried there, only 38 years later, at All Saints' (it has a memorial). She used the area in her first novel, *Anderby Wold*, and in her last, *South Riding*, the story of left-wing headmistress Sarah Burton, at odds with the community and with her husband.

South Riding reflects Winifred's own political interests, which took root in Yorkshire and grew at Somerville College, Oxford, where she became a close friend of Vera Brittain.

Vera's tribute to Winifred, *Testament of Friendship*, was the second volume of Brittain's trilogy. In 1933 she had published *Testament of Youth*, an intensely moving account of the years 1900 to 1925. *Testament of Experience* would follow in 1957.

While rural Yorkshire and the Ridings have the Brontës, Ted Hughes, Phyllis Bentley and Winifred Holtby, the modern industrial cities have their own writers. Bradford has J. B. Priestley; Leeds has Alan Bennett and Barbara Taylor Bradford; Bingley has John Braine. Hull has 17th-century poet Andrew Marvell and 20th-century Philip Larkin.

Larkin came to the city in 1935 as university librarian and stayed till he died 30 years later. He averaged only three poems a year, yet he became the leader of the 1950s New Poetry Movement and embodied its 'ordinariness' in his most popular poem, *The Whitsun Weddings*, based on a train journey from Hull.

Andrew Marvell was three when his family moved to Hull in 1624 after his father, the vicar of Winestead, was appointed to Holy Trinity church. He attended the Old Grammar School (now a her-

itage centre) and served as MP for Hull from 1659 until his death in 1678. Most of his adult life was spent in London and abroad, but he still had Hull in mind as he wrote his best-known poem

*V*era Brittain, born in Newcastle under Lyme, 1893. She grew up at Buxton and published her First World War experiences in Testament of Youth.

*M*etaphysical poet Andrew Marvell (1621-1678) came from Winestead, near the mouth of the Humber.

*H*ull, where Marvell's father was vicar of Holy Trinity (left), has an annual literature festival that features local people from Marvell to Larkin, Stevie Smith and current authors.

J. B. Priestley relaxing in 1941 between his popular wartime broadcasts. During his English Journey *(1934) he returned to his native Bradford, noting that it still 'has the good fortune to be on the edge of some of the most enchanting country in England.'*

To His Coy Mistress –

*Had we but World enough,
   and Time,
This coyness Lady were no
   crime...
Thou by the Indian Ganges
   side
Should'st Rubies find: I by the
   Tide
Of Humber would complain...
But at my back I alwaies hear
Times winged Chariot
   hurrying near.*

Bradford City Hall's bell tolled every minute for an hour when John Boynton Priestley died in 1984. He hadn't lived in the city for 70 years, but he was – like his statue – robust, round-faced, and rooted in Bradford.

He was born in Mannheim Road in 1894, moved to Saltburn Place 10 years later and went to Belle Vue Boys' School (it has a memorial window in the Priestley Hall). He worked as a wool-office clerk in the city and left to fight in the 1914-18 war.

'Part of me is still in Bradford, can never leave it,' he wrote years later. It had given him a love of the theatre, pubs, and the moors. He made it the model for Bruddersford in *The Good Companions*, about a troupe of actors on the road, which made Priestley's name as a popular writer in 1929.

Though he personified the bluff, no-nonsense Yorkshireman, Priestley's work had international appeal. He produced hundreds of books, articles, scripts and plays, including *An Inspector Calls* and the Yorkshire-based comedy *When We Are Married*.

Priestley's statue in Bradford, the city known as Bruddersford to Jess Oakroyd and The Good Companions.

Like Priestley, Barbara Taylor Bradford was a journalist before her block-buster novel *A Woman of Substance* made her a household name in 1979. She was born in Leeds in 1933, worked on the *Yorkshire Evening Post* and moved on to papers and magazines in London.

She had been living in America for some years when she used Leeds and the Yorkshire Dales as the background for her rags-to-royalties story of Emma Harte. Emma becomes a woman of such substance that her empire stretches all the way from a Leeds department store to America and Australia. When it passes to her granddaughter, in *Hold the Dream* and *To be the Best*, Paula carries on the business and the links with Yorkshire.

Leeds was also the birthplace, in 1934, of playwright Alan Bennett whose wry, self-deprecating (almost Eeyore-ian) humour carefully expresses his North Country background.

From school in Leeds, Bennett went to Oxford

J.B.PRIESTLEY O.M.

and became part of the university review *Beyond the Fringe*, produced for the Edinburgh Festival of 1960. After two stage plays, *Forty Years On* and *Getting On*, Bennett turned to screen writing, with the *Talking Heads* series (one set in Harrogate) and *A Private Function*. But he has since scored more stage successes with *The Madness of George III* and an outstanding adaptation of Kenneth Grahame's *The Wind in the Willows*.

Bingley, a wool town on the edge of Ilkley Moor, is the setting for one of the classics of 1950s anti-romantic fiction, *Room at the Top*, written by Bradford-born John Braine. It charts Joe Lampton's ruthless rise

from the narrow streets of a typical northern town, to a house on a hill and a wealthy marriage – abandoning Alice, the woman he used to meet on Ilkley Moor.

'I've always loved Bingley,' and *Room at the Top* was really Joe Lampton's 'affair with a little Yorkshire town', Braine explained. He thought Bingley's section of the Leeds-Liverpool canal 'the loveliest stretch of canal in the whole of England', and he was buried in the local cemetery in 1986.

When *Room at the Top*

appeared in 1957 it put Braine among the best of the Angry Young Men: a wave (they rejected 'group' status) of new, mostly provincial, young writers.

Between 1953 and 1960, they subjected complacent, class-ridden Britain to a full-frontal attack: starting with *Hurry on Down* by John Wain, born in Stoke-on-Trent, and *Lucky Jim*, Kingsley Amis's first and best book, based on a 'redbrick' university. Then came John Osborne's *Look Back in Anger*, set in Birmingham, and Alan Sillitoe's Nottingham-based *Saturday Night and Sunday Morning*. And finally there was *A Kind of Loving* in fictional Cressley, by Stan Barstow, who was born at Horbury, south-east of Bradford, and has returned to live at Haworth.

NORTH-WEST PASSAGES

John Masefield, Poet Laureate 1930 to 1967, came to Liverpool as a boy of 13 and joined a merchant navy training ship. He gave up the sea four years later and tried various careers before making his name as a writer. When he did, in 1902, it was with a volume of *Salt Water Ballads*, including 'Sea Fever', in which he explains his coming to Merseyside.

He would write almost 100 volumes of plays, poems, novels and articles, some closely associated

> *I must go down to the seas*
> *again, to the lonely sea and*
> *the sky,*
> *And all I ask is a tall ship,*
> *and a star to steer her by*
>
> John Masefield, *Sea Fever*.

John Masefield (1878-1967) sailed round Cape Horn at the age of 15, before becoming a poet, novelist, dramatist, friend of W. B. Yeats and the 'Dymock Poets'.

Ilkley Moor gave John Braine the background to one of the powerful 1950s regional novels, Room at the Top, *which he followed with* Life at the Top *in 1962.*

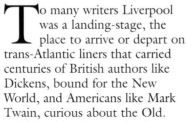

*N*ear Liverpool's Albert Dock, now an award-winning museum, American novelist Nathaniel Hawthorne (below right, 1804-1864) worked in an office on the corner of Brunswick Street.

*H*erman Melville, born in New York City 1819, published Moby-Dick in 1851, but died in obscurity 40 years later, before completing Billy Budd.

with Ledbury, his childhood home, and Oxford, where he lived later. But his enduringly popular work is his children's fantasy, *The Box of Delights* (the spine-tingling scenes 'When the Wolves were Running' predate, and are at least as good as, C. S. Lewis's *Narnia*), and the poems, like *Cargoes*, based on the voyages that began by the docks.

To many writers Liverpool was a landing-stage, the place to arrive or depart on trans-Atlantic liners that carried centuries of British authors like Dickens, bound for the New World, and Americans like Mark Twain, curious about the Old.

The oddest literary landing was radical writer Tom Paine's in 1819: his ardent apostle William Cobbett returned from America bringing Paine's bones in a box with his baggage.

Cobbett had exhumed them determined that they should be repatriated with greater honour. Unfortunately, he could get neither permission to re-bury them, nor money for a monument 'to the common sense of the great man'. After Cobbett's death in 1835, Paine's mortal remains were somehow mislaid. Most arrivals

caused less of a stir among the grand buildings that still line Liverpool's waterfront.

Herman Melville shipped here as a cabin boy in 1839 and described the voyage in *Redburn*, where his young hero spends six weeks exploring Liverpool.

A decade later Melville was in England again (shortly before publishing *Moby-Dick*), though his account of the trip did not appear until long after his death in 1891.

Melville dedicated *Moby-Dick* to his compatriot and friend Nathaniel Hawthorne, who came to Liverpool as American consul in 1853. Leaving America just after he published *The Scarlet Letter* and *The House of the Seven Gables*, Hawthorne stayed four years. He didn't entirely enjoy working here but it gave him material for his essays *Our Old Home* and *Passages from the English Notebooks*, published posthumously in 1870.

Harriet Beecher Stowe had an enthusiastic reception when she arrived in Liverpool in 1853, the year after she published *Uncle Tom's Cabin*. She wrote up her visit as *Sunny Memories of Foreign Lands*, called on Mrs Gaskell in Manchester and, on her second visit, was honoured by Queen Victoria.

Samuel Langhorne Clemens, better known as Mark Twain, also

received a royal reception when he came to Britain in 1907. It was one of several trips before and after he wrote *The Adventures of Tom Sawyer* and *Huckleberry Finn*. This time he was on his way to Oxford to receive an honorary degree.

For lots of authors Merseyside has been far more than a port of call. Wilfred Owen's family lived here for almost a decade, in the Birkenhead district, and the Central Library has a memorial window to the First World War poet. They arrived in 1898 and in 1907 returned to Shropshire where Wilfred had been born.

For Beryl Bainbridge and Helen Forrester Liverpool was a home and a community with a history to write about.

Beryl Bainbridge was born here in 1934 and from her first novel in 1967, *A Weekend with Claude*, to *The Dressmaker*, and the bittersweet story of *An Awfully Big Adventure* (based on her time at the Liverpool 'rep' theatre) she is, she says, 'committing to paper episodes I have lived through'.

Helen Forrester, now writing best-sellers in Canada, was a child in 'the struggling, poverty-stricken Liverpool of the 1930s'. She sets several novels in the city – *Thursday's Child*, *Liverpool Daisy*, and *Three Women of Liverpool*; and tells of her own Liverpool story in four volumes of autobiography, including *Twopence to Cross the Mersey*.

By the beginning of the 1960s,

the most inventive writing round Merseyside was coming from the 'Liverpool Poets' – Adrian Henri, Roger McGough and Brian Patten, whose joint volumes *The Mersey Sound* and *The Liverpool Scene* appeared in 1967.

They were part of the young, exuberant, 'non-square' Mersey culture that swept Britain with the music of the Beatles, whose own verses include some of the loveliest lyrics of the 20th century. Tracking the Beatles round Merseyside, down 'Penny Lane' and Mathew Street (tours and site details from the Tourist Information Centre) naturally leads through the landscape of the 'Liverpool Poets'.

Knowsley, north-east of Liverpool, is the birthplace of some of the most comical books in English. *Illustrations of the Family of Psittacidae* is not one of them. It is a serious folio of brilliant bird pictures, drawn at London Zoo in 1831. But without it Edward Lear would never have come to Merseyside and might never have produced *A Book of Nonsense*.

Lear's exquisite bird books caught the eye of Lord Stanley, who had formed a private menagerie at Knowsley Hall (now open as Knowsley Safari Park) and he commissioned Lear to draw his rare animals. From 1832 to 1837, Lear spent most of his time at Knowsley either painting or entertaining the Stanley children with comic animal sketches, rhymes and limericks.

Gathering them together, with

W. Holman Hunt's portrait of Edward Lear, whose genius for comic rhymes came to light in Liverpool, is part of the collection in the city's Walker Art Gallery. By popular demand Lear enlarged his Book of Nonsense *twice and it went into 30 editions before he died in 1888.*

William Harrison Ainsworth (1805-1882) had already written The Tower of London, Old St Paul's *and* Windsor Castle *before his tale of local sorcery made him 'The Lancashire Novelist'.*

Tatton Park, near Knutsford, the original for Cumnor Towers in Mrs Gaskell's last novel Wives and Daughters.

Conditions in Old Manchester, deplored by Victorian novelists, are recreated, complete with sewer, in the city's museum.

more verses and drawings, he published *A Book of Nonsense* in 1846 (the year he was summoned to give Queen Victoria drawing lessons on the Isle of Wight). In 1871 came *Nonsense Songs, Stories, Botany and Alphabets*, containing 'The Jumblies' who 'went to sea in a sieve' and:

> *The Owl and the Pussy-cat*
> *went to sea*
> *In a beautiful pea-green boat,*
> *They took some honey, and*
> *plenty of money*
> *Wrapped up in a five-pound*
> *note.*

Manchester in the 1840s seemed to Benjamin Disraeli's young hero *Coningsby* a dream city where modern machinery, steam and science were propelling the nation into a new era of prosperity.

To Mrs Elizabeth Gaskell and her young heroine *Mary Barton*, it was a place of poverty, disease and death. And Mrs Gaskell had the edge over Disraeli – even over reformers like Dickens and Carlyle: she was living in the middle of it.

Elizabeth had moved here in 1832 when she married William Gaskell, Unitarian minister of Cross Street Chapel. Twelve years later she wrote *Mary Barton: A Tale of Manchester Life*, one of the most powerful mid-19th-century 'condition of England' novels. Soon she was hosting one of the leading literary salons outside London. At her home in Plymouth Grove (number 84,

used by Manchester University for students) she entertained Charlotte Brontë, Harriet Beecher Stowe, Charles Dickens and many others.

Dickens was not always complimentary about Mrs Gaskell, yet he serialised her stories in his weekly journal *Household Words* from its March 1850 launch onwards. In September 1854, he began running her second Manchester novel *North and South*. It wasn't entirely

her fault that magazine sales dropped. Dickens said the book was too long; she wouldn't cut it. Yet *he* chose to publish it straight after his own strikingly similar *Hard Times*, the story of Thomas Gradgrind's industrial city Coketown, based partly on Preston.

If Mrs Gaskell's Manchester is now to be found only in the city's award-winning Museum of Science and Industry, her *Cranford* is alive and well at Knutsford, one of the prettiest, Georgian towns in Cheshire.

Elizabeth grew up there with an aunt (her mother died soon after Elizabeth was born, in London, in 1810) living in a handsome, brick house (with a plaque) facing the heath, in what is now Gaskell Avenue.

Knutsford remains as she described it, a 'pleasant little country town', where 'life moved gradually, not in a hurry'. It is still a place to saunter among the many 18th-century shops and houses she knew, along the two parallel roads known locally as 'top' and 'bottom' streets.

It is easy to picture the *Cranford* ladies meeting 'at the door under the carriage way' to the inn, ready to see the magician. Or modest Molly, in *Wives and Daughters*, wandering through the town, renamed Hollingford. In the centre are a Gaskell Memorial Tower and St John the Baptist's church where Elizabeth married William Gaskell.

At the bottom of the hill is Brook Street chapel where Elizabeth worshipped until she moved to Manchester. She set several scenes here in her story *Ruth*; and was buried at the chapel in 1865.

The hanging of the Pendle Witches at Lancaster Castle (left) depicted in a 17th-century woodcut. Their story, preserved in a court report, was used by Ainsworth for his novel, and is now on video in Pendle Heritage Centre, Barrowford.

Manchester gave a mayoral dinner in the Town Hall for novelist William Harrison Ainsworth in 1881, the year before he died. It also bestowed on him the title 'The Lancashire Novelist', partly on account of his thrilling story of *The Lancashire Witches*, which he had published over 30 years before.

Ainsworth was born in King Street in 1805 and went to Manchester Grammar School, in premises then near the cathedral. At 19 he left for London to finish his legal training but went into publishing and writing within a couple of years. He wrote numerous historical novels, packed with characters, romance and melodrama that Victorian readers found irresistible.

The Lancashire Witches was based on legends of witchcraft at Pendle Hill, beside ruined Whalley Abbey, where crone rivalry came to a head in 1612. When a passing pedlar died, caught in the crossfire of curses, the Pendle witches were brought to trial and hanged at Lancaster Castle (the court rooms and dungeons are open).

All Saints' church at Daresbury in Cheshire has a large, colourful window to Lewis Carroll, creator of the Mad Hatter, the Dormouse, the March Hare, and the Gryphon who 'Alice did not quite like the look of'. Carroll, pen-name of Charles Lutwidge Dodgson, was born at Daresbury parsonage on January 27, 1832 and lived there till he was 11. On Sundays he would sit listening to Papa preach from the Jacobean pulpit, still in place at All Saints', richly carved with angels and, some say, a gryphon.

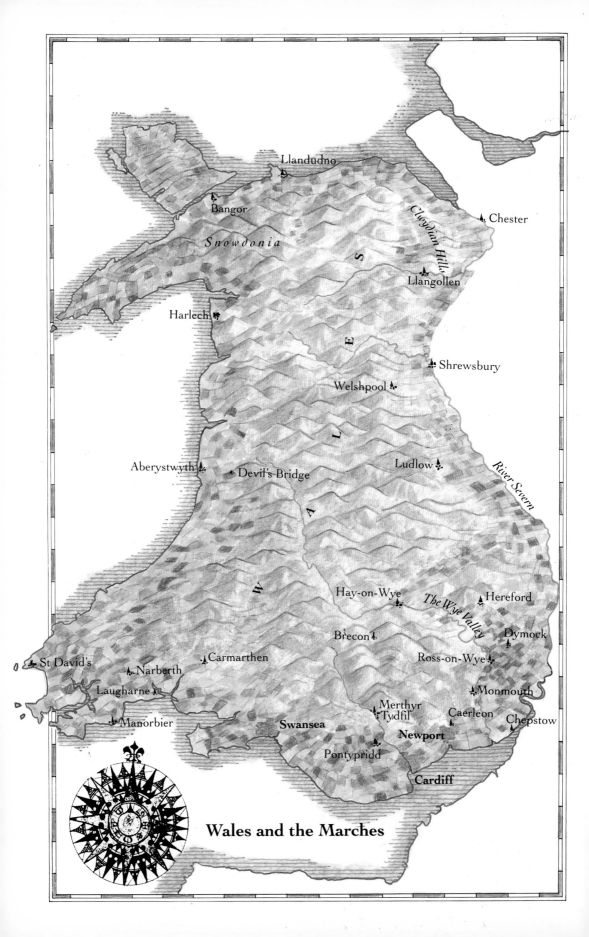

Wales and the Marches

CHAPTER 8

WALES AND
THE MARCHES

CELTIC MYTHS AND CHRONICLES

Of all the literature Wales has produced, its greatest contribution to European culture is the legend of King Arthur.

Arthur's first 'chronicler' was Geoffrey of Monmouth, believed to be a Benedictine monk born around 1100, who became Archdeacon of Monmouth. He was made Bishop of St Asaph in North Wales as well, but died before entering the diocese.

Geoffrey's so-called *History of the Kings of Britain*, written in Latin shortly before 1150, introduced the story of King Arthur to the world. It was romantic invention rather than history and it became the most popular book of the age. Behind it lie 500 years of folk-tales and sagas, handed down by poets and professional storytellers since the 6th-century Welsh songs of Taliesin and Aneirin - who lived within a generation or two of Arthur himself.

Taliesin was a Mid-Wales poet whose reputation was so great that a village, Tre-Taliesin, grew up near his supposed grave, a few miles north of Aberystwyth. He even became part of Arthurian legend, named as one of the Round Table in Lord Tennyson's poem *Idylls of the King*.

Aneirin is an equally shadowy figure, but as he and Taliesin sang the praises of great lords like Arthur, mourned the dead in battle, and encouraged

Wales has the oldest literary tradition in Europe - unbroken from the 6th-century Celtic folk-tales and Arthurian legends preserved in The Mabinogion, *to the present-day poetry of R. S. Thomas.*

Harlech Castle, Gwynedd, the setting for Branwen Daughter of Llyr, *one of* The Mabinogion *folk-tales.*

Narberth Town Hall houses the Landsker Visitor Centre and a colourful exhibition on The Mabinogion *stories.*

A story-board (right) re-tells the tale of Pwyll Prince of Dyfed, one of two local tales full of Celtic magic and humour that are shown in Narberth's exhibition.

ancient Britons to continue the struggle against the invading English, they began the traditions of a heroic age and the conventions of Welsh court-poetry and bardic culture.

Stories of Arthur and his warriors gradually became part of the professional storytellers' standard repertoire, told around the hearth fires on winter nights. Some of the oldest are among the 11 tales known as *The Mabinogion*, recorded in prose in the 11th century; though they preserve much older oral traditions. They tell of local figures and magicians, as well as Arthur, and conjure up an enchanted world of Celtic mystery, based in the Welsh countryside.

Narberth in Pembrokeshire takes its name from Arberth, named in *The Mabinogion* as the place where Pwyll, Prince of Dyfed, held court. At the Landsker Visitor Centre, in Narberth, large colourful storyboards tell two of the local *Mabinogion* tales - how Pwyll, great lord of Dyfed, feasted with the beautiful Rhiannon; and how Monawydan threatened to hang a pregnant mouse for ruining his crops and found a seven-year spell had been cast over his lands.

Geoffrey of Monmouth's inventive *History* pulls together folk-tales and references to Arthur from earlier chronicles and converts them into the romantic figure who eventually emerges as T. H. White's *Once and Future King,* the fully-fledged hero of *Camelot.*

Where some legends claimed Arthur's court was in Cornwall, Geoffrey sets it down in Caerleon, among the remains of the Romans' huge barracks, ramparts, baths and amphitheatre, known locally as King Arthur's Table.

Thomas Malory took the same line in the 15th century in *Le*

Morte Darthur, and Tennyson followed suit. In 1856, working on his lengthy poem *Idylls of the King*, Tennyson came to Caerleon and put up at the Hanbury Arms pub, a place much favoured by local novelist, master-of-the-macabre Arthur Machen (born Arthur Jones) in the 1890s.

Geoffrey of Monmouth claimed Carmarthen as Merlin's birthplace. The name can be translated into Merlin's Town and the country-

side around is dotted with places named for Arthur's magician.

Carmarthen civic hall and the county museum (outside the town) each have a small, sad lump of wood from Merlin's Oak, a tree that stood for centuries in the town centre until it was condemned as a traffic hazard.

Behind the town, rising steeply from the valley, is Merlin's Hill - said to cover the cave where the wizard counsellor is entombed for ever. In an ancient Welsh text known as *The Black Book of Carmarthen*, Merlin wanders around for 50 years after Arthur's death, till he teaches his spells to a wily woman named Vivien and is himself spell-bound inside the cave.

The hill is pierced with old lead mines, whose entrances can be seen half hidden among trees from the road to Llandeilo. This is Mary Stewart's *Hollow Hill* where young Myrddin, born the bastard son of a Welsh princess, pulls back the overhanging branches and finds 'a globe lined with diamonds, a million burning diamonds' in the enchanted world of the *Crystal Cave*.

While Geoffrey of Monmouth was creatively writing history, his near contemporary, Gerald of Wales, was carefully recording a *Journey through Wales* in 1188.

Gerald was the foremost Welsh scholar of his day. He was born at Manorbier Castle around 1146. His grandmother was Princess Nest, his father Lord of Manorbier. As a younger son, Gerald became a priest and his powerful Welsh and Norman family helped him to high office.

He travelled widely in the service of the Church and the king, yet to Gerald, Manorbier and the

Cyfarthfa Castle near Merthyr Tydfil, home of Lady Charlotte Guest, has an exhibition on The Mabinogion, *the 11 medieval Welsh tales which she translated and published in English for the first time. When they appeared between 1838 and 1849 they fuelled the Victorians' passion for Arthurian Romance and became a source for Lord Tennyson's poem* Idylls of the King.

coast of Pembroke remained 'the fairest place in all Wales'.

Looking up from the sheltered little beach towards the castle, it is not difficult to see why. The castle, though smaller than today's great stronghold, was 'excellently well defended by turrets and bulwarks'. He describes the winding valley, the 'stream of water which never fails', the mill and the circular dovecote - so large it could have fed 40 people on pigeon pie twice a week.

As a writer Gerald was prolific. But his ambitions lay in ecclesiastical reform at Brecon, where he was archdeacon, and at St David's, on the far south-west tip of Wales, where he was twice denied the bishopric.

*G*erald of Wales, *Gerald de Barri (c.1146-1223) - 'You may never find anyone worse than a bad Welshman, but you will certainly never find anyone better than a good one.'*

*M*anorbier Castle, *home of the powerful de Barri family, still stands on the Pembrokeshire coast.*

St David's, the smallest cathedral city in Britain, where Gerald was administrator of the diocese from 1176 to 1184.

Remote and ruined Strata Florida Abbey (right), traditional burial place of Dafydd ap Gwilym, greatest of Welsh medieval poets.

Dafydd ap Gwilym (below) is one of the Heroes of Wales in the Marble Hall, Cardiff.

The tiny cathedral settlement of St David's, founded by the patron saint of Wales, Dewi Sant, had become the richest diocese in Wales. It was partly due to its popularity with pilgrims: two journeys here equalled one to Rome, three counted as a trip to Jerusalem.

Gerald's aim was to make St David's more powerful and put himself in charge. When he finally failed he retired to Lincoln to spend the rest of his life writing and editing. But his tomb is said to be in St David's, marked by the faceless figure in the south choir aisle.

Gerald's *Journey through Wales,* in the spring of 1188, had taken him to Llanbadarn Fawr near Aberystwyth, where the monastery produced some of the earliest and finest Welsh manuscripts. Inside the village's 13th-century church is an exhibition about the monastery, its scriptorium, Gerald's visit and another great figure in Welsh literature: Dafydd ap Gwilym.

Born a few miles away at Penrhyn-coch, Dafydd ap Gwilym was the most gifted of all the medieval poets in Wales. The site of his birthplace, Bro Gynin, is sign-

posted from the village and marked with a slate plaque. He came from a family of poets and knew the age-old bardic styles and conventions. Yet when Dafydd sang, around 1320 to 1370, he broke through traditional forms. He uses brilliantly fresh and vivid images to praise nature and women, especially his mistresses, like Morfudd, wife of a local official.

His poems tell of secret love affairs and self-mocking disasters when he tries to keep trysts in the birchwoods. He seems endlessly lost - at night, in mist, in bogs. At

an inn he stumbles around in the dark (in an episode worthy of *Tom Jones*) trying to find a girl's room after buying her dinner and fine wine, only to wake the dogs and the entire household. In *The Girls of Llanbadarn,* he gets a crick in his neck eyeing them from behind his hat in church on Sunday.

Dafydd sang his way through various parts of Wales, sometimes as official poet in the houses of the gentry. But his burial place is debatable. Many believe he lies in the medieval ruins of Strata Florida Abbey, near Tregaron, where a tablet is set in the shade of an ancient yew.

DYLAN THOMAS

'To begin at the beginning', as *Under Milk Wood* does, Dylan Marlais Thomas was born on October 27, 1914, at No.5 Cwmdonkin Drive, in Swansea - 'an ugly, lovely town,' he wrote later, 'crawling, sprawling, slummed...by the side of a long and splendid curving shore'.

No.5 is an unassuming semi on a steep suburban hill in the Uplands area, hemmed in by respectable streets and houses. At the top of the Drive is a flight of steps that leads higher still until the whole of Swansea Bay spreads out below like a map. 'This sea was my world,' he recalled.

Away to the right lies the Gower Peninsula: the countryside and pubs Dylan explored from Mumbles to Rhossili and The Worm, 'the very promontory of depression'.

To the left the River Tawe spills into the sea beside the Maritime Quarter and the brightly-muralled Little Theatre where Dylan made some of his earliest stage appearances. Beside it his statue sits in the square looking across the new marina to a statue of 'Blind Captain Cat' hauling on his bell rope, for ever bent on hearing 'what the women [of Llareggub] are gabbing round the pump'.

As a child in the Uplands, Thomas had discovered a 'world within a world of the sea town': Cwmdonkin Park, 'a place full of terrors and treasures' with 'miniature jungles' ideal for playing Cowboys and Indians. After he died, two friends placed a stone beside the miniature pond, inscribed with a verse from his poem *Fern Hill*,

Dylan soon brought his bride, Caitlin Macnamara, back to Wales to show her off to his family and friends after their wedding in Cornwall in 1937.

> *Oh, as I was young and easy*
> *in the mercy of his means*
> *Time held me green and*
> *dying*
> *Though I sang in my chains*
> *like the sea.*

Fern Hill recalls childhood holidays in the valley of the Towy, around Llangain and Llanstephan, west of Swansea. As always, Dylan was deeply influenced by his surroundings and images of Carmarthenshire fields and shores seep into his poetry.

But the place that most famously influenced him lies further west at Laugharne, a quiet little coastal town described by Dylan as 'the strangest town in Wales'.

In *Under Milk Wood, a play for voices* he transformed Laugharne, pronounced 'larn', into Llaregyb.

The National Library of Wales, Aberystwyth, has an outstanding collection of ancient Welsh books and illuminated manuscripts, some permanently on show. Among the rarest are the 12th-century Black Book of Carmarthen *and the 14th-century* Red Book of Hergest, *containing* The Mabinogion *stories.*

Wales is the only country in the
world that makes a poetry competi-
tion and crowning of the bard into
the centre-piece of its biggest national
event. The Royal National Eisteddfod
preserves the time-honoured customs in a
gathering dedicated to poetry, literature,
music and the arts. It is held in different
parts of the country each year and
enjoyed by thousands - including many
non-Welsh speakers listening to
simultaneous translations.

The Museum of Welsh Life at
St Fagans, Cardiff, has a collection
of bardic chairs, crowns and
Druids' regalia, used at previous
eisteddfodau. Among the 'village' of
traditional buildings re-erected in
St Fagans's grounds is a typical
miners' institute, founded to help
bring books and learning to the miners in The Valleys.

from their cottage in Gosport
Road to a larger house closer to
his and nearer 'the fishingboat-
bobbing sea'.

The lilt and inventiveness of
Thomas's poetry was indebted to
Gerard Manley Hopkins, but the
idea for *Under Milk Wood* was
straight James Joyce. Dylan was
planning, he told Hughes, the

Dylan Thomas's
grave,
Laugharne.

The reverse spelling of Llaregyb
makes Dylan's attitude quite clear
enough without the 'Llareggub'
spelling often used now to make it
more obvious.

When Dylan and Caitlin moved
to Laugharne in 1938, the year
after they were married, Richard
Hughes was living by Laugharne
Castle. Writing there, looking out
on the garden, Hughes had
already earned an international
reputation with what Dylan called
his 'cosmopolitan stories' *A High
Wind in Jamaica* and *In Hazard*.

Pretty soon Hughes arranged
for Dylan and Caitlin to move

story of a town lasting just 24
hours, a 'Welsh Ulysses'.

In fact, he spent almost a
decade wandering and working on
it before he and Caitlin returned
settled at the 'seashaken house on
a breakneck of rocks' that is now
preserved as The Boat House.

Dylan spent his last four years
writing in the tiny blue-painted
work shed, perched on the rocks
even more precariously than the
house. Looking
over the estuary's
'heron priested
shore', he reworked
Under Milk Wood
till it acquired its
famous cast of
Laugharne charac-
ters: Polly Garter,
Organ Morgan,
Dai Bread, Captain
Cat, Mrs Ogmore-
Pritchard and
the Reverend Eli
Jenkins.

The Boat House
(above right)
became Dylan and
Caitlin's home beside
the 'heron priested
shore' in 1949.

Thomas's work shed,
Laugharne. When
he left for his last trip to
America in October
1953, he was working
on two new poems, In
Country Heaven *and*
Elegy.

Here he wrote perhaps his best-remembered poem, *Do Not Go Gentle into that Good Night*. And he drank - heavily: at Brown's Hotel, at the pub on the Grist (since re-named The Under Milk Wood), and throughout his last lecture tour of America, where he died in New York in November 1953, only 39 years old.

He was brought back to Laugharne and buried beneath a simple white cross at St Martin's church, in the new cemetery reached by the footbridge.

THE VALLEYS

Richard Llewellyn's emotionally-charged coal-mining saga, *How Green Was My Valley,* is probably the most popular novel ever written in English by a Welshman.

Set in south-east Wales at the turn of the century, it is the story

of the break-up of Huw Morgan's family; of a chapel-going, choral-singing community divided by unemployment and strikes; and a landscape destroyed by the spread of the mines.

The author was born Richard Llewellyn Lloyd, not in the valleys but far west at St David's in 1906. He came to Gilfach Goch near

Pontypridd to spend a few months as a collier before writing the book in 1938.

Huw, the narrator, watches the big pit wheels spread across the countryside as new collieries poke their 'skinny black fingers out of the bright green' and more houses spread 'on both sides of the road round the mountain'. In fact, the valleys he mourned - 'Beautiful are the days that are gone, and O, for them to be back' - are greening over again. As the mines closed the colliery yards have been demolished and 'landscaped', though the new-green-grass doesn't entirely hide the scars where 'black gold' was gouged out of the ground.

Huw's world is to be found now in mines-turned-museums, like Rhondda Heritage Park at Lewis Merthyr Colliery, closed down in 1983 and re-opened as a visitor centre with exhibitions, an underground tour and a reconstructed miner's house.

Roald Dahl's father, Harald, a prosperous Norwegian ship-broker, who settled in Cardiff in the 1880s, had a theory that if a pregnant mother constantly looked at beautiful things her 'baby would grow up to be a lover of beautiful things'. On that basis and judging by the gruesome characters Roald loved to create for children, and the spooky events in his *Tales of the Unexpected*, Mrs Dahl must have had a horrific time in Cardiff in 1916.

Dahl was born that year 'in a fine house in the village of Llandaff', which was rapidly becoming a Cardiff suburb,

Richard Llewellyn (1906-1983).

Rhondda Heritage Park, Trehafod, tells the history of the mining communities that Richard Llewellyn portrayed in How Green Was My Valley.

Roald Dahl (1916-1990) described his Cardiff childhood in his memoir Boy.

Cardiff Bay's Norwegian Church, restored with help from Roald Dahl, is now an arts centre with a programme of storytelling, poetry and exhibitions.

and christened in the white-boarded Norwegian church in Cardiff Bay.

The church was built in traditional Norwegian-village style as a mission to seamen and a centre for the Scandinavian families who settled in Cardiff in the 19th century. In the current massive Cardiff Bay development, it has become a landmark - a waterside visitor centre with a coffee shop that could one day become a Roald Dahl centre.

W. H. Davies (opposite) the 'supertramp' poet, pictured in 1930 with the Mayor of Newport, outside the pub where he grew up.

Dannie Abse, one of Wales's best-known modern writers is strongly tied to Cardiff. Going back there brings

In 1995, Ty Llen, the first purpose-built literature centre in Britain, opened at the Dylan Thomas Centre in Swansea. It occupies the historic Guildhall overlooking the Maritime Quarter and combines galleries, library, theatre, bars and restaurants, even rooms for writers to hire. Officially named the National Literature Centre for Wales, it is open all year round and provides a 'platform' for literally any type of literary event - or just a place to sit and read in Dylan Thomas's home town.

on a poem, *Down the M4* - 'Me! dutiful son going back to South Wales...'

'I was born in a smoky house', he doesn't remember the number, in Whitchurch Road, and lived in two more in Albany Road. His autobiographical novel, *Ash on a Young Man's Sleeve* (the title is from T. S. Eliot's *Little Gidding*) describes a real and imaginary childhood in a Jewish family, watching rugby at Cardiff Arms Park, taking trips to the seaside: 'Porthcawl was the place. Posh. The Figure of Eight and the Ghost Train.' He recalls, too, a day on Barry Island, where 'The sea crinkled its lace petticoat up the beach...'

W. H. Davies, the super-tramp poet who wrote, 'What is this life if, full of care, We have no time to stand and stare...', was born in 1871 in Newport; and the town has a symbolic statue of him in Commercial Street designed to make passers-by do just that.

Davies describes his South Wales childhood in *The Autobiography of a Super-Tramp*, which he wrote at the suggestion of poet Edward Thomas and published with the help of George Bernard Shaw.

William Henry was brought up by his grandparents and lived for a time at their docklands pub, Church House (marked by a plaque). When his grandmother died and left him 10 shillings a week he set off for America, working the boats, begging and tramping; until he lost his left foot jumping a ride on a train. As the *Renfrew Mercury* reported on March 24, 1899: 'His intention had been to beat his way to Vancouver, and then go on to the Klondike. Davies says that as soon

as able to be out of hospital, he will return to his home in the old country.'

Back in Britain he lived in doss houses in London before moving to Kent, again helped by Edward Thomas, and gradually gained recognition for his simple, lyrical verses.

During 1914 he stayed with the Dymock Poets near the Wye. He went on to marry *Young Emma*, and spent his last years in Gloucestershire, once more near his native country:

Can I forget the sweet days that have been,
When poetry first began to warm my blood,
When from the hills of Gwent I saw the earth
Burned into two by Severn's flood.

NORTH WALES

In 1774, the year after Dr Johnson's memorable Highlands and Islands journey with Boswell, he set off to North Wales with his friend Mrs Hester Thrale and her husband.

The tour had its moments, especially when they explored the spectacular castle ruins at Denbigh, Caernarvon and Beaumaris.

But it is clear from Johnson's *Journey into Wales* that he wasn't inclined to write another full-length travelogue. Both he and Mrs Thrale were disappointed to find that the childhood home she had just inherited at Tremeirchion, near Denbigh, was dismally dilapidated.

After her second marriage, to an Italian musician named Gabriel Piozzi (Johnson totally disapproved), Mrs Thrale built a new house on the site and lived there happily until Piozzi died. The plaque in Tremeirchion church nonetheless refers to her as 'Dr Johnson's Mrs Thrale'.

'*Stand and Stare'*, Newport's symbolic sculpture of W.H.Davies.

Dr Samuel Johnson toured North Wales with Mr and Mrs Thrale in 1774.

'*Perhaps in the whole world there is no region more picturesquely beautiful than Snowdon*' - George Borrow, Wild Wales.

Johnson brightened up when the party stayed near Denbigh at Gwaenynog Hall. 'It was truly the dinner of a country gentleman,' he decided. Mrs Thrale recorded in her diary: 'The dinner was splendid and we had ices in the dessert.' Their host was so flattered by the great Doctor's visit he erected a monumental urn in the grounds. Johnson wasn't too happy with it, confiding to Mrs Thrale that it 'looks like an intention to bury me alive'.

It was left to Beatrix Potter to provide merrier memorials of Gwaenynog, in *The Tale of the Flopsy Bunnies*, published 1909. It had become the home of her Aunt Harriet and Uncle Fred Burton, and Beatrix visited them for many years, despite Aunt Harriet's aversion to her bringing 'Sammy, Hunca Munca and Mrs Tiggy', her pet rat, mouse and hedgehog.

Beatrix in turn was not especially keen on her aunt's family. But the house made 'a week's change every spring' and in September 1905 it provided an instant refuge from her parents, in the sad period after the unexpected death of Norman Warne, whom Beatrix had agreed to marry a few weeks earlier.

Gwaenynog also supplied

subjects Beatrix liked to paint. It had, she wrote, 'the prettiest kind of garden where bright old fashioned flowers grow amongst the currant bushes'. She drew it again and again, in watercolour and pencil, and in *The Flopsy Bunnies*, the

walled garden and stone-built gardener's cottage are clearly recognisable as 'Mr McGregor's'.

The walled garden has been recreated and opened at Gwaenynog Country World. Johnson's urn and his walk through the estate can also be seen during visits to Broadleys Farm (which produces its own ice cream good enough to have softened the Great Doctor's heart).

If Johnson wasn't inspired to write a full account of his Welsh travels, George Borrow certainly was. Borrow came to Wales in the summer of 1854, taking the train as far as Chester. He brought his wife and stepdaughter from their home in Suffolk and spent nearly four months walking throughout the country. The result was a classic, *Wild Wales*.

Borrow had no obvious Welsh connections. Yet his fondness for the people, their language (he was fluent enough in the north to be mistaken for a man of the south) and the country hugs every line of his journal. He took the title from the best-loved poem in medieval

gypsies, exploring and recording his walks.

Starting at Llangollen, he went to Plas Newydd, home of Lady Eleanor Butler and the Hon. Sarah Ponsonby, the celebrated Ladies of Llangollen who had shocked society by setting up house together in 1780.

For almost 50 years (they had gone by Borrow's time) they entertained a stream of literary visitors in their handsome black-and-white house overlooking the valley (where the International Eisteddfod is now held every summer).

Wordsworth wrote them a sonnet in the garden. Sir Walter Scott, Shelley, Lord Byron, Thomas De Quincey all paid visits. So did Mrs Hester Piozzi, coming with her new husband from their new house at Tremeirchion.

George Borrow used the old city of Bangor as a base to walk through Snowdonia, 'a region of mountains, lakes, cataracts and groves in which Nature shows herself in her most grand and beautiful form'.

Snowdon by moonlight had made a similar impact on

The Bridge at Llangollen, drawn by Welsh artist Wil Rowlands for a 1995 edition of George Borrow's travelogue Wild Wales, *first published 1862.*

Elizabeth Mavor's book Life with the Ladies of Llangollen *draws on the journals and letters of the two Irish ladies who lived at Plas Newydd (left) at the end of the 18th century.*

John Cowper Powys (1872-1963).

Welsh (often, but wrongly, ascribed to Taliesin):

> *Their lord they shall praise,*
> *Their language they shall keep,*
> *Their land they shall lose,*
> *Except wild Wales.*

Day after day with boundless energy Borrow tramped, sometimes alone, up to 30 miles, talking to local people, tinkers and

Wordsworth when he climbed it in 1791 and the region would again exert its powerful magic on John Cowper Powys. John, eldest of the three prolific Powys brothers, was born in England in 1872 but claimed ancient Welsh ancestry.

He lived the last 30 years of his life in the mountains at Corwen and Blaenau Ffestiniog, absorbed in Welsh mythology, writing massive novels and essays, some published in his collection *Obstinate Cymric.*

He had just finished *Morwyn or the Vengeance of God* when he wrote from Corwen to his brother Llewellyn: 'I bring Socrates into it and Taliesin and the Marquis of Sade and Torquemada and Rabelais.'

J. B. Priestley (hardly noted for brevity either) called Powys a 'huge sprawling genius'. To Henry Miller he was 'one of the few persons I shall always revere, whom I shall feel forever indebted to.'

George Borrow, heading south, went to Devil's Bridge, as Coleridge and Wordsworth had, and decided the spectacular Mynach Falls crashing through the gorge were 'one of the most remarkable locations in the world'.

He called at Hafod, nearby on the banks of the Ystwyth, Thomas Johnes's legendary marble paradise in the mountains. Johnes lavished a fortune on his Gothic mansion and grottoes for his ornamental gardens, laid out on Picturesque principles with the help of Richard Payne Knight and Uvedale Price, his friends and the leaders of the Picturesque movement.

Coleridge, on a marathon walk round Wales in 1794, would cer-

The Mynach Falls at Devil's Bridge, near the legendary Hafod estate on which Thomas Love Peacock probably based his satire of the Picturesque movement, Headlong Hall.

Llandudno, Gwynedd, keeps much of the Victorian seaside style that Alice Liddell and her family knew in the 1860s.

tainly have come across Hafod when he stayed at Devil's Bridge, even if he hadn't heard of it before; and Hafod's 'stately pleasure domes' could well be among the images that drifted through his opium-dream of *Kubla Khan.*

Johnes went bankrupt proving 'the wilderness shall flourish'. He even rebuilt the house after a disastrous fire. In time it was demolished. But Hafod's legacy still lingers in the lovely wooded valley he planted (where the Forestry Commission has marked a trail). And in Elisabeth Inglis-Jones's supreme biography of a house and its visionary owner, *Peacocks in Paradise.*

On the seafront at Llandudno stands a statue of Lewis Carroll's White Rabbit. It is a memorial to the real *Alice in Wonderland* and her family, the Liddells, who came regularly for holidays.

Llandudno was purpose-built as a resort in the mid-19th century and soon became fashionable among Victorian society. Alice's parents spent their honeymoon here. In 1861 they brought the children and rented a house, now St Tudno's Hotel. When they wanted a permanent summer home, Dean Liddell had a house built (now part of Gogarth Abbey Hotel) on the West Shore.

Their guests were the great and good: Matthew Arnold, William Gladstone and (so the story goes) Lewis Carroll, writing and reading aloud Alice's adventures. The facts are as hard to pin down as smoke from the Caterpillar's hookah.

Some pages are missing from Carroll's diary, razored by an unknown hand, and they cover this part of his relationship with the Liddells: 'a very anxious subject' as he put it. One fellow-guest, however, claims Carroll was present and local tradition agrees.

Certainly on Llandudno's broad beaches the Walrus and the Carpenter could have 'wept like anything to see Such quantities of sand'. The White Knight's scheme

'To keep the Menai bridge from rust By boiling it in wine', also owes its origins to North Wales. The jury may be out on this one, but the town has a small Rabbit Hole to visit as well as the statue and hotels. In walk-through tableaux with life-size characters it presents several of the most popular Wonderland scenes: the Mad Hatter's tea party, the Red Queen's kitchen, and the Trial to decide Who Stole the Tarts?

Gerard Manley Hopkins left less than 1,500 lines of poetry, not one published in his lifetime, and his theme was

always *God's Grandeur*. Yet he was one of the most important poets of the 19th century. In 1874 he entered the Jesuit seminary of St Beuno's in the Vale of Clwyd (one of several he attended in training to be a priest) and the three years he spent in North Wales were crucial to his style and awareness of God in nature.

Hopkins's meticulous, almost obsessive obedience to his calling had previously prompted him to burn all his poetry. Now, delighting in the sound of the Welsh language, he discovered the 'sprung rhythm' he wanted for poems intended 'less to be read than heard'. In the Clwydian countryside he found the *Pied Beauty* of the landscape; the imagery for *The Windhover* - 'striding high there, how he rung upon the rein of a wimpling wing'; and the subject for a verse drama at St Winefride's Well, nearby in Holywell. It was left unfinished when he died, but saved with the rest of his poetry and published later by his friend and fellow-poet at Oxford, Robert Bridges.

At Harlech, Robert Graves records in his memoir *Goodbye to All That*, written in the 1920s, 'I found a personal peace

The Clwydian countryside inspired Gerard Manley Hopkins with its Pied Beauty *and the story of St Winefride's Well*

The Walrus and the Carpenter - Sir John Tenniel's illustration for Lewis Carroll's Through the Looking Glass.

Robert Graves (1895-1985) - poet, novelist and critic.

Gerard Manley Hopkins (1844 - 1889).

R. S. Thomas, born in Cardiff 1913, and ordained in 1937, published his first major collection, Song at the Year's Turning, *in 1955.*

independent of history or geography. The first poem I wrote as myself concerned those hills'. He went on to produce more poetry, novels and criticism; to spin new stories out of the classics - *I Claudius, The Greek Myths.* And to write a major history of poetic myths, *The White Goddess,* drawing heavily on the Celtic mythology he had grown to love in Wales.

His mother had a house at Harlech and Graves's childhood holidays were nearly all spent on the beach - 'good, hard sand for miles, safe bathing, sandhills for hide-and-seek' - or climbing round Harlech Castle, between the mountains and the sea. In the spring of 1914 he was mountaineering in Snowdonia. In the summer, having just left school, he was in Harlech again as war broke out over Europe. 'A day or two later I decided to enlist' - and went off to fight at the Front, where he was so badly wounded, in 1916, that *The Times* reported him dead.

On the same Harlech beach that same summer of 1914, seven-year-old Daphne du Maurier was holidaying at Llanbedwr with her sisters and cousins. The cousins were 'older than us and therefore to be admired and envied, even loved', Daphne wrote later, adding

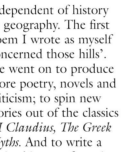

their names: 'George, Jack, Peter, Michael, Nico'. They were the Llewellyn Davies brothers, the 'lost boys' who had inspired J. M. Barrie's fantasy *Peter Pan* and been 'adopted' by Barrie after their parents died.

Priest and poet R. S. Thomas, the first Welsh poet nominated (1995) for the Nobel Prize for Literature, was born in 1913 in Cardiff. In 1942 he became rector of Manafon, near Welshpool, where most of his first three volumes of poetry were written; and where he invented his alter ego, the local peasant Iago Prydderch - 'Just an ordinary man of the bald Welsh hills'.

Thomas's later work, still essentially religious and concerned for *Welsh Landscape* and the Welsh - 'We were a people, and are so yet' - owes its origins to the Lleyn Peninsula, where his small, simple stone cottage overlooks the sea.

THE MARCHES

Across the borderlands that unite Wales and England, the Celts, Romans and Saxons struggled for possession for centuries. Soon after 1066 William the Conqueror shared out its rolling hills and lush valleys among his barons - the powerful Marcher Lords.

The warring went on in the 12th century as King Stephen and the Empress Maud battled for the throne. This is the period that Shropshire writer Ellis Peters picked for her best-selling medieval whodunits, the *Chronicles of Brother Cadfael.*

Cadfael is an imaginary

The Lleyn Peninsula, where R. S. Thomas, living and working as preacher and poet, has continued to voice his grave fears for Wales and Welsh culture.

Benedictine monk who comes to Shrewsbury Abbey and takes the cowl after years Crusading and sailing the high seas. In the comfort-zone of the cloisters he potters happily in the herbarium preparing potions for sick patients. At the Shrewsbury Quest centre in part of the abbey ruins, Cadfael's medieval garden and 'potting shed' are faithfully recreated alongside a hands-on scriptorium and the sounds-and-smells of abbey life.

But Cadfael is a medieval cross between Inspector Morse and Miss Marple, a Holmes in monk's habit. His skills and wise counsel keep drawing him away from the abbey, over the bridge, up steep Wyle Cop, into Dogpole and the heart of the town.

The route is the same today. Shrewsbury's street plan has hardly changed and its narrow roads

plunge up and down hill inside the old town walls while the River Severn loops tightly round below.

Tiny alleys, known as 'the shuts', sidle between medieval buildings where Cadfael's author said she pictured her characters. Half way up Wyle Cop was Martin

Bellecote's woodyard in the *Monk's-Hood* murder. Beside St Mary's church is Drapers' Hall, home of Hugh Beringar the stalwart sheriff (Watson to Cadfael's Holmes).

In Shrewsbury's pavements metal 'footprints' have been placed as 'clues' to the crime sites and there are several car-tours (from the Tourist Information Centre) following Cadfael's casebook as he sleuths his way around the Marches applying the fine turn of ancient Welsh law that Ellis Peters made her hallmark.

The news of Wilfred Owen's death in France reached his home in Shrewsbury on Armistice Day, November 11, 1918. The poet whose poignant verses of despair raged at the waste of young men's lives was killed in battle at the age of 25, leaving his poem *Strange Meeting* unfinished at the line, 'Let us sleep now...'.

'Mahim', Monkmoor Road, Shrewsbury, where the Owen family lived (his attic room at the front looks out to the Wrekin) has a plaque. Shrewsbury Abbey churchyard also has a memorial to Owen.

Council House Court, near Shrewsbury Castle, is the Aurifabers' yard in the Chronicles of Brother Cadfael.

Ellis Peters, pen-name of Edith Pargeter (1913-1995), creator of the 'Rare Benedictine' super-sleuth Brother Cadfael.

Shrewsbury Quest visitor centre has planted a Cadfael herb garden in the shadow of the Abbey Church.

Alfred Edward Housman, aged 35, at the time of writing A Shropshire Lad *and working as Professor of Latin at University College London.*

St Laurence's church, Ludlow. Housman's ashes were buried against the north wall on July 25, 1936.

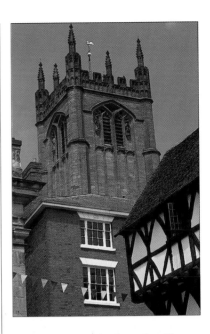

A.E. Housman's poems have become so closely associated with Shropshire it is hard to remember that *A Shropshire Lad* was mostly written in a villa in Highgate, London.

At first the slim volume of 63 short poems, published in 1896 at the author's expense, made little impact. It was the coming of the 1914-18 war that made their melancholy air, idealised country-side and military themes so poignant (Siegfried Sassoon kept a copy in his knapsack while he fought in the trenches). Ever since, Housman's verses have stayed among the best-loved lines in English poetry: 'In summer time on Bredon The bells they sound so clear'; and 'Loveliest of trees, the cherry now Is hung with bloom along the bough...'

Housman was born, grew up and went to school in various places in the Bromsgrove area south of Birmingham, until he went up to Oxford in 1877; and Bromsgrove has a statue, trail and an exhibition in the museum about the Housmans and their local connections.

From one home, Perry Hall (since extended and turned into a hotel) he could look to the Clees, the 'blue remembered hills' of Shropshire and his 'land of lost content'.

'Shropshire was our western horizon,' he explained, 'which made me feel romantic about it.' In his poems he describes the long wooded scarp of Wenlock Edge and the villages nearby, 'Clunton, Clunbury, Clungunford and Clun, Are the quietest places under the sun'.

The 'blue remembered hills' of A Shropshire Lad *also dominate Mary Webb's novels* The Golden Arrow *and* The House in Dormer Forest *as well as* Precious Bane.

226

He refers to Ludlow frequently, picturing 'When smoke stood up from Ludlow', and the town still has the Monday market and the chimes he mentions:

> Or come you home of Monday
> When Ludlow market hums
> And Ludlow chimes are
>   playing
> 'The conquering hero comes'.

Yet, as is hinted on the plaque in St Laurence's church, Ludlow, where he is buried, Housman put his academic work - teaching classics at Cambridge - first. Poetry came second. The precise locations were not so important to him as the spirit of the borderlands and the ancient feuding of the Welsh Marches which he echoes in his ballad-style verses.

P. G. Wodehouse, Plum to his friends and fans, claimed that the timeless, comic world of Wooster and his omniscient

gentleman's gentleman, Jeeves, was 'an artificial world of my own creation'. To invent it, though, he plundered all the people and

places he knew. Blandings estate, owned by Lord Emsworth and home of his pig the Empress of Blandings, seems to be based on Weston Park near Shifnal. Plum lived for a time at Stableford less than 10 miles away and Weston Park's terraces, lake and gardens fit the Blandings frame exactly. According to Wodehouse fans (Evelyn Waugh called him 'The Master') that makes the little hamlet of Weston-under-Lizard into Blandings Parva. So Shifnal becomes Market Blandings with the railway station used by nitwit nephews making dawn escapes from fire-breathing aunts.

But Blandings Castle itself Wodehouse apparently imported from Sudeley in Gloucestershire. He may also have added a touch of Corsham Court near Bath and then put the whole thing down in sight of the Wrekin at Weston Park, amid Shropshire's pleasant 'Vale of Blandings'.

Mary Webb's stories from the depths of rural Shropshire, written in the 1920s, have always had admirers. Rebecca West called her a genius when *Gone to Earth* was published. Prime Minister Stanley Baldwin (Rudyard Kipling's cousin) wrote thanking her 'a thousand times' for the pleasure of reading *Precious Bane*, the story of gentle, disfigured Prue Sarne and her love for the debonair Kester.

Mary's love affair with 'Salop' lasted from her birth in 1881, close to the county's famous

Weston Park near Shifnal, one of P.G. Wodehouse's models for Blandings, home of Lord Emsworth. Emsworth himself owes more to the 8th Duke of Devonshire who lived with his prize pig at Chatsworth, Derbyshire.

A.E. Housman memorial, at St Laurence's church, Ludlow

Sir Pelham Grenville Wodehouse (1881-1975) described his novels as 'a sort of musical comedy without music and ignoring real life altogether'.

Milton's poetic drama Comus, 'A Maske presented at Ludlow Castle' *was first performed by the Earl of Bridgewater's children 'on Michaelmasse night 1634'. It was written to celebrate the earl's entry as Lord President of Wales and the Marches. The story is set in an enchanted forest where a lady, played by young Lady Alice, becomes separated from her brothers one night and is waylaid by Comus, a pagan god invented by Milton. The song that summons Sabrina, goddess of the River Severn, to help the children - 'Sabrina fair, Listen where thou art sitting Under the glassy, cool, translucent wave,' - is the most famous passage in the masque. During Ludlow's summer festival the ruined castle is used for open-air performances of Shakespeare.*

' *H* ow oft, in spirit, have I turned to thee,
O sylvan Wye!' -
William Wordsworth,
Tintern Abbey.
Further up river is the small country town of Hay-on-Wye, the largest second-hand book centre in the world and the scene of one of Britain's best literary festivals, held in May each year.

hump, the Wrekin; through childhood near Much Wenlock; marriage at Holy Trinity in Moele Brace; homes at various places around Pontesbury, Lyth and Bayston hills; until she was buried in Shrewsbury cemetery in 1927.

Her poetry and novels are full of rustic passion and poverty, easily matching the drama of Shropshire's landscape. But they are less popular now than Stella Gibbons's *Cold Comfort Farm*, a hilarious send-up of Mary's earthy, primitive *Precious Bane*.

THE WYE VALLEY

I n 1800, both a fourth and fifth edition appeared of William Gilpin's *Observations on the River Wye and Several Parts of South Wales, etc, Relative Chiefly to Picturesque Beauty: made in the summer of the year 1770.* Evidently the Rev. Gilpin's 'little work' was, 'still thought worth the notice of the public, a new edition of it in large octavo hath been printed, with a set of new etchings, as the old plates were too much worn to be of farther use. A small edition hath also been printed, as a more portable companion to those who wish to take it with them, in their travels through Wales.'

It is unthinkable that Wordsworth had not read such a best-seller when he came to the Wye in 1793. He returned five years later with Dorothy, and wrote *Lines Composed a Few Miles Above Tintern Abbey.* When

Coleridge 'did' Tintern in 1794 towards the end of his first walk round Wales, his companion Hucks, a fellow-undergraduate from Cambridge, had already had enough so Coleridge pressed on to Tintern alone.

By the end of the century the cult of walking tours, observing nature and searching for Picturesque views was in full stride. But when Gilpin made the journey from Ross-on-Wye down to Chepstow in 1770 (he added the upper reaches from Hay-on-Wye later), he was still formulating the principles of Picturesque taste.

In a stream of essays and poems Gilpin, Uvedale Price and Richard Payne Knight set out the new aesthetic and tried to define the perfect Picturesque landscape. Reacting against the regularity of classical taste enjoyed by the

Augustans, they 'explained' how the roughness and irregularity of natural beauty could be 'improved' with man-made waterfalls, follies and grottoes.

Tintern's ruined Cistercian abbey, Gilpin decided, was 'the most beautiful and picturesque view on the river'; and Hafod, Thomas Johnes's estate near Devil's Bridge, he advised travellers, 'you should by no means pass by... such scenery is rarely met with.'

Naturally their ideas could be taken to absurdity. Jane Austen pokes gentle fun in *Northanger Abbey*, though her family frequently used Gilpin's guides on expeditions. Other writers went for fullscale ridicule. But it didn't deter the next generation, like Francis Kilvert, from flocking to make their own Picturesque assessments. In his diary Kilvert notes, 'Tintern Abbey at first sight seemed to me to be bare and almost too perfect to be entirely picturesque.'

The Rev. Kilvert served as curate at Clyro, close to Hay-on-Wye, from 1865 till 1872; and as vicar of Bredwardine, a few miles the other side of Hay, for two years until he died suddenly in 1879, aged 38.

Kilvert's Diary was written during the last 10 years of his life and is one of the most enjoyable of English journals. Not that he ever intended it for publication: in fact most of it was destroyed by his family. It was too personal a picture of the Victorian parishes, and their vicar - a gently erring and forgiving man who loved life and pretty faces.

He was born in Wiltshire but his heart was in the Welsh Borderlands. He loved long walks along the Wye and the Golden Valley. He loved snow 'falling thickly in enormous feathers'; playing croquet on the lawn at Hay Castle; reading Robert Browning; and the chimes of 'the sweet bells of Clyro'.

Most of all he loved dancing quadrilles with Daisy Thomas and daydreaming about her as he sat writing sermons. His study at Clyro, in Ashbrook House (now the Kilvert Gallery) looks over the lane to St Michael's. But his 'prospects' weren't good enough for Daisy's father and when eventually he married (Elizabeth) it was little more than a month before his death. He was buried at Bredwardine in the churchyard

Tintern Abbey ruins (left and cenre) would be more Picturesque, William Gilpin thought, with 'A mallet judiciously used (but who durst use it?)'

The Rev. Francis Kilvert (1840-1879).

Sitting in Ashbrook House (left) Kilvert noted: 'Whitsun Tuesday, 1870 - Up early and writing in my bedroom before breakfast. The swallows kept on dashing in at the open window...'

Edward Thomas was writing prose before he joined the Dymock Poets and went on to produce his poignant First World War poetry.

where he had enjoyed 'the singing of the birds and the brightness and gladness of the spring'.

In Dymock church a small exhibition records the group of writers who came to live or visit each other in the Leadon Valley on the eve of the 1914-18 war.

Drawn together as friends and fellow-poets, they included Robert Frost, Edward Thomas, Rupert Brooke and W. H. Davies. They shared a passion for the countryside and, to some extent, a simple colloquial style. They were inspired by the woods and hills between the Malverns and the Wye.

St Mary's church, start of a Poets' Path that links the haunts of the Dymock Poets.

They would walk, meet, talk, spend evenings drinking cider in each others' cottages or lodgings - and help each other write.

To American poet Robert Frost goes the credit for Edward Thomas becoming a poet. Thomas had spent years pouring out prose and reviews, including a favourable one on W. H. Davies which marked the start of Davies's career as a poet and their long friendship. In October 1913, when Thomas and Frost first met, Thomas was suffering his worst period of restlessness and depression; though it is hard to realise from his essays, *Literary Pilgrim in England,* how much mental anguish he suffered.

Frost had come to Britain in search of a publisher and in spring

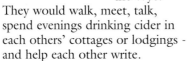

1914 he moved to Leddington to settle among the 'Dymock Poets', who had become a sort of off-shoot of Harold Monro's London Poetry Bookshop and the 'Georgian Poets'.

Soon Thomas arrived from his Hampshire home for the first of many visits and Frost urged him to recognise the essential poetry in his writing. Thomas recorded the journey there via Adlestrop station:

Yes, I remember Adlestrop -
The name, because one after
*   noon*
Of heat the express-train drew
*   up there*
Unwontedly. It was late
*   June.*

The station, near Stow-on-the-Wold, has gone but the railway sign and the poem are on show in the village bus-shelter.

Frost returned to America early in 1915. Thomas had planned to go too. Instead he enlisted and his poetry, like Rupert Brooke's, turned to war. In April 1917 he was killed in action, shortly before most of his poetry, including *Lights Out,* was published.

The Priory Church, Great Malvern (right), all that remains of the monastery where William Langland was educated, before he gave up the priesthood for marriage and his poetry.

'In a summer season when soft was the sun' Piers Plowman sets out to walk the Malvern Hills and he dreams 'a marvelous dream'. Piers is the narrator of a series of visions that reveal the 'sad pageant of men's miseries', poverty and injustice and the corruption of the Church. Written by Chaucer's contemporary William Langland, it is generally agreed to be the finest allegorical poem of the period (Bunyan's more entertaining *Pilgrim's Progress* was yet to come). About Langland himself almost nothing is agreed except that he wrote and re-wrote around 1370 and spent some time at Great Malvern Priory, whose partly-Norman church has survived as one of the town's chief attractions.

Since 1929 Great Malvern has been the setting for an annual Festival of Drama and Music. It was started by Sir Barry Jackson as a platform for George Bernard Shaw's plays and Sir Edward Elgar's music. They made an unlikely pair (Lady Elgar disapproved of Shaw's radical socialism), but were nevertheless firm friends for years.

Tretower Court near Brecon, one of the best-preserved 15th-century houses in Britain, was the family seat of the Vaughans. Metaphysical poet Henry Vaughan and his twin, Thomas, were born at one of the family's neighbouring estates in 1621 and both became writers. Henry's religious and pastoral poems - *I saw Eternity the other night* - were a major influence on Siegfried Sassoon. On Vaughan's gravestone at Llansantffraed, almost hidden by a tree behind the church, he is named as the 'Silurist', on account of his love for Breconshire, originally inhabited by the Silures tribe.

Henry Vaughan's ancestor, Sir Roger, was the richest commoner in Wales when he began building Tretower Court in the late 15th century.

Hereford Cathedral, on the banks of the River Wye, has some outstanding literary treasures. The early 17th-century Chained Library is the finest in the world and contains nearly 1,500 ancient volumes, still chained, row on row, in wooden presses. There are over 200 manuscripts dating from about 800AD to 1500, including The Hereford Gospels *handsomely illuminated in similar style to the* Book of Kells. *And, as befits the 'capital' of the cider country, there is a rare 15th-century Cider Bible, whose English translator used the unorthodox wording 'strong cider' instead of 'strong drink' in a passage about John the Baptist. A new exhibition centre at the cathedral also displays Hereford's priceless 1289 Mappa Mundi in which the world is drawn flat with Jerusalem at the centre.*

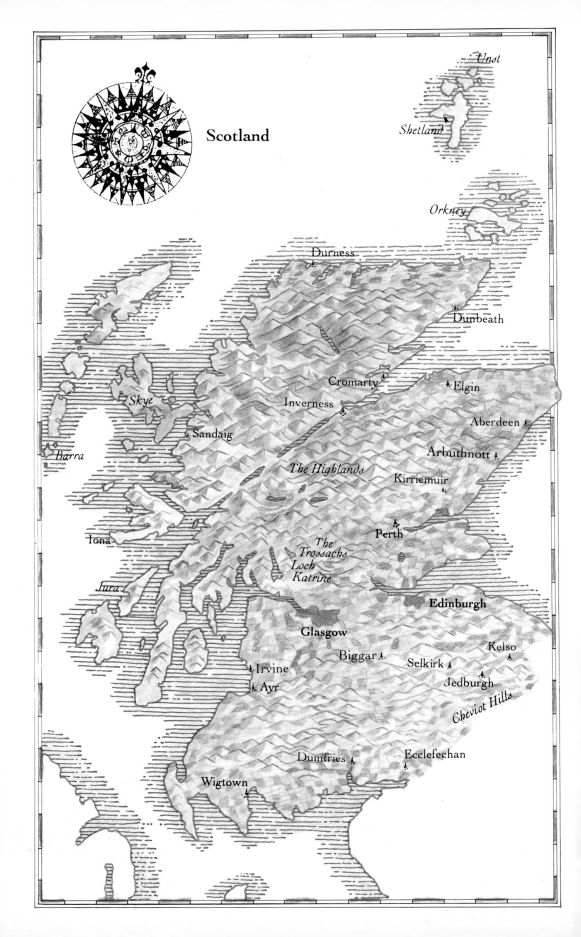

CHAPTER 9

SCOTLAND

✦

EDINBURGH

I don't wonder that anyone residing in Edinburgh should write poetically.

Washington Irving, 1817, visiting Walter Scott.

At one end of Edinburgh's 'Royal Mile', running down the ridge of the Old Town, the castle stands on top of its great rock. At the other lies the Palace of Holyroodhouse.

Walk the length of the Mile and you come to the Writers' Museum, St Giles's Cathedral (several literary memorials), three great libraries, and scores of tall old tenement houses where writers lived and worked beside the crowded, cobbled streets.

Late in the 15th century, when William Dunbar was court poet at Holyroodhouse, the Mile was a pathway, bustling, noisy, smelly, teeming with traders, footpads, booths and ballad-mongers.

By the early 18th century, Daniel Defoe thought it 'the largest, longest, and finest street for Buildings and Number of Inhabitants...in the World.'

It was still appallingly dirty but, Tobias Smollett reported in 1766, it was also 'a hot bed of genius'. Staying with his sister, above the archway to St John Street, he met the leading writers and thinkers of the Scottish Enlightenment, Adam Ferguson, David Hume, Adam Smith. They were, Smollett decided, as interesting to meet as to read, and he gave an approving account in his last and best book, *The Expedition of Humphrey Clinker*, published five years later.

Edinburgh Castle, the setting for R. L. Stevenson's novel St Ives, *and George Borrow's boyhood memories in* Lavengro, *after his father was quartered at the castle in 1813.*

In the Palace of Holyroodhouse, William Dunbar – Chaucer's successor as Britain's best poet – celebrated the wedding of King James IV and Queen Margaret in The Thrissill and the Rois *[The Thistle and the Rose], 1503.*

St Giles, the High Kirk, at the centre of the Old Town, has a bronze relief to Stevenson with his poem: 'Home is the sailor, home from sea, And the hunter, home from the hill.'

Allan Ramsay (1686-1758) poet, publisher and founder of Scotland's first lending library, lived at 'Goose Pie' house. His statue is in Princes Street Garden, with Scott's and the Stevenson memorials.

The Writers' Museum, Lady Stair's House, contains Stevenson's hand printing-press, as well as the Ballantyne press that produced Scott's novels.

In the next courtyard off Canongate – the lower part of the Mile – James Boswell and his cousin Margaret took a flat in Chessel's Buildings soon after their wedding in November 1769. Boswell (son of an Edinburgh judge) had been born near St Giles in 1740, and he and Margaret made their main home in the city, though they later inherited estates in the Lowlands.

By 1773, when Dr Johnson came at the start of his Highland tour with Boswell, they were living in James Court, off the Lawnmarket, the upper part of the Mile. Margaret, more sensible than her husband, and less keen on Johnson, nonetheless made the Great Doctor welcome.

Their flat in James Court has disappeared. So has Robert Burns's first lodging (a plaque marks the site) nearby in the Lawnmarket. But a house known as Gladstone's Land has been restored and opened to show how life was lived along the Mile in the 18th century.

Burns came to Edinburgh in 1786 to find a printer who would produce a follow-up to the Kilmarnock edition of his

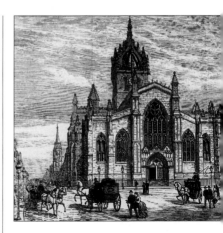

poems. William Smellie (producer of the first *Encyclopaedia Britannica* in 1768) obliged; another plaque records Smellie's shop in Anchor Close and the tavern he and Burns frequented. Mrs Agnes MacLehose also obliged Burns – with at least *Ae Fond Kiss*.

He met her on a return visit to the city, wrote to her as 'Clarinda', and produced the song *Ae Fond Kiss* when they parted in 1791, while he was staying at the White Hart in the Grassmarket.

Other writers came to Edinburgh to study at the university. Boswell, Walter Scott and R. L. Stevenson read law. Thomas Carlyle read arts and theology. Oliver Goldsmith and Arthur Conan Doyle read medicine. Doyle, born in the city in 1859, was a contemporary and friend of J. M. Barrie, whose recollections of the university, *An Edinburgh Eleven*, included R. L. Stevenson as well. Doyle's memories were put to more popular effect: he used the brilliant deductive methods of his tutor for his detective Sherlock Holmes.

Near the university stand two of Edinburgh's grand libraries. The National Library of Scotland has priceless archives including manuscripts of Hugh MacDiarmid, Robert Garioch (author of the *Edinburgh Sonnets*) and other moderns. Edinburgh's Central Library has a Scottish and an Edinburgh room with collections on city-based writers.

Less grand and less well known is the Scottish Poetry Library, tucked away off the Mile in Tweeddale Court. It is a gem, definitely not to be missed for an hour's quiet reading, and it sells the only local literary map, showing everyone from William Dunbar to Sydney Goodsir Smith, via Allan Ramsay, Robert Fergusson and Robert Burns.

Burns has two memorials in St Giles, the High Kirk of Edinburgh: a brashly modern window and an aptly simple stone, which John Knox's statue seems about to set his Calvinist heel on. The cathedral also has plaques to R. L. Stevenson and to Mrs Oliphant, born near the city in 1828.

Left a widow at 31 with three young children, Margaret Oliphant wrote her way out of debt with 100 novels. Her Cranford-esque *Chronicles of Carlingford* had quite a following for a time. Yet before she died in 1897, she cast one eye on George Eliot and ruefully remarked: 'Should I have done better if I had been kept, like her, in a mental greenhouse and looked after?'

Outside the cathedral there is a heart-shaped design in the pavement to mark the site of the Tolbooth prison, the *Heart of Midlothian* that gave Sir Walter Scott the title and setting for the tragic tale of Effie and Jeanie Deans.

There is more about Scott in the Writers' Museum at Lady Stair's House, one of few 17th-century originals still in James Close. It has three complete collections, about Scott and Stevenson, both sons of the city, and Robert Burns.

Here among the portraits, pens and letters are touching little trinkets like Scott's chess-board, Jean Armour's (Mrs Burns) gloves and a lock of 'Highland Mary's' hair. But Burns belongs to the Lowlands, and his life and loves can be followed there. Scott's heart was elsewhere, too – in the Borders, building his baronial fantasy at Abbotsford.

If the museum captures one writer who cannot easily be found elsewhere, it is Robert Louis Balfour Stevenson (always Lewis to his family). Edinburgh was his birthplace in 1850 and Lady Stair's House has his only relics in Britain. They were brought back from Samoa where he died, aged only 44, after spending his

'You and Barrie and Kipling are my Muses three,' R. L. S. wrote to Henry James from Samoa in 1892. Edinburgh made a fourth: 'sights and thoughts of youth pursue me', he added, recalling the Hawes Inn at South Queensferry, where David Balfour's Kidnapped journey begins.

Burns's meeting with young Walter Scott in 1789 at Sciennes Hill House, near The Meadows (it has a tablet), is recorded in a painting now kept at Abbotsford.

last seven years overseas, bundled abroad for the sake of his health by his American wife.

Poor Fanny. Divorced *and* a decade older than Lewis, she never had a good 'press' in Britain, except from Henry James. Yet Lewis loved her brave free-wheeling spirit, just as he loved and endlessly wrote about Edinburgh and Scotland.

In *Kidnapped*, David Balfour and Alan Breck's 200-mile journey, and its sequel *Catriona*, Stevenson covered Scotland with classic adventure stories. In his unfinished masterpiece *Weir of Hermiston*, he used villages he had known near Edinburgh: Colinton with its wooded walks and Swanston on the edge of the Pentland Hills.

Edinburgh's Classical New Town, built to replace Robert Fergusson's 'Auld Reekie' and the narrow streets known to Tobias Smollett and his character Matthew Bramble.

In *The Strange Case of Dr Jekyll and Mr Hyde* he conjured up Edinburgh itself, even though it was allegedly set in London, and written in Bournemouth. His 'shilling shocker' (Fanny thought it far beneath him) was the result of six days' frantic writing, a nightmare, and his childhood fascination with the darker conflicts of the Calvinist city.

Jekyll and Hyde were based on a real-life Edinburgh figure,

Deacon Brodie, who lived in Brodie's Court. By day a respectable councillor and cabinet maker, by night a notorious criminal, gambler and womaniser, Brodie was caught and hanged near St Giles in 1788 after he bungled a raid on the excise office in Chessel's Court.

Stevenson's Edinburgh childhood was also responsible for *A Child's Garden of Verses*, containing his much-loved lines, 'I have a little shadow that goes in and out with me', and 'Faster than fairies, faster than witches'.

The house he grew up in, 17 Heriot Row (it has a plaque) stands in Edinburgh's New Town, the elegant suburb begun in 1767 and laid out with wide, straight streets and sweeping crescents. It soon became, and stayed, the most fashionable part of the city.

In 1811, Percy Bysshe Shelley took a flat there in George Street, at No.60 (the shop has a plaque) with his runaway teenage bride, Harriet. Kenneth Grahame was born at No. 32 Castle Street (another plaque) in 1859, and Sir Walter Scott used No. 39 as his town house for almost 30 years. Only his financial crash in 1826 would force him to leave it.

The following year, round the corner at the Assembly Rooms – still a miracle of ballrooms and halls with chandeliers dripping from ornate ceilings – Scott made his curious 'confession' at a banquet that he was the author of *Waverley*. No one had doubted it for years, though at first he kept it secret, fearing the role of novelist didn't match his legal standing and his reputation as a serious man of letters.

Round the next corner in Hanover Street is Milne's Bar, the

legendary meeting place of the poets who led Scotland's modern literary renaissance: Hugh MacDiarmid, Norman MacCaig, Sorley Maclean and Sydney Goodsir Smith. Down the steps in the semi-basement bar, nick-named the Little Kremlin, the walls are covered with their framed photos and poems, among them, of course, MacDiarmid's *In an Edinburgh Pub* and Sorley Maclean's *Springtide.*

There is also Iain Crichton Smith's poem *Jean Brodie's Children,* recalling novelist Muriel Spark and her Edinburgh-based book about *The Prime of Miss Jean Brodie* and her 'crème de la crème' 1930s schoolgirls.

Born in the city in 1918, Spark had attended James Gillespie's School for Girls. It was one of several schools that made Edinburgh famous for education. Jane Carlyle had attended Miss Hall's in Leith Walk early in the 19th century. Rebecca West went to George Watson's Ladies College in George Square (described in her novel *The Judge,* 1922).

Hugh MacDiarmid, Muriel Spark and Rebecca West were just three of the galaxy of writers who turned up in 1962 for the first writers' conference held during the Edinburgh International Festival. It wasn't so much a con-ference as a mutual demolition job. Literary 'hack' took on new meaning as delegates rubbished each other from the platform.

The festival, begun in 1947 and held each August, had already grown into one of the best in Europe. But the writers' event was new and uncertain. J. B. Priestley thought it safer to stay away. Kingsley Amis, Stephen Spender and Angus Wilson decided to brave it.

So did Henry Miller, Norman Mailer and Mary McCarthy, though she rapidly realised this was one 'Group' she could do without. As Angus Wilson's biographer, the novelist Margaret Drabble, explains, Angus had recently written a dismissive review of McCarthy who naturally retaliated, demolishing his arguments.

*W*alter Scott (1771-1832) pictured in 1805, when The Lay of the Last Minstrel *was published.*

*T*wo of Sir Walter's many statues stand in Selkirk (right) and Edinburgh (below), near the railway station named after his Waverley *novels.*

Nowadays a special literature programme is held every second year during the festival, and though it is not always as dramatic as the original gathering, it is equally unpredictable.

SIR WALTER SCOTT'S COUNTRY

Breathes there the man, with soul so dead,
Who never to himself hath said,
This is my own, my native land!

Sir Walter Scott, The Lay of the Last Minstrel, *Canto 6.*

Thirty miles south of Edinburgh and its ornate Scott Monument, deep in the Borders between Scotland and England, a simple statue of Sir Walter stands in the small grey-stone market place beside Selkirk courtroom. Edinburgh's monument marks a man born in the city who re-invented Scottish culture and restored the country to royal favour (while

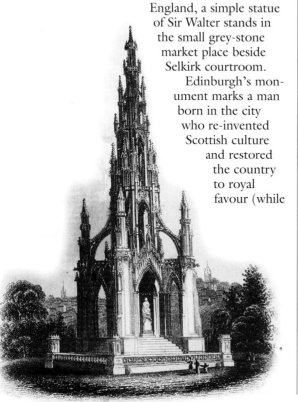

the Jacobite uprising was still just within memory). The Selkirk statue salutes a child of the Borders who served as sheriff for 33 years, became a friend of the 'Ettrick Shepherd' poet, and laird of Abbotsford.

In the courtroom, restored as a museum, a figure of Sir Walter sits reminiscing about his life and work as sheriff: 'From eleven till half past eight in Selkirk taking precognitions about a row, came home famished and tired. Can the Sheriff neglect his duty that the author may mind his?' he pondered in his journal.

He was appointed sheriff in 1799, two years after his marriage, and held the post till his death in 1832. He was never specially successful at the job, nor did he like it. But it kept him in the borderlands where he had grown up listening to heroic folk-tales and balladry.

The Borders were in Scott's blood. His ancestors lived around the Tweed and Teviot rivers and before he was three, Scott was sent to live on his grandfather's farm beside Smailholm Tower.

Looking down from the 16th-century tower the borderlands ripple away south and westwards to the Cheviot Hills and the Ettrick Valley. There stands Kelso, the town where Scott lived for a time with an aunt and went to school; and Melrose, the beautiful ruined abbey he helped restore. And there is Jedburgh, where he appeared in court soon after qualifying as an advocate in 1792.

Beyond lies the Liddesdale landscape Scott 'raided' gathering ballads for his *Minstrelsy of the Scottish Border* (1802) and inspiration for his first original poem, *The Lay of the Last Minstrel*. Some people thought it wasn't original enough and owed a mite too much to Coleridge's poem

Christabel. Scott was still defensive about it 25 years later, explaining how he first heard 'the charming fragments', and refuting Lord Byron's charge that he had published an 'unfriendly review' of *Christabel* in order to try to kill it.

Scott's greater debt was to James Hogg, the self-taught shepherd poet of the lovely Ettrick and Yarrow valleys which meet just above the county town of Selkirk.

Hogg, born at Ettrick in 1770

Smailholm Tower, next to Sandy Knowe farm, where Scott grew up recovering from childhood illnesses.

(a monument marks the site), grew up like Scott in the rich oral tradition of Border ballads and folklore. Influenced by Burns and Allan Ramsay as well, Hogg was already publishing poems when he (and his mother) were introduced to Scott as a good source of material for *The Minstrelsy*.

It became almost a life-long friendship and collaboration. Scott helped publish more of Hogg's work. Hogg supplied Scott with tales and guided him around the valleys visiting Bowhill, Newark Castle and St Mary's Loch (a statue of Hogg is nearby).

At Aikwood, a fine 16th-century Peel tower near Ettrickbridge once owned by Hogg's family, there is an exhibition about him; and in Selkirk at Halliwell's House museum (a few yards from Scott's Courtroom) there is another.

On Bemersyde Hill, Scott's carriage horses, drawing his funeral hearse, paused out of habit for 30 minutes at the spot, now Scott's View, where he would sit looking at the Eildon Hills.

When mass for Kilmeny's soul had
    been sung,
When the bedesman had prayed, and
    the deadbell rung
Late, late in a gloaming when all
    was still,
When the fringe was red on the
    westlin hill...
When the ingle lowed wi' an eiry
    leme -
Late, late in the gloaming Kilmeny
    came hame!

James Hogg, *Kilmeny*.

James Hogg *(1770-1835)*

At Dryburgh Abbey Scott was buried beside his wife, Margaret Charpentier. They had married in Carlisle Cathedral on Christmas Eve 1797 and she died at Abbotsford in 1826.

Abbotsford, Scott's feudal-style home (below), where he welcomed Washington Irving, Maria Edgeworth and Wordsworth. At his desk (right) Scott created a romantic version of Scottish history based on borderland ballads, folk-tales and fantasy.

Halliwell's also sets out the sad story of Flodden Field, the battle where Scotland's King James IV was killed in 1513. Only one Selkirk man escaped, riding back with the remnants of the flag, now kept in the museum.

Flodden was the subject of Scott's next narrative poem *Marmion*, published in 1808. Soon after came *The Lady of the Lake*, set at Loch Katrine in the Trossachs, 50 miles north-west of Edinburgh. Both verse romances were phenomenally popular and both were written by the Tweed, where Scott lived each summer from 1804 in a house near Clovenfords (the village has another statue).

In 1811 Scott bought a farm six miles down river near Melrose known as the 'Clarty Hole' (Dirty Hole). He renamed it Abbotsford and began transforming the run-down farm into a mock-baronial mansion.

It took 13 years before Abbotsford was ready for a grand

Christmas house-warming. The improvements helped to ruin him in 1826 (the year his study was finished) and the toil of writing his way out of bankruptcy helped hasten his death.

But Scott adored the place and it remains the best showcase for his medieval fantasy world – a treasure house of Scottish antiquities. In the armoury are Rob Roy's broadsword, dirk and sporran purse; in the library, Helen Macgregor's silver brooch, Flora Macdonald's pocket book, and thousands of Scott's books.

At Abbotsford he began the novels that made his first fortune. *Waverley* appeared in 1814 and by 1820 there were six, including *Rob Roy*, now his most famous, and *Heart of Midlothian*, possibly the best. Sitting in the galleried study he wrote *Woodstock* and more *Tales of my Landlord*.

Scott said later that he turned to novels because 'Byron beat me' at poetry. More important, perhaps, they increased his popularity and earnings. In 1820 King George IV made him a baronet and two years later Scott arranged the king's grand visit to Edinburgh. In 1831 when Scott was advised to take a winter cruise, the government provided a ship. If anything it worsened his health.

He died, back at Abbotsford, in September 1832 and was buried among the ruins of Dryburgh Abbey, which stands in a tree-lined loop of the Tweed.

Though Scott is generally linked to the Borders, the region he originally popularised was the Trossachs and Loch Katrine, north of Stirling, where an antique steamer, 'Sir Walter Scott', regularly plies the loch round Ellen's Isle.

First with his poem *The Lady of the Lake*, then the novels *Waverley* and *Rob Roy*, Sir Walter did for the Trossachs what Thomas Hardy would do for Wessex nearly a cen-

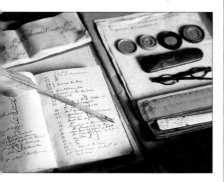

tury later. In 1810, almost as soon as they read the story of Ellen Douglas, travellers came flocking to Loch Katrine to find the setting

of *The Lady of the Lake* and:

The stag at eve
had drunk his fill,
Where danced the
moon on Monan's
rill,
And deep his midnight
lair had made...

Scott had toured the area, from Stirling to Loch Lomond, staying with local lairds, meeting crofters and shepherds, gathering material for the poem as early as 1801.

In *Waverley*, (Scott explained later) he pictured the waterfall, where Flora MacIvor sits singing and strumming her harp, as the falls at Ledard near Aberfoyle. And in *Rob Roy*, he returned again to the glens and lochs of the Trossachs, in his romanticised version of the murdering, cattle-rustling clan Macgregor.

The Rob Roy and Trossachs Visitor Centre in Callander and the Breadalbane Folklore Centre in Killin have details of all the Rob Roy sites.

Rob Roy Macgregor's statue, Stirling.

Ben Venue looms over Loch Achray at the heart of the Trossachs countryside surrounded by Rob Roy sites, from his birthplace in Glengyle by Loch Katrine, to his grave at Balquhidder.

ROBERT BURNS AND THE LOWLANDS

Robert Burns began his brief life the son of a tenant farmer, born at Alloway near Ayr on January 25, 1759.

At the age of 27 he was lionised in Edinburgh as 'Caledonia's Bard', an overnight success with his first volume of *Poems, Chiefly in the Scottish Dialect.* Published at Kilmarnock in 1786, it contained:

> But Mousie, thou art no thy
> lane
> In proving foresight may be
> vain:
> The best-laid schemes o' Mice
> an' Men
> Gang aft a-gley.

Rabbie Burns and the characters in his rustic poems: A Cotter's Saturday Night, Highland Mary, Holy Willie's Prayer *and* Tam o' Shanter.

He travelled the country gathering Scottish songs and lyrics, from Linlithgow, where he was made a freeman of the burgh, to Culloden battlefield, and Dunfermline Abbey, where (ever the patriot) he knelt by the grave of Robert the Bruce.

At 37 he was dead and his long funeral procession through Dumfries made front-page news. Wordsworth and Keats both came to see the Ploughman Poet's grave. And he is still remembered around the world at Burns Suppers (on his birthday) when his health is drunk to the simple toast: 'The Immortal Memory'.

Burns's revolutionary political views and his real achievements (preserving Scots dialect and traditional lyrics) are sometimes obscured by Scotch spirit and stories of his amorous adventures. But there is ample evidence of the real Rabbie in the western Lowlands.

From Alloway north to Irvine and south to Dumfries, the region is dotted with Burns museums and memorials. Almost all of them witness his failed efforts to farm the worked-out, poverty-stricken land, before he became an excise man.

His birthplace in Alloway, now a southern suburb of Ayr, is a low, two-room 'auld clay biggin' (a traditional stone and clay

The birthplace cottage, Alloway (right), simply furnished as an 18th-century 'cotter's' home.

Over the Brig O'Doon Tam o' Shanter *makes his night ride, escaping after he gate-crashes a coven of carousing witches, but leaving in their hands the tail of his old grey mare.*

farm dwelling) that his father built. The museum next door has the fullest collection of songs, manuscripts and belongings of all the many Burns museums in Scotland.

Along the road is the Tam o'Shanter Experience, a visitor centre that turns the sound-and-light treatment on Burns's rollicking poem of drunken Tam. Opposite are the 'haunted ruins' of the Auld Kirk, in which Tam 'saw an unco sight! Warlocks and witches in a dance'. And crossing the river is the ancient Brig o'Doon, over which Tam reaches safety at the end of his wild ride.

In 1766, Burns's family moved over the Brig o'Doon to a farm just north of Kirkoswald, the village where Tam's real-life prototype, Douglas Graham, is buried in the old graveyard. Just across the road

is the home of Tam's 'ancient, trusty, drouthy crony', his friend the shoemaker. Souter Johnnie's Cottage is open, with relics of the original cobbler, and there are stone figures of Tam and the other characters seated 'by the ingle bleezing brightly' in the restored ale-house in the garden.

Burns was 18 when the farm failed, and the family moved again, north of Ayr (the town has a Burns statue and the Auld Kirk in

Souter Johnnie's Cottage, Kirkoswald, has stone figures of Tam and Johnnie – 'Tam lo'ed him like a vera brither' – seated by the fire while 'The storm without might rair and rustle'.

which he was baptised). They settled at a farm near Tarbolton and Mauchline; Tarbolton preserves, with relics, the house now known as the Bachelors' Club, where Burns took dancing lessons, helped set up a debating society and, in 1781, became a Freemason.

Outside the town is a memorial to 'Highland Mary', one of the many loves in Burns's life before and after his marriage to Jean Armour. When Jean was expecting their third child in 1788, Burns married her in Mauchline and installed her in a house that is now another Burns House Museum. By the time they left the town four of their children were buried in the churchyard, near the tavern, Poosie Nansie's, where Burns often drowned his sorrows.

Before he settled in Mauchline, Burns tried his hand at flax dressing in Irvine, on the coast north of Troon. But that didn't work out

Burns statue, Dumfries. He died in the town aged 37 in 1796.

Glasgow (right) where A. J. Cronin became a doctor, returning to the region to write Dr Finlay's Casebook *in the countryside north-west of Glasgow and Dumbarton, Cronin's home town.*

either, hence the lines –

> O, Why the deuce should I
>   repine,
> And be an ill forboder,
> I'm twenty three and five
>   foot nine,
> I'll go and be a sodger
>   [soldier].

Burns had arrived at Irvine in June 1781 as a partner in the flax business, and lodged and worked in an area known as Glasgow Vennel. After the business failed Burns stayed on till March, enjoying life in Irvine (museums at the Burns Club and Glasgow Vennel tell all) before he returned to farming and Mauchline.

Moving south from Mauchline, Burns gave farming one last go, at Ellisland Farm (now a museum) north of Dumfries. Yet again he ran

The Globe Inn, Dumfries, little changed since it was 'Burns's Howff', a short walk from his home and his Mausoleum, erected at St Michael's by world-wide subscription.

into money trouble. He could have accepted payment for collecting and revising old Scottish songs: more than 200 of the best – *Auld Lang Syne, O my luve's like a red, red rose, Ye Banks and Braes* – are Burns's work. But he refused, calling it his patriotic duty. Instead he took a full-time post as an excise officer and moved into Dumfries town.

His last home, from May 1793 until his death in July three years later, stands in a Dumfries back street (re-named Burns Street), filled with exhibitions and relics. Together with volumes of his poems are his sword-stick, Masonic apron, toddy ladles, chair; his autograph scratched in the study window; and the brightly coloured miniature Jean Armour kept of him, living on here as a widow for 34 years.

At the end of the street is St Michael's Kirkyard, where he was buried. By the river, in a restored watermill, is a Robert Burns Centre detailing his links with the town, and the High Street has a Burns statue. But the place to end a Burns tour is in the warmth of the old Globe Inn, Burns's favourite 'howff', among the wood-panelled rooms where he sat many an evening, drinking and singing in the snuggery.

At Auchinleck, near Ayr, where James Boswell's family were landowners for centuries, the former parish church has become a Boswell Museum, with the family mausoleum alongside. James was born in Edinburgh

Modern Glasgow is the 'grey but gold city' of novelist James Kelman, of William McIlvanney's *Laidlaw*, and Alasdair Gray's cult vision *Lanark*. McIlvanney, born at Kilmarnock in 1936, read English at Glasgow University in the 1950s, soon after Alistair MacLean, author of *Where Eagles Dare*. MacLean, son of a Scots minister from Inverness, had attended Glasgow's Hillhead High School. Then he did wartime service in the navy – which supplied the first and grimmest of his stories, *HMS Ulysses* – before enrolling as a student in 1946. The vast Victorian university (one of Gilbert Scott's grand designs) now has a visitor centre running tours of the colleges where novelists John Buchan and A. J. Cronin were also students: Buchan reading law, Cronin medicine, like his character Dr Finlay.

in 1740, and lived most of his life with 'the great, the gay and the ingenious' in Edinburgh and London. Yet he was immensely proud of his Auchinleck inheritance.

Boswell lived here for a while after his marriage in 1769 and brought Dr Johnson to visit his father, Lord Auchinleck, in 1773. James might have guessed the visit would be a failure: father and son rarely agreed about anything, certainly not wives and friends. After James became laird himself, in 1782, he spent long periods at Auchinleck, staying six months in 1794, the year before he died in London.

Lanark by Alasdair Gray, a landmark in the new wave of Glaswegian writing that includes Liz Lochhead's poetry and James Kelman's How late it was, how late, *Booker Prize winner 1994.*

THROUGH THE BORDERS

Up a track on the side of a hill near Biggar, sheltered by rowan trees, is a two-room labourer's cottage where poet Hugh MacDiarmid spent the last 27 years of his life.

Brownsbank was little more than a hut – no water, no electricity – when MacDiarmid moved in, rent-free, with his wife Valda in 1951. A kitchen and bathroom of sorts were built on later but it is

'*The rose of all the world is not for me I want for my part Only the little white rose of Scotland That smells sharp and sweet and breaks the heart.*' Hugh MacDiarmid's The Little White Rose, *engraved by the door of his cottage.*

A large steel 'book' on the hillside is MacDiarmid's memorial at Langholm, where he was born in 1892, and buried in 1978. After he returned to the Borders, he travelled the world, saw Brecht's widow in Germany, Ezra Pound in Italy; and was in turn visited by countless writers, including Yevtushenko.

still a small, damp, scruffy shrine to a man of enormous, rebellious genius.

Born Christopher Murray Grieve (he adopted the pseudonym in 1922) he became Scotland's leading 20th-century poet, ranked among the greatest with Robert Burns and William Dunbar, Scotland's Chaucer. MacDiarmid was the central figure in the Scottish literary and cultural revival, an ardent nationalist and communist; and his complex personality still fills the tiny cottage, along with his papers, pictures and possessions.

Round his bed, by the fireplace, above his chair are row upon row of books – all the detective novels (Raymond Chandler, Agatha Christie) that he would read at a sitting. One room is his, the other Valda's; her shelves house Dorothy L.Sayers, some dated from Whalsay in the 1930s, when they lived in Shetland.

If Shetland saw MacDiarmid writing at his best, Brownsbank was the period of his greatest influence. Returning to the Borders, where he was

born at Langholm in 1892, he made Brownsbank his permanent home.

From here he set off on lecture tours around the world that made him an international figure; or took the bus to Edinburgh to sit talking and drinking with fellow authors – Sorley Maclean and Norman MacCaig – in Milne's Bar. More often, especially in later years, the world came to him at Brownsbank.

'Hundreds of people from pretty well all over the world made their pilgrimage to that little home,' MacCaig recalled.

In 1926 MacDiarmid's masterpiece, *A Drunk Man Looks at the Thistle*, appeared. The year before, he published a volume of lyrics, *Sangschaw*, with a preface written – unlikely as it seems – by the hero of the Establishment, John Buchan.

John Buchan (1875-1940) pictured for Vanity Fair *magazine, made the country near Moffat (centre) the scene of the chase in* The Thirty Nine Steps, *written at Broadstairs.*

John Buchan and Hugh MacDiarmid's politics, personalities and writing could hardly have been more contrary: what they shared was a background in the Borders.

Barely five miles from Brownsbank is the old Free Church at Broughton where Buchan's parents met and married in 1874 (Buchan Senior was stand-in minister for six months); and where John worshipped during childhood holidays and return visits.

The church has been turned into a John Buchan Centre, covering all his various careers: publisher, biographer, politician, diplomat, First Baron Tweedsmuir of Elsfield, Governor

General of Canada, Chairman of the Church Commissioners for Scotland – and author of *The Thirty Nine Steps*.

Buchan dearly wanted to be remembered as a serious man of letters, or at least for his historical novels: *Midwinter*, set in Oxfordshire, and *Witch Wood*, his favourite, based here at Broughton in the 17th century.

The Thirty-Nine Steps put paid to that. Buchan dismissed it as a 'shocker', written in 1914 to while away time when he was convalesc-

ing. It contains what for millions is the most thrilling chase in fiction. Richard Hannay's trek through the heather, hunted down by the Black Stone Gang, takes him cross-country through Dumfries and Galloway. He passes Drumlanrig Castle, delivers his speech in Lockerbie, stops at Moffat and heads towards Broughton and the River Tweed.

It was a landscape Buchan knew from countless holidays and return visits, staying at family homes in Broughton, Biggar and Peebles. The Buchan Centre at Broughton details them all, and his overseas visits, from South Africa to Ottawa, mostly with photos and family history, but a few posses-sions, too: Buchan's uniforms, kilt and the rods he used, fishing in the beautiful Tweeddale valley.

In a small, odd-shaped house in an obscure village near Dumfries hangs a testimonial, dated 1875, signed by Robert Browning, Charles Darwin, George Eliot, Thomas Hughes, G. H. Lewes, Anthony Trollope and a host of lesser-known Victorians.

It is a tribute to 'a teacher whose genius and achievements have lent radiance to his time': Thomas Carlyle, born the son of a stonemason in The Arched House at Ecclefechan, 80 years earlier. His reputation has evaporated since his death in 1881, but to many Victorians in London Carlyle was 'the sage of Chelsea', venerated as essayist, critic and philosopher.

Not everyone accepted his doom-laden criticism of the age. Queen Victoria was not amused. Anthony Trollope lampooned him in *The Warden* as Dr Pessimist Anticant, 'a Scotchman, who had passed a great portion of his early days in Germany ... and began the great task of reprobating every-thing and everybody'. And later generations have objected to many of his political and social views, along with his admiration for strong leaders like Frederick the Great.

The Arched House has copies of the lengthy lives he wrote of Frederick and of Oliver Cromwell, and some furniture from the London home he shared (in a state of almost constant irritation) with his Scottish wife, Jane Welsh Carlyle.

Jane's more mid-dle-class birthplace, at Haddington,

Thomas Carlyle. His stern Calvinist background helped make him 'the Diogenes of his day'.

The Arched House, Carlyle's birth-place, Ecclefechan. He came back to live near Dumfries when he married and wrote Sartor Resartus before moving to London.

J. M. Barrie (1860-1937, knighted 1913) had five plays running in London at once, including The Admirable Crichton, Dear Brutus *and* Quality Street – *so popular that the chocolates were named after it, with graphics based on his costumed characters.*

Behind Barrie's birthplace is the wash-house that he said inspired Wendy's house in Peter Pan, *easily his most successful play. It has been a moneyspinner for Great Ormond Street Hospital ever since Barrie granted the copyright benefits to the hospital, which has a gallery of* Peter Pan *memorabilia.*

where she lived from 1801 until her wedding in 1826, has also been restored as a museum.

Both Thomas and Jane chose to be buried in their native towns. Thomas refused a place in Westminster Abbey and lies with his family in Hoddam Churchyard, within yards of his birthplace and statue at Ecclefechan. Jane, who died in 1866, was buried at St Mary's, Haddington, near Edinburgh.

THE NORTH-EAST

On May 9, 1860 at No. 9 Brechin Road in Kirriemuir there was one major event, and one – apparently – minor. Downstairs in the modest little house, 'six hair-bottomed chairs' arrived. Upstairs and up-staged, as he always believed, J. M. Barrie was born.

Barrie was, after all, his parents' ninth child. The chairs marked a fresh era, when his father's weaving loom moved out of the four-roomed cottage and more furniture moved in for his mother's first genteel parlour.

The chairs are still in Barrie's

Birthplace with other furniture and displays (some perhaps meant only for children) that detail his early years in Kirriemuir and many return visits long after *Peter Pan* made him London's most sought-after play-wright.

Behind it is the wash-house that his mother shared with neighbours in the Tenements. Barrie said it was his model for 'the little house the Lost Boys built in Never Land for Wendy'.

James Matthew Barrie's story – best read by the fire in the Birthplace tearoom, sitting on the wooden settle brought here from his London home – is a rags to riches tale. Not only was Barrie a linen-maker's son, but his first successful stories were based on his home town, renamed *Thrums* – the weavers' word for waste threads.

A Window in Thrums, published 1889, tells the story of Jess sitting by the window watching for her son to come home, just like Barrie's mother hoping to see her favourite son, David, who died when James was six.

Barrie knew he could never replace him. David was a boy who would never grow up – and the idea haunted Barrie for the rest of his life. At its best it became his triumphantly popular children's fantasy *Peter Pan,* staged in 1904 and based on stories he told to the Llewelyn Davies boys he 'adopted'.

By then Barrie was a London celebrity, a fashionable writer with several stage hits behind him.

Robert Louis Stevenson thought him a genius with a journalist at his elbow. But Peter Pan, Wendy, the Darling family, Nana the dog and Tinker Bell were very different from Barrie's previous work and some friends thought he had gone out of his mind.

Barrie went on to more popular plays and novels, several times reworking the sentimental theme of lost and dying children, till the fantasy finally collapsed in a late play, *The Boy David*. Only one

thing makes it memorable, the agreement he made with his 'collaborator', which hangs in Barrie's Birthplace.

During a visit to Kirriemuir in 1933, Barrie had attended Princess Margaret Rose's third birthday party at Glamis Castle, five miles away. Sitting by her at tea he promised her a royalty of a penny a performance from his next play, in return for using some of her words.

Though the play flopped, there were payments owing and Barrie was delighted to receive a demand from the royal solicitors in 1937. He prepared a bag of pennies to take to Buckingham Palace, but died before he could deliver them. He was buried at the cemetery on Kirriemuir Hill.

North-east of Kirriemuir, towards Stonehaven, lie the village of Arbuthnott and the uplands of the Howe of the Mearns, where Lewis Grassic Gibbon based his trilogy *A Scots Quair*.

In *Sunset Song, Cloud Howe* and *Grey Granite*, published 1932-4, Gibbon (pen name of James Leslie Mitchell) gives breathtaking descriptions of the area as he portrays the breakdown of crofting life during the early part of the century.

His story of Chris Guthrie, torn between her love of the land and her longing to escape from the small rural community, moves through the period of the Great War, the General Strike and the Thirties hunger marches.

Gibbon was born into a crofting family in Aberdeenshire in 1901 and spent his childhood at Hillhead of Seggat. By the time he wrote the three novels he was 'in exile' in London. The years in between, living at a croft near Arbuthnott, shaped Gibbon's

Glamis Castle (left), where Barrie attended Princess Margaret's birthday party, is traditionally the site of King Duncan's murder, the 'bloody deed' committed by Macbeth.

...you'd waken with the peewits crying across the hills, deep and deep, crying in the heart of you and the smell of the earth in your face, almost you'd cry for that, the beauty of it and the sweetness of the Scottish land and skies.
Lewis Grassic Gibbon, *Sunset Song*.

thinking as well as supplying the scenes for his stories, and *Sunset Song* is his tribute to the town, renamed Kinraddie.

When Gibbon died suddenly in 1935 before he was 34, he was buried at Arbuthnott church and there is a Grassic Gibbon Centre nearby showing his life and work and the history of the crofting community he described.

A JOURNEY THROUGH THE HIGHLANDS

D octor Johnson must have cut a remarkable figure riding through the Highlands with James Boswell in the late summer of 1773. Still tall, broad and massively strong for his 64 years, wearing a Highland bonnet and broadsword, he bulked over the little Shetland ponies he rode once they were off the coach roads.

Johnson was in his element, at least at first. He had become so famous he was feted wherever they went. He had his pension, freedom to travel and the company of his young friend, admirer and future biographer Boswell.

James was the ideal companion: Scots by birth, sociable, knowl-

edgeable and, like Johnson, happy to record their travels. Johnson wrote them up as *A Journey to the Western Islands of Scotland*, published two years later. Boswell's more amusing version, *Journal of a Tour of the Hebrides*, only appeared after Johnson's death, in 1785.

From Edinburgh they went north to Aberdeen where Johnson was awarded the freedom of the town, and on August 23 they set off north by coach along the coast.

In Boswell's account, still a good guide to the route, they stayed at Slains Castle, now an impressive cliff-top ruin beside Cruden Bay. Boswell swore he slept badly at Slains because his pillow was stuffed with the 'feathers

of some sea fowl'. A century later, 'Bram' Stoker deserved to sleep badly at Cruden Bay: he was here in 1895 – one of several visits – writing *Dracula* and evidently had Slains Castle and the coast in mind for Castle Dracula.

On the coast near Lossiemouth, Boswell and Johnson stopped at Elgin, 'though it rained much', to see the towering remains of Elgin Cathedral, once the loveliest cathedral in Scotland, known as the 'Lantern of the North'.

Around Lossiemouth, Victorian writer, poet and preacher George MacDonald set several books for adults. MacDonald was born at Huntly in Aberdeenshire in 1824 and wrote volumes of religious and supernatural poems, allegories and novels, often in local dialect. Then in 1871 he published the first of several children's fantasies, *At the Back of the North Wind*.

With *The Princess and the Goblin* and *The Princess and Curdie*, MacDonald developed a cult following. Lewis Carroll became a close friend (he used MacDonald's children to test-run *Alice*); and G. K. Chesterton, C. S. Lewis, J. R. R. Tolkien and Sir John Betjeman all claimed MacDonald as a major influence.

Leaving Elgin, Johnson and Boswell whiled away the journey to Cawdor Castle inventing parodies of *Macbeth*, 'Thane of Cawdor', and his sleep-walking, hand-wringing wife.

Shakespeare wrote *Macbeth* for the Globe Theatre, London, around 1605, and Cawdor Castle's treasures include a copy of the Second Folio of Shakespeare's work (1632) and a rare Third Folio, issued after the Restoration in 1660 and the re-opening of London's theatres.

Heading west to Inverness, Boswell and Johnson passed Culloden Moor, perhaps the saddest site in Scotland. Less than 30 years earlier, on an icy April day in 1746, Bonnie Prince Charlie had led his Jacobite followers to their deaths on the battlefield.

Waverley, Sir Walter Scott's story of the uprising, was rapturously received in 1814 and sold out four editions in its first year. But in truth, no fiction matches the terrible facts of the battle. No words can equal the awful silence of the battlefield or the sound of the wind whistling over the heather and the grey-cold water of the Moray Firth.

James Boswell told Johnson two years before their tour of the Highlands that he'd been gathering notes for a 'life' of the Great Doctor ever since they met in London in 1763.

Elgin's ruined cathedral.

Cawdor Castle, famous for Macbeth, *had other memories for Lord Byron: 'I remember Lady Cawdor was a sweet pretty woman.' Byron had grown up with his Scots mother in Aberdeen (the grammar school has a statue).*

Puffins on the cliffs of Shetland, where Stevenson found the shape of Treasure Island.

Neil Gunn (1891-1973). The Gunn Trail follows his books along the Caithness coast.

Barbara Cartland made it to The Guinness Book of Records *with 26 books written in 1983. Behind the frothy pink image and bat-wing eyelashes, the 'Queen of Romance' (if not Hearts) mines a rich seam in 'real love not sex' and has worldwide sales topping 650 million.*

At Inverness, the coach road ran out. Dr Johnson, with some misgivings, took to a pony and they turned south-west beside Loch Ness, heading for Skye and the Western Isles.

North of Inverness, on the tip of the Black Isle, is the home of the 'Cromarty Stonemason', Hugh Miller.

It is a low, thatched house, with tiny windows deep-sunk in thick walls. It was already a century old when Miller was born there in 1802. Today it is preserved as a monument to a man who became not only a master stonemason and lay reader of the Free Kirk, but an eminent geologist and man of letters. He was much admired by Dickens, Darwin, Ruskin and Carlyle, who called Miller's suicide in 1856 'the world's great loss'.

Around the Caithness coastline and the village of Dunbeath is the countryside where Scottish writer Neil Gunn based his best-known novels. Gunn was born at Dunbeath in 1891 (the village has a bronze memorial by the harbour) and published his first popular novel *Morning Tide* in 1930.

When *Highland River* confirmed his reputation in 1937 he turned to writing full-time and settled in a farmhouse in the hills above Dingwall. In 1941 came his most successful book, *The Silver Darlings*, set among the herring fishing community of the Caithness coast, where Catrine journeys between Dunbeath, renamed Dunster, and Helmsdale.

A few miles north of Dunbeath,

the Clan Gunn Heritage Centre has details of his life and work. A few miles south at Helmsdale, Timespan Heritage Centre has a display about a remarkably different writer - record-breaking romantic novelist Barbara Cartland.

In honour of her regular holidays in the area, the centre has a model of Dame Barbara in one of her trade-mark pink gowns, surrounded by make-up, flowers, family photos and books. Born in 1901, she brought out her first book, *Jigsaw*, at 21. She called it 'Mayfair with the lid off'. What followed is an inimitable oeuvre: 625 titles, chiefly love stories about chaste young ladies, written at breakneck speed ('a book a fortnight for 20 years') for an army of ardent readers.

Strathnaver Valley on the northern-most coast of the Scottish mainland, near Durness, is the setting for Iain Crichton Smith's story *Consider the Lilies*. Published in 1968, it is a disturbing account of the Highland Clearances, the wholesale eviction of crofters at the end of the 18th century by estate owners eager to make money from sheep farming.

Award-winning poet, critic and novelist, deeply concerned for the survival of the Gaelic language, Iain Crichton Smith was born in Glasgow in 1928. He grew up on the Hebridean island of Lewis, the setting for another novel, *The Last Summer*, and now lives in Argyll.

TREASURED ISLANDS

Robert Louis Stevenson spent a week in June 1869 sailing round the puffin-crowded cliffs of Shetland and Orkney with his father. They were inspecting lighthouses, some of 88 the Stevenson family business had designed and installed, and as they mapped their route round the coast it is easy to see where Stevenson spotted *Treasure Island*.

The outline of Unst, most northerly of all Shetland's far-flung islands, fits exactly the size and shape of Captain Flint's island. It looks, as young Jim, Squire Trelawney and Dr Livesey discover, 'like a fat dragon standing up' with Burra Firth clearly separating the dragon's head and tail. It also has some of the loveliest and loneliest sand beaches in the world (Unst Heritage Centre has walkers' guides to the coast).

Stevenson wrote gleefully about *Treasure Island* as he progressed the plot, 'If this don't fetch the kids, why, they have gone rotten since my day.' It was his first full-length work of fiction and when it appeared in 1883, whether or not it fetched the kids was immaterial: it brought him serious recognition as a writer.

In Royal Deeside, one of the thickly wooded valleys of the central Highlands, are Braemar Castle (above), Braemar village and the mountain of Lochnagar. At a rented house in Braemar, one wet August day in 1881, R. L. Stevenson invented Treasure Island *to entertain his stepson. Another wet holiday nearly a century later at neighbouring Balmoral Castle prompted Charles, Prince of Wales, to write the tale of* The Old Man of Lochnagar.

On Shetland's Whalsay island, Hugh MacDiarmid made his home in the 1930s. MacDiarmid came to Shetland in May 1933 driven by despair to a self-imposed exile on the 'edge of the world'.

During his nine years here with his wife and baby son, living among the fishing families and white-washed crofts, watching seals basking on the rocks, he recovered from a nervous breakdown and wrote much of his finest work.

The isles and seas of Shetland inspired MacDiarmid as much as the lowland countryside of his

Whalsay, the 'Whale island', where Hugh MacDiarmid wrote On a Raised Beach.

The Grieve House, Hugh and Valda MacDiarmid's home on Whalsay. 'Shetland is my best discovery yet,' he told Neil Gunn in June 1933, soon after they arrived.

Compton Mackenzie, pictured 1919, already popular for his novels Carnival *and* Sinister Street.

George Mackay Brown, poet and novelist of the fishing and farming communities, Fishermen with Ploughs, *on Orkney.*

childhood. The poems of these years, from *Stony Limits and Other Poems* to *The Kind of Poetry I Want* (published later) include the short lyrics 'On the Ocean Floor' and 'Skald's Death'.

His rough stone cottage, since named The Grieve House, has become a 'bod', one of Shetland's chain of camping-barns, ideal for visitors who want to sample Shetland's simple life.

George Mackay Brown, the Bard of Orkney, was born at Stromness in 1921 and has spent almost all his life on the islands to which the Norsemen brought their rich tradition of storytelling over a thousand years ago.

As poet, novelist and playwright, Brown has kept alive their narrative tradition, drawing on rural life and the Orkneys' rugged landscape as well as the legacy of folklore and Norse sagas.

From *A Calendar of Love*, published 1967, to *Greenvoe* in 1972, and the 1995 collection *Winter Tales*, Brown's stories seem steeped in peat smoke, whisky and bannocks. In *Beside the Ocean of Time*, set in the 1930s, he covers almost the entire history of the Orkneys in the daydreams of young Thorfinn, a crofter's son on the island of Norday.

The sinking of the SS Politician in February 1941 has gone down as one of the funniest nights in Hebridean history – thanks to Sir Compton Mackenzie's novel *Whisky Galore!*

When the Politician foundered on a hidden shoal just off the tiny islands of Eriskay and Barra in the Outer Hebrides, she was bound for America with 264,000 bottles of best Scotch whisky.

It was a cash-rich cargo designed to help Britain's war effort. But by the time the islanders had helped to salvage it, 100,000 bottles had been 'liberated'. The Politician bar on Eriskay has proof.

Mackenzie turned the episode into *Whisky Galore!* in 1947, writing from his home on Barra, overlooking the windswept beach.

He had a fondness for islands and had lived on Capri for a time around 1919. D. H. Lawrence was there, too, and, as Mackenzie recalled in an interview in 1972, Lawrence 'wrote a thing about me called *The Man who Loved Islands*'.

Mackenzie died soon after the interview and was buried on Barra, while a lone piper played a last lament.

> *I have known all the storms
>   that roll.
> I have been a singer after the
>   fashion
> Of my people – a poet of
>   passion.
> All that is past.
> Quiet has come into my soul.
> Life's tempest is done.
> I lie at last
> A bird cliff under the
>   midnight sun.*
>
> Hugh MacDiarmid, *Skald's
> Death*

'It was early spring when I came to live at Camusfearna for the first time, and the grass at the burn side was gay with thick-clustering primroses and violets, though the snow was still heavy on the high peaks and lay like lace over the lower hills of Skye across the Sound.'

Gavin Maxwell's Camusfearna was Sandaig on the mainland near the new bridge to Skye, looking across the Sound of Sleat to the snow-capped Cuillin mountains. He tried at first to disguise the identity of the *Ring of Bright Water* by re-naming it, though it wasn't long after the book appeared in 1960 that readers worked out where it must be.

Maxwell was born in Scotland

in 1914, near Wigtown on the south-west Lowland coast (described in *The House of Elrig*, his autobiography). He tried shark fishing on the tiny island of Soay, writing in London and travelling abroad before he returned to Britain with the first of his otter-cubs.

At the house at Sandaig he sat 'with an otter on its back among the cushions', while he wrote *Ring of Bright Water.* After that came *Rocks Remain* and *Raven Seek Thy Brother.*

The house burned down in 1968 (the site has a memorial) and the following year Maxwell died.

The spectacular, sparse scenery of Jura, one of the southern-most isles off Scotland's west coast, is well matched to the bleak theme of George Orwell's political satire *Nineteen Eighty-Four.*

The island has only one road running along the coast and linking the straggle of shore-side villages. When it runs out, before the northern end of the island, it is still seven miles short of the house where Orwell lived from 1946 to 1949 and wrote his last novel.

He had already published *Animal Farm*, portraying Stalin as the boar Napoleon. On Jura he sat down to write another attack on a totalitarian state, 'Oceania', posing not only the threat of Big Brother (Stalin again) but propaganda and 'Newspeak'.

In 1949, the year *Nineteen Eighty-Four* appeared, Orwell was forced to leave Jura for hospital in London and died a few months later.

George Orwell, pen-name of Eric Arthur Blair, made his home on Jura while he worked on his last masterpiece, Nineteen Eighty-Four.

Crossing the Cuillin Mountains (left) to Dunvegan Castle, Johnson and Boswell spent a month on Skye (September 1773). They pushed on past Fingal's Cave on Staffa, where Keats and Wordsworth came later, and reached the climax of their tour at St Columba's 'sacred site' on Iona.

GAZETTEER

The gazetteer lists places of interest that are open to the public on a chapter by chapter basis, following the nine regions. Under each chapter heading places appear in alphabetical order. The names in bold are the author(s) associated with each place. All authors and places appear in the general index. When planning a visit please telephone to confirm seasonal and daily opening times. For information on places not listed here telephone the local Tourist Information Centre.

CHAPTER 1

Assembly Rooms
(Museum of
  Costume)
Bennett Street
Bath
Avon
Tel: 01225 46111
Jane Austen

Clevedon Court
Tickenham Road
Clevedon
Avon
BS21 6QU
Tel: 01275 872257
**Samuel Taylor
  Coleridge**

Coleridge Cottage
35 Lime Street
Nether Stowey
Bridgewater
Somerset
TA5 1NQ
Tel: 01278 732662
**Samuel Taylor
  Coleridge**

Dartington Hall
  Gardens
Dartington
Nr Totnes
Devon
Tel: 01803 862271
**Agatha Christie
Sean O'Casey**

Dartmoor National
  Park High Moorland
  Visitor Centre
Dutchy Buildings
The Square
Princetown
Yelverton
Devon
PL20 6QF
Tel: 01822 890414
**Sir Arthur Conan
  Doyle**

Guildhall
Butchers Row
Barnstaple
Devon
Tel: 01271 388583
(Barnstaple TIC, by
appointment only)
John Gay

Jamaica Inn
Bolventor
Launceston
Cornwall
PL15 7TS
Tel: 01566 86838
Daphne du Maurier

Lanhydrock House
Bodmin
Cornwall
Tel: 01208 73320
Daphne du Maurier

No. 1 Royal
  Crescent
Bath
Avon
BA1 2LR
Tel: 01225 428126

Prior Park College
Ralph Allen Drive
Combe Down
Bath
BA2 5AH
Tel: 01225 837491
**Alexander Pope
Samuel Richardson
Henry Fielding**

St Michael's Mount
Marazion
Nr Penzance
Cornwall
TR17 0HT
Tel: 01736 710507
George Eliot

The Museum of
  North Devon
The Square
Barnstaple
EX32 8LN
Tel: 01271 46747
**John Gay
Henry Williamson**

Pump Room (and
  Roman Baths)
Abbey Church Yard
Bath
Tel: 01225 462831
**Jane Austen
Samuel Pepys
Oliver Goldsmith**

Tintagel Castle
Tintagel
Cornwall
PL34 0HL
Tel: 01840 770328
Alfred Lord Tennyson

Torquay Museum
529 Babbacombe
  Road
Torquay
Devon
TQ1 1HG
Tel: 01803 293975
Agatha Christie

Torre Abbey Historic
  House and Gallery
The Kings Drive
Torquay
Devon
TQ2 5JX
Tel: 01863 293593
Agatha Christie

Trelissick Gardens
Feock
Nr Truro
Cornwall
TR3 6QL
Tel: 01872 862090
Winston Graham

Trerice
Nr Newquay
TR8 4PG
Tel: 01637 875404
Winston Graham

CHAPTER 2

Athelhampton
  House and Gardens
Athelhampton
Dorchester
DT2 7LG
Tel: 01305 848363
Thomas Hardy

Carisbrooke Castle
Newport
Isle of Wight
P30 1XX
Tel: 01983 522107
William Wordsworth
John Keats

Charles Dickens
  Birthplace Museum
393 Old
Commercial Road
Portsmouth
PO1 4QL
Tel: 01705 827261
Charles Dickens

Christchurch Priory
Quay Road
Christchurch
Dorset
BH23 1BU
Tel: 01202 485804
Percy Bysshe Shelley

Clouds Hill
Wareham
BH20 7NQ
Tel: 01929 405616
T. E. Lawrence

Dorset County
  Museum
High West Street
Dorchester
DT1 1XA
Tel: 01305 262735
Thomas Hardy

Farringford Hotel
Bedbury Lane
Freshwater Bay
PO40 9PE
Tel: 01983 752500
Alfred Lord Tennyson
Lewis Carroll
Edward Lear

Farnham Castle
The Castle
Farnham
Surrey
GU9 0AG
Tel: 01252 721194
William Cobbett

Gilbert White's
  House and Garden
The Wakes
Selborne
Alton
Tel: 01420 511275
Gilbert White

Hardy's Cottage
Higher Bockhampton
Dorchester
Dorset
DT2 8QJ
Tel: 01305 262366
Thomas Hardy

Jane Austen's House
Chawton
Alton
Hampshire
GU34 1SD
Tel: 01420 83262
Jane Austen

Lyme Regis Museum
Bridge Street
Lyme Regis
Tel: 01297 443370
John Fowles
Jane Austen
George Cruikshank
Henry Fielding

Max Gate
Alington Avenue
Dorchester
Dorset
DT1 2AA
Tel: 01305 262538
Thomas Hardy

Osborne House
East Cowes
Isle of Wight
PO32 6JY
Tel: 01983 200022
A. A. Milne
Robert Graves
Edward Lear

Shelley Rooms
Beechwood Avenue
Boscombe Manor
Bournemouth
BH5 1NE
Tel: 01202 303571
Percy Bysshe Shelley
Mary Shelley

Sherborne Old
  Castle
Castleton
Sherborne
Dorset
D19 5NR
Tel: 01935 812730
Sir Walter Ralegh

Sherborne Abbey
The Close
Sherborne
Dorset
DT9 3LQ
Tel: 01935 812452
Sir Thomas Wyatt

Stonehenge
Amesbury
Salisbury
Wiltshire
SP4 7D4
Tel: 01980 623108
Thomas Hardy
Samuel Pepys

Wilton House
Wilton
Salisbury
Wiltshire
SP2 0BJ
Tel: 01722 743115
Mary Sidney
Sir Philip Sidney

CHAPTER 3

Allington Castle
Allington
Maidstone
Kent
ME16 0NB
Tel: 01622 54080
Sir Thomas Wyatt

Bateman's
Burwash
Etchingham
East Sussex
TN19 7DS
Tel: 01435 882302
Rudyard Kipling

Bleak House
Fort Road
Broadstairs
Kent
CT10 1HD
Tel: 01843 862224
Charles Dickens

Canterbury
  Heritage Museum
Poor Priests
  Hospital
Stour Street
Canterbury
Tel: 01227 452747
Joseph Conrad

Canterbury Tales
  Visitor Centre
St Margaret's Street
Canterbury
Kent
CT1 2TG
Tel: 01227 454888
Geoffrey Chaucer

Charles Dickens
  Birthplace
393 Old
  Commercial Road
Portsmouth
PO1 4QL
Tel: 01705 827261
Charles Dickens

Charles Dickens
  Centre
Eastgate House
High Street
Rochester
Kent
Tel: 01634 844176
Charles Dickens

Charleston
Firle
Lewes
East Sussex
BN8 6LL
Tel: 01323 811265
Virginia Woolf
Lytton Strachey
John Maynard
  Keynes

Chartwell
Westerham
Kent
TN16 1PS
Tel: 01732 866368
Sir Winston Churchill

Darwin Museum
Down House
Luxted Road
Downe
Nr Farnborough
Kent
BR6 7TY
Tel: 01689 859119
Charles Darwin

Dickens House
  Museum
2 Victoria Parade
Broadstairs
Kent
Tel: 01843 862853
Charles Dickens

Folkestone Library
Grace Hill
Folkestone
Tel: 01303 850123
H. G. Wells

Gad's Hill School
Higham
Nr Rochester
Kent
ME3 7PA
Tel: 01474 822366
(by appointment
only)
Charles Dickens

Goodnestone Park
Wingham
Canterbury
Kent
CT3 1PL
Tel 01304 840107
Jane Austen

Great Maytham Hall
Rolvenden
Cranbrook
Kent
TN17 4NE
Tel: 01580 241346
Frances Hodgson
  Burnett

Groombridge Place
Groombridge
Royal Tunbridge
  Wells
Kent
TN3 9QG
Tel: 01892 863999
Sir Arthur Conan
  Doyle
Edmund Waller

Guildford Museum
Castle Arch
Quarry Street
Guildford
Surrey
GU1 3SX
Tel: 01483 444750
Lewis Carroll

Guildhall Museum
Priory Park
Priory Road
Chichester
Tel: 01243 784683
John Keats

Historic Dockyard
Chatham
ME4 4TE
Tel: 01634 812551
Charles Dickens

Igtham Mote
Ivy Hatch
Sevenoaks
Kent
TN15 0NT
Tel: 01732 810378
Anya Seton

Knole House
Sevenoaks
Kent
TN15 0RP
Tel: 01732 450608
Vita Sackville-West
Virginia Woolf

Lamb House
West Street
Rye
East Sussex
TN31 7ES
Tel: 01892 890651
Henry James
E. F. Benson
Rumer Godden

Lympne Castle
Hythe
Kent
CT21 4LQ
Tel: 01303 267571
Russell Thorndyke

Monk's House
Rodmell
Lewes
East Sussex
BN7 3HF
Tel: 01892 890651
Virginia Woolf

Museum of Kent
Life
Cobtree
Lock Lane
Sandling
Maidstone
Kent
ME14 3AU
Tel: 01622 763936
H. E. Bates

Penshurst Place
Penshurst
Nr Tonbridge
Kent
TN11 8DG
Tel: 01892 870307
Edmund Waller
Sir Philip Sidney

Polesden Lacey
Great Bookham
Dorking
Surrey
RH5 6BD
Tel: 01372 458203
**Richard Brinsley
  Sheridan**

Rochester Castle
The Lodge
Rochester-upon
  Medway
Medway
Kent
ME1 1SX
Tel: 01634 402276
Charles Dickens

Rottingdean's Grange
  Museum and Art
  Gallery
The Green
Rottingdean
Brighton
BN2 7HA
Tel: 01273 301004
Rudyard Kipling

Royal Pavilion
Old Steine
Brighton
BN1 1UE
Tel: 01273 603005
**Sir Arthur Conan
  Doyle**

Shipley Windmill
Shipley
Horsham
West Sussex
Tel: 01403 730439
Hilaire Belloc

Sissinghurst Castle
Sissinghurst
Cranbrook
Kent
TN17 2AB
Tel: 01580 712850
Vita Sackville-West

Southover Grange
  Gardens
Southover Road
Lewes
East Sussex
BN7 1UF
Tel: 01273 472555
John Evelyn
**William Harrison
  Ainsworth**

Uppark
South Harting
Peterfield
Hampshire
GU31 5QR
Tel: 01730 825415
H. G. Wells

CHAPTER 4

Banqueting House
Whitehall
London
SW1A 2ER
Tel: 0171 839 8919
Ben Jonson
Samuel Pepys

British Museum and
  British Library
  Reading Room
Great Russell Street
London
WC1B 3DG
Tel: 0171 636 1544
John Keats
Thomas Gray
William Cowper
Karl Marx
George Eliot
Robert Browning
Oscar Wilde
H. G. Wells
Bertrand Russell
George Gissing
Angus Wilson
Charles Dickens

Carlyle's House
24 Cheyne Row
London
SW3 5HL
Tel: 0171 352 7087
Thomas Carlyle

Chiswick House
Burlington Lane
Chiswick
London
W4
Tel: 0181 995 0508
Alexander Pope

Dickens House
  Museum
48 Doughty Street
London
WC1N 2LF
Tel: 0171 405 2127
Charles Dickens

Dr Johnson's House
17 Gough Square
London
EC4A 3DE
Tel: 0171 353 3745
Dr Samuel Johnson

Dulwich Picture
  Gallery
College Road
London
SE21 7AD
Tel: 0181 693 5254
Edward Alleyn

Highgate Literary
  and Scientific
  Institute
11 South Grove
London N6
Tel: 0181 340 3343
**Samuel Taylor
  Coleridge**

Highgate Cemetery
Swains Lane
London N6
Tel: 0181 340 1834
**G. H. Lewes
George Eliot
Karl Marx**

Imperial War
  Museum
Lambeth Road
London
SE1 6HZ
Tel: 0171 416 5000
Ian Fleming

Keats's House
Wentworth Place
Keats Grove
London
NW3 2RR
Tel: 0171 435 2062
John Keats

Kelmscott House
26 Upper Mall
London
W6 9TA
Tel: 0181 741 3735
William Morris

Kensal Green
  Cemetery
Harrow Road
London
W10 4RA
Tel: 0181 969 0152
**Anthony Trollope
William Makepeace
  Thackeray
Wilkie Collins
Leigh Hunt
Terence Rattigan**

Kenwood
Hampstead Lane
London
NW3
Tel: 0181 348 1286
Charles Dickens

London Zoo
Regents Park
London
NW1
Tel: 0171 722 3333
Edward Lear

Marble Hill
Richmond Road
Twickenham
Middlesex
TW1 2NL
Tel: 0181 892 5115
Alexander Pope

National Portrait
  Gallery
2 St Martin's Place
London
WC2H 0HE
Tel: 0171 306 0055

Natural History
  Museum
Cromwell Road
London
SW7 5BD
Tel: 0171 938 9123
Beatrix Potter

Shakespeare's Globe
  Exhibition
New Globe Walk
Bankside
London
SE1 9EB
Tel: 0171 928 6406
William Shakespeare

Sherlock Holmes
  Museum
221B Baker Street
(actually at 239)
London
NW1 6XE
Tel: 0171 935 8866
**Sir Arthur Conan
  Doyle**

Sherlock Holmes Pub
1011 Northumberland
  Street
London
WC2N 5DE
Tel: 0171 930 2644
**Sir Arthur Conan
  Doyle**

Southwark Cathedral
Montague Close
London
SE1 9DA
Tel: 0171 407 2939
**Geoffrey Chaucer
John Gower
John Fletcher
Philip Massinger**

St Paul's Cathedral
St Paul's Churchyard
London
EC4M 8AD
Tel: 0171 248 2705
John Donne

St Mary's University
  College
Waldegrave Road
Strawberry Hill
Twickenham
Middlesex
TW1 4SX
Tel: 0181 892 0051
Horace Walpole

Theatre Museum
Russell Street
London
WC2
Tel: 0171 836 7891
**Agatha Christie
'Mrs Pat' Campbell
Dame Ellen Terry
Terence Rattigan
Noel Coward**

Tower of London
Tower Hill
London
EC3N 4AB
Tel: 0171 709 0765
Sir Walter Ralegh

Victoria and Albert
  Museum
Cromwell Road
London
SW7 2RL
Tel: 0171 938 8500
Beatrix Potter
William Morris

William Morris
  Gallery
Lloyd Park
Forest Road
London
E17 4PP
Tel: 0181 527 3782
William Morris

Westminster Abbey
(Poets' Corner)
Parliament Square
London
SW1P 3PA
Tel: 0171 222 5152

CHAPTER 5

Bedford Library
Harper Street
Bedford
Tel: 01234 350931
John Bunyan

Bunyan Museum and
  Bunyan Meeting
  House
Mill Street
Bedford
Bedfordshire
MK40 3EU
Tel: 01234 358075
John Bunyan

CAMBRIDGE
Christ's College
John Milton
Charles Darwin
C. P. Snow

The Fellows'
  Garden
Christ's College
C. P. Snow

Girton College
Virginia Woolf

King's College
M. R. James
E. M. Forster
Rupert Brooke

Magdalene College
Samuel Pepys
C. S. Lewis

Newnham College
Virginia Woolf

Pepys Library
Magdalene College
Samuel Pepys

St John's College
William Wordsworth

Trinity College
Lytton Strachey
Bertrand Russell
G. E. Moore
A. E. Housman
Lord Byron
Thomas Gray
Francis Bacon
George Herbert
Andrew Marvell
John Dryden
A. A. Milne

Wren Library
Trinity College
Lord Byron
George Eliot

**For details of when
colleges are open to
public visitors contact
Cambridge TIC:**
Tel: 01223 322640

Cecil Higgins Art
  Gallery
Castle Close
Bedford
Bedfordshire
MK40 3NY
Tel: 01234 211222
John Bunyan

Cowper and
  Newton Museum
Gilpin House
Market Square
Olney
Berkshire
MK46 4AJ
Tel: 01234 711516
William Cowper
Rev. John Newton

D. H. Lawrence
  Birthplace
8A Victoria Street
Eastwood
Nottingham
NG16 3AW
Tel: 01773 763312
D. H. Lawrence

Eastwood Library
Wellington Place
Nottingham Road
Eastwood
Nottinghamshire
NG16 3GB
Tel: 01773 712209
D. H. Lawrence

Fitzwilliam Museum
Trumpington Street
Cambridge
CB2 1RB
Tel: 01223 32900

Gorhambury House
St Albans
Hertfordshire
AL3 6AH
Tel: 01727 854051
Francis Bacon

Houghton House
Ampthill
Bedford
Tel: 01234 824195
John Bunyan

Hughendon Manor
High Wycombe
Buckinghamshire
HP14 4LA
Tel: 01494 532580
Benjamin Disraeli

Milton's Cottage
Dean Way
Chalfont St Giles
Buckinghamshire
HP8 4JH
Tel: 01494 872313
John Milton

Moot Hall
Elstow
Bedford
Tel: 01234 266889
John Bunyan

National Horseracing
  Museum,
99 High Street
Newmarket
Tel: 01638 667333
Dick Francis

Newstead Abbey
Nottingham
NG15 8GE
Tel: 01623 793557
Lord Byron

Shaw's Corner
Ayot St Lawrence
Welwyn
Hertfordshire
AL6 9BX
Tel: 01438 820307
George Bernard Shaw

Sherwood Forest
  Visitor Centre
Edwinstowe
Mansfield
Nottinghamshire
NG21 9HN
Tel: 01623 823202

Stockwith Mill
Harrington Road
Hagworthingham
Spilsby
Lincolnshire
PE23 4NE
Tel: 01507 588221
Alfred Lord Tennyson

Tennyson Research
  Centre
Lincoln Castle
Castle Hill
Lincoln
LN1 3AA
Tel: 01522 511068
Alfred Lord Tennyson

The Usher Gallery
Lindum Road
Lincoln
LN2 1NN
Tel 01522 527980
Alfred Lord Tennyson

CHAPTER 6

Anne Hathaway's
  Cottage
Cottage Lane
Shottery
Stratford-upon-Avon
Warwickshire
Tel: 01789 292100
William Shakespeare

Arbury Hall
Nuneaton
Warwickshire
CV10 7PT
Tel: 01203 382804
George Eliot

Batsford Park
Moreton-in-Marsh
Gloucestershire
GL56 9QF
Tel: 01608 650722
Nancy Mitford

Bodleian Library
Broad Street
Oxford
OX1 3BG
Tel: 01865 277165

City Museum
Bethesda Street
Hanley
Stoke on Trent
ST1 3DW
Tel: 01782 202173
Arnold Bennett

Eton College
Windsor
Berkshire
SL4 6DW
Tel: 01753 671000
Thomas Gray
Horace Walpole
Henry Fielding
Percy Bysshe
  Shelley
Algernon Charles
  Swinburne
Aldous Huxley
John Le Carré
Ian Fleming
George Orwell

Gladstone Working
  Pottery Museum
Uttoxeter Road
Longton
Stoke on Trent
Staffordshire
ST3 1PQ
Tel: 01782 319232
Arnold Bennett

Hall's Croft
Old Town
Stratford-upon-Avon
Warwickshire
Tel: 01789 292107
William Shakespeare

Hampton Court
East Molesey
Surrey
KT8 9AU
Tel: 0181 781 9500
Jerome K. Jerome

Harvard House
High Street
Stratford-upon-Avon
Warwickshire
Tel: 01789 204507
Marie Corelli

Izaak Walton
  Cottage Museum
Shallowford
Stone
Staffordshire
Tel: 01785 760278
Izaak Walton

Jerome K. Jerome's
  Birthplace Museum
Belsize House
Bradford Street
Walsall
West Midlands
WS1 1PNl
Tel: 01922 653116
Jerome K. Jerome

Kelmscott Manor
Kelmscott
Nr Lechlade
Gloucestershire
GL7 3HJ
Tel: 01367 252486
William Morris

Kenilworth Castle
Kenilworth
Warwickshire
CV8 1NE
Tel: 01926 52078
Sir Walter Scott

Mapledurham House
Mapledurham
Reading
Berkshire
RG4 7TR
Tel: 01734 723350
Alexander Pope

Mary Arden's House
and the Shakespeare
Countryside Museum
Wilmcote
Stratford-upon-Avon
Warwickshire
CV37 6EP
Tel: 01789 293455
William Shakespeare

New Place/Nash's
House
Chapel Street
Stratford-upon-Avon
Warwickshire
Tel: 01789 292325
William Shakespeare

Nuneaton Library
Church Street
Warwickshire
CV11 4DR
Tel: 01203 384027
George Eliot

Nuneaton Museum
and Art Gallery
Riversley Park
Nuneaton
Warwickshire
CV11 5TU
Tel: 01203 376158
George Eliot

OXFORD
Balliol College
**Samuel Taylor
Coleridge
Robert Southey
Gerard Manley
Hopkins**

Christ Church
**Lewis Carroll
John Ruskin
W. H. Auden**

Exeter College
**William Morris
J. R. R. Tolkien**

Hertford College
Evelyn Waugh

Magdalen College
**C. S. Lewis
Oscar Wilde
John Betjeman**

Merton College
Louis MacNiece

Oxford Union
Library
William Morris

St John's College
**Kingsley Amis
Philip Larkin**

Somerville College
Dorothy L. Sayers

University College
**Percy Bysshe Shelley
Stephen Spender**

Wadham College
Cecil Day-Lewis

**For details of when
colleges are open to
public visitors contact
Oxford TIC:**
Tel: 01865 726871

Perrott's Folly
Waterworks Road
Edgbaston
Birmingham
West Midlands
B16 9AL
Tel: 0121 643 2514
(Birminghan TIC)
J. R. R. Tolkien

Rousham House
Rousham
Nr Steeple Aston
Bicester
Oxfordshire
OX6 3QX
Tel: 01869 347110
**Alexander Pope
John Gay
Jonathan Swift**

Royal Shakespeare
Theatre
Stratford-upon-Avon
Warwickshire
CV37 6BB
Tel: 01789 296655

Samuel Johnson
Birthplace Museum
Breadmarket Street
Lichfield
Staffordshire
WS13 6LG
Tel: 01543 264972
Dr Samuel Johnson

Sarehole Mill
Cole Bank Road
Hall Green
Birmingham
West Midlands
Tel: 0121 777 6612
J. R. R. Tolkien

Shakespeare's
Birthplace
Henley Street
Stratford-upon-Avon
Warwickshire
CV37 6QW
Tel:01789 204016
William Shakespeare

Stanton Harcourt
Manor
Stanton Harcourt
Nr Witney
Oxfordshire
OX8 1RJ
Tel: 01865 88928
Alexander Pope

The World of
Shakespeare
13 Waterside
Stratford-upon-Avon
Tel: 01789 69190
William Shakespeare

The Oxford Story
6 Broad Street
Oxford
Oxfordshire
OX1 3AJ
Tel: 01865 728822

Tom Brown's
  School Museum
The Old School
Broad Street
Uffington
Faringdon
Oxfordshire
SN7 7RA
Tel: 01367 820259
Thomas Hughes
Sir John Betjeman

University of Keele
Keele
Staffordshire
ST5 5BG
Tel: 01782 621111
Arnold Bennett

Walsall Museum and
  Art Gallery
(Garman Ryan art
  collection)
Central Library
Lichfield Street
Walsall
West Midlands
WS1 1TR
Tel: 01922 653116

CHAPTER 7

Abbot Hall
Kirkland
Kendal
Cumbria
LA9 5AL
Tel: 01539 722464
Arthur Ransome
John Cunliffe

Albert Dock
  Museum
Strand Street
Liverpool
Merseyside
L3 4AA
Tel: 0151 708 8854
Nathaniel Hawthorne
Thomas Paine
Herman Melville

Alnwick Castle
Alnwick
Northumberland
NE66 1NQ
Tel: 01665 510777
Sir Thomas Malory

Bamburgh Castle
Townfoot
Rothbury
Northumberland
NE65 7SP
Tel: 01669 620314
Sir Thomas Malory

Beatrix Potter
  Gallery
Main Street
Hawkshead
LA22 0NS
Tel: 015394 36355
Beatrix Potter

Beatrix Potter's
  Lake District
Packhorse Court
Keswick
Cumbria
A12 5JB
Tel: 017687 75173
Beatrix Potter

Bede's World
Church Bank
Jarrow
Tyne & Wear
NE32 3DY
Tel: 0191 489 2106
The Venerable Bede

Brantwood
Coniston
Cumbria
LA21 8AD
Tel: 015394 41396
John Ruskin

Brontë Parsonage
  Museum
Church Street
Haworth
Keighley
West Yorkshire
BD22 8DR
Tel: 01535 642323
Charlotte, Emily and
  Anne Brontë

Castle Howard
Coneysthorpe
York
YO6 7DA
Tel: 01653 648444
Sir John Vanburgh
Evelyn Waugh
Jane Austen

Dove Cottage &
  Wordsworth
  Museum
Town End
Grasmere
Ambleside
Cumbria
LA22 9SH
Tel: 015394 34455
William Wordsworth

Hill Top
Near Sawrey
Hawkshead
Cumbria
LA22 0LF
Tel: 015394 36269
Beatrix Potter

Keswick Museum
Fitz Park
Station Road
Keswick
Cumbria
CA12 4NF
Tel: 017687 73263
William Wordsworth

Knowsley Safari Park
Prescot
Merseyside
L34 4AN
Tel: 0151 430 9009
Edward Lear

Lingholm Gardens
Lingholm
Keswick
Cumbria
CA12 5UA
Tel: 017687 72003
Beatrix Potter

Mirehouse
Underskiddaw
Keswick
Cumbria
CA12 4QE
Tel: 017687 72287
Alfred Lord Tennyson

Museum of Science
and Industry
Liverpool Road
Castlefield
Manchester
Tel: 0161 832 2244
**Mrs Elizabeth
Gaskell**

Oakwell Hall and
Country Park
Birstall
Batley
West Yorkshire
WF17 9LG
Tel: 01924 474926
Charlotte Brontë

Pendle Heritage
Centre
Park Hill
Barrowford
Lancashire
BB9 6JQ
*Tel: 01282
695366/611718*
**William Harrison
Ainsworth**

Red House Museum
Oxford Road
Gomersal
Cleckheaton
West Yorkshire
BD19 4JP
Tel: 01274 872165
Charlotte Brontë

Richmondshire
Museum
Ryders Wynd
Richmond
North Yorkshire
Tel: 01748 825611
James Herriot

Rydal Mount
Ambleside
Cumbria
LA22 9LU
Tel: 015394 33002
William Wordsworth

Shandy Hall
Coxwold
North Yorkshire
YO6 4AD
Tel: 01347 868465
Laurence Sterne

Shibden Hall
Godley Lane
Halifax
West Yorkshire
HX3 6XG
Tel: 01422 352246
Charlotte Brontë

South Shields
Museum
Ocean Road
South Shields
Tyne and Wear
NE33 2JA
Tel: 0191 456 8740
Catherine Cookson

Tatton Park
Knutsford
Cheshire
WA16 6QN
Tel: 01565 750250
**Mrs Elizabeth
Gaskell**

Thirsk Museum
14-16 Kirkgate
Thirsk
YO7 1PQ
Tel: 01845 22755
James Herriot

Windermere
Steamboat Museum
Rayrigg Road
Windermere
LA23 1BN
Tel: 015394 45565
**Beatrix Potter
Arthur Ransome**

The World of
Beatrix Potter
The Old Laundry
Crag Brow
Bowness-on-
Windermere
Cumbria
LA23 3BX
Tel: 015394 88444
Beatrix Potter

Wallington
Cambo
Morpeth
Northumberland
NE61 4AR
Tel: 01670 774283
John Ruskin

Walker Art Gallery
William Brown Street
Liverpool
L3 8EL
Tel: 0151 207 0001
Edward Lear

Wood End
The Crescent
Scarborough
North Yorkshire
YO11 2PW
Tel: 01723 367326
**Edith, Osbert and
Sacheverell Sitwell**

Wordsworth House
Main Street
Cockermouth
Cumbria
CA13 9RX
Tel: 01900 824805
William Wordsworth

Wray Castle
Low Wray
Ambleside
Cumbria
LA22 0JB
Tel: 015394 323200
Beatrix Potter

CHAPTER 8

Bromsgrove
Museum
26 Birmingham Road
Bromsgrove
Worcestershire
Tel: 01527 831809
A. E. Housman

Caerleon
Newport
Gwent
Tel: 01633 430777
**Geoffrey of
Monmouth**
Thomas Malory
Alfred Lord Tennyson

Carmarthen
Museum
Carmarthen
Abergwili
Dyfed
Tel: 01267 231691
**Geoffrey of
Monmouth**

Cyfarthfa Castle
Merthyr Tydfil
Mid Glamorgan
Tel: 01685 723112
Mabinogion Tales

Dylan Thomas Boat
  House
Dylan's Walk
Laugharne
SA33 4FD
Tel: 01994 427420
Dylan Thomas

Gwaenynog
  Country World
Gwaenynog Hall
Denbigh
LL16 5NU
Tel: 01745 812991
Beatrix Potter
Dr Samuel Johnson

Harlech Castle
Castle Square
Gwynedd
Tel: 01766 780552
Mabinogion Tales

Kilvert Gallery
Ashbrook House
Clyro
Hereford
HR3 5RZ
Tel: 01497 820831
Rev. Francis Kilvert

Landsker Visitor
  Centre
High Street
Narbeth
Pembrokeshire
SA67 7AR
Tel: 01834 860061
Mabinogion Tales

Ludlow Castle
Ludlow
Shropshire
Tel: 01584 873947
John Milton

Manorbier Castle
Manorbier
Nr Tenby
Pembrokeshire
Tel: 01834 871394
Gerald of Wales

Museum of Welsh
  Life
St Fagans
Cardiff
Tel: 01222 569441

National Library of
  Wales
Penglais Hill
Aberystwyth
SY23 3BU
Tel: 01970 623816

Plas Newydd
Hill Street
Llangollen
Clwyd
Tel: 01978 861314
George Borrow
Elizabeth Mavor

Rhondda Heritage
  Park
Coed Cae Road
Trehafod
Mid Glamorgan
Tel: 01443 682036
Richard Llewellyn

Shrewsbury Quest
193 Abbey Foregate
Shrewsbury
Shropshire
SY2 6AH
Tel: 01743 243324
Ellis Peters

Sudeley Castle
Winchcombe
Gloucestershire
GL54 5JD
Tel: 01242 602308
P. G. Wodehouse

Tintern Abbey
Tintern
Gwent
Tel: 01291 689251
William Gilpin
William Wordsworth
Rev. Francis Kilvert

Tretower Court
Brecon
Tretower
Powys
Tel: 01874 730279
Henry Vaughan

Weston Park
Weston-under-
  Lizard
Shifnal
Shropshire
TF11 8LE
Tel: 01952 850207
P. G. Wodehouse

CHAPTER 9

Abbotsford House
Galashiels
Borders
Tel: 01896 752043
Sir Walter Scott

Aikwood
Nr Selkirk
Ettrickbridge
Borders
TD7 5HJ
Tel: 01750 52253
James Hogg

Bachelor's Club
Tarbolton
Strathclyde
Tel: 01292 541940
Robert Burns

Barrie's Birthplace
9 Brechin Road
Kirriemuir
Tayside
Tel: 01575 72646
J. M. Barrie

Boswell Museum
131 Main Street
Auchinleck
Ayr
Tel: 01290 20757
James Boswell

Breadalbane
Folklore Centre
The Falls of Dochert
Killin
Perthshire
Tel: 01567 820254
Sir Walter Scott

Brownsbank
Candy Mill
Biggar
Strathclyde
Tel: 01899 860327
Hugh MacDiarmid

Burns Cottage and
  Museum
Alloway
Strathclyde
Tel: 01292 41215
Robert Burns

Burns Club
Wellwood
Irvine
Ayrshire
Tel: 01294 313886
(Irvine TIC)
Robert Burns

Burns House
  Museum
Castle Street
Mauchline
Ayr
Tel: 01290 50045
Robert Burns

Burns Monument
Alloway
Strathclyde
Tel: 01292 41321
Robert Burns

Burns House
Burn Street
Dumfries
Tel: 01387 55297
Robert Burns

Carlyle's Birthplace
The Arched House
Ecclefechan
Lockerbie
Tel: 01576 300666
Thomas Carlyle

Cawdor Castle
Cawdor
Highland
Tel: 01667 404615
William Shakespeare

Clan Gunn Heritage
  Centre
Latheron
Caithness
Tel: 01593 721325
Neil Gunn

Edinburgh Castle
Castle Rock
Top of the Royal
  Mile
Edinburgh
Tel: 0131 244 3101
**Robert Louis
  Stevenson**

Edinburgh's Central
  Library
George the Fourth
  Bridge
Edinburgh
Tel:0131 225 3584

Ellisland Farm
Dumfries
Tel: 01387 74426
Robert Burns

Gladstone's Land
447b Lawnmarket
Royal Mile
Edinburgh
Tel: 0131 2265856
Robert Burns

Glamis Castle
Forfar
Tayside
Tel: 01307 840242
J. M. Barrie

Glasgow Vennell
10 and 4 Glasgow
  Vennell
Irvine
Strathclyde
Tel: 01294 75059
Robert Burns

Grassic Gibbon
  Centre
Arbuthnott
Lawrencekirk
Grampian
AB30 1YB
Tel: 01561 361668
**Lewis Grassic
  Gibbon**

Halliwell's House
  Museum
Halliwell's Close
Market Place
Selkirk
Tel: 01750 20096
Sir Walter Scott

Hugh Miller's
  Cottage
Church Street
Cromarty
Highland
Tel: 01381 600245
Hugh Miller

Jane Welsh Carlyle's
  Museum
Welsh Street
Haddington
East Lothian
Tel: 016282 2531
Thomas Carlyle
Jane Welsh Carlyle

John Buchan Centre
Broughton
Biggar
Strathclyde
Tel: 01899 221050
John Buchan

National Library of
  Scotland
1 George The
  Fourth Bridge
Edinburgh
Tel: 0131 226 4531
Hugh MacDiarmid
Robert Garioch

Palace of
  Holyroodhouse
Foot of the Royal
  Mile
Edinburgh
Tel: 0131 556 1096
William Dunbar

Rob Roy and
  Trossachs Visitor
  Centre
Ancaster Square
Callander
Central
Tel: 01877 30342
Sir Walter Scott

Robert Burns
  Centre
Mill Road
Dumfries
Tel: 01387 64808
Robert Burns

Scottish Poetry
   Library
Tweeddale Court
14 High Street
Edinburgh
Tel: 0131 557 2876

Scottish National
   Portrait Gallery
Queen Street
Edinburgh
EH2 1JD
Tel: 0131 556 8921

Smailholm Tower
Smailholm
Borders
Tel: 0131 244 3101
Sir Walter Scott

Souter Johnnie's
   Cottage
Kirkoswald
Strathclyde
Tel: 01655 6603
Robert Burns

Tam o'Shanter
   Museum
High Street
Ayr
Tel: 01292 269794
Robert Burns

Timespan Heritage
   Centre
Dunrobin Street
Helmsdale
Sutherland
Highlands
Tel: 01431 82327
Barbara Cartland

University of Glasgow
   Visitor Centre
Glasgow
G12 8QQ
Tel: 0141 3305511
**John Buchan,
A. J. Cronin**

Writers' Museum
Lady Stair's House
Lady Stair's Close
Lawnmarket
Edinburgh
EH1 2PA
Tel: 0131 529 4098
**Robert Burns
Sir Walter Scott
Robert Louis
   Stevenson**

St Giles' Museum
On the Royal Mile
Edinburgh
Tel: 0131 225 9442

INDEX

Figures in italics refer to captions

PICTURE ACKNOWLEDGMENTS

Photographs used in this book have been supplied by the English Tourist Board's *Britain on View* picture library. The publishers would also like to thank the following for their generous help with visual material.

A

Aberdeen Tourist Board 249 (bottom), 251, 253

All Saints' Church, Daresbury 209

B

Bath Tourism/Unichrome 30 (bottom), 32 (bottom), 34 (bottom), 35 (top)

Jonathan Berg/Birmingham Picture Library 159 (both pictures)

Birmingham Museums and Art Gallery (Kilhwych, the King's Son by Joseph Gaskin) 211

Bloodaxe Books 224 (top)

Brighton Reference Library 88 (bottom), 89 (bottom)

By permission of The British Library 67 (Harley MS 4866, f.88.), 149 (80.1.13), 192 (Cotton MS Nero DIV 139)

C

Canongate Books Ltd/Alasdair Gray, Lanark 245

Canterbury Tales centre 67

City of Cardiff 214 (bottom)

The Charleston Trust, © The Estate of Vanessa Bell 12, 84

Val Corbett 191 (centre)

Cornish Tourist Board 11 (bottom), 15 (top), 17 (centre)

D

Dartmoor National Park Authority 23 (bottom)

Darwin Museum, Down House 68

Dean Prior 22

Ditchling Museum 86

Dumfries and Galloway Tourist Board 246 (top), 247 (centre)

Durham County Council 192 (top), 193 (top)

E, F

East Sussex County Council 72 (centre), 77 (centre), 86 (centre)

Edinburgh Tourist Board 233 (bottom), 236

English Heritage Photo Library 42 (bottom), 44 (centre), 48 (top)

Museum of Farnham 42 (centre)

G

Gloucestershire County Council 162 (bottom), 163 (bottom), 164 (centre), 165 (top), 230 (centre)

The George Eliot Fellowship 158 (all pictures)

Grassic Gibbon Centre 250 (top)

Groombridge Place 75

Guildford Borough Council 95 (bottom)

Gwaynynog Country World 220

H

Hampshire County Council 41 (centre)

HarperCollins 159 (top)

Headline/Talbot Whiteman 225

The Dean and Chapter of Hereford and the Hereford Mappa Mundi Trustees 231

Heritage Projects (Oxford) Ltd 168 (bottom)

High Cross House 22 (top)

Hulton Deutsch Collection

I, J

Island Photos, Don French 45 (top & centre), 46 (centre)

Huw John/Swansea City Council 218

(bottom)

Jonathan Cape/Miriam Berkeley 115

K

Kent County Council 69 (bottom), 71 (all pictures), 72 (centre), 79 (bottom), 81, 85

The Kilvert Gallery 229 (bottom)

King's School, Canterbury 67

The Kipling Society 74 (centre & bottom)

Wendy Kress 217 (bottom)

L

Lancashire Heritage Trust 209 (top)

Andrew Leah, Max Gate 51

Lichfield City Council 154 (centre)

Loch Lomond, Stirling and the Trossachs Tourist Board 241 (bottom)

Lightwork, Barry Stacey 185 (top), 186 (top & centre), 189, 190 (bottom)

M

Magdalene College, Cambridge 131

Manchester Central Library Local Studies Unit 208 (bottom)

Mary Evans Picture Library

Cailean Maclean 255 (bottom)

Michael Buselle 194 (top)

Michael Joseph Ltd 217 (top)

Mirehouse/Clare Spedding 186

John Morrison 196 (bottom), 201, 202 (bottom)

Museum of Welsh Life 216 (top)

N

By courtesy of the National Portrait Gallery, London 11, 23, 72, 81, 201

The Trustees of the National Library of Scotland 252

National Trust for Scotland 243 (top)

National Trust Photo Library 5 (bottom), 10 (top), 18 (top), 70 (bottom), 74 (top), 77 (bottom), 83 (bottom & centre)

Newport Borough Council 219 (top)

Newport Museum and Art Gallery 219 (centre)

Norwegian Church Arts Centre, Cardiff 218 (top)

Nottinghamshire County Council 140

Nuneaton and Bedworth Borough Council 157 (bottom)

O

Oakwell Hall 202

Martin O'Neill/West Sussex County Council 90, 91, 92, 93

Old Swan Hotel, Harrogate 195 (top)

Oxfordshire Photographic Archive 164 (bottom), 165 (bottom)

Oxford Picture Library 170 (bottom),172 (bottom), 177 (both pictures)

P

Jack Partington 56 (centre), 58 (bottom), 59 (top), 60 (top), 61 (top)

Penguin Books Ltd 75

The Philpot Museum 57

Puffin Modern Classics 82

R

Range/Bettmann/UPI 165 (centre), 170 (top)

© Vernon Richards 255 (centre)

Rochester Tourism and Marketing Civic Centre 64

Wil Rowlands/Gomer Press 221 (top)

Royal Institution of Cornwall 18 (bottom)

Royal Shakespeare Theatre 151 (centre)

S

Samuel Johnson Birthplace Museum 154, 155, 219

Scottish Borders Tourist Board 240 (bottom)

Line illustration by E. H. Shepard , © under the Berne Convention, reproduced by permission of Curtis Brown, London and (U. S.) © 1928 E. P. Dutton, renewed © 1956 by A. A. Milne. Used by permission of Dutton Children's Books, a division of Penguin Books USA Inc. 73, and (U. S.) © 1933 Charles Scribner's Sons, renewed © 1961 E.H. Shepard, by permission of Simon and Schuster. 179

Scottish National Portrait Gallery 237 (bottom)

Shakespeare's Globe, Richard Kalina 103 (bottom)

Shepway District Council 80 (centre)

Shetland Islands Tourism 253 (bottom), 254 (top)

The Shrewsbury Quest 225 (centre)

Somerset Archaeological and Natural History Society 56

South Pembrokeshire District Council 212 (all pictures)

Courtesy of the City Museum and Art Gallery Stoke-on-Trent 153 (all pictures)

Surrey Hills Visitor Project 95 (top)

Surrey Local Studies Library 94 (centre)

T

© Charles Tait 254 (bottom)

Tate Gallery Archive, Vanessa Bell photographic collection 83

Tatton Park/Cheshire County Council 208 (centre)

Telegraph Colour Library 116 (bottom)

Thanet District Council 65 (centre)

Thearle Photography, Ryde, Isle of Wight 47 (centre)

Tilling Society/Cynthia Reavell 78

Trinity College, Cambridge 130

V

Victoria Art Gallery, Bath 32, 33

Viewfinder Colour Photo Library 5 (centre), 8 (bottom), 9 (bottom), 11 (top), 14 (bottom),15 (bottom), 17 (top), 21, 28 (top)

The Vintage Magazine Picture Library 87

W

Wales Tourist Board 213 (top), 215 (bottom), 217, 221, 222, 224

Walker Art Gallery, Board of Trustees of the National Museums and Galleries on Merseyside 207

Walsall Metropolitan Borough Council 76 (bottom), 89 (top), 92 (centre), 160 (bottom),160/1, 174 (top)

Walter Scott (Bradford Ltd) 203 (bottom)

Warrillow Collection, Keele University Library 152 (bottom & top)

© Frederick Warne & Co, 1930 163 (top), 1903, 1987 59 (bottom) 1904 189 (top)

Warwickshire County Council 161 (bottom)

Paul Watts 8 (top), 9 (centre), 13 (centre)

West Country Tourist Board 26 (centre)

West Somerset District Council/ T. King 25 (centre)

Roy J. Westlake 29 (top & centre)

William Morris Society 175 (bottom)

Wiltshire Photograph Collection 43 (bottom)

Winchester City Council 39, 44 (top)

TEXT ACKNOWLEDGMENTS

The publishers and author are grateful to the following for permission to publish extracts from copyright material:

Dannie Abse: *Ash on a Young Man's Sleeve*, copyright © Dannie Abse, 1978 first published Penguin Books; 'Down the M4' from *White Coat, Purple Coat*, copyright © Dannie Abse, 1989, first published Hutchinson, by permission of the author. **Richard Adams:** *Watership Down*, Penguin Books and (U.S.) Macmillan, Inc., Simon and Schuster, Paramount Publishing. **Hilaire Belloc:** 'The Four Men' from *Hilaire Belloc: An Anthology*, Mercury Books, and 'The South Country' from *Complete Verse*, Random House, The Peters Fraser & Dunlop Group Ltd. **Arnold Bennett:** *Anna of the Five Towns*, A. P. Watt Ltd. on behalf of Madame V. M. Eldin; and The Arnold Bennett Papers, Keele University Library. **John Betjeman:** Desmond Elliott, Administrator of the Estate of Sir John Betjeman; *Collected Poems*, John Murray (Publishers) Ltd.; *Collins Guide to English Parish Churches*, William Collins Sons and Co. Ltd. **Laurence Binyon:** *For the Fallen – September 1914*, Mrs. Nicolete Gray and The Society of Authors on behalf of the Laurence Binyon Estate. **Charles Causley:** *Collected Poems 1951-1975*, Macmillan Publishers Ltd., by permission of the author. **G. K. Chesterton:** *The Innocence of Father Brown, Charles Dickens* and *Love and Friendship*, A. P. Watt Ltd. on behalf of The Royal Literary Fund. **Agatha Christie:** *The Mystery of the Blue Train*, copyright Agatha Christie 1928, and *The Plymouth Express* from *Poirot's Early Cases*, copyright © Agatha Christie Limited 1974. **Roald Dahl:** *Boy*, the Estate of Roald Dahl and Jonathan Cape. **W. H. Davies:** *The Complete Poems of W. H. Davies*, the Estate of W. H. Davies and Jonathan Cape. **T. S. Eliot:** *The Complete Poems and Plays*, Faber and Faber Ltd., and (U.S.) Harcourt Brace and Company. **Ford Madox Ford:** *Collected Poems*, Oxford University Press, 1913 and *The Saddest Story*, Arthur Mizener, 1972, The Bodley Head. **E. M. Forster:** King's College Cambridge and The Society of Authors as the literary representatives of the E. M. Forster Estate. **John Fowles:** *A Short History of Lyme Regis*, 1982, by permission of the author. The Dovecote Press, copyright © The Friends of Lyme Regis Museum, 1982. **Kenneth Grahame:** *The Wind in the Willows*, copyright Kenneth Grahame, Curtis Brown, London. **Robert Graves:** *Goodbye to All That*, 1929, Carcanet Press Ltd. **Thomas Hardy:** The Trustees of the Estate of Miss E. A. Dugdale. **A. E. Housman:** The Society of Authors as the literary representative of the Estate of A. E. Housman. **Ted Hughes:** 'Torridge' from *River*, copyright © 1983 by Ted Hughes, Faber and Faber Ltd. in association with James and James, and (U.S.) Harper & Row Publishers, Inc., 1984; *Remains of Elmet*, copyright © 1979 by Ted Hughes, Faber and Faber Ltd., and (U.S.) Harper & Row 1979. **Jerome K. Jerome:** *Three Men in a Boat*, A. P. Watt Ltd. on behalf of The Society of Authors. **Rudyard Kipling:** *Sussex, If* and *Something of Myself*, A. P. Watt Ltd. on behalf of The National Trust for Places of Historic Interest or Natural Beauty. **D. H. Lawrence:** *The Letters of D. H. Lawrence*, Cambridge University Press, Laurence Pollinger Ltd. and the Estate of Frieda Lawrence Ravagli. **Laurie Lee:** *Cider With Rosie*, copyright © Laurie Lee 1959, Hogarth Press/Penguin Books. **Hugh MacDiarmid:** *Selected Poetry*, Carcanet Press Ltd., and *Letters of Hugh MacDiarmid*, Deirdre Chapman. **John Masefield:** The Society of Authors as the literary representative of the Estate of John Masefield. **Daphne du Maurier:** *Vanishing Cornwall*, copyright © 1967 Daphne du Maurier, Victor Gollancz, and *Myself When Young* copyright © 1977 Daphne du Maurier, Curtis Brown, London, on behalf of the Estate of Daphne du Maurier. **Gavin Maxwell:** *Ring of Bright Water* copyright © 1974 by Gavin Maxwell, Penguin Books. **A. A. Milne:** *When We Were Very Young*, copyright A. A. Milne, Curtis Brown, London on behalf of The Trustees of the Pooh Properties, and (U.S.) Dutton Children's Books; *The Enchanted Places* copyright © 1974 by Christopher Milne, Curtis Brown, London. **Rosamunde Pilcher:** *The Shell Seekers*, copyright © 1987 by Rosamunde Pilcher, New English Library Ltd., and (U.S.) St. Martin's Press, Inc. **Beatrix Potter:** *The Tailor of Gloucester*, copyright © Frederick Warne & Co., 1903; *The Tale of Mrs. Tiggy-Winkle*, copyright © Frederick Warne & Co., 1905; Judy Taylor, *Beatrix Potter – Artist, Storyteller and Countrywoman*, Frederick Warne and Co., 1986. **J. B. Priestley:** *Instead of the Trees, Margin Released, Rain on Godshill* and *English Journey*, The Peters Fraser & Dunlop Group Ltd. **Gwen Raverat:** *Period Piece*, Faber and Faber Ltd. **Victoria Sackville-West:** Nigel Nicolson. **G. B. Shaw:** The Society of Authors on behalf of the Bernard Shaw Estate. **John Steinbeck:** *Steinbeck, A Life in Letters*, William Heinemann, 1975, Elaine Steinbeck and Robert Wallsten. **Dylan Thomas:** 'Fernhill' from *Collected Poems 1934-1953, Reminiscences of Childhood, Under Milk Wood* and *The Collected Letters of Dylan Thomas*, ed. Paul Ferris, The Trustees for the copyrights of the late Dylan Thomas, J. M. Dent and Sons Ltd. (London), and New Directions (U.S.). **R. S. Thomas:** *Selected Poems 1946-68*, Bloodaxe Books (1986) Ltd., by permission of the author. **Flora Thompson:** *Lark Rise to Candleford*, 1945, and *Still Glides the Stream*, 1948, Oxford University Press. **J. R. R. Tolkien:** *The Hobbit* and *The Two Towers*, and *J. J. R. Tolkien: A Biography* Humphrey Carpenter, HarperCollins Publishers Ltd. **Virginia Woolf:** The Society of Authors as the literary representative of the Estate of Virginia Woolf.

The author and publishers offer their apologies to any copyright holders not named above whom they were unable to identify or contact before publication; and we would be pleased to hear from them, in order to rectify any mistakes in subsequent editions.